Rhinegold Study Guides

A Student's Guide to A2 Religious Studies

for the **Edexcel** Specification

by

Peter Freeman

Rhinegold Publishing Ltd
241 Shaftesbury Avenue
London WC2H 8TF
Telephone: 01832 270333
Fax: 01832 275560
www.rhinegold.co.uk

Rhinegold Religious Studies Study Guides
(series editor: Lucien Jenkins)
A Student's Guide to AS Religious Studies for the AQA Specification
A Student's Guide to AS Religious Studies for the Edexcel Specification
A Student's Guide to AS Religious Studies the OCR Specification

A Student's Guide to A2 Religious Studies for the AQA Specification
A Student's Guide to A2 Religious Studies for the Edexcel Specification
A Student's Guide to A2 Religious Studies for the OCR Specification

Rhinegold Music Study Guides
(series editor: Paul Terry)
Student's Guides to GCSE, AS and A2 Music for the AQA, Edexcel and OCR Specifications

Listening Tests for Students: AQA, Edexcel and OCR GCSE Music

A Student's Guide to Music Technology for the Edexcel AS and A2 Specification

Rhinegold Publishing also publishes Classical Music, Early Music Today, Music Teacher, Opera Now, Piano, The Singer, British and International Music Yearbook, British Performing Arts Yearbook, Music Education Yearbook, Rhinegold Dictionary of Music in Sound.

First published 2003 in Great Britain by
Rhinegold Publishing Ltd
241 Shaftesbury Avenue
London WC2H 8TF
Telephone: 01832 270333
Fax: 01832 275560
www.rhinegold.co.uk

© Rhinegold Publishing Ltd 2003

All rights reserved. No part of this publication may be reproduced, stored in a retrieval system, or transmitted in any form or by any means, electronic, mechanical, photocopying, recording or otherwise, without the prior permission of Rhinegold Publishing Ltd.

Rhinegold Publishing Ltd has used its best efforts in preparing this guide. It does not assume, and hereby disclaims, any liability to any party for loss or damage caused by errors or omissions in the Guide whether such errors or omissions result from negligence, accident or other cause.

You should always check the current requirements of the examination, since these may change. Copies of the Edexcel specification may be obtained from Edexcel Examinations at Edexcel Publications, Adamsway, Mansfield, Notts, NG18 4FN
Telephone 01623 467467, Fax 01623 450481, Email publications@linneydirect.com
See also the Edexcel website at http://www.edexcel.org.uk

A Student's Guide to A2 Religious Studies for the Edexcel specification
British Library Cataloguing in Publication Data.
A catalogue record for this book is available from the British Library.

ISBN 1-904226-14-0

Printed in Great Britain by Perfectaprint

Contents

Introduction 5

Philosophy of religion 12

    Argument for the existence of God, 12

    Beliefs about life after death, 15

    Religious language, 18

Old Testament/Jewish Bible 22

    Key concepts (prophecy, mercy, justice, righteousness, kingship), 22

    Key people (Solomon, Hosea, Amos, Jeremiah), 25

Religious ethics 31

    A study of the relationship between religion and morality, 31

    Ethical theories, 33

    Ethical language, 35

    Moral discourse and applied ethics, 36

New Testament 40

    Luke, 40

    The fourth Gospel, 47

    The early Church, 54

Christianity 60

    The Reformation in England, 60

    The Reformation in Europe, 66

    Christian thought and developments in Europe, 74

    Liberation Theologies, 83

    Christian belief and practice, 89

World religions 98

    Buddhism, 98

    Hinduism, 104

    Islam, 109

    Judaism, 115

Issues in Religion 122

The author

Peter Freeman teaches Religious Studies and Psychology at the Tuition Centre in Hendon, London. Prior to this he has worked at the Leys School, Cambridge, as Head of Department at Tonbridge Grammar School for Girls and at Paston Sixth Form College. He has worked closely with the Edexcel specification for several years.

Acknowledgements

With thanks to Abi, Beth, Claire and Lucy, at whose gentle insistence a first version of some of the material in this book was created, and to whom, as promised, this book is dedicated. And also to Lucien Jenkins, Emma Whale and Hugh Sadleir, with whom it has been a pleasure to work.

In the writing of a guide such as this many people have contributed. The author and publishers are grateful to the following people for their specific advice, support and expert contributions: Hallam Bannister, Susan Gillingham, Esmond Lee, Abigail Walmsley and Keith Ward. But the author is also conscious of having drawn on a lifetime's reading. More recently the growth in use of the Internet has made an unparalleled amount of exciting information and challenging opinion widely available. Although every attempt has been made to acknowledge both the primary and secondary sources drawn on, it is impossible to do justice to the full range of material that has affected the creation of this book. The author would therefore like to apologise if anyone's work has not been properly acknowledged. He would be happy to hear from authors or publishers so that any such errors or omissions may be rectified in future editions.

Warning. Photocopying any part of this book without permission is illegal.

Introduction

This guide has been written for students who have completed the AS level Edexcel specification in Religious Studies and are going on to take the A2 Edexcel course.

When you studied for the AS exam you would have focused on two modules taken from a choice of five: Philosophy of Religion, the Old Testament *or* Religious Ethics, the New Testament, Christianity and World Religions.

Almost certainly you will want to make the same selection again for the A2 course, as the A2 modules build on and develop the material covered in the AS modules. However you are free to choose any of the modules and options within the modules. If you do choose different modules from those that you took at AS, you will have to make sure that you have covered the material in the AS specification before tackling the A2, and this will take quite a lot of time. You should only consider this possibility if you have an exceptionally strong interest in a different area of the course, and if you are sure that you have the time and resources to do the necessary extra study. This is especially important in light of the demands of Module 12.

> Throughout this guide you will find references to *A Student's Guide to AS Religious Studies for the Edexcel specification* by Peter Freeman (Rhinegold 2003). For simplicity's sake, this will be referred to as the Edexcel AS Guide.

A2 examination structure

You will have three examinations to assess what you have learnt on this course:

- There will be two 1½-hour examinations, one on each of the two modules you have studied. As with the AS examinations, you will have a choice of two questions out of five. Each of the two examinations is worth a maximum of 15% of your final A-level mark

- There will be a special examination on Module 12 of the specification, which is compulsory. This module is called 'Issues in Religion' and is designed to test your ability to link together different aspects of the course. In this examination you answer just one question in the 1½ hours you are given, and your answer will be worth a maximum of 20% your final A-level mark.

> The Issues in Religion examination presents its own particular challenges. Detailed advice and discussion on this module is included in this guide. See pages 122–125.

Unlike at AS, there is no coursework element to the A2 course.

What's the difference?

According to the specification, the difference between AS and A2 is as follows:

> The Advanced GCE specification requires students to demonstrate a wider range and greater depth of knowledge and understanding, a greater maturity of thought and expression and more developed analytical skills in a further three units of assessment (A2).

We can break this statement down into its constituent parts to help define the exact nature of this difference:

- **Wider range and greater depth of knowledge and understanding.** There are more facts to learn (and appreciate the signifi-

> Warning. Photocopying any part of this book without permission is illegal.

cance of) at A2, both in terms of the range of topics covered in a module and in the amount of material that is in each topic

- **Greater maturity of thought and expression.** The A2 modules can be seen as a bridge between AS and university study. At AS a great deal of support is given to help you understand the material, and only limited analysis and criticism is expected in the examinations. During the study of A2 you should become more able to think for yourself and to express what you have learnt in your own way, in a more sophisticated manner. This will help you at university, where students are expected to discover and explore further the work of major scholars with relatively little guidance and to write in a way that shows a profound engagement with the scholars' work.

- **More developed analytical skills.** In your A2 year you should be moving towards a more independent approach to the work, forming more of your own opinions about the issues involved, opinions that you can support with evidence and argument. While studying for A2 you should be able to work with texts at a greater depth, being able to say more about how a particular piece of writing fits into the topic in general, and demonstrating a very good awareness of – and the ability to criticise – the arguments and evidence contained in the writing.

Gaining these skills

Your A2 year should see a considerable development in your academic abilities. Certainly as far as Religious Studies is concerned, this development can be achieved by gradually building on the skills that have been learnt at AS. Given the right sort of material to study, your ability to work at A2 level should climb fairly naturally until it reaches its peak in the second or even third term of the year (hopefully in time for the exams!). The standard of work ought to be more demanding from the start of the course, but you should not feel that it is impossibly difficult. On the other hand, if you feel that you are not facing a greater challenge than that of AS, then this might indicate that the work is not demanding enough.

How to prepare for the examinations

Studying for A2 is an opportunity to deepen your knowledge and understanding of Religious Studies as a subject – as well as giving you the chance to gain a very useful qualification. To get the best grade you can you need to know how to turn your knowledge and understanding of the subject into marks in the final three examinations. Doing this requires an awareness of what the examiners want you to be able to show you can do.

An important way of getting this awareness is to be familiar with the 'trigger words' used in the examinations and listed in the specification. Trigger words are found at the start of examination questions and they indicate what the examiners are expecting from you.

AO1 trigger words

Your examination questions are likely to contain the following words:

- Analyse
- Clarify
- Comment critically

Warning. Photocopying any part of this book without permission is illegal.

- Compare
- Contrast
- Define
- Distinguish between
- Examine
- Explain.

As you will probably remember from studying for AS, 'AO1' stands for 'Assessment Objective 1', which asks you to 'Select and demonstrate clearly relevant knowledge and understanding through the use of evidence, examples and correct language and terminology appropriate to the course of study.' The big difference between the AS and A2 is that the A2 trigger words and phrases demand that you show understanding as well as knowledge.

To give an example of this distinction, let's compare the AS and the A2 in an area where they deal with similar material. Arguments for the existence of God appear in the Philosophy of Religion modules in both and this provides a good area for us to look at.

If you were doing Philosophy of Religion at AS then you might have been asked to 'Describe' or 'Outline' either the design argument or the cosmological arguments, for example. This would require you simply to state what the argument was without necessarily making any further comment.

In the A2 examination you might be asked to 'Analyse' or 'Comment critically' on the argument from religious experience or the ontological argument, for example. This would require you to state what the argument was and to write some more about the argument. This additional material *might* include:

- How different aspects of the argument relate together
- Whether there are different versions of the argument and if so how they differ
- The intellectual background to the argument, including issues of whether it is based on experience or pure reasoning
- Different perspectives on the argument from different scholars
- How the historical context in which the argument arose might affect our understanding of it.

Not all of these aspects will apply to every module and to every question, and other aspects may be appropriate depending on the module and the question being asked. The example is meant to give you some idea of the way in which AO1 at A2 differs from AO1 at AS. AO1 is obviously more demanding at A2. It is still important not to *evaluate* when providing AO1 material, as you should be just showing knowledge and understanding.

Your examination questions are likely to contain the following words:

- Assess
- Consider critically

AO2 trigger words

Warning. Photocopying any part of this book without permission is illegal.

- ✦ Criticise
- ✦ Discuss
- ✦ Evaluate
- ✦ Interpret
- ✦ Justify
- ✦ To what extent
- ✦ Why.

Again these are quite different from the AS trigger words, which were: comment on, consider, how far. The A2 trigger words indicate that a more rigorous evaluation is needed than was required at AS. So it is important as you work through the A2 material to be aware of this more demanding requirement.

Sample examination essays with comments

The following essays are sample well-written A2 exam answers. They are all approximately 900 words long, which is a typical length for a strong A2 answer. Note how the candidates address the relevant Assessment Objectives in their approach to the question.

The existence of God

'An analysis of arguments for the existence of God will result in valid philosophical reasons to believe in God.' Discuss and assess this claim with reference to the following two arguments for the existence of God:

(a) religious experience argument

(b) ontological argument.

The question is taken from the Specimen Papers with Mark Schemes provided by Edexcel (download from www.edexcel.org.uk). The question can be found on page 21 and the mark scheme on page 104.

Keep material for AO1 assessment separate from material for AO2. This has the advantage of making sure that the distinction between AO1 and AO2 material is clear for you and the examiner. 60% of the essay is AO1 and 40% AO2 and this mirrors the marks available for either section.

Make sure you tackle each part of the question. Here, not only does the ontological argument and the argument from religious experience need to be covered, but also issues about 'valid philosophical reasons' and what is meant by 'belief in God'.

Warning. Photocopying any part of this book without permission is illegal.

In order to answer this question I will first clarify what is meant by 'valid philosophical reasons'. Taken in its strongest sense, valid philosophical reasons will be a chain of correct deductions from first principles that cannot be doubted which will give logical proof of the truth of the proposition under question. Such arguments are 'a priori' as they are purely deductive without appeal to experience. The philosophies of Descartes and Spinoza are examples of attempts to provide this absolute level of philosophical proof.

In its weaker sense, 'valid philosophical reasons' can refer to features of a proposition such as its coherence, or the fact that it can be shown to be probably true. Such reasons fall short of proving a proposition to be correct, but, in the view of the philosopher defending the truth of the proposition, belief in its truth is justified. Such arguments are 'a posteriori' or inductive arguments based on experience.

The ontological argument attempts to prove the existence of God. One form of the ontological argument, first stated by Anselm, is that God can be defined as the greatest conceivable being. A being that exists in reality is greater than one that exists in thought alone. Therefore God must exist in reality as if God existed in thought alone God would not be the greatest conceivable being, as has been stated in the first part of the argument.

Descartes put forward another form of the argument. He stated that as soon as we conceive of a triangle we realise that its internal angles must add up to 180 degrees. In the same way, as soon as we conceive of the existence of a perfect being (God) we realise that such a being must include existence as part of its perfection.

[Clearly summarise the important aspects of the arguments of key scholars.]

The argument from religious experience is an example of the second sort of 'valid reason' for believing in God. For Swinburne the existence of God becomes probable once the strength of the argument from religious experience has been accepted. By 'religious experience' Swinburne means the type of experience that is exemplified by an overwhelming sense of the presence of God or a vision of a religiously significant person or object.

[Keep the wording of your answer close to the wording of the question. This will ensure that your answer remains relevant.]

Swinburne argues that it should be accepted that these sorts of experiences are of realities beyond the experiencing mind. He based this conclusion on two principles. The first of these is the 'principle of credulity'. This states that 'what appears to be the case probably is the case'. So if it appears to you that you are experiencing God or some supernatural vision then that is probably what is actually happening. The 'principle of testimony' is that if someone who you know to be trustworthy claims to have had an experience of God or some other religious object, then the truth of that claim should be accepted. On this basis Swinburne believes that the otherwise equally balanced likelihood or unlikelihood that God exists is swung in favour of the existence of God by the fact of religious experience and so the rational individual should believe in God.

[Cite authorities effectively.]

As a concluding point to this part of the essay, we note that we have taken 'believing in God' to mean 'to believe in the existence of God.' 'Believing in God' might also mean 'having faith in the good character of God' and this possibility will be discussed below.

[Target all aspects of the question.]

Evaluating the above points, we note that the attempt to provide deductive proof of the existence of God is not taken very seriously today. Kant provided what is generally taken to be the best refutation of the ontological argument. He stated that the argument assumes that existence is a predicate, a property that a being can have. Kant denied this, and stated that a being must logically exist before it can have predicates, so existence cannot be one of its predicates. Aside from Kant's specific rejection of the ontological argument, philosophy is now much more concerned with experience and the use of language rather than matters of strict deductive proof.

[Use relevant terminology to back up your arguments.]

Swinburne's attempt to show that it is probable that God exists can also be criticised. For example, according to Hick, to say that the nature of the universe leads to the conclusion that God probably exists implies that we can compare this universe with a number of others the nature of which suggest that God does not exist, and this cannot be done. As well as this example of a general criticism, more specifically both the principle of credulity and the principle of testimony seem very weak when applied to religious

[Show awareness of conflicting views.]

Warning. Photocopying any part of this book without permission is illegal.

experience. As Vardy suggests, if we were talking about a bus going down a street then they are fine, but the claim to have directly experienced God or another religious object surely requires a far greater degree of scepticism.

So I conclude that neither the ontological argument nor the argument from religious experience provide valid reasons for believing in the existence of God, either in terms of a priori proof or of a posteriori inductive reasoning. However if we take 'believing in God' to mean having faith and confidence in God then both arguments are effective. As Barth suggested, the ontological argument helps the believer see what from their point of view is the perfection of God. The argument from religious experience helps the believer realise what is, from their point of view, the transcendence of God.

> *In the final paragraph give a specific answer to the question and make sure it is supported by all the previous paragraphs. Put forward your own opinion.*

Nirvana in Buddhism

'Nirvana is unconditioned, free from self, suffering and change.' Analyse and evaluate this claim illustrating your answer from the set texts.

Buddhists believe that nirvana is a state that is 'unconditioned'. This contrasts with existence in samsara, which is totally conditioned by previously existing factors. For example, every one of the factors that go together to make up a human being has arisen because of what has happened previously. It is this conditioning which Buddhists see as the most powerful aspect of dukkha, the first noble truth of Buddhism. We are conditioned in this way because of our cravings, and that is the second noble truth of Buddhism. Nirvana is offered as release from this conditioned existence (the third noble truth) and the noble eightfold path is the way to find that release (the fourth noble truth). Interpreted in this way, the four noble truths as the most basic teaching of Buddhism can be seen as providing a path from the conditioned to the unconditioned bliss of nirvana. These noble truths are found in the 'Deer Park Sermon'.

Another aspect of nirvana is that it is 'free from self'. It is part of Buddhist teaching that what we think of as the self exists as a set of constantly changing factors. It is because we mistake this self for something permanent and real that we feel ourselves to be in opposition to the rest of reality, and so suffering arises. In the state of nirvana this delusion is no longer there and is replaced by bliss. The best illustration of this idea is found in the set texts, in the illustration of the chariot from the 'Questions of King Milinda'. King Milinda is confused by Nagasena's claim that he has no real self. Nagasena asks Milinda to name the parts of a chariot. Milinda does so, and Nagasena asks him whether any part of the chariot is the chariot itself. Milinda says not, and Nagasena goes on to list some of the parts of a human being. None of these parts is the self, Nagasena concludes, and so nothing that corresponds to the word 'self' has a permanent existence.

The concept of nirvana as a state of being which is free from suffering is probably the most obvious meaning of nirvana to a

> *The question is taken from the Specimen Papers with Mark Schemes provided by Edexcel (download from www.edexcel.org.uk). The question can be found on page 36 and the question and mark scheme on page 138.*

> *A strong answer will immediately get to grips with the terms of the question. Don't waste time on an irrelevant introduction.*

> *Use the wording or layout of the question to help you structure your answer: here, look at the beginning of the first three paragraphs.*

> *Refer to your set texts where they are a relevant and cogent way of backing up your analysis.*

Warning. Photocopying any part of this book without permission is illegal.

Buddhist. As we have already explained, teaching about nirvana is the third of the four noble truths, and is the medicine for the illnesses the Buddha has diagnosed in the first and second noble truths, those of suffering and craving, found in the 'Deer Park Sermon'. In 'The Questions of King Milinda' nirvana is likened to, among other things, water that cools the passions which cause suffering, and the lotus which is 'unstained by all the defilements' of selfishness and delusion which cause suffering.

> Again, illustrate each point from the set texts as the question requests.

- Finally nirvana is held to be free from change. For Buddhists, one of the 'three marks of being' is impermanence. No state of affairs lasts, and so even if we could gain the greatest happiness possible without following the Buddha's teaching, that happiness would not last. Nirvana is a state of being which is absolutely stable and unchanging. Again this aspect of nirvana is illustrated in 'The Questions of King Milinda' in which nirvana is likened to space, as it is a state of being which is unborn and does not grow old, and it is like a mountain peak which is 'unshakeable'.

> The correct Pali term (anicca) would have been useful here, though not essential.

- One way in which this claim can be evaluated is in terms of whether the Buddhist is to seek the state of nirvana only for him or herself. Theravada Buddhism has always seen the quest for nirvana as a matter for the individual. Mahayana Buddhism has seen the role of the Bodhisattva to put off their own arrival into the state of nirvana until all sentient beings have been released from suffering. This is made clear in the 'Lotus Sutra', which speaks against the urge of anyone 'to win a private nirvana for just for himself'. In my view, there is no doubt that the original teaching of the Buddha was that you sought nirvana for yourself, but with the Buddha's teaching on compassion the development of the Mahayana view was both inevitable and justified.

> Keep a clear distinction between knowing and understanding about Buddhist teaching on nirvana (AO1) and evaluating it (AO2), and signal when you change from AO1 to AO2.

> Include a personal opinion with some justification in each evaluation.

A second issue from which the statement about nirvana can be evaluated relates to whether the state can be fully achieved in this present life. Theravadan Buddhism suggests that the final entry into nirvana comes after death and the number of people on earth in a position to make that final entry is very small as numerous lives are needed to become pure enough. The Mahayanan philosopher Nagarjuna, however, states that 'samsara is nirvana'. In other words, the Buddhist who realises the ultimate emptiness of the ordinary everyday world has reached the state of nirvana which is identical to the world of suffering, no-self and impermanence. It is all a question of how we see the world. In this case my opinion is that the Theravadan view has an important truth for Buddhists, even if the idea of many rebirths is only a symbol of the great struggle needed to gain nirvana. Mahayana views are at risk of being misunderstood as an easy way to happiness.

> It is vital that you can recognise the diversity within the major world faiths. Make sure you deal with the perspectives of more than one sect.

My conclusion is that the claim that nirvana is 'unconditioned, free from self, suffering and change' is a vital part of the teaching of Buddhism, whether these descriptions of nirvana are seen as complete in themselves or as the starting point for the development of ideas about nirvana and the bodhisattva and nirvana as achievable in this present life.

> Give an overall conclusion following the wording of the question very closely.

Warning. Photocopying any part of this book without permission is illegal.

Three very good books that deal with all the issues in this section are: *The Puzzle of God* by Peter Vardy (Fount 1999); *Philosophy of Religion* by John Hick (Prentice Hall 1989); *Reason and Religious Belief* ed. Michael Peterson and others (Oxford University Press 1998). A good starting-point could also be *Philosophy of Religion for A level* by A. Jordan, Neil Lockyer and E. Tate (Thornes 1999)

> **Further study**
>
> William James in *The Varieties of Religious Experience* (Penguin 1983) writes about a wide range of religious experiences. James was a founder of modern psychology and of 'Pragmatism', a philosophy which suggests that 'truth' should be connected with what helps human beings thrive. Get hold of a copy of *Varieties* and see why it is regarded as one of the most interesting books on religion ever written.

See *The Existence of God* by Richard Swinburne (Oxford University Press 1979) for more on the principles of credulity and testimony.

Criticisms

See *God and Philosophy* by Anthony Flew (Hutchinson 1966).

For example if someone said, 'I saw an angel on my way to school' you would be justified in requiring a greater number of witnesses and a more thorough checking of their truthfulness than if someone else said 'I saw a milkman on my way to school'.

> **Warning.** Photocopying any part of this book without permission is illegal.

Philosophy of religion

Philosophical arguments for the existence of God

The religious experience argument

The type of religious experience most often discussed in the context of arguments for the existence of God is that of an individual having an intense inner experience which they take to be God communicating directly with them. The Christian philosopher **Richard Swinburne** has identified two principles which, in his view, make it reasonable to accept that such experiences do come directly from God, and consequently demonstrate that God exists. These are:

◆ The **principle of credulity**, which states that if something appears to be the case then, in the absence of contradictory evidence, it should be taken to be the case. So, if God seems to be the cause and the object of a religious experience, then, as it cannot be proved that God is not behind the experience, it should be accepted that the experience is genuinely of God

◆ The **principle of testimony**, which states that we should believe what someone tells us unless there is a good reason not to. So if someone claims to have had a direct experience of God then, knowing them to be otherwise truthful people, we should accept what they say.

Swinburne believes that we live in a world in which it is very difficult to decide whether or not God exists. It is very unlikely that God does, but it is even less likely that the world as it is came about without having a creator and designer. For Swinburne the key reason for thinking like this is the fact that so many people have religious experiences, the reality of which, according to his principles of credulity and testimony, we should accept. In a godless world religious experiences would not happen.

Swinburne's attempts to show that religious experiences can be accepted as evidence for the existence of God have been rejected by many other thinkers. For example the British philosopher **Anthony Flew** argues that a religious experience, which by its nature must be personal and subjective, cannot be used to give us objective information. **Peter Vardy** maintains that the principles of credulity and testimony may apply to day-to-day events, but the claim to have had a direct experience of God is so extraordinary that people are entitled to be more sceptical and to require greater levels of proof.

Another reason some people are sceptical of the claim that religious experiences demonstrate that God exists is that such experiences can be held to have very natural explanations. Freud argued that certain types of religious experience represent the attempt of unhappy people to recreate the first months of life when the universe was nothing but 'I' and life was a blissful unity. He called this the **oceanic feeling**. Also, sociologists suggest that religious experiences play a key role in societies that are insecure and threatened, as demonstrated by the visions of the children in former Yugoslavia during the 1980s and 1990s.

The ontological argument

Ontological arguments hold that God's existence can be proved by defining the meaning of the term 'God'. The definition of God necessitates the existence of God. Once you define what God is, it is impossible to maintain that God does not exist. The argument is most usually associated with **St Anselm** (1033–1109), Archbishop of Canterbury from 1093, and can be stated like this:

> For a detailed discussion of this see *The Many-Faced Argument* ed. John Hick and A. McGill (MacMillan 1968).

- God is defined as the most perfect being of which we can conceive
- To exist in reality is better than to exist in the mind (eg the fact that we can eat real apples but not imaginary ones makes the real ones better)
- If God existed in the mind alone then God would not be the most perfect being of which we can conceive, as a God who existed in reality would be more perfect that a God who existed in the mind alone
- But, according to our definition, God *is* the most perfect being of which we can conceive
- Therefore God must exist in reality.

René Descartes (1596–1650) expressed this argument differently. He argued that God must be ultimately perfect in every way in order to be God. To be completely perfect, God must exist – existence is thus a **predicate** (defining characteristic) of perfection. He used the analogy of a **triangle** to illustrate this: as soon as you have a mental image of a triangle, you know that by necessity it must have three sides. In the same way, as soon as you have a mental concept of a perfect being, you know that by necessity such a being must exist, or else it would not be perfect.

Descartes' triangle

> 'Existence can no more be separated from the essence of God than the fact that its three angles equal two right angles can be separated from the essence of a triangle, or than the idea of a mountain can be separated from the idea of a valley.' René Descartes.

One of the most famous modern forms of the ontological argument is that of Alvin Plantinga. Plantinga proposes that we consider that, given an infinite number of possible worlds, there must be one possible world in which there is a being possessing maximal excellence. Maximal excellence (says Plantinga) comprises such God-like qualities as being all powerful, all knowing and morally perfect. But to be maximally great, such a being must possess maximal excellence in every possible world, it must exist necessarily and be necessarily maximally excellent. (This builds on an aspect of Anselm's argument, that central to God's status as the greatest being is his being independent of the processes of time and space: he is a **necessary** being, not a **contingent** one. This is the cornerstone of what is usually called Anselm's 'second ontological argument'.)

> See *The Nature of Necessity* (Oxford 1974).

However are people who do not already accept the claim that there is a being which possesses maximal greatness likely to be persuaded by this reasoning? The argumentative process looks as if it is circular, couldn't they turn the logic on its head and prove the very reverse of what Plantinga believes he has proved?

Consider the following three criticisms of ontological arguments:

Criticisms

A priori arguments. Ontological arguments are a priori, which means the premises and conclusions within them are not depend-

Kant's objection to the ontological argument is clearly set out in *The Puzzle of God* by Peter Vardy (Fount 1999).

Further study

Hold a class debate on the issue 'The concept of necessary existence is senseless'.

Even Richard Swinburne, who, as a Christian philosopher of religion, is anxious to justify belief in God, dismisses the ontological argument as the argument of 'mere philosophers', and notes that 'the greatest theistic philosophers of religion have on the whole rejected this type of argument'. See *The Existence of God*, pages 9–10.

For a useful discussion of this argument, see section 2 of chapter 6 in *An Interpretation of Religion* by John Hick (Macmillan 1991).

Further study

Find a basic introduction to 'proof' and 'probability' as they are used in mathematics, and see whether the mathematical use of these terms can be applied to the question of the existence of God with or without changing their mathematical significance.

ent on external evidences or experiences, but rather on logic, and initial premises that are instead intuitively true (such as all wives have husbands). But who is to say that the initial premise here, that God is the greatest being conceivable, is actually true?

Gaunilo's island. Gaunilo of Marmoutier (c.994–1083) held that Anselm's argument was absurd in that it could be applied to any number of things, and gave the example of a lost island. He imagined a lost island in which there was an abundance of good things, the greatest island conceivable. According to Anselm's theory, this island must exist (Anselm replied that his argument was only intended to apply to necessary beings – islands are contingent).

Immanuel Kant. Kant (1724–1804) rejected the idea that existence is a predicate at all. It does not tell us anything about what something/someone is like, it is not a quality in the same way as 'red' or 'large' are. Knowing that someone/something exists does not really add to or detract from its concept or essence.

Concepts of proof and probability

The two arguments for the existence of God that we have just discussed are very different. The ontological argument claims to be a proof of God's existence, so that anyone who is capable of understanding the starting point of the argument and of following its logical steps will come to the conclusion that God must exist. However this sort of a priori proof is almost universally rejected. **St Thomas Aquinas** argued against it when he claimed that intellectual knowledge is based on the knowledge of the world we get from the five senses. This is an **a posteriori** argument, one whereby the premises and conclusions within it are dependent on external evidence or experiences. Furthermore modern philosophers are much more interested in language as a human invention rather than an expression of timeless logical truths. A modern theologian like **Karl Barth** (1886–1968) values the ontological argument not because it is proof of God's existence, but because it tells us something about the God in which theists believe.

Arguments from religious experience are very different. Swinburne states there is a very small probability that this world was created by the sort of God of which theists conceive. However he says that it is even less probable that this world is just here with no supernatural cause. So it is more probable that God does exist than that God does not. For Swinburne, it is the fact of religious experience that swings the balance of probabilities in favour of God. If there is a God, he says, then we would expect people to have just the sort of religious experiences that they do have. If there was no God then people would not have the religious experiences they have. Hence the fact of religious experience makes it more probable that God exists.

Probability is also a vital factor in certain types of philosophical arguments. As well as being a priori or a posteriori, arguments can be defined as **inductive** or **deductive**. Deductive arguments run to a logically necessary conclusion. Inductive arguments are not logically necessary, but probable.

The non-existence of God and critiques of religious belief

Arguments for the non-existence of God include:

- Sciences such as astronomy and genetics have shown the universe to be a self-contained reality that does not need the supernatural to explain how it came into, or is maintained in, existence

- The existence of evil and suffering in the world is incompatible with the existence of God

- Religious belief and behaviour is an aspect of life that can be more easily explained by, for example, neuroscience, psychology and sociology than by the real existence of a God who is the 'object' of that religious belief and behaviour.

See *The Selfish Gene* by Richard Dawkins (Oxford University Press 1989) for an account of the world which excludes God. John Hick discusses sociological and psychological theories of religion in *Philosophy of Religion* (Prentice Hall 1989).

Critiques of religious belief include:

The agnostic critique. Agnostics hold that there is insufficient evidence for concluding that God exists, so believing in God means the irrational acceptance of a belief that cannot be shown to be true. Agnostics do not *deny* the existence of God, they simply refuse to accept it in the absence of proof.

For a selection of the writings of the founder of agnosticism and the inventor of the term see *Agnosticism, Christianity and Other Essays* by Thomas Henry Huxley (Prometheus Books 1992).

The humanistic critique. Religion has been and still is a major contributor to the forces of ignorance, superstition and violence. Many wars have been caused by religious intolerance and, through out-dated approaches to issues such as abortion, euthanasia and contraception, religion still leads to suffering in the world. Religion has always tried to hold back scientific and technical progress in its attempt to protect its own superstitious practices even though we depend on science and technology for much of our current and future happiness.

For an exploration of the possible superiority of humanism over religion see *A Celebration of Humanism and Freethought* by David Allen Williams (Prometheus Books 1995).

The Marxist critique. Karl Marx (1818–1883) famously described religion as the 'opium of the masses'. Religion acts as a social painkiller, a way to alleviate the suffering of the poor and oppressed, but one whose effects are only temporary. Through their dependence on concepts of a utopian afterlife, the poor are discouraged from rising against their oppressors to create a utopia in the present. Religious belief is nothing more than the projection of human hopes, dreams and ideals, objectified in terms of the state, the church and ultimately God.

The psychoanalytical critique. Sigmund Freud (1856–1939) believed that all religious behaviour is the result of sexual neurosis. The idea of God springs from an ancient tribal **Oedipus** moment when the young men of a tribe killed their chief and took his wives. Their extreme guilt ensured they replaced this killed father with God the Father: religious sacrifices were thus a way of overcoming their guilt. This has been passed down and kept alive by each new generation. Freud argued that now that humans have become more rational and 'grown up', the illusion must be destroyed and the unhealthy repression that religion embodies replaced.

According to Freud, every child goes through one crucial moment whereby they wish to have sex with the parent of the opposite sex and displace the other. This is the Oedipus moment. His views on the 'primal horde' are not popular among scholars.

For more on Marx and Freud's views on religion, see page 32.

Beliefs about life after death

Belief in life after death

Dualistic arguments for life after death depend on the idea that

Death and Eternal Life by John Hick (Macmillan 1976) deals with this topic in a very comprehensive, clear and helpful way.

Arguments for life after death

'Dualism' is a word that has more than one meaning in philosophy. In this context, dualism is the belief that human beings are made up of body and spirit as opposed to just one or the other.

See *Discourse on Method* by René Descartes (Penguin 1968) and Plato's 'Phaedo' in *The Last Days of Socrates* (Penguin 1993) for the original arguments of these two philosophers.

For more on Kant's ethical theory see the Edexcel AS Guide, pages 42–43.

Hick discusses parapsychology in his *Philosophy of Religion* (Prentice Hall 1989), and there is also some material on it in *Reason and Religious Belief* ed. Michael Peterson and others (Oxford University Press 1998).

Arguments against life after death

See 'The Self and the Future' by Bernard Williams in *Personal Identity* ed. John Perry (University of California Press 1975). Hick's reply to the sort of arguments made by Williams can be found in *Death and Eternal Life*.

For Cupitt's views see his *Reforming Christianity* (Polebridge Press 2001).

Reincarnation

Warning. Photocopying any part of this book without permission is illegal.

a human being is more than just a physical body. Dualists hold that we have a soul that is able to exist independently of the body and that will survive the death of the body. **Plato** (428–347 BCE) argued that mental and physical life are distinct and that it is impossible for the one to turn into the other. Hence the source of our mental life, the soul, must exist both before and after physical life. Plato believed that the soul became trapped in the physical body at birth and was released again at death.

Descartes maintained a dualist position when he claimed that a mind can exist without a body. This, he argued, shows that we are really non-physical and that the body is disposable.

Kant argued that all humans should adhere to a universal moral law based on duty. To do so is to achieve the *summum bonum*, the greatest good. But being good does not in itself make us happy. The concept of the afterlife acts as the link between virtue and happiness, it is the reward for our striving.

Aquinas argued that human beings are designed to be able to achieve their ultimate purpose, which is lasting happiness. He suggested that as we are not happy in this life there must be another life in which that happiness can be achieved.

Moreover some people such as **John Hick** have argued that parapsychology, which investigates issues like near-death experiences, might be seen as experimental evidence for life after death.

A strong argument against believing in life after death is the question of how we would know whether we were the same person after death as we were before death. Psychology suggests that who we are depends at least in part on what is happening in our brains. At death our brains stop working and so it would seem that at death whatever it is that makes a person who they are is lost forever.

The philosopher **Bernard Williams** argues that it is an essential part of a person's identity that their lives can be traced through the time and space of this world. We cannot conceive of a person without that person possessing the qualities that come from being part of this world. Therefore it is impossible for a person to enter another way of existing, as belief in life after death requires, without them becoming a different person. If they are a different person then it is not really life after death.

The radical Christian theologian **Don Cupitt** puts forward a pragmatic argument for not believing in life after death. This is that belief in life after death makes us take this life less seriously. If we rejected all arguments for any sort of afterlife then we would be fully committed to the life that we have and attempt to get the best from it.

The nature of life after death

This is the traditional Hindu belief in life after death, which has become increasingly popular in western culture. Reincarnation states that each one of us is a spiritual reality clothed in a body and personality particular to the life that we currently have. When this body and personality die the spiritual reality is reborn with another personality and body. The quality of rebirth is determined by the moral choices we have made in previous lives. When we have made enough moral progress then we no longer need to be reincarnated and our true spiritual self is united with the universal good to enjoy an eternity of bliss. Reincarnation in non-Hindu culture can become the hope of having another chance in another life, but this ignores the fundamental Hindu idea that, although life can be good and enjoyable, ultimately we should aspire to escape the circle of birth and death.

See, for example, the relevant chapter in *The Essential Teachings of Hinduism* ed. Kerry Brown (Arrow Books 1990).

Rebirth is the Buddhist approach to reincarnation. The basic concept is the same, which is that there is a chain of cause and effect from one life to the next, and that the aim is to escape the chain by living a good life. Where rebirth and reincarnation differ is the fact that Buddhists believe that there is no 'spiritual self' that goes from one life to another. Instead rebirth is purely a matter of causes. The choices you make in this life will determine the quality of your next life in the same way as where you point a torch will determine where the torch beam shines. Traditional Buddhists believe that rebirth takes place in one of six realms: the realms of ghosts, hell-creatures, animals, titans, gods and humans. It is believed that the best rebirth is into the human realm, as it is here that one has the optimum chance of acting morally and thus exhausting the chain of cause, effect and rebirth to find enlightenment (nirvana). Most forms of Buddhism depend upon concepts of rebirth to make sense of life, although one modern western Buddhist, Stephen Batchelor, argues that a Buddhist does not have to believe in literal rebirth.

Rebirth

Buddhism by John Snelling (Element 1996) has a helpful section on rebirth.

See pages 98–104 for more on Buddhism.

See *Buddhism Without Beliefs* by Stephen Batchelor (Bloomsbury 1998) for his personal interpretation of Buddhism.

Resurrection is a form of belief in life after death that is found in the traditional forms of the Abrahamic religions. The basic idea is that the body dies, but at some time in the future God will bring the body back to life. This event is associated with a Final Judgement, at which God will judge all human beings that have ever lived. Those who are saved will spend eternity in heaven while the rest will not. Life in heaven is generally seen as a bodily affair, although, for example, in Christianity the Apostle Paul makes clear (1 Cor 15) that the resurrected body will bear the same resemblance to the earthly body as a full grown plant does to the seed from which it came.

Resurrection

For traditional Christians, Jews and Muslims the belief in the resurrection of the body presents no intellectual problems as it is part of the revealed truth of their religions. However, as discussed *above*, there are philosophical difficulties with the idea.

Hick gives a philosophical defence of the idea of resurrection in *Death and Eternal Life*.

The Ancient Greeks were the first to give the idea of the immortality of the soul intellectual substance. Earlier books in Jewish scripture make no mention of the immortality of the soul. The later 'Wisdom' books include discussions of the relationship between this life and the next (Wis 1–5). The Wisdom of Solomon, originally written in Greek, probably by a Hellenised Alexandrian Jew in the 1st or 2nd century BCE, asserts that immortality is a reward for holy living but punishment is the consequence of sin. Through the influence of Greek thinkers on the Church, the immortality of the soul became an important concept in Christianity, although there is a distinct tension between concepts of immortality of the soul and resurrection of the body.

Immortality of the soul

Note that although Wisdom asserts the immortality of the human soul, it has nothing to say about the resurrection of the body: see by contrast Dan 12: 12 and 2 Mac 7: 9. Psalms which seem to teach immortality include Pss 16, 17, 49 and 73).

Warning. Photocopying any part of this book without permission is illegal.

> **Further study**
>
> Make a wall chart which compares and evaluates the various beliefs in life after death discussed in this section.

We have noted *above* the arguments of Plato and Descartes for the immortality of the soul. The idea has been much criticised in modern philosophy on the basis that nobody can identify a way in which an agreed description of the soul can be put together.

Religious language

Analogy

When theists talk about God they use words that usually refer to things in this universe. For example theists state that God is 'powerful', 'knowing' and 'present', qualities that are also held by kings, queens, presidents and prime ministers. Philosophers have raised the question of how theists can know that God is powerful, knowing and present when they also say that God exists beyond the physical universe.

A distinction is made between the univocal, equivocal and analogical use of language:

+ Univocal: a word is only used with one meaning: eg 'carpet'
+ Equivocal: a word is used with two completely unconnected meanings: eg 'bat' means 'something to hit a ball with' and 'flying mammal'
+ Analogical: combines the univocal and equivocal use of language.

One answer theists have put forward is that when language is used to describe God it is being used in an analogical way. For instance a word like 'powerful' can be used of an earthly ruler and of God. The power of God and an earthly ruler are completely identical and completely different at the same time. They are completely identical because in both cases 'power' means that they are able to control things. But they are also completely different because, as supreme being, God's power is of a completely different nature to that possessed by an earthly ruler. We can draw an analogy between the power of God and the power of the earthly ruler so that we can speak of the power of God as a matter of fact, but have no idea what God's power is actually like.

Peter Vardy describes two types of analogy which are found in Aquinas. The first of these is the **analogy of proportionality**. This means that God has some of the same qualities as us, but that in the divine nature they exist to the highest degree possible. Hence, like kings, God is powerful, but God's power is without limit. The second kind of analogy is the **analogy of attribution**. This means that God has whatever qualities are needed to create the world and to maintain it in existence.

The Puzzle of God by Peter Vardy (Fount 1999) offers a clear treatment of this topic.

Vardy states that it is logical to accept that the two types of analogy do give us a basis for saying what God is like in human language. The problem he sees with it is that we have no idea of what the qualities God is said to have are actually like. To say that God is, for example, powerful to the nth degree as the analogy of proportionality suggests, or that God has whatever power is needed to create the world as the analogy of attribution suggests, is to give us no real idea what God is like as we have no way of knowing what power in those terms really is.

A more fundamental criticism of the idea of analogy is that it cannot show that God exists, and so the whole idea of analogy is dependent on the assumption that God exists, a idea that for many is itself philosophically incoherent. Arguably, analogical language about God is best seen as a language game (see *below*) that allows believers to speak about God at the same time as recognizing the basic mystery of God's nature.

> **Warning.** Photocopying any part of this book without permission is illegal.

Language games

Most people believe in the **correspondence theory** of truth. This suggests that we can know that language is true or false by comparing it with the reality that it is meant to describe. So if I say 'That is a table' and it really is a table then I have made a true statement. But if it is a chair then I have made a false statement.

The Austrian philosopher **Ludwig Wittgenstein** (1889–1951) carried out his early philosophical work on the correspondence theory of truth, but later came to reject it completely. The following example of a table is useful in helping to explain why. Imagine a community of people who sailed on small rafts with a post at each corner for holding on to. To us, one of their rafts would be an upside-down table. But to them, one of our tables would be an upside-down raft. Wittgenstein saw that it would be impossible to decide whether one of these objects is 'really' a raft or a table. In one culture it would 'really' be a raft, in another it would 'really' be a table. He invented the phrase 'language game' to suggest that, like the board and pieces of a game such as chess, words get their meanings from the way that they relate to each other, and not from the way in which they relate to some reality outside of the game. This is the **coherence theory** of truth.

Wittgenstein's early conclusion is written up in the *Tractatus Logico-Philosophicus* (Routledge 2001). His later views are in *Philosophical Investigations* (Blackwell 2002) which can either be easy to understand or impossible to interpret, depending on which section you read and your general views of the issues involved. There is an excellent discussion of Wittgenstein in Peter Vardy's *What is Truth?* (John Hunt 2003).

Wittgenstein's work led to a distinction being made between 'Realists' and 'Anti-realists' or 'Non-realists'. Realists believe in the correspondence theory of truth and argue that the task of language is to describe a real world that exists independently of language. Anti-realists adhere to the coherence theory of truth and accept Wittgenstein's statement that 'the limits of my language are the limits of my world'.

Religious philosophers such as D. Z. Phillips and Gareth Moore (1948–2002) have taken up Wittgenstein's work with enthusiasm, suggesting that talk about God is a language game of its own and that the task of religious philosophy is to explain the rules about using God-talk. The language game of religion cannot be judged by, for example, the language game of science, as the two language games work in different ways. In fact, we can never step outside language games to decide which one is 'really' true as any judgement would itself be part of another language game.

D. Z. Phillips has written very widely on the issue of religious language. His *The Concept of Prayer* (Blackwell 1981) attempts to show the difference that believing that God is not some sort of quasi-real object makes to the religious life. Gareth Moore's *Believing in God* (T&T Clark 1996) is a straightforward explanation of the anti-realist position.

Myth and symbol

In the context of religion, myth can be taken to mean a story about God believed to have vital meaning for an individual, community, nation or cosmos. The language of myth can be a powerful tool for creating and expressing what people believe about God, as, for example, the opening chapters of the Book of Genesis in the Bible suggest. However, while many people consider that evolutionary theory and Big Bang theory do not have the poetic appeal of the creation stories in Genesis, these theories do use language which has the support of scientific evidence and so seem more objective. Responses to the tension between the language of myth and the language of science include:

Myth

See the relevant chapter in John Hick *An Interpretation of Religion* (Macmillan 1991) on the relationship of religious truth and myth. You could also look at *God Talk* by John Macquarrie (SCM 1967).

♦ Abandon the language of myth and try to get as close as you can to a scientifically rational view of the world. This is the approach adopted by **Richard Dawkins**. **Peter Atkins**, a profes-

See *Creation Revisited* by Peter Atkins (Penguin 1994).

sor of chemistry at Oxford University, argues that the facts of science are always to be preferred to the myths of religion

Nietzsche: Life as Literature by Alexander Nehamas (Harvard University Press 1990) is useful on Nietzsche's ideas on truth, especially the chapter 'Untruth as the Condition of Life'.

✦ Abandon any idea of having an objectively 'true' view of the world and go for the myth that you like best. This approach was supported by the philosopher **Friedrich Nietzsche** (1844–1900)

✦ Try to reconcile the language of myth and science. Many people find this impossible to do, but look at the work of Keith Ward, John Polkinghorne, Richard Swinburne and John Hick.

Symbol

A symbol represents a reality, and helps individuals and communities participate in that reality. For instance, a flag both represents a country and helps people feel that they are part of that country. Talk about God uses many symbols, such as Father, King, Shepherd, Lord, Creator. These symbols allow believers to develop a rich sense of what believing in God means, but also raise the question of how we can know what the real God behind the symbols is like, or, to put it another way, how do we know that we are using the right symbols? An answer was provided by the theologian **Paul Tillich** (1886–1965), who suggested that only one expression is literally true: God is 'being-itself' or 'ultimate reality'. Other language about God is simply symbolic, and is based on this one literal truth.

For more on Tillich's views of symbols see his *Dynamics of Faith* (Perennial 2001). There is also a short section on Tillich in *Philosophy of Religion* by John Hick (Prentice Hall 1989).

In his 1967 book *The Symbolism of Evil*, philosopher **Paul Ricoeur** noted the dependency of religious language upon symbol and metaphor. He argued that this 'double-level language' ensured that when reading religious texts we must employ two types of **hermeneutics**. By reading the Bible with a **hermeneutic of suspicion** (asking tough critical questions about the validity of the text and the motivation of its authors, for example) and a **hermeneutic of retrieval** (listening with a 'post-critical openness' to what symbols have to say) we can find a 'post-critical faith'.

Hermeneutics is the science of interpretation.

Debates about verification and falsification

The debate about God and language came to a head during the last century. **Logical Positivism**, a school of philosophy that first developed in Austria and Germany in the early decades of the 20th century, suggests that for a statement to have a meaning it must relate to the physical world. So, the statement 'the universe has doubled in size' is meaningless as it makes no difference to anything anyone can know about through their senses. Logical Positivists argue that this test renders all language about God meaningless. The British philosopher and atheist **A. J. Ayer** (1910–1989) built upon the work of the Logical Positivists to establish what is known as the **Verification Principle**. Ayer argued that something is true only if it can be properly verified (by the five senses). Thus for Ayer the statement that 'God exists' is not true or false but simply senseless because there is no way of checking the validity of the claim.

For more on this, see *20th-century religious thought* by John Macquarrie (SCM 2001) and a good summary in Vardy's *Puzzle of Ethics*.

Ayer's most famous work is his *Language, Truth and Logic* (Penguin 2001), which he completed at the age of 24. See also page 33–34.

Anthony Flew established the **Falsification Principle**. Flew maintained that if a theist wants us to accept that language about God has meaning then they have at least to make clear what would cause them to accept that their statements about God might be false, asking the question, 'What would have to occur or to have occurred to constitute for you a disproof of the love of, or of the existence of God?' Flew used the example of a child dying of cancer, whose parents claim that, despite this tragedy, God is really a loving God. Flew argued that if theists are in all circumstances going to maintain that God is a loving God then their statements about God ultimately become meaningless.

Flew's ideas on falsification are put forward in *New Essays In Philosophical Theology* ed. Anthony Flew and Alasdair MacIntyre (Macmillan 1956).

Theists realised that all language about God was under threat from the supporters of verification and falsification. They came up with a number of responses:

- Those who supported traditional Catholic thinking claimed that the idea of analogy showed how at least some language about God can be shown to pass the tests of verification and falsification

- **Alvin Plantinga** put forward the idea of **Reformed Epistemology**. The argument here was that the statement 'God exists' is 'foundational'. In other words it is something you have to assume to be true before you can make sense of anything else. Language about God must have a meaning or else no language has a meaning

- Anti-realists seized on the later philosophy of Wittgenstein and argued that language about God is meaningful to believers who use it as it should be used. It is not meant to be a language which can pass philosophical tests.

Further study

Read a philosophical description of God, such as the first chapter of *Classical and Contemporary Readings in the Philosophy of Religion* by John Hick (Prentice Hall 1991), alongside some more religious descriptions of God, such as Genesis 1, Psalm 23 and 93, Isaiah 6. Think about whether one type of description is capable of being 'true' in a way which the other is not. Or can both be true but in different ways? Or are neither true?

Test yourself

1. Outline the argument for the existence of God based on religious experience. Is religious experience too subjective to be the basis of such an argument?

2. Summarise one version of the ontological argument for the existence of God. What, if any, value does this argument have in the attempt to prove that God exists?

3. Does it make more sense to be an atheist or an agnostic, or is there no important difference between the two positions?

4. Summarise one critique of religious belief and evaluate its success in attempting to show that religious belief is a mistake.

5. Give an outline of two or more arguments that support belief in life after death and two or more arguments that counter belief in life after death. Which side has the stronger case?

6. Outline what Wittgenstein meant by his concept of 'language games'. If talk of God can be shown to be a language game does this guarantee or destroy the truth of language about God?

7. Demonstrate the difference between verification and falsification. Have theists been able to put up a convincing case that religious language can be meaningful in response to these two challenges?

The prophetic books form part of the second section of the Tenakh, the Neviim (prophets). They are subordinate in status to the Torah but are nonetheless of great significance in their own right.

See Harry Mowvley *Guide to Old Testament Prophecy* (Lutterworth 1979) and Robert R. Wilson *Prophecy and Society in Ancient Israel* (Fortress Press 1980) for two clear guides to this topic.

The specification uses 'Hebrew' to describe the religion of the Jewish Scriptures. Often scholars reserve the term 'Hebrew' for the early development of the religion in Canaan, describing its later development as 'Israelite'. Towards the end of the period of the Jewish Scriptures it becomes appropriate to speak of 'Judaism' and 'Jews'.

See *How To Read The Prophets* by Jean Pierre-Prévost (SCM 1996) for a useful discussion of what prophecy actually is.

Early prophets

See 1 Kings 20: 35–42, where an anonymous member of a guild of prophets denounces King Ahab's actions to his face. See also 2 Kings 4: 38; 6: 1.

Prophecy and established religion

Warning. Photocopying any part of this book without permission is illegal.

Old Testament/Jewish Bible

Prophecy

Nature and importance of prophecy

Prophecy in Hebrew religion can best be understood as God inspiring certain people, enabling them to proclaim a message that showed more than human knowledge and understanding. You should note that prophets were called by God and did not choose the job. Some of them don't even seem obvious candidates for the job (Moses may have had a speech impediment) but the task is given, not earned. Thus their authority is not personal: it comes entirely from God. Deutero-Isaiah implied this when he declared 'The spirit of the Lord is upon me' (Is 61: 1). When denounced by the priest Amaziah before Jeroboam, Amos replies: 'I am no prophet, nor a prophet's son; but I am a herdsman, and a dresser of sycamore trees, and the Lord took me from following the flock, and the Lord said to me, 'Go, prophesy to my people Israel' (Amos 7: 14–15). Amos here distances himself from the prophetic guilds, and places the emphasis on God's peculiar and unexpected choice of him as a prophet.

Although prophecy existed in a variety of ancient cultures, the subject the Hebrew prophets dealt with was always the divine covenant with Israel. The prophets thus confronted departures from Judaism, such as idolatry.

Biblical prophets spoke of the future and people consulted them much as they might turn to necromancers and astrologers (see for example Deut 18: 9–22 and 1 Sam 28: 3–25). However if you look at Hosea, Amos or Jeremiah, you will find that none of them was very interested in making **predictions**: it was the present that occupied all three. They were keener to pursue a political (raising issues of social justice) and religious (calling for a return to the covenant) agenda. Where they did address the future it was to warn that current behaviour was bound to bring divine punishment on the Pentateuchal model of the Egyptian plagues. Thus Amos cited invasion (Amos 3: 11) earthquake (Amos 8: 8) and drought (Amos 4: 7–8).

Some prophets were associated with Israel's cultic centres, such as Bethel and Jerusalem. These had a **liturgical role**, presenting the prayers of the people to God and communicating his response.

Israel's prophets had a key religious and political role (Samuel is central in first Saul's and then David's rise to the throne: 1 Sam 8–12; 15–16), but they cannot be seen as being 'career' prophets. Indeed, some later prophets, including Isaiah, Jeremiah, Ezekiel, Hosea and Amos, come across as working outside the mainstream and the establishment, and thus as lonelier figures. Jeremiah particularly makes much of his isolation (Jer 10: 20), as if recognising it as central to his calling.

But beware of assuming that there is a single and distinct prophetic attitude with regard to organised religion or the political establishment. Jeremiah was frequently in conflict with the politicians because of his willingness to speak of the overrunning of Jerusalem by the Babylonians (in 597 BCE and then again ten years later), behaviour that the authorities regarded as treason. Amos and Hosea were both opposed to the central religious establishment, including the Temple, but other prophets supported it: Ezekiel came from a priestly family.

Forms and functions of prophecy

Early Hebrew prophecy shared features with prophecy as it is found in other religions. We can see this similarity when we look at some of the terms used in Jewish scripture to describe prophets and prophetic activity:

- **Nabi**: this term comes from the Hebrew for 'one who has a message'. In 1 Samuel 10: 9–13 a group of charismatic 'nabis' meet Saul

- **Roeh**: this means 'seer' and is closely linked with 'qosem' which means 'diviner'. This ability to see into the future is a common aspect of prophesy in religion and often various equipment, such as entrails, is needed to do it. The outlawing of this in the Torah is a later tradition and is a response to its popularity

- The **war prophets**: these are people like Gideon and Samson who were spoken to by God (see for example Judges 6: 11–18) and so were able to act as leaders of the people.

Foreign influences on prophecy

When Hebrew religion was emerging after the settlement in Canaan it still had many things in common with the religion of its neighbours and those further afield. So it is not surprising that Hebrew prophecy at this stage was influenced by, for example, the divination and charismatic inspiration found in other religions. Of particular interest in this respect are the inscriptions found in the city of Mari in Mesopotamia as they show features of prophecy similar to those of Hebrew religion.

Development of the prophetic tradition

The prophetic tradition spanned five crucial centuries. This period begins after the division of the monarchy between Israel in the north and Judah in the south after the death of Solomon. It concludes with the return from the Babylonian exile under the Persian ruler Cyrus the Great in 538 BCE and the reconstruction of the Temple. The prophetic tradition is divided into two groups: the major prophets and the minor prophets.

> **Further study**
>
> The prophets of the Jewish Scriptures make an interesting contrast with the 'prophets' of the current religious right who are predicting the imminent end of the world. If you visit an evangelical Christian bookshop you should find a range of such books. Compare the two different types of prophecy.

A transitional phase of Israelite prophecy is identifiable with the change from early Hebrew prophecy (see *above*) to classical Hebrew prophecy (see *below*). These transitional prophets include Samuel and Elijah. In their ability to work miracles to show the presence of God in action (eg 1 Kings 18) they are like the early prophets. In speaking the word of God to the nation they are like the later, classical prophets (eg 1 Sam 7: 3–4).

Elijah

The rise of prophecy is characterised by the appearance of specific, named prophets. These individuals, most notably Elijah and Elisha, act as a bridge between the 10th- and 9th-century BCE (often anonymous) prophets and the writing prophets of 8th century BCE and beyond. The individual prophets served to guide

Prophecy in the 8th century BCE

'Early critical scholars tended to see the prophets as inspired individuals who were responsible for creating the purest form of Israelite monotheism. This view of prophecy gave rise to works that concentrated on the intellectual and theological aspects of prophecy, with the result that little attention was given to the prophet as a human figure intimately connected with his social setting.' Robert R.Wilson *Prophecy and Society in Ancient Israel* (Fortress 1980).

A classic here is *A History of Israelite Religion* by Georg Fohrer (SPCK 1973). Also very good is *The Faith of the Old Testament* by Werner H. Schmidt (Blackwell 1983).

Mercy

In modern Judaism the congregation becomes the priest, the symbols of the festival serve as the psychological means of becoming 'at one' with God and a reading from Leviticus 16 is accompanied by one from Isaiah 57, which places the emphasis on justice, helping the poor and striving for righteousness. See also Lev 4.

Justice

Righteousness

Warning. Photocopying any part of this book without permission is illegal.

Israelite religion through the several social, political and theological crises of the 8th, 6th and 4th centuries BCE.

The final group of Israelite prophets is known as the 'classical', 'canonical' or 'literary' prophets. It is these prophets whose names we find on the books of the prophets in the Hebrew Scripture, such as Amos, Isaiah and Jeremiah. The classical prophets represent the final break of the Hebrew religion with its Canaanite origins. Many times in the classical prophets we find laments about the unfaithfulness of Israel to God and warnings of what would happen to her if she did not mend her ways. It was through the inspiration of one of the classical prophets, known to scholars as Deutero-Isiah ('Second Isaiah'), that Israel finally expressed the belief that only one God existed who had created the world, rather than that there was one God to be worshipped and other gods rejected (Isaiah 40: 18–31). See *below* for notes on three classical prophets.

God and Israel

Nature of God

Animal sacrifice is common in primitive religion. For the Israelites, animal sacrifice developed as atonement for sin. Once a year, on the Day of Atonement the high priest would go into the Holy of Holies in the Temple and sacrifice a bull so that God, in his mercy, could forgive the sins of his people (Lev 4).

As the religion developed the sense of God's mercy to the whole of Israel remained important. After the Exile, when the Israelites returned to Jerusalem and Judea, Deutero-Isaiah saw God's mercy in what had happened: 'But now thus says the Lord, he who created you, O Jacob, he who formed you O Israel: "Fear not, for I have redeemed you; I have called you by name, you are mine"'. (Is 43: 1). The suffering itself becomes a means of God's mercy as it enables the Israelites to see that their God is working in history for their good.

In the early form of Israelite religion neither God nor his people showed much concern for justice. God was a tribal god who helped his people to win wars, giving permission for necessary slaughter (Deut 20: 15–18). However when the Israelites had settled in Canaan a belief developed in the just nature of God. The concern in the law codes that justice be done (Lev 19) shows this. The **Psalms** praise God for his justice many times and a prophet like Isaiah sees justice as firmly established as one of God's major characteristics (Is 5: 16). The message of Amos, the first classical prophet, had as one of its important themes God's anger at the unjust society his people had created (Amos 5). In Job, Elihu, faced with Job's rather worrying claim that God may not be just after all (Job 19: 7), asserts that 'the Almighty will not pervert justice' (Job 34: 12).

Righteousness means 'doing the right thing', a commitment to what is good, fair and honourable. As with the belief in a just God, Israel's belief in a righteous God took some time to develop. God's righteousness means that Israelites can hope to be delivered by him (Ps 31: 1). God's righteous judgments will save Israel (Ps 36: 6). The righteousness of God leads to the messianic belief that a king will arise who will rule in righteousness (Is 32: 1), and when the day of the righteous God arrives 'the sun of righteousness shall arise, with healing in its wings' (Mal 4: 2).

As God is believed to be righteous, so his people should show this quality, for 'The Lord loves righteousness and justice' (Ps 33: 5). Obedience to the Law is the 'righteousness' of Israel (Deut 6: 25). The whole sacrificial system that took place in the Temple was an expression of Israel's righteousness (Deut 33: 19). God will reward people for their righteousness (1 Sam 26: 23). The book of Proverbs makes several references to the importance of a righteous life (Prov 11: 5, 6, 18). Most strikingly, 'the way of righteousness leads to life' (Prov 12: 28).

> **Further study**
>
> Wisdom literature is particularly rich in discussions on the issue of justice, both social and divine. Look at the opening of Wisdom and note the way that the developing emphasis on justice encouraged the theology of life after death to grow in this late work.

In the early days the Israelites had no king. It was only after the Israelite monarchy had established itself that the Israelites could think of God as a king. Isaiah had a vision of the Lord sitting on a throne (Is 6: 1), and the Psalms, which reflect the developing themes of the Israelite religion, refer to God as 'King': 'God is the great king over all gods.' (Ps 95: 3). The prophets express the belief that God is the King of Israel: 'I am the Lord, your holy one, the Creator of Israel, your king', (Is 43: 15) who is present with his people: 'the King of Israel, the Lord, is in your midst' (Zeph 3: 15). Deutero-Isaiah looks forward to salvation coming to earth as an expression of God's kingship: 'Behold I [God] am doing a new thing… I will make a way in the wilderness and rivers in the desert' (Is 43: 19). In the last of the Jewish scriptures, God is king of heaven as well as earth: 'Praise and honour the King of Heaven, for all his works are right and his ways are just' (Dan 4: 37).

Kingship

> 'The twofold notion of sovereignty and communion that was basic to the relationship between God and man determined the religious attitude of man before Yahweh (God). There are always two complementary reactions or notions: fear and love, absolute trust and communion, dependence and sharing in God's sovereignty.' Georg Fohrer *The History of the Israelite Religion* (SPCK 1973).

King Solomon

1 Kings 1–11 tells the story of Solomon from the dying days of his father David to the visit of the Queen of Sheba. His reign was characterised both by increasing prosperity and by a tension between traditional religious demands and political commitment to a foreign policy of engagement with Israel's neighbours.

> The self-revelation of God in his word is a basic characteristic of the Old Testament understanding of God. It catches distinctively the difference between God and man: God speaks, man hears. Because God himself is known by name, man himself is able to call upon him. With his self-introduction God gives man a commission, and the one addressed obeys.' Werner H. Schmidt *The Faith of the Old Testament* (Blackwell 1983).

Inheriting a unified and prosperous kingdom, Solomon was able metaphorically and literally to build on his father's achievements, establishing a professional army and system of government, and developing trade. The building of the Temple shows the prosperity of the country, but note that King Hiram of Tyre supplied not only cedar wood but also architects and artisans: Israel had no experience of such a massive building project. It also encapsulates the political/religious tension of the reign: 1 Kings 6: 11–13 shows God telling Solomon that if the Temple is built according to God's rules, and if Solomon obeys God's commandments, then God will stay loyal to his people and his covenant. Read Solomon's dedicatory prayer carefully (1 Kings 8: 22–61) and you will notice that this is a genuinely religious project. However you should also note that the building of the Temple is only part of a grand building scheme that includes a new royal palace (1 Kings 7: 1–12; 1 Kings 9: 1 indicates that there were other building works). At the end, God warns Solomon that although the Temple was good, it was no substitute for the king and his descendants remaining loyal to the covenant (1 Kings 9: 1–9).

Building the Temple

See *King Solomon* by Frederic Thieberger (East and West Library 1947).

Successes

Solomon asked for **wisdom** rather than longevity or wealth (1 Kings 3: 5–15) and God was pleased. The passage emphasises the role of dispensing justice as a king's task. As a result of this reputation, Solomon has both part of the canonical book of Proverbs and the apocryphal book of Wisdom attributed to him.

This is demonstrated in the subsequent passage, where Solomon is asked to decide which of two women who were both claiming that a baby was hers was telling the truth. He said that the baby should be cut in two. The real mother immediately identified herself by surrendering the baby to the other woman rather than allowing it to be harmed (for more on his reputation for wisdom, see 1 Kings 4: 29–34).

Solomon also succeeded in **keeping intact the kingdom** he inherited from his father. He used his dynastic marriages to strengthen his kingdom. He developed a centralised government and a professional army (he had 12,000 horsemen), thus making Israel much more state-like and easier to defend. As a result the population lived in safety (1 Kings 4: 25–26).

His reign was one of **prosperity and territorial expansion** (1 Kings 4: 20–21; 1 Kings 10: 23–24) and trade enhanced both the wealth and the status of Israel. The king is said to have made silver as common in Jerusalem as stones, and cedar as plentiful as sycamore trees in the foothills (1 Kings 10: 27).

He ordered the **building** of the first of the great temples in Jerusalem, thus providing a focus for political and religious unity. Should we see this as an achievement or a folly, what we might today call a 'prestige project'? Frederic Thieberger comments favourably:

> The king himself, the architect of the Temple, knew that without a central spiritual force, the security of his kingdom would be precarious. What he did not know was that the spiritual legacy of his own life would be powerful enough to keep the nation alive even after the destruction of the kingdom.

See *below* however for the political consequences of this building project.

Failures

It is argued that among the failures of his reign is his having been too open to the influence of foreign religions. He was naturally visited by foreign dignitaries, and he built a palace for Pharaoh's daughter. His many dynastic marriages to foreign wives were not universally welcome.

Foreign gods

Marriages are specified to Ammonites, Edomites, Hittites, Moabites, Sidonians and of course Egyptians in the shape of Pharaoh's daughter, see 1 Kings 11: 1–12. As a result of this uxorious reputation, Solomon has the Song of Songs attributed to him.

You should note the way that the narrator specifically states that the nations listed are those that God had forbidden the Israelites from intermarrying in case they drew the Israelites away from God and into the service of foreign gods (1 Kings 11: 2). Accordingly, in old age, his wives did indeed draw him into the service of their own gods. On a hill east of Jerusalem, Solomon built a high place for the Moabite god Chemosh and for the Ammonite god Molech. He himself is recorded as having followed Molech and the Sidonian goddess Ashtoreth. He also built holy places for his other foreign wives, who burned incense and offered sacrifices to their gods (1 Kings 11: 1–8). Solomon is thus accused of disloyalty to the covenant.

Taxation and unrest

Solomon's enemies included: Hadad the Edomite, from the royal line of Edom (1 Kings 11: 14); Rezon, son of Eliada, who had fled from his master, Hadadezer, king of Zobah (1 Kings 11: 23) and Jeroboam, an Ephraimite and one of Solomon's officials (1 Kings 11: 26).

On the social front, Solomon's building projects led to harsh taxation and the use of forced labour. Opposition to this led to a weakening of loyalty by some of the Israelites. There were rebellions and the divisions that resulted from Solomon's policies meant that the united kingdom of Israel only survived a short time after his death. The northern tribes formed their own kingdom. Although 2 Samuel generally shows Solomon as a good king, his death (in c.926–922 BCE) was followed by the revolt of the northern tribes. Kept to heel by Solomon himself, they felt able to reject his son Rehoboam so that the briefly unified and successful kingdom split into two parts that were more liable to conquest and invasion. Accordingly the northern kingdom eventually fell victim to the Assyrians in 721 BCE and the southern kingdom to the Babylonians in 587 BCE. These events form the background of the work of the prophets to whom we now turn.

Three prophets

Hosea

Hosea is unique among the corpus of prophets because its author came from the northern kingdom of Israel in the period following the division of the monarchy. It is thought that he was active between about 750 BCE to 725 BCE. During the reign of Jeroboam II, the political situation was one of anxiety about the growing power of Assyria, which was in fact to lead to the conquest of Israel in 721 BCE. Israel was not keeping the covenant she made with God, since the Israelites still followed Canaanite religious practices and worshipped Ba'al.

Context

Hosea by Hans Walter Wolf (Fortress Press 1974).

There are several references to God threatening to judge and punish Israel for this unfaithfulness:

Judgement

✦ 'Now I will uncover [Israel's] immorality in the sight of her lovers [the false gods], and no one shall rescue her out of my hand. And I will put an end to all her mirth, her feasts, her new moons, her Sabbaths, and all her appointed feasts. And I will lay waste her vines and her fig trees' (3: 10–12)

✦ 'Their [Israel's] heart is false; now they must bear their guilt. The Lord will break down their altars and destroy their pillars' (10: 2)

Hosea's life became a living expression of his message to Israel. He was told by God to marry Gomer, a prostitute (Hos 1: 2–3): this may be genuinely autobiographical or it may be that the figure of Gomer is an allegorical one that Hosea uses as a metaphor for Israel's infidelity to God. Hosea is thus able to praise God's faithfulness to the covenant in wooing the wife (Gomer/Israel) who had deserted him. Their first child, a son, was called Jezrel, a name that means 'God plants', and refers to God's decision to put an end to the kingdom of Israel (Hos 1: 4–5). The second child, a daughter, was called Loruhamah, meaning 'Not pitied' referring to God's decision to show no more pity to Israel (Hos 1: 6). The third child, a second son, was called 'Loammi', meaning 'Not my people', because of God's decision to abandon his people (Hos 1: 8–9).

Hosea's personal life

Some commentators have suggested that Gomer was actually a cultic prostitute in the service of Baal (perhaps Hos 2: 8 retains a hint of this). Not all authorities accept the idea of 'sacred prostitution': there is a brief outline of the debate in *Wisdom and the Book of Proverbs* by Bernard Lang (Pilgrim Press 1986).

The naming of the three children of this marriage is taken by some commentators to suggest that the story of Gomer is largely metaphorical. But biblical children are given symbolic names: see 1 Sam 4: 21 for the naming of Ichabod, 'where is the glory'.

God's determination to destroy Israel was a consequence of Israel's choice to be unfaithful to the covenant. Like a lot of people with relationship problems, God felt ambivalent about his partner. In 11: 1–4 Israel is spoken of as a beloved child and in 11: 8 there is the impassioned cry from God: 'How can I give you up, O Ephraim! How can I hand you over, O Israel!' If Israel would return to God then she would know his love and prosper:

Reconciliation with God

> I will heal their faithfulness; I will love them freely, for my anger has turned from them. I will be as dew to Israel; he shall blossom as the lily, he shall strike root at the poplar; his shoots shall spread out.' (Hos 14: 4–6)

Warning. Photocopying any part of this book without permission is illegal.

Old Testament/Jewish Bible

Amos

Context

The splendid buildings and costly ivory inlays of Phoenician or Damascene origin unearthed at Samaria show that Amos did not exaggerate the luxury that Israel's upper classes enjoyed.

Amos was active as a prophet around the years 765 and 750 BCE. It was during this time that the northern kingdom was at its strongest (see 2 Kings 14: 21–15: 12), despite having undergone a period of severe instability after the division of the Israelite settlement. Able leadership and favourable regional conditions resulted in a staggering increase in prosperity, optimism and confidence. It is clear from the words of Amos that at least some Israelites were living in considerable luxury: 'Woe to those who lie upon beds of ivory, and stretch themselves upon their couches… who drink wine in bowls, and anoint themselves with the finest oil (6: 4, 6). The wealthy were not ignoring the cult completely and in fact made many sacrifices, but they were failing to keep faithfully to the demands of the covenant. The failure was firstly in terms of behaviour in the religious places: '[Men and women] lay themselves down beside every altar upon clothes that have been religiously dedicated; and in the house of their God they drink the wine of those who have been fined' (Amos 2: 8). Secondly, the sacrifices and other cultic activities continued in a society which was full of injustice (see *below*).

Amos preached an unpopular message, which went against the political grain. Consequently he was denounced by representatives of the Jerusalem establishment (note the fact that Amaziah is a priest). Amos responds with the significant rejoinder that he is not a prophet at all but a herdsman and landowner (Amos 7: 14–15). This gives a meaning to the term 'prophecy' that moves it away from anything cultic or official, leaving it as the vocation of anyone who is inspired by God to preach a particular message.

Moral and social righteousness

Amos has some of the best-known words in scripture on the theme of righteousness: 'I [God] hate, I despise your feasts, and I take no delight in your solemn assemblies. Even though you offer me your burnt offerings and cereal offerings I will not accept them, and the peace offerings of your fatted beasts I will not look upon them. Take away from me the noise of your songs; to the melody of your harps I will not listen. But let justice roll down like waters, and righteousness like an ever flowing stream' (5: 21–24). Social justice had been just as much a part of the covenant agreement as the Temple system of sacrifices and Amos insists that to ignore the former is to make the latter worthless. Amos explicitly denounces established religion, recollecting the experience of apostasy in the desert before the settlement in Canaan. This must be set within a context where feasts and offerings were associated with the Temple in Jerusalem and with the work of the priests in particular. Amos goes on to criticise the ruling authorities in 6: 1–3.

Joel and Amos by Hans Walter Wolf (Fortress Press 1977).

Nature of God

Amos' emphasis is on the original covenant with Abraham. This is indicated by the way that Amos opens: 'The Lord roars from Zion, and utters his voice from Jerusalem' (Amos 1: 2). This introductory theme is picked up in Chapter 3 in what is rightly regarded as almost the birth charter for classical Israelite prophecy: 'Does the lion roar in the forest when he has no prey?… Surely the Lord God does nothing, without revealing his secret to his servants the prophets' (Amos 3: 4, 7).

Warning. Photocopying any part of this book without permission is illegal.

God's position with regard to Israel is declared by Amos 3: 2: 'You only have I known of all the families of the earth; therefore I will punish you for all your iniquities.' This threat of judgement is a familiar theme in the book. It is repeated in Amos 5: 2: 'Fallen, no more to rise is the virgin Israel; forsaken on her land, with none to raise her up.' It is further repeated in the dramatic visions of Chapter 7 when Amos sees locusts, fire and a plumbline. But the most famous image occurs at the beginning of Chapter 8. Amos sees a basket of summer fruit, which in Hebrew is very similar to the word for end or destruction. The basket is held to mean that 'the end has come upon my people Israel'.

The Israelites at whom the words of Amos were directed had become very casual in their attitude to God and his covenant and cult: 'Woe to you who are at ease in Zion, and to those who feel secure on the mountains of Samaria' (6: 1). They had assumed that God would give them prosperity by the very fact of the covenant having been created, no matter how people behaved. But Amos taught that the persistent breaches of the covenant would lead God to punish his people. He echoes in this the original mutuality of the covenant agreement in which Israel was offered election in return for covenant obedience.

By this time in the development of Israelite religion an eschatological belief had arisen that at some point in the future there would be a 'day of the Lord' when the enemies of Israel would be destroyed by a direct intervention of God. Amos warns that it is the Israelites who will be judged on this day: 'Woe to you who desire the day of the Lord! Why would you have the day of the Lord? It is darkness, and not light' (5: 18). Amos insists that the Day of the Lord is imminent but that it will be a time of disaster and not deliverance.

But the purpose of Amos' preaching, as he understood it, was not simply to be a prophet of doom but to give his people the chance to repent:

> Seek good, and not evil, that you may live; and so the Lord, the God of hosts, will be with you, as you have said. Hate evil, and love good, and establish justice in the gate; it may be that the Lord, the God of hosts, will be gracious to the remnant of Joseph (Amos 5: 14–15).

Jeremiah

Jeremiah contains a wealth of biographical material that helps us reconstruct the life of the author. Jeremiah was active as a prophet between about 628 BCE and 586 BCE. He was from a priestly family and supported the reforms made by King Josiah in 721 BCE. He lived in Jerusalem, which, during this time, was coming under increasing pressure from the Babylonians. In 605 BCE the battle of Carchemish made it clear that the Babylonians were a serious threat to Israel. Jeremiah sent his secretary Baruch to read a scroll of prophecy in the Temple, from which Jeremiah himself was banned. King Jehoiakim ordered the scroll to be burned. Jeremiah began work on a lengthier second version (Jer 36: 32). The Babylonians took some Jews as prisoners before they attacked Jerusalem itself in 587 BCE. The Temple was destroyed and many Jews were exiled to Babylon.

Jeremiah taught that these disasters were God's punishment for

---

Further study

Amos says clearly that he is neither a prophet nor a prophet's son (Amos 7: 14). Think about what this tells us about the concept of what a prophet was in the 8th century BCE. Can you distinguish between prophets and priests?

Relationship with God

'In making his heavy emphasis upon doom, Amos leaned over backward to counteract the false optimism of his time. Later on, when the desperate political situation drove people to fanaticism or despair, the prophets were to proclaim a message of hope. But the age of Jeroboam II did not need to hear the divine promise, for the people already believed that 'God is with us' (Amos 5: 14). What they needed to hear was the word of divine judgment that would shatter their complacency and false security. Then, perhaps, they would understand that the promise rests, not on political and economic factors, but on the gracious dealings of God with his people.' *Understanding the Old Testament* by Bernard W. Anderson (Prentice Hall 1986).

See Amos 9; compare with Lev 26: 14–33.

Context

Warning. Photocopying any part of this book without permission is illegal.

Jeremiah by William L. Holladay (Fortress Press Vol 1 1986, Vol 2 1989).

repeated breaches of the covenant. He anticipated further disaster in the period leading up to the exile and his prophecies won him few friends. Jeremiah initially stayed in Jerusalem after the exile. Against his will, he was eventually taken to Egypt, where he died, it is reported, with words of judgement on his lips.

Jeremiah suffered greatly for his message. His words were unpopular and putting up with this unpopularity caused him much psychological pain: 'O Lord, you deceived me and I was deceived; you overpowered me and prevailed. I am ridiculed all day long; everyone mocks me' (Jer 20: 7). He received death threats for the message he brought to Judah.

Judgement

> 'No braver or more tragic figure ever trod the stage of Israel's history than the prophet Jeremiah. His was the authentic voice of the religion of Moses speaking, as it were, out of season to the dying nation. It was his lot through a long lifetime to say, and say again, that Judah was doomed and that that doom was God's righteous judgement upon her for breach of covenant.' *A History of Israel* by John Bright (SCM 1964).

As with the other prophets, Jeremiah brought warning to the people of Israel that disaster would follow if they did not change their ways: 'Therefore thus says the Lord of hosts: Because you [Judah] have not obeyed my words, behold I will end for all the tribes of the north, says the Lord, and for Nebuchadrezzar the king of Babylon, my servant, and I will bring them against this land and its inhabitants, and against all these nations round about: I will utterly destroy them, and make them a horror, a hissing, and an everlasting reproach' (25: 8–9).

However Jeremiah's foretelling was not solely a matter of doom and gloom, it contained an important element of optimism. Jeremiah posits God as saying: 'I [God] will put my law within them, and I will be their God, and they shall be my people. And no longer shall each man teach his neighbour and each his brother, saying 'Know the Lord,' for they all shall know me, from the least of them to the greatest, says the Lord; for I will forgive their wrongdoing, and I will remember their sin no more.' (31: 33–34) This passage must have been shocking in Jeremiah's day and thereafter; after all, the passage implies that God will draw up a fresh contract without the defects of the old, implying in turn that he could improve on the old one. One could argue that the affirmation of Deutero-Isaiah, 'The word of our God will stand for ever' (Is 40: 8) was intended as a reassurance against these implications. On the other hand, the idea had been prepared for by Hosea's words about a fresh covenant to be given by Yahweh (Hos 2: 20) and it is likewise true that the crisis of the fall of Jerusalem and exile was so severe that the word 'new' features largely in the hopeful words.

Jeremiah 31: 31–34.

Jeremiah by William L. Holladay (Fortress Press Vol 1 1986).

Test yourself

1. What does an understanding of the prophets contribute to an understanding of the Jewish Scriptures?

2. (a) How are the themes of the mercy, justice, righteousness and kingship of God presented in the Jewish Scriptures?

    (b) Are there any tensions between these different presentations of the nature of God?

3. Should Solomon be considered as a success or a failure?

4. Is the loving nature of God the main theme of Hosea?

5. (a) Why was the prophetic message of Amos needed in Israel at the time that he lived?

    (b) What is the unique message of Amos compared with the other prophets you have studied?

6. To what extent is the description of Jeremiah as a prophet of doom justified?

Religious ethics

The relationship between religion and morality

The moral argument for the existence of God

There are in fact a range of moral arguments for the existence of God. The most important of these can be postulated from the ethical reasoning of the philosopher **Immanuel Kant** (1724–1804). His argument, illustrated by a quotation from *The Critique of Practical Reason* (1788), runs as follows:

> Now it was seen to be a duty for us to promote the highest good...

Kant is arguing that as human beings we have a rational nature. As rational individuals we have a duty to do what is morally correct, and this means that we have a duty to act in such a way that will bring about the highest possible good.

> ...consequently it is not merely allowable, but it is a necessity connected with duty as a requirement, that we should assume that the highest good can be brought about in reality...

This idea is summarised as 'ought' implies 'can'. For Kant we cannot be morally obliged to achieve the impossible. But the fact that we have a moral duty to pursue the highest good means that the highest good must be obtainable.

> ...and this is possible only on the condition of the existence of God...

If the highest good is possible then there must be a being who is capable of bringing that highest good into existence. As only a being with the attributes of God could bring the highest good into existence then, Kant concludes:

> ... it is morally necessary to assume the existence of God.

Mackie is not convinced by this argument. He writes: 'The most glaring weakness of the argument is in the step from the proposition that "we ought to seek the highest good" to the claim that "it must therefore be possible". Even if, as Kant argues elsewhere, "ought" implies "can" the thesis that we ought to seek the highest good implies only that we can seek to promote it, and perhaps, since rational seeking could not be completely fruitless, that we can to some extent actually promote it.' Once this connection between what we ought to do and therefore what must be the case is broken then, in Mackie's view, the argument fails. This line of argument is very widely accepted.

Morality is sometimes seen as such a strange and overwhelming aspect of human life that it can only be explained by the existence of a God. For example, Newman saw the fact of the conscience as an indication that God exists. The conscience seems to have the power to tell us what is right and wrong regardless of our background and inclinations. It appears to express an objective and superhuman reality. Newman believes that it is appropriate to describe this reality as 'God'. C. S. Lewis made much the same point when he argued that in moral values we find a reality that cannot be explained in human terms, a reality that is exactly what we would expect to find if the world was created by a God who

---

> If you choose to answer questions in the exam on religious ethics, you will not be able to answer questions on the Old Testament/Jewish Bible.

The Puzzle of Ethics by Peter Vardy and Paul Grosch (Fount 1999) is a good introduction to this topic.

It is vital that you note that Kant never actually put forward a moral argument for the existence of God. The word 'postulate' is vital here – Kant recognised that the existence of God could be assumed from his ethical reasoning, but he did not think it could be proved. He argued that the human mind was incapable of having direct knowledge of reality, therefore no attempt to establish God could be successful on that basis.

> 'Morality, according to Kant, requires not only that we obey what is our duty, but that in doing so we see ourselves as bringing forth the highest good, a world in which virtue is necessarily accompanied by happiness. It is not within our own power to bring this about by our own efforts, but we must view our actions as contributing to its realization. This gives rise to a "need of reason" to believe in the conditions under which the highest good would be the result of our actions. These conditions are the existence of a personal God, who sees into our hearts and arranges the laws of nature so that happiness will be the reward of virtue.' *Encyclopedia of Ethics* (Routledge 2001), page 993.

See J. L. Mackie, *The Miracle of Theism* (OUP 1983).

Newman and Lewis

Further study

Do we have to posit the existence of a God to explain why we act morally, or can psychology and sociology offer better explanations? Find out what Freud and Nietzsche had to say about the origins of morality.

wished human beings to have the possibility of freely deciding what is good.

A slightly different form of the argument is that if God did not exist and there was no Last Judgment after death then we would have no motivation for being moral and anarchy would result.

Critiques of links between religion and morality

Kant argued that morality had to be 'autonomous', which means that moral actions should be motivated by considerations of moral duty and nothing else. If a person is choosing to behave in a particular way because they believe that God has told them what to do or because God will reward them, then they are trying to pretend that they are not morally autonomous beings who can work out what their duty is through the use of their rational natures.

For some of these other perspectives on the moral argument, see Michael Peterson et al, *Reason and Religious Belief* (OUP 1998) and John Hick, *Philosophy of Religion* (Prentice Hall 1990).

Theoretical critiques

See 'Autonomy, Obligation and Virtue: An Overview of Kant's Moral Philosophy' by J. B. Schneewind in *The Cambridge Companion to Kant* ed. Paul Guyer (Cambridge University Press 1992).

The autonomy of morality is supported by the **Euthyphro dilemma**. This suggests that there are two possible relationships between God and ethics. In the first of these, morality depends on what God decides is right and wrong. However, why should we accept the moral standards of God? What if God were to decide that murder was morally acceptable? The second possibility is that God accepts a moral standard independent of God (eg that murder is wrong). But if this is the case we do not need God to tell us what is right and wrong: we can discover moral standards on our own. In the first instance, God is not all-good, in the second, God is all-good, but not all-powerful.

A good source for investigating the Euthyphro dilemma on the internet is: www.str.org/free/commentaries/apologetics/evil/euthyphr.htm

Practical critiques

Three very influential thinkers argued that the link between religion and morality was inherently flawed, if not dangerous:

See page 15.

♦ **Sigmund Freud** (1856–1939) argued that religious morality can be a major factor in creating mental health problems. Many people have been taught by religion that their desires are evil and that their animal natures are something of which to be ashamed. Freud believed that the energy of our animal natures has to go somewhere. If religious people cannot find ways of expressing it outwardly, due to some sense of shame, then it gets suppressed and causes problems such as depression and compulsive disorders

For Freud's attack on religious morality see his *Civilisation and Its Discontents* (Penguin 2002).

♦ **Karl Marx** (1818–1883) argued that religious morality is used by the bourgeoisie to control the proletariat. By promising the less well-off that they will go to heaven if they live 'moral' lives, the bourgeoisie are able to oppress their natural desire for social revolution

For more on Marx's views on the link between religion and morality, see *Marx and Ethics* by Philip J. Kain (Clarendon Press 1991). See also page 15 of this guide.

♦ **Friedrich Nietzsche** (1844–1900) argued that religious morality is a 'safety first' way of looking at the world that destroys human potential. For Nietzsche, the fact that 'God is dead' (ie no longer relevant to life) means that if we are strong enough we can create a world where human life is of value because of what it is, rather than because of God. Nietzsche saw Christianity as indicative of a 'herd mentality' that encouraged people to be cowardly and conformist.

Nietzsche's Ethics and His War on 'Morality' by Simon May (Oxford University Press 2002).

Ethical theories

Deontology

Deontology suggests that ethics is a matter of duty and obligation. Deontological thinkers believe that we should decide whether an action is right without considering its consequences. The murder of an evil dictator for instance might bring some important benefits (freedom for thousands of people, an end to oppression), but it would still be an act of murder and therefore inherently wrong. The best-known proponent of the deontological approach to ethics is Kant, who believed that it was the possession of a good will that made a moral person. Kant stated:

> It is impossible to conceive of anything at all in the world, or even out of it, which can be taken as good without qualification, except a good will.

In other words, the only thing we can be certain of when making moral decisions is that our will is intending either good or bad; we are either choosing our duty or we are not. If we act with the intention of doing our duty then we are being morally good.

The Blackwell Guide to Ethical Theory ed. Hugh LaFollette (Blackwell 1999) has some useful material on all of these theories.

Strengths	Weaknesses
◆ It seems to be common sense that moral behaviour must involve at least some attempt to do our duty	◆ Can supporters of deontological ethics show *why* duty is important or even what our duty is?
◆ Deontological ethics might be thought to fit in well with religious views about morality as duty to God	◆ Deontological ethics runs the risk of lacking humanity, suggesting that one should care more about doing one's duty than about other people
◆ Sometimes a morality based on the idea that 'the end justifies the means' is used to justify acts of evil (eg genocide).	◆ Thinking about the consequences of one's actions seems to be an essential part of morality.

Evaluation

See *Ethics* by William K. Frankena (Prentice Hall 1988) for a useful discussion of deontology and other aspects of ethical theory.

Emotivism

Emotivism was an ethical theory put forward by the British philosopher **A. J. Ayer** (1910–1989). He argued that the only way we can know whether or not language has a **meaning** or not is if its truth makes any difference to the world as we observe it. So the statement 'The universe has just doubled in size' is meaningless because it is impossible to see the difference this would make if it were true. Ayer applied this idea to moral statements such as 'stealing is wrong'. We can't actually see the difference this makes to the world, so the statement, even though it sounds like a fact, is really meaningless. Ayer held that moral statements that sound as if they mean something are really just expressions of emotion: 'stealing is wrong' is just another way of saying 'I don't like stealing'. Emotivism is often known as the boo-hooray theory of ethics, as it posits that all ethical statements are a matter of either booing or cheering moral actions.

For more on Ayer's ideas see page 20. He first set out his emotive argument in *Language, Truth and Logic* (Penguin 2001).

Evaluation

Strengths	Weaknesses
◆ Some philosophers accept that Ayer is right in claiming that ethical language does not tell us anything about the world ◆ Emotivism helps explain why there are moral disagreements: people are arguing about subjective feelings when they think that they are establishing facts ◆ Emotivism can be seen as a creative approach to ethics, as it suggests that ethics is about deciding what we like rather than doing what we are told.	◆ Some philosophers argue that ethical language does tell us about the real world (see *below*) ◆ People do not just use moral language to try to state moral facts. They also use it to influence the actions of others, and emotivism does not take this into account ◆ If emotivism is correct then we live in a world in which 'anything goes' and the morality of behaviour is simply a matter of personal taste.

Intuitionism

Moore's *Principia Ethica* (Cambridge University Press 1993) puts forward the basic arguments for Intuitionism.

Intuitionism is also known as 'Non-naturalism'.

Intuitionism is closely associated with the British philosopher **G. E. Moore** (1873–1958). Moore argued that it is impossible to define what is ethically good. The idea that we could take the concept of 'good' apart and find out what it is in the same way as we can take apart a table, for example, is for Moore an example of the **naturalistic fallacy**. Good is not a natural object but a non-physical reality which cannot be defined or described in other terms. We know that good exists because we have an ability to know intuitively that it is a reality. If someone asks us 'Why is stealing wrong?', the best answer, according to Intuitionists, is that 'I know that it is wrong and I need no arguments to tell me so'. Moore also believed that the more we can intuit and promote goodness in society, the better society will become.

Evaluation

Strengths	Weaknesses
◆ Many people might well agree that we somehow know what is good without having to try to define it ◆ Intuitionism avoids difficult arguments that try to show how the physical world and moral world relate to one another. Moral values such as 'good' are real but do not have the same reality as physical objects which we know through use of our senses ◆ Intuitionism allows ethics to be objective. As moral statements are about what really exists they can be correct or incorrect, rather than just a matter of opinion.	◆ Why should we accept that moral values such as 'good' have a real existence when there is no evidence for them? ◆ Intuitionism depends on one set of intrinsic, unified moral values. But if you are an Intuitionist in one part of the world then your values might well be different from those of an Intuitionist in another part. Intuitionism seems culturally dependent and thus subjective ◆ Intuitionists assume that moral language is about trying to describe the world, but perhaps it is about expressing our feelings or affecting how others behave.

Natural moral law

There is a full discussion of natural moral law in *The Puzzle of Ethics* by Peter Vardy and Paul Grosch (Fount 1999).

Natural moral law is an attempt to answer the question: 'How should human beings live?' It is based on the theory that there is an ideal way to be and behave as a human being. The medieval theologian **Thomas Aquinas** (1225–1274) argued that human beings were created by God to achieve their ultimate purpose or *telos*: to be happy. Aquinas held that it is possible, as a matter of objective fact, for us to order our thinking and actions in a way that brings us closer to fulfilling this ultimate purpose, by using our bodies in the proper way, for example. Genitals, to use one of Aquinas' examples, were designed by God to help us find happiness through sexual intercourse in marriage. But if we use our genitals for homosexual activity, then we are breaking natural moral law and moving away from our ultimate fulfillment.

Strengths	Weaknesses
◆ It gives a clear sense of the meaning and value of human life, and avoids moral confusion by providing a set of hard-and-fast rules to live by ◆ It is a moral system which depends on rationality, rather than the powerful and dangerous forces of emotion ◆ Although natural law theories are usually associated with Christianity, the concept of a universal moral law is non-sectarian and provides a useful meeting-point for members of many different faiths.	◆ The idea that there is a basic human nature that we all share has been criticised by many. Existentialists suggest that we make up what it means to be a human being as we go along ◆ Natural moral law can be used as a form of social control against minority groups ◆ Natural moral law does not account for the fact that human beings are more than just the sum of their parts. It breaks human beings into their working components.

Evaluation

> **Further study**
>
> Choose a current ethical issue and judge whether a deontological or a natural law perspective would be the best approach to the moral dilemma concerned. See for example *Contemporary Moral Problems* ed. James E. White (Wadsworth 2002) for a range of interesting essays on important applied ethical issues.

Ethical language

'Is-ought'

'Is-ought' is one of the most famous distinctions in ethical theory. It was first made by the Scottish philosopher **David Hume** (1711–1776), who argued that it was incorrect to leap from statements of fact ('is' statements) to making moral judgments ('ought' statements) about those facts. For example if I were to steal a woman's purse, she would be upset. No sensible person would deny that the unhappiness of the victim 'is' part of the real world, a fact. However some people would deny that there is any logical connection between the statements 'she is upset' and 'you ought not to have stolen her purse'. One could go on describing facts about the event – such as the woman's distress – forever, but even if one described the most terrible pain that one human being can cause to another, this does not show that it was wrong to cause that pain. There is no logical link between facts and values. Other people disagree. They think that you can make a logical move from physical pain to making a moral judgment about that pain.

Those who make this distinction between 'is' and 'ought' are known as non-cognitivists. They believe that moral statements cannot give us information about the world, that there are no moral facts. Ayer's emotivist theory is a non-cognitive position. The **prescriptivism** of **R. M. Hare** (1919–2002) is another example of non-cognitivism. Hare suggested that moral language is about trying to get ourselves and others to act in certain ways. Moral concepts are not part of nature, but acquired through custom and upbringing.

The second group of people are known as cognitivists. They believe that moral facts exist and that moral language refers to actual qualities. Some cognitivists are naturalists who believe that the existence of pleasure and pain, or of a God, can be the basis for making moral judgments. Other cognitivists, such as Moore, are non-naturalists who think that moral values really exist as part of the universe but are not bound up with pleasure and pain or God, they are just simply 'themselves'.

'Hume's fork' was set out in his *Treatise of Human Nature* (Oxford University Press 2000).

See *A Treatise of Human Nature* by David Hume (Oxford University Press 2000) for the original is/ought distinction.

Cognitivists and non-cognitivists

See *The Language of Morals* by R. M. Hare for a discussions of the issues raised here and of Hare's own moral theory.

The meaning of 'good'

'Good' is one of the key terms used in ethical theory. If we can work out what we mean by 'good' then we will have a pretty good grasp of what ethics is about. Here are the suggestions of some prominent thinkers:

There is a useful discussion of the meaning of 'good' in Ethics *by William K. Frankena (Prentice Hall 1988).*

- Moore suggested that 'good' is a value that cannot be defined but really exists, just not in the same way as a table or an apple exists in the physical world. We know it is there by our own intuition

For more on Bentham's theory of Utilitarianism, see page 43 of the Edexcel AS Guide.

- The Utilitarian Jeremy Bentham (1748–1832) argued that 'good' is an objective moral value, and held that an action or object is good to the degree to which it causes pleasure

- Aquinas believed that God is the ultimate good. God has created human nature so that human beings can behave in good ways, which means in ways that will help them to achieve their ultimate good of being eternally happy

- The atheistic philosopher J. L. Mackie (1917–1983) maintained that 'good' is whatever human beings decide that it is

- Ayer argued that calling something 'good' is just another way of saying that you like it.

The meaning you give to 'good' will depend on whether you are a cognitivist or a non-cognitivist (see the distinction *above*). If you are a cognitivist then you will think that 'good' is an objective reality which has its source in things like pleasure, God, or non-natural realities. But if you are like most non-cognitivists, you will be of the opinion that good is either something which human beings invent or is an expression of emotion.

Being Good: A Short Introduction To Ethics by Simon Blackburn (Oxford University Press 2001) has a good deal to say explicitly and implicitly about the meaning of 'good'.

Concepts in moral discourse and applied ethics

Objectivity, relativism, subjectivism

Compare these two statements:

- London is the capital of England
- Yellow is the best colour.

There is an excellent series of articles on objectivity and subjectivity in Introduction to Philosophy: Classic and Contemporary Readings *ed. Louis P. Pojman (Wadsworth 1999). The whole book is an outstanding introduction to philosophy, and contains articles relevant to other areas of the specification.*

The first statement is a matter of fact. It is objectively true and its truth does not depend on who is making the statement. The second statement is a matter of opinion. It may be true for the person who is making the statement but it is not necessarily true for anyone else. It is a subjective statement. A big issue in ethics is whether moral statements are objective or subjective. Is, for instance, the statement 'stealing is wrong' an objective statement?

Objectivists believe that moral statements can be a matter of fact. There are different grounds for being an objectivist:

- The belief that moral values are logically related to states of affairs in the world. For example stealing is objectively wrong because it causes pain

- There is a God who has the authority to make some values objectively valid

Warning. Photocopying any part of this book without permission is illegal.

✦ Intuitionists argue that some objective values, such as 'good', exist and although we are unable to know these things by our senses, we are aware of them intuitively.

Subjectivists believe that moral statements are a matter of opinion rather than fact. The 'argument from queerness' made by Mackie suggests that objectively existing values do not fit in easily with other sorts of existence that we know of: they are just too strange to be true. Mackie also argues that if moral values were objective then we would expect to have the same sort of agreement about them that we have about other factual aspects of the world. Nobody argues about what a chair or table is. But we find that a person's moral values are relative to, among other things, where and when they live.

> 'If there were objective values, then they would be entities or qualities or relations of a very strange sort, utterly different from anything else in the universe'. J. L. Mackie *Ethics: Inventing Right and Wrong* (Penguin 1990).

This is the argument from relativity, which also suggests that moral values are not objective. Cultural relativists hold that moral values are determined by social norms, which differ from place to place and from era to era. The historian **Herodotus** (c.480–c.425) demonstrated this when describing King Darius of Persia. Darius asked some Greeks if they would ever eat the bodies of their dead fathers for money. They were horrified by the idea. He than asked a tribe called the Callatiae, who were known for eating the dead bodies of their parents, if they would consider cremating them instead, again for money. They were equally horrified. Herodotus thus demonstrated how the most inbuilt moral values are perhaps simply dependent on one's culture, and thus subjective.

Applied ethics

Applied ethics is the study of how ethical decisions are made in real-life situations. Sometimes these decisions concern what is and is not legal. In order to make laws, governments have to have authority. Two types of authority can be identified:

Authority

✦ **De jure** authority is when someone has the power *in law* over others (though they may not be able to use it in practice)

✦ **De facto** authority is when someone has the power *in practice* to make others do what they want (though their power may be held illegally).

Governments need to have de facto authority if they are to be recognised as morally sound. Traditionally the de facto authority of governments was held to come from the ultimate de facto authority of God. In his *Summa Theologica* Thomas Aquinas quotes St. Paul, who wrote in Romans 13 that all governmental authority comes ultimately from God. Aquinas says that 'the duty of obedience [to the state] is for the Christian a consequence of the derivation of the authority from God'. Luther makes much the same point in his *An Admonition to Peace*. Although Luther was theologically radical, he was politically conservative, and had no hesitation in backing the violent suppression of peasant revolts by the state. In the modern world de facto authority is often thought of as resulting from the expression of the will of the people expressed through democratic means. Some Christians are in favour of passive or active resistance to what they see as unjust government.

Jacques Maritain, a leading Catholic philosopher of the 20th century, offers some interesting insights into how traditional Christianity relates to modern democratic ideas. See his *Christianity and Democracy* (Ignatius 1986).

For more on this, see the notes on Liberation, Black and African Theology on pages 83–89.

Distributive justice

A government uses its authority to distribute a number of good things in society. The question of how these goods should be shared out comes under the heading of distributive justice. One basis of distributive justice is **natural law**, based on meeting as many of the needs of human beings as they exist in nature. Aquinas writes in *Summa Theologica* that 'Laws may be unjust... by being contrary to human good'. By this 'good' Aquinas means what is appropriate to human nature as God wills is to be. So as we have a natural need to eat, a law which left some people hungry would be unjust.

> One problem with ideas based on natural law is that philosophers find it hard to say just what this 'natural' human nature really is. It is widely held today that human nature is a product of language and society.

Another basis for distributive justice is **utilitarianism**, which suggests that distribution should result in the greatest happiness of the greatest number. This is widely accepted as an important basis for justice in modern society, but can be criticised on the grounds that utilitarianism can only take into account what can be measured, and this may lead to injustice. For example, building new roads reduces journey time, which can be measured, but the extent of damage caused by the new roads might be a much more subjective judgement.

John Rawls (1921–2002) suggested that distributive justice would be achieved if the person distributing was aware of the fact that they could end up in the same position as any of those who would be affected by the distribution. This is called the 'Original Position'. The person in the Original Position should also not know any of those who will be affected by the distribution, and this 'Veil of Ignorance' should again ensure fairness. From a Christian perspective, Rawls' theory may well seem too optimistic, as no one can be free enough from the effects of sin to make an unbiased distribution.

> See John Rawls, *A Theory of Justice* (OUP 2002), plus the articles on 'Justice' and 'Justice, Distributive' in *The Routledge Encyclopaedia of Philosophy* (Routledge 1997).

Positive law

In order to express its authority to act justly, a government must pass laws. Aquinas saw a chain of law which began with the eternal law of God. He believed that natural law expresses how human beings can best live the life that God has given them, and saw positive law, the sort of law passed by Parliament, as trying to enable society to live as close to the natural law as possible. This means that positive law can be paternalistic and so can pass laws that interfere directly with people's private lives even if the people concerned are not hurting anyone else.

> Mill's *On Liberty* (Penguin 1982) is seen as a classic on this issue.

The Utilitarian John Stuart Mill (1806–1873) rejected this view, and argued that the only reason a government should pass laws is to stop its citizens hurting each other. He strongly disagreed with the idea of paternalistic government. In our modern society, we are used to an emphasis on governments only interfering in the lives of individuals when there is an obvious reason. Some issues relevant to this debate in recent years have included the decision to pass laws forcing passengers to wear seatbelts in cars, and the legal difficulties faced by sado-masochists who hurt each other, but with full consent. In both these cases the issue is whether the government should interfere in a private activity to stop people hurting themselves.

Punishment

If people break the law then the government has the option to punish them. Punishment is based on the idea of 'just desserts', which is making someone suffer for the wrong they have done. This idea plays an important part in the Bible and traditional Christian thinking. If one causes suffering then it is right that one should suffer oneself. People who hold a this type of view concerning punishment think that prisons in particular should not be too comfortable; some would like them to be really very nasty indeed. This view of punishment is also one of the major arguments marshalled by those who support capital punishment.

Utilitarians hold that the concept of punishment is ethically justified. Bentham made this point in his *Rational of Punishment*. He argued that an enlightened society was not likely to cause suffering that had no good effect or purpose. The work of the Utilitarians led to the modern radical view of the use of prisons. Prisons are necessary so that those who commit crimes can be withdrawn from society to protect it, others can be deterred and, most importantly, the prisoner can have the opportunity to be rehabilitated.

Look up 'punishment' in the index of *The Metaphysics of Morals* by Immanuel Kant (Cambridge University Press 1996) for the classic statement of punishment based on 'just desserts', and Bentham's 'Rational of Punishment', especially chapter 4 ('Cases Unmeet for Punishment'), at www.constitution.org/jb/pml.htm.

Test yourself

1. What reasons are there for thinking that ethics should stand apart from religion and what reasons are there for thinking that ethics depends on religion?

2. Is there a convincing case to be made for making duty the most important consideration when making moral decisions?

3. Was Ayer right to claim that all ethical statements do is express emotion?

4. Assess the strengths and weaknesses of natural law as a basis for moral decision making.

5. Outline a case for thinking that moral values are objective. Secondly, outline a case for thinking that moral values are subjective and relative. Which case is the stronger?

6. Does political authority ultimately come from God?

The New Testament

The Gospel according to Luke

The purposes and characteristics of the Gospel

Purposes

> Use of a good commentary is essential for Luke. Two good commentaries are: *St Luke* by G. B. Caird (Penguin 1990) and *Luke* by Leon Morris (IVP 1988).

Discussion of the purpose of the Gospel can be related to two key aspects. The first is the Preface (Lk 1: 1–4), in which Luke claims to be writing an 'orderly account' for his reader, Theophilus, which is based on material from eyewitnesses. One argument takes at face value both the Preface and Luke's concern to put the events of Jesus' life in their proper historical context (see for example Lk 2: 1–2 and 3: 1–2). Scholars such as Marshall who argue in this way maintain that even if Luke can be shown to have a clear theological purpose, and even if ancient writers did not perceive the division between historical fact and interpretation in the same way as we do today, that Luke's main aim was nonetheless to record the major facts of Jesus' life. An alternative argument to Marshall's has been receiving some attention recently. This is based on the work of Talbet, who compares Luke with ancient epics, such as Virgil's *Aeneid*, and concludes that Luke's theological message was far more important to him than the recording of historical facts.

> See *Luke: Historian and Theologian* by I. H. Marshall (Paternoster 1970).

> C. H. Talbet's views are described and discussed in *The Past as Legacy: Luke-Acts and Ancient Epic* by Marianne Palmer Bonz (Fortress Press 2000).

The second aspect revolves around key texts in the Gospel that indicate that a major purpose of Luke was to bring the message of the Gospel to the Romans. A particularly important text in this regard is Luke 2: 32, in which Simeon thanks God for the birth of Jesus who is a 'light to the gentiles'. Moreover Luke traces the genealogy of Jesus back to Adam (3: 23–38), thus demonstrating that Jesus came to save the whole of humankind and not just the Jews. Luke is always anxious to demonstrate that Christians wished to be on good terms with the Romans: he portrays centurions in a good light in 7: 2–10 and 23: 47, and Pilate is shown to be blameless in the execution of Jesus – Luke has him state on three occasions that Jesus had done no wrong (23: 4, 14, 22).

Characteristics

Central characteristics of the Gospel are:

> Leon Morris covers the characteristics of Luke very well in his introduction. See *Luke* (IVP 1988).

- ✦ **Universalism.** The Gospel shows a concern for humanity as a whole. This theme is summarised in the final story of the Gospel in which the resurrected Jesus instructs the disciples to take the message of Christianity to 'all nations' (24: 47)

- ✦ **Concern for those at the margins of society.** Often quoted in this respect is the story of the prostitute who washed the feet of Jesus at the house of Simon the Pharisee (7: 36–50), the story of the Good Samaritan which shows the failings of the socially acceptable Priest and Levite (10: 29–37), the story of the tax collector who received God's forgiveness and of the proud Pharisee who did not (18: 9–14), and the three stories of the lost: the Lost Coin, the Lost Sheep and the Lost Son (15: 1–32), told, according to 15: 1, to the tax collectors and sinners 'who were drawing near'. Finally there are the words of Jesus to the criminal crucified alongside him: 'Today you will be with me in paradise' (23: 43)

> **Warning.** Photocopying any part of this book without permission is illegal.

- **Emphasis on women.** Luke shows interest in the lives of women, such as Mary and Elizabeth in the Birth Narratives in Chapters 1 and 2, and in the story of the woman who lost a coin (15: 1–10).

Relationship to the Synoptics

Jesus' teaching

The Kingdom of God had been a key theme of Israel's religion from the time of the Old Testament onwards. Israel had come to believe that God was the Creator King of the universe, but they had also developed the desire that God's kingship should be made real on Earth, leading to the overcoming of evil in the world. In Luke 4: 43 Jesus tells his disciples that his role is to 'preach the good news of the Kingdom of God'. Here are some key texts from Luke about the Kingdom:

The Kingdom of God

- **6: 20.** The poor are told that the Kingdom of God belongs to them

For more on these passages, see references to the 'Kingdom of God' in the index of *St Luke* by G. B. Caird (Penguin 1990).

- **9: 27.** Jesus says that some of his listeners will not die 'before they see the Kingdom of God', referring to its complete coming at the end of time

- **9: 62.** The disciples are warned that if they turn back once they have decided to follow Jesus they are not 'fit for the Kingdom of God'

- **11: 2.** The disciples are told to pray for the coming of the Kingdom

- **11: 20.** Jesus says that 'If it is by the finger of God I cast out demons, then you know that the Kingdom of God has come upon you'. The power of Jesus to defeat evil is a sign that the age of the Kingdom is beginning

- **13: 19.** The Kingdom of God is like a mustard seed. Just as a mustard tree is far larger than the original seed, so the Kingdom of God will grow from the teaching and actions of Jesus and his disciples into something that changes the world

> **Further study**
>
> One of the most controversial Kingdom sayings in Luke is 17: 21: 'The Kingdom of God is within you'. This has been used by many spiritual writers to suggest that Jesus was talking of a subjective spiritual experience. However for some Protestant commentators this makes us rather over familiar with God and they have consequently tried to translate the verse 'The Kingdom of God is in the midst of you' ie 'you' as in the Christian community. Use commentaries to come to your own conclusion on what Luke meant by this statement.

- **14: 15–24.** This is the parable of the Great Banquet or Great Supper. Those originally invited refuse, so the socially unacceptable are made to attend. This suggests that the Kingdom of God is not for those who consider themselves too good for it, but for those who would not think themselves good enough

- **22: 16.** During the Last Supper Jesus looks forward to the great banquet that will celebrate the final coming of the Kingdom.

Kummel states the following about Luke's teaching on the Kingdom:

> Jesus gives no more exact time, since the coming of the kingdom cannot be determined beforehand by the observation of signs and calculations. But when it comes, God will destroy this old world, ruled and corrupted by the devil, and create a new world. Men are also to share in this transformation and become like angels.

Weiss places emphasis on the power of Jesus demonstrated by Luke's Gospel:

See *The New Testament* (SCM Press 1970) by Werner Geog Kummel, page 229. Pages 226–244 contain Kummel's discussion on the Kingdom and eschatology.

Warning. Photocopying any part of this book without permission is illegal.

See *Jesus' Proclamation of the Kingdom of God* by Johannes Weiss (SCM Press 1971), page 76.

...if Jesus speaks of a Kingdom of God which is present, it is not because there is present a community of disciples among whom God's will is done, as if God's rule were realized from the side of men. Rather Jesus does so because by his own activity the power of Satan, who above all others is the source of evil, is being broken.

Salvation

See *The Theology of the Gospel of Luke* by Joel B. Green (Cambridge University Press 1995), page 94.

According to Green, 'Luke uses the language of salvation more than any other New Testament writer'. Prominent examples of this are:

◆ **1: 69.** Zechariah thanks God for the 'salvation' he has given to his people

◆ **2: 30.** Simeon thanks God that he has seen Jesus: 'for my eyes have seen your salvation'

See chapters 3 to 8 of *Luke: Historian and Theologian* by I. H. Marshall (Paternoster Press 1970) for a thorough discussion of this topic.

◆ **3: 6.** Luke equates the prophesy of Isaiah that 'all flesh shall see the salvation of God' with the coming of Jesus

◆ **4: 18–19.** Jesus reads from Isaiah in the synagogue in Nazareth. The poor, the captives, the blind and the oppressed are all going to be saved by the one on whom the Spirit of the Lord rests. Jesus states that 'Today this scripture has been fulfilled in your hearing'

◆ **5: 32.** Jesus says that he has come to save sinners rather than those who are righteous

◆ **15: 11–32.** In the story of the Lost Son it is the younger son who is saved from his life of poverty through the love and forgiveness of his father

> 'We have seen that the ultimate source of salvation is God the Saviour, that His Son Jesus has been born into the world as Saviour to bring men peace and to lead them to glorify God, that this salvation is for God's people but also reaches to the Gentiles, that salvation is in accord with the divine promises of the Old Testament... It is our claim that these are the ideas that run through the work of Luke as a whole and constitute its main theme.' H, Marshall, *Luke: Historian and Theologian*, page 102.

◆ **19: 1–10.** When the hated tax collector Zacchaeus receives Jesus into his house and promises to change his ways, Jesus says 'Today salvation is come to this house'

◆ **23: 43.** The dying thief who asks Jesus to remember him when he comes into his kingdom is promised salvation: 'Today you will be with me in paradise.'

These texts make plain that Jesus was sent by God to save humanity, and that the promise of salvation is a cause for joy and celebration. In fact, salvation is so prevalent a theme in Luke's Gospel that Marshall argues that it is *the* central theme of the Gospel.

Prayer

For more on prayer, use the index of *St Luke* by G. B. Caird (Penguin 1990).

Luke maintains a strong sense that God is active in history and the world. So prayer, as one would expect, plays an important part in the Gospel. For example:

◆ **1: 13.** Zechariah is told by the angel that his prayer for a son has been answered

Further study

These three prayers have been set to music many times and there are many recordings from which to choose. The Magnificat and the Benedictus can both be heard in the Anglican service of Evensong; the Benedictus and Nunc Dimittis both occur in the Roman Catholic Mass. SIGCD002 contains examples of all three prayers set by Thomas Tallis (1505–1585), but look out for recordings of Bach's setting of the Magnificat and his B-Minor Mass.

◆ **1: 46–55, 68–79; 2: 29–32.** The Birth Narratives contain three prayers unique to Luke which take the form of hymns of praise: the prayers of Mary (the Magnificat), Zechariah (the Benedictus) and Simeon (the Nunc Dimittis)

◆ **6: 12; 9: 28; 22: 39–45.** At key times, before choosing the disciples, at the Transfiguration and just before his death, Jesus spends time in prayer

◆ **18: 1–8.** Luke includes the story of the Unjust Judge, told 'to the effect that they [the disciples] ought always to pray and not to lose heart'.

Plymale emphasises Jesus' awareness of the power of prayer, commenting that:

> Reflecting on the prayer example and teaching presented by Luke through Jesus' life and ministry, one gets a clear picture of a Jesus who was directed and empowered by God to accomplish an assigned task in the plan of salvation. Jesus, aware of the role of prayer, taught his followers by word as well as example to rely upon prayer.

See *The Prayer Texts of Luke-Acts* by Steven F. Plymale (Peter Lang 1991), page 110.

The Sabbath

Luke's understanding of the role of the Sabbath is summarised in the story in 6: 1–5. Jesus allows his disciples to rub corn between their hands to produce the grain to be eaten. The Pharisees object to this as it breaks one of the traditions that developed in order to prevent contravention of the actual Law (in this case, the Fourth Commandment, which prohibited work on the Sabbath). This practice of establishing traditions is known 'as making a fence around the Law'. But Jesus tells the Pharisees that 'the Sabbath was made for man, not man for the Sabbath'. In other words, the Sabbath was created to benefit human beings and not to cause them more suffering. Thus the Sabbath is presented as an issue that helps to define the conflict between Jesus, who understands that the true purpose of the Law is to benefit humanity, and the Jewish leaders, who have created unnecessary human traditions around the Law. The Jewish leaders are presented as either ignoring these traditions themselves or keeping them as an expression of spiritual pride. In either case they do not help the common people.

Eschatology

'Eschatology' comes from the Greek for 'last things'. When used in New Testament studies, it refers to the belief (dominant for most of the New Testament period) that the end of the world was imminent. This would be the result of the **parousia** (the second coming of Jesus), and would be marked by the resurrection of the dead and the Last Judgement. Followers of Jesus would be rewarded with everlasting happiness. Prominent eschatological texts in Luke are:

For more on eschatology, see *The Theology of the Gospel of Luke* by Joel B. Green (Cambridge University Press 1995), pages 97–101.

- **1: 67–79.** In Zechariah's song of praise for the birth of his son John the Baptist anticipates a time of complete salvation

- **3: 17.** John the Baptist warns his listeners of the coming judgment: 'His [Christ's] winnowing fork is in his hand, to clear his threshing floor, and to gather the wheat in his granary, but the chaff he will burn with unquenchable fire'

- **12: 35–40.** Luke's readers are warned by Jesus to remain alert as 'the Son of Man [Jesus] is coming at an hour you do not expect'

- **21: 5–36.** In the 'Apocalyptic Discourse' Jesus speaks of the great trouble and strife that will arise before his second coming.

This discourse has been the subject of considerable debate. See references to it in *St Luke* by G. B. Caird (Penguin 1990) and *Luke* by Leon Morris (IVP 1988).

Jesus' relations with the religious and political authorities

The religious authorities

The society in which Jesus lived was dominated by religion. Jewish religious leaders had tremendous power over the lives of ordinary people, power which brought them prestige and wealth. The Gospels present Jesus as an individual who stood up against the abuse of power by the Jewish religious leaders, who, as a result, had him arrested and put to death.

Luke tends to divide the Jewish leaders into the Pharisees and

See chapter 3 of *The Death of Jesus in Luke-Acts* by Joseph B. Tyson (University of South Carolina Press 1989) for a discussion of the different groupings of Jewish leaders.

the chief priests, though there are also other groups that are associated with both, such as the scribes and the elders.

In a number of stories in Luke Jesus argues with the Pharisees (see, for example, the notes on the Sabbath on page XX), while in others, such as 11: 42–44, he simply speaks out against them. Luke also puts in a note of his own which condemns the Pharisees for their hypocrisy. In general, the disputes with the Pharisees occur in Galilee and revolve around the Pharisees' insistence that the extra rules and traditions they have developed to protect the Law should be maintained.

The chief priests are based in Jerusalem, and it is they who are behind the arrest, trial and death of Jesus. They are provoked by Jesus' teaching in the Temple in the days after he has thrown out the money changers (19: 45–48), and begin to seek a way to destroy him. It is also the chief priests who accept Judas' offer to betray Jesus (22: 3–6) and who take part in Jesus' arrest (22: 52). Jesus denounces them for not arresting him in the Temple when he was with the crowds. The chief priests and the scribes bring Jesus to trial (23: 66) and are the main accusers of Jesus in front of Pilate (23: 4). Overall, Luke presents the chief priests as finding Jesus an intolerable threat to their pre-eminence in the religious hierarchy.

The political authorities

Jesus lived in a country that was part of the Roman Empire. The Romans could be a very intolerant ruling power if their authority was challenged, as is noted in Luke 13: 1: 'There were some present at that time who told him [Jesus] of the Galileans whose blood Pilate had mingled with their sacrifices.'

In the Gospels, the Jewish leaders are concerned that Jesus will be seen by the Romans as a political threat, and that, as a result, the whole nation would suffer reprisals (see Jn 11: 42–53). But Luke presents Jesus as a law-abiding citizen capable of positive relations with the Romans. In Luke 7: 1–10 Jesus heals a centurion's servant and says of the centurion, 'I tell you, not even in Israel have I found such faith'. Jesus also makes clear that the people must pay their taxes to Caesar, thus demonstrating that he accepts the (secular) legitimacy of Roman rule (Lk 20: 19–26).

For more on this see *Conflict in Luke* by Jack Dean Kingsbury (Fortress Press 1991).

In Luke it is Pilate who represents Roman political authority. Luke has Pilate declare three times that Jesus is innocent (23: 4, 14 and 22) and suggests that it is really the Jewish leaders who are responsible for Jesus' death. Luke thus tries to avoid any suggestion that Jesus clashed with the Roman authorities, and that Christians might be troublemakers.

The Passion Narratives and the death of Jesus

The death of Jesus is a prominent theme throughout Luke's Gospel. Shortly after Jesus' birth Mary is warned by Simeon that 'a sword will pierce through your own soul also' (2: 35), a reference to the pain that Mary will feel at the crucifixion of her son. Once Peter has recognised Jesus as the Messiah, Jesus predicts his own suffering and death, and tells his disciples that following him will mean they will have to take up their own crosses (9: 18–23). And, in 9: 51, Jesus resolves to travel to Jerusalem because he is aware that his death is imminent.

Warning. Photocopying any part of this book without permission is illegal.

In preparing his readers for the story of the crucifixion of Jesus Luke makes clear that Jesus was not a helpless victim of circumstance and that Jesus' death was not brought about by human beings acting independently of God. Rather, Luke expresses the essential Christian teaching that Jesus' death is a <u>key element in God's plan to bring salvation to humankind</u>. The crucifixion was the culmination of the role of the Jews in this salvation history and the foundation of the message of the Church for all humankind.

The significance that Luke places on the crucifixion is demonstrated by the detailed treatment that he affords it:

- **23: 18–25. Barabbas** is released and Jesus is condemned. Luke makes clear the innocence of Jesus, who does not deserve to die

- **23: 26. Simon of Cyrene** is made to carry Jesus' cross. This emphasises Jesus' complete helplessness following his mistreatment by the soldiers (22: 63). The suffering and humiliation of Jesus recalls the **Suffering Servant** of Isaiah 53 who was disfigured and despised before being recognised as the saviour of his people

- **23: 27–31.** Women from Jerusalem follow Jesus, weeping and lamenting. Jesus warns them of the greater trials that are to come, and this demonstrates that even in his weakened state Jesus is able to think compassionately of others

- **23: 33.** Jesus is crucified at **Golgotha**, the place of the skull, which was outside the walls of Jerusalem. This shows that Jesus died as a common criminal, again recalling the role of the Suffering Servant

- **23: 34.** The soldiers cast lots for the clothes of Jesus, which means that he died with no possessions. This recalls Psalm 22, which describes the intense suffering of a victimised individual. The Passion Narratives of Mark and Matthew include the words of Psalm 22:1: 'My God, my God, why have you forsaken me?' However Luke omits these words, perhaps because they do not support his presentation of Jesus as being aware of his Father's presence

- **23: 36.** The offering of vinegar to Jesus recalls Psalm 69: 21. Psalm 69 also speaks in very intense terms of the suffering of an innocent

- **23: 39–43.** One of the criminals who is crucified with Jesus asks to be remembered by him. Jesus replies: 'Truly, I say to you, today you will be with me in paradise.' This demonstrates that the salvation that Luke believes to be available to all humanity is present at the death of Jesus

- **23: 44.** There is three hours of darkness as Jesus hangs on the cross. The triumph of evil seems to be complete

- **23: 45.** The Temple curtain is torn. This curtain separated the Holy of Holies, where the presence of God was believed to dwell, from the rest of the Temple. But Jesus' death means that in future there will be no barrier between God and humankind.

Luke does not explicitly mention the concept of **atonement** in the terms of 'Jesus died to forgive our sins'. However Morris considers

The crucifixion

> Luke sees Jesus as our Saviour and that by the way of the cross. If the atoning significance of Christ's suffering is not stressed at least it is there, and Luke does not hint at any other significance. In view of his clear interest in salvation the question may well be asked, Why does Luke so stress the cross unless because of its saving significance? Leon Morris, *Luke* (IVP 1988).

> 'Luke will interpret Jesus' resurrection and ascension as his being "raised up", his exaltation. Among the many transpositions that so characterize his Gospel, herein we come face-to-face with what is for Luke the definitive reversal: the Righteous One [Jesus] repeatedly declared innocent by the Roman authorities, is executed in the way reserved for those of low status, by crucifixion, only to be raised up by God. God raises up the lowly, vindicates the faithful.' *The Theology of the Gospel of Luke* by Joel B. Green (Cambridge University Press 1995), page 68.

Further study

To enhance your knowledge and understanding of the Resurrection Narrative in Luke, do a comparative study with the story in Matthew and Mark. You might find *The Resurrection in Matthew, Mark and Luke* by Norman Perrin (Fortress Press 1977) helpful for this.

---

that the key role of the crucifixion in the Gospel and the way that Luke emphasises its importance demonstrates that he did have the standard Christian meaning in mind.

The Resurrection

All four Gospel writers include stories about the Resurrection, which is not surprising given its great significance to Christianity. However there are important differences between the four Resurrection Narratives. These range from fairly minor differences over detail of exactly what happened on the first Easter Sunday morning to more major disagreements in the stories about the resurrected Jesus and about the period of time between the Resurrection and the Ascension.

One point on which Luke and the other Gospel writers do agree is that the Resurrection occurred on the Third Day after the crucifixion. This detail recalls the story of Jonah (Jon 1: 17), who spent three days in the belly of the whale before being returned to life. Hence the truth of the Resurrection had already been indicated in God's relationship with the Jews.

This insistence that the Resurrection, just as much as the crucifixion, is part of God's plan for humanity is a major feature of Luke's Resurrection Narrative. In 24: 4–7 the two men in dazzling clothes at the tomb tell the women that they should not be surprised that Jesus has returned to life, as he himself had predicted this would happen. On the road to Emmaus the unrecognised Jesus 'beginning with Moses and all the Prophets... interpreted to them in all the scriptures concerning himself'(24: 27), and in his closing words to the disciples Jesus tells them that 'it is written that Christ should suffer and on the third day rise again from the dead' (24: 46).

Other features of Luke's Resurrection Narrative are:

- The description of the 'two men in dazzling clothes' (24: 4) recalls very closely the wording used by Luke at the Transfiguration (9: 29) and Ascension (Acts 1: 10), and is obviously meant to indicate that something supernatural is going on

- The beautiful story of the walk to Emmaus (24: 13–35) expresses in miniature the truth of the Resurrection for Christians. The disciples are at first in darkness and unable to understand. They invite Jesus to share food with them and, in a symbolic representation of the Eucharist, their eyes are opened and they recognise Jesus

- The story of Jesus eating fish in front of his disciples (24: 36–43) to prove that his physical body has returned to life represents an interesting development from the earliest surviving writing about the Resurrection: the Apostle Paul's account in 1 Corinthians 15: 1–8. In this Paul places no particular emphasis on Jesus' resurrected body, and the accounts of Paul's conversion (Acts 9: 1; 22: 6) describe the risen Jesus as a bright light. By the time Luke was writing it was possible to doubt the occurrence of the Resurrection, so Luke may have stressed its physical nature in an attempt to persuade those who did not believe the story

- Luke reminds the readers (23: 44–49) that the Resurrection, along with the crucifixion, is at the heart of the message of salvation for humanity. This passage suggests that the power of the Resurrection will be made available to the disciples through the spirit: 'stay in the city, until you are clothed with power from on high.'

Test yourself

1. Why did Luke write his Gospel?
2. Is salvation the dominant theme of the Gospel of Luke?
3. What can we learn from the Gospel of Luke about eschatology? To what extent does Luke wish his readers to be concerned with salvation as an expected event in the future as opposed to seeing salvation as something experienced in the present?
4. How does Luke's presentation of the relationship of Jesus with the religious authorities of his day contrast with his presentation of the relationship of Jesus with the political authorities of his day?
5. What theological purposes does Luke achieve in his Resurrection Narrative?

The Fourth Gospel

The purposes and characteristics of the Fourth Gospel

Guthrie notes the following purposes:

- John 20: 31 states that the book was written so 'that you may believe that Jesus is the Christ, the Son of God, and that by believing you may have life in his name'. The major purpose of the book was to enable its readers to come to belief in Jesus as the Christ and the Son of God.

- John was fighting against **Gnosticism**. Gnostics refused to believe that what was divine could become truly human. There are several references to the physical humanity of Jesus (for example, the blood and the water which flowed from his pieced side – 19: 34) that might show that the Gospel was written to admonish the Gnostic view

- John meant to show that it was wrong to follow **John the Baptist**. Acts 19: 1–7 confirms that John the Baptist had followers for some years after his death. Passages such as John 3: 30, where John the Baptist says 'He [Jesus] must increase and I must decrease', suggest that John was concerned to show that Jesus rather than John the Baptist was the one to be followed

- John wished to emphasise spiritual truths that the Synoptics had not covered. Guthrie quotes **Clement of Alexandria** (150–215 CE): 'Last of all John, seeing that the external facts had been set out in the other Gospels, at the insistence of his disciples and with the inspiration of the Spirit, composed a spiritual Gospel.' Indeed, John makes frequent use of 'spiritual' terms such as 'light' and 'darkness' in a way that the Synoptics do not

- John was presenting a **Hellenised** Christianity. The Gospel was written in terms that would have been immediately recognisable to those familiar with Greek ways of thinking. This has been a popular view for many years, although some scholars have recently re-emphasised the Jewish elements in the Gospel.

Good introductory commentaries are: *The Gospel of St John* by John Marsh (Penguin 1991) and Kenneth Grayston's *The Gospel of John* (Epworth Press 1990). A good discussion of the Fourth Gospel is *John: Evangelist and Interpreter* by Stephen Smalley (Paternoster 1998).

See *New Testament Introduction* by Donald Guthrie (Apollos 1990), pages 283–297.

Gnosticism (Greek: *gnosis*, 'knowledge') taught that the present material world was evil and only the world of the spirit was good, and that the god who created the world was inferior to the god who redeemed it. Some scholars see Gnosticism as a heresy within Christianity, others as a separate religion that predated Christianity.

'Hellenic' and 'Hellenised' refer to all things Greek. The conquests of Alexander the Great resulted in the dissemination of Greek language and culture throughout much of the Mediterranean, and the Greek influences continued even after many of these areas were conquered by the Romans. Hellenic culture had a great influence on the development of Judaism and Christianity.

Characteristics

See *The Gospel of John* by John Marsh (Penguin 1990).

Marsh divides the characteristics of the Fourth Gospel into 'Greek' and 'Hebrew'. The Greek characteristics include its **Platonism**, with its emphasis on a lower and an upper world, and the elements the Gospel shares with Gnosticism (knowledge, life, light, truth, the sacraments). The Hebrew elements are linked by Marsh to the **Dead Sea Scrolls**, which stress, like the Gospel, the moral distinction between good and evil and the need to become 'sons of light'.

Another approach to the characteristics of the Fourth Gospel is to compare it with the Synoptics. John does not contain any parables, and misses out many of the major Synoptic stories, including the virgin birth, Jesus' baptism, temptation and transfiguration, and the Last Supper. Overall, the presentation of Jesus in the Fourth Gospel is much more directly theological. Hence John does include dialogues with, for example, Nicodemus and the Samaritan woman, which are not in the Synoptics and which make explicitly theological points. The same can be said of chapters 14–17 where Jesus speaks in a long unbroken passage first to the disciples and then to God. By contrast, where there are long speeches in the Synoptics (eg the Sermon on the Mount, Mt 5–7), these can be shown to be the result of various redactors' efforts to bring otherwise scattered material together.

For more on this see the section on the Farewell Discourse on page 51.

The Prologue

See *The Gospel According to John* by C. K. Barrett (SPCK 1970), and *The Gospel of John: A Commentary* by Rudolf Bultmann (Blackwell 1971). The page references come from these two editions.

The Prologue is the name given to one of the best-known of all Christian texts. In it John uses some terms which are key to understanding his presentation of Jesus and Christianity. All scholars of the Fourth Gospel have commented on the Prologue, but here we will concentrate on the views of two of the most well-known, **Barrett** and **Bultmann**.

The Word: John 1: 1–4, 14. Barrett, along with other commentators, sees the opening phrase 'In the beginning' as based on Genesis 1: 1. In Genesis it is the word of God that creates the world, and in John Jesus-the-Word has the same function. Barrett also points out that in the Old Testament the Word is 'the prophet's message, that is, the means by which God communicates his message to his people' (page 27). Jesus obviously has this function in the Fourth Gospel. Bultmann, on the other hand, is more interested in the Greek idea of the Word as a divine being, 'an intermediary between God and the world, whose purpose is to explain how the step from the transcendent divinity to the formation of the world was possible' (page 25). Also, Bultmann notes, in Greek philosophy and religion, the Word does not only make the world, but it is through knowledge of the Word that it is possible for human beings to escape this world of darkness and return to the spiritual world of light, their true home. This, for Bultmann, provided a model for the presentation of Christ in the Fourth Gospel.

This belief that there are two worlds, a good spiritual world and a bad physical world, is called 'dualism'. There are several other meanings for dualism in religion and philosophy, so be careful in the way you use it.

Light and life: John 1: 4–9. Barrett comments:

> The words light and life are among the most characteristic of the gospel. Later Jesus claims that he is the life and that he is the light of the world… Light and life are essential elements in the Old Testament creation narrative. God gives light and is the source of life and wisdom… The words light and life are almost equally characteristic of Hellenistic religious and philosophical thought. Many of the popu-

lar religions were in some degree based upon mythologies treating of the conflict of light and darkness; light was thus inevitably an element in cosmogony and redemption (page 131).

'Cosmogony' is a technical term in religious studies and refers to beliefs and stories about the beginning of the universe.

Bultmann's views of the significance of light and life in the Gospel are similar. He states that:

> The life of the Word is not compared with the light: it is the light... Brightness... is the illumined condition of existence, of my own existence. So brightness is necessary for life; so that from the first, and throughout the ancient world, light and life, darkness and death, are seen as belonging together (pages 40–41).

Truth: John 1: 14. Barrett comments:

> It [truth] means the Christian revelation brought by and revealed in Jesus... It is saving truth (8: 32); it is perceived only through the work of the Spirit (16: 13)... this truth is Jesus himself, who being God is the fulfilment and revelation of God's purposes (page 139).

Glory: John 1: 14. Barrett states that: 'In the Septuagint glory often renders a particular Hebrew word, and denotes particularly the visible manifestation (often of light) accompanying an appearance of God' (pages 138–9). Bultmann comments: 'It is those who, as believers, allow him to be for themselves what he [Jesus] is, who see his glory. The vision of faith takes place in the process of upturning all man's natural aims in life, a process which is described in verse 12 as becoming "children of God"' (page 69).

Jesus' teaching

John presents this world as a place of darkness and evil in which human beings need to be saved through belief in Jesus. Examples are:

Salvation

- **1: 12.** Salvation comes through belief and it means becoming a child of God through a spiritual rebirth

- **3: 1–21.** Nicodemus is told by Jesus that salvation means being 'born again' or 'from above' by water and the Spirit. Jesus has come into the world so that it can be saved

- **4: 22.** Jesus tells the Samaritan woman that 'salvation is from the Jews'. In other words, the Jews rather than the Samaritans kept the truth about God which Jesus the Jew showed fully to the world

- **4: 42.** The people of Samaria recognise that Jesus is 'the Saviour of the World'

- **6: 35.** Jesus is the bread of life who brings full satisfaction

- **8: 12.** Jesus is the light of the world, and his followers will have the light of life

- The stories of the **healing of the blind man** and the **raising of Lazarus** (chapters 9 and 11 respectively) portray what salvation means to John. It is receiving spiritual sight instead of being blind and spiritual life instead of being dead.

Eternal life is is a key concept in John. 20: 31 states that the book was written so that the reader might have 'eternal life'. In John the expressions 'eternal life' and 'life' are used with no difference in meaning. Dodd suggests that 11: 25–26 shows a tension in the way

Eternal life

> Warning. Photocopying any part of this book without permission is illegal.

There is a good discussion of eternal life in *The Interpretation of the Fourth Gospel* by C. H. Dodd (Cambridge University Press 1968), pages 144–150.

that John thought about eternal life. In 11: 25 Jesus says 'he who believes in me, though he die, yet shall he live' suggesting that eternal life is something after death. But in 11: 26 Jesus claims 'whoever lives and believes in me shall never die' suggesting that eternal life can be experienced as part of this present life. Other significant references to eternal life in the Gospel are:

- ◆ **3: 14–15.** Jesus is going to be lifted up on the cross so 'that whoever believes in him may have eternal life'

- ◆ **5: 21.** The gift of life is given by the Son to whoever he chooses

- ◆ **6: 54.** To have eternal life it is necessary to eat the body and drink the blood of Jesus: ie to take part in the Eucharist

- ◆ **11: 25; 14: 6.** Jesus is himself the 'life' and so is the one who can give life to others.

Eschatology

Eschatology is the study of beliefs about what will happen at the end of our lives and the end of time, topics which are often closely related in religious thought. Sometimes John uses the language of contemporary Jewish eschatology. For example:

- ◆ '...the hour is coming when those who are in the tombs will hear [the son of Man's] voice and come forth, those who have done good to the resurrection of life, and those who have done evil, to the resurrection of judgement' (5: 28–29)

- ◆ 'And when I [Jesus] go and prepare a place for you [in heaven], I will come again and take you to myself, that where I am you may be also' (14: 3).

But at other times John speaks as if judgement and eternal life have been made real in this life. For example: 'Truly, truly, I say to you, the hour is coming and now is, when the dead will hear the voice of the Son of God, and those who hear will live' (5: 24). The 'dead' that John refers to here are not the physically dead but the spiritually dead.

See *The Theology of the Gospel of John* by Dwight Moody Smith (Cambridge University Press 1995), page 149, and *The Gospel of John: A Commentary* by Rudolf Bultmann (Blackwell 1971), page 261.

Conservative commentators such as Moody Smith hold that John believed in both future and realised eschatology: 'the possession or gift of eternal life in the believer's present existence is integrally related to the assurance of its permanence... the overcoming of death relates first of all to physical death.' For liberal commentators such as Bultmann, John believes totally in realised eschatology and the future eschatology in his Gospel is there as mythology or, in the case of 5: 28, an editorial addition which is 'an attempt to reconcile the dangerous statements in 5: 24 with traditional eschatology'.

Jesus' relations with the religious and political authorities

Religious authorities

John makes over sixty references to 'the Jews' in his Gospel. The Jewish leaders in John both represent and are responsible for what John sees as the failure of Judaism to recognise the truth about Jesus. Examples are:

> **Further study**
>
> For an interesting discussion of the relationship between Jesus and the Jews in the Gospel of John see *Understanding the Fourth Gospel* by John Ashton (Oxford University Press 1993), pages 124–159.

- ◆ The ignorance of the Jewish leaders is shown most clearly in the example of Nicodemus, 'a man of the Pharisees... a ruler of the Jews' (3: 1). When he shows his confusion about Jesus' teaching about being 'born again', Jesus says to him, 'Are you a teacher in Israel, and yet you do not understand this?' (3: 10)

- Jesus argues with the religious leaders in Chapter 8 about the value of their being descendents of Abraham, and in Chapter 9 about the miracle of the healing of the blind man. In 8: 44 John has Jesus say of the Jewish leaders 'You are of your father the devil, and your will is to do your father's desires'

- In 10: 31 the Jewish leaders are represented as being on the point of stoning Jesus for his 'blasphemy'

- It is the high priest Caiaphas who decides that Jesus must die: 'You know nothing at all; you do not understand that it is better for you that one man should die for the people, and that the whole nation should not perish' (11: 50)

- The Jewish leaders insist that Jesus should die in spite of Pilate's unwillingness to condemn him to death. For example, 19: 12: 'Upon this Pilate sought to release him, but the Jews cried out, "If you release this man, you are not Caesar's friend; every one who makes himself a king sets himself against Caesar"' (19: 12).

The Gospel according to John by C. K. Barrett (SPCK 1970), page 143.

John takes a negative view of the ordinary lives of men and women, as is shown in 3: 19, where he says, 'And this is the judgement, that the light has come into the world, and men loved darkness rather than light, because their deeds were evil'. As a result the Fourth Gospel is overwhelmingly concerned with psychological/supernatural themes to do with escaping from the dark world of unsaved humanity. From John's point of view, politics is trivial compared with this task. Hence in the Gospel references to political authority are few and far between:

Political authorities

- Following the story of the Feeding of the Five Thousand, John writes: 'Perceiving then that they were about to come and take him by force to make him king, Jesus withdrew again to the hills by himself'(6: 15). Jesus thus prevents any politicising of his mission

- In John, **Pilate** represents political authority in this world. However Jesus tells him that 'You would have no power over me unless it had been given to you from above' (19: 11). Jesus submits to political authority on the earth, but in the full knowledge that it is God who holds ultimate authority. John, unlike the Synoptic writers, has Pilate sitting down 'on the judgement seat on the place called The Pavement' (19: 13), and it is quite possible that this is ironical: Pilate appears to be in a place of judgement, but the real judge is God.

Further study

John's presentation is one of a number of sources we have for the life of Pilate. For a chapter on John's Pilate and a consideration of the figure of Pilate as a whole see *Pilate in History and Interpretation* by Helen K. Bond (Cambridge University Press 1998). Also useful are pages 593–610 of *The Gospel of St John* by John Marsh (Penguin 1991).

The Farewell Discourse

Following John's version of the Last Supper in chapter 13, chapters 14–16 consist of a speech or discourse made by Jesus to his disciples. This is followed by a prayer in chapter 17. Scholars treat chapters 14–17 as a continuous whole, and call it 'The Farewell Discourse' because in the Gospel story Jesus at this time is close to his death, resurrection and ascension. Farewell scenes are common in ancient literature, and the Farewell Discourse of John has features that it shares with, as well as features that contrast with, other literature of this type. Only very conservative scholars argue that the Discourse is a record of the actual words of Jesus; most

Warning. Photocopying any part of this book without permission is illegal.

scholarly debate tends to centre on the extent to which the Discourse is a literary creation.

Chapter 14 begins with Jesus reassuring the disciples that they will find final salvation by following him (1–3). Jesus is 'the way, the truth and the life' and it is through him that the Father is known (4–11). The spiritual experience of the disciples will not suffer because Jesus is going to his Father; rather it will be strengthened because after he is gone the Father will send 'the Holy Spirit, the Counsellor' to them (12–31).

Chapter 15 opens with the illustration of the vine and the branches. The branches of a vine can only bear fruit if they are linked to the main stem of the vine, and so the disciples are to be totally united with Jesus (1–11). The disciples are to love one another as friends, and are to love Jesus as his friends rather than as his servants. This will allow them to bear fruit (12–17). The disciples are to expect persecution and hatred, but the Holy Spirit of truth will be sent to them (18–27).

Chapter 16 starts with further warnings of persecution and a repeated reassurance that because Jesus is going away the Counsellor will come (1–15). The departure of Jesus will cause the disciples misery at first, but they will rejoice later. They will receive whatever they ask from the Father so that their 'joy may be full'. Jesus has overcome the world (16–33).

Chapter 17 begins with Jesus praying to his Father, saying that the 'hour is come' and asking that the Father should glorify the Son as he has 'accomplished the work' that God gave him to do (1–5). Jesus prays that the disciples should be one as he and the Father are one, and that they should be kept from evil and be made pure (6–19). Lastly Jesus prays for those who will become his followers through the witness of the disciples, that they may be one also. Jesus has known the Father and has made his name known to the disciples (20–26).

The following analysis of the Discourse is based on the very useful breakdown and commentary in Marsh: see The Gospel of St John *by John Marsh (Penguin 1991).*

The Interpretation of the Fourth Gospel by C. H. Dodd (Cambridge University Press 1968), page 399. Dodd's general discussion of the Farewell Discourse can be found on pages 390–423.

Dodd argues that John had a double intention when composing these discourses: 'first, to interpret the death and resurrection of Jesus as an eschatological event in the fullest sense, and in doing so reinterpret the eschatological beliefs of the early Church; and, secondly, to set forth the nature of the new life into which the disciples (and all Christians) are brought through Christ's death and resurrection.'

Dodd divides John's Gospel into the Prologue (1: 1–18), the Book of Signs (1: 19–13: 38) and the Book of the Passion (14: 1–20: 30). He sees the Farewell Discourse as developing some of the major themes of the Book of Signs. This development is most evident in the expression **agape** which appears over thirty times in the Farewell Discourse, but only a few times in the Book of Signs. The situation is reversed for the terms 'life' and 'light'. So it is in the love shared by the Father, the resurrected Jesus, the Spirit and all believers, as shown in the Farewell Discourse, that the salvation through life and light spoken of earlier in the Gospel is made real.

Agape is a three-syllable Greek word (A-gap-e) for spiritual love. In the Fourth Gospel it refers to the Christian love revealed by Jesus, which desires the best for others irrespective of their personal qualities.

The death of Jesus

Religious features. Jesus is described as 'the King of the Jews' (19: 19), showing his kingship over the people who rejected him (1:11). The quotation in 19: 24 ('They parted my garments among them, and for my clothing they cast lots') is taken from Psalm 22: 18 and demonstrates that the death of Jesus fulfilled the Jewish Scriptures. 'I thirst' (19: 28) is taken from Psalm 69, which, like Psalm 22, expresses the pain of terrible and undeserved suffering. Also the quotation 'Not a bone of him shall be broken' is taken from Exodus 12: 46, which again shows that scripture was being fulfilled.

Helpful on this are: *Understanding the Fourth Gospel* by John Ashton (Oxford University Press 1993), pages 485–510, and *The Theology of the Gospel of John* by Dwight Moody Smith (CUP 1995), pages 115–124.

Theological significance. John places the story of the plot against Jesus after the raising of Lazarus (11: 45–52), thus demonstrating the connection between the death of Jesus and the return of life to humanity. Paradoxically, the death of Jesus reveals his glory to the world: 'The hour has come for the Son of Man to be glorified. Truly, truly unless a grain of wheat fall into the earth and dies, it remains alone; but if it dies, it bears much fruit' (12: 23–24). It is by the death of Jesus that salvation will come to humankind: 'If I be lifted up from the earth I will draw all people to me' (12: 32). But the death of Jesus is also the judgement of the Earth (12: 31) as there is no longer any excuse for those who choose to stay in the darkness of evil. Hence only John has Jesus cry 'It is finished' (19: 30) at the moment of his death. This is also a cry of triumph, as the Greek word used by John – **telestai** – means 'I've done it!'. Furthermore Dodd suggests that the reference to the water and blood coming out of the side of Jesus after it is pieced with a spear (19: 34) refers to the Eucharist: 'From the crucified body of Jesus flows the life-giving stream: the water which is the Spirit given to believers in Him (7: 38–9), the water which a man is to drink if he is never to thirst again (4:14) and the blood which is "drink indeed" (6:55).'

The death and resurrection of Jesus

The Interpretation of the Fourth Gospel by C. H. Dodd (Cambridge University Press 1968), page 428.

There are several features of the Resurrection Narrative in the Fourth Gospel that are unique to John. He alone has the recognition of Jesus by Mary Magdalene (20: 11–18) and the appearance of Jesus to the disciples, firstly without Thomas, and then, a week later, with Thomas (20: 19–31). However chapter 21 is written in a different style to the rest of the Gospel and scholars doubt that it is the work of the original writer.

The Resurrection

Ashton notes the following themes in John's Resurrection Narrative:

Understanding the Fourth Gospel by John Ashton (Oxford University Press 1993), pages 506–511.

- ✦ **Faith** (20: 1–10). Ashton comments that: 'By leaving the angels out of this story John opens the door to faith. He is able to record the response the beloved disciple makes, not to the voice of an intermediary, but to a vision of emptiness'

- ✦ **Recognition** (20: 1, 11–18): 'A divine nimbus surrounds [Jesus] even while he is on earth… John, unlike Mark, may be thought to require a recognition scene in order to establish the identity-in-difference between the earthly and the resurrected Jesus'

- ✦ **Mission** (20: 19–23): 'Recognition and mission are two sides of a door that opens out from the closed world of the Gospel to that of Christian believers… the first side looks back to the earthly life of Jesus, the second side forward to the life of the community.'

Another key feature of the Resurrection Narrative in John is the declaration of faith by Thomas, who was absent from Jesus' first

For very detailed discussion and understanding there are three 'heavyweight' commentaries: C. K. Barrett *The Gospel According to John* (SPCK 1970), Rudolph Bultmann *The Gospel of John* (Blackwell 1971) and C. H. Dodd *The Fourth Gospel* (CUP 1953). These commentaries are difficult for the unaided student to use, but very interesting if you get 'into' the subject.

appearance, after he has seen the resurrected Jesus (20: 19–31). He proclaims Jesus to be 'My Lord and my God' (20: 28). Jesus recognises this as true belief (20: 29), but says that those who believe without seeing are 'blessed' in a way that Thomas is not. So the readers of the Gospel are led to understand that true belief is found in acknowledging Jesus as Lord and God, but this must be done without the certainty of sight.

Test yourself

1. What do you understand to be the main characteristics of the Fourth Gospel?

2. How does the writer of the Fourth Gospel present Jesus' relations with the religious and political authorities with whom he came into contact? What is the writer of the Gospel trying to achieve by presenting these relationships in this way?

3. What are the main features of the 'Farewell Discourse'? To what extent does the Farewell Discourse fit in with the other parts of the Fourth Gospel you have studied?

4. What use does John make of the Jewish Scriptures when telling the story of the death of Jesus? What is the theological significance of the death of Jesus in the Fourth Gospel?

5. What is the point of the stories of the resurrected Jesus in John 20?

The early Church as reflected in Acts, 1 Corinthians and Romans 13

Paul's life and work as reflected in Acts

An excellent source for understanding the various ways in which the early church developed is *The Primitive Church* by Maurice Goguel (Allen and Unwin 1964).

Before conversion

Barnabas Lindars' essay 'Paul' in volume 25 of *The Encyclopaedia Britannica* is excellent and gives you a great deal of what you need to know about Paul for this section.

Paul was born a Jew and a Roman citizen in Tarsus, probably during the first years of the 1st century AD. He was a tentmaker by trade and at some point in his life became a Pharisee who, when the new group of Christians began to spread, persecuted them enthusiastically (see Acts 22: 1–5, Phil 3: 5–6). Sanders writes:

Paul by E. P. Sanders (Oxford University Press 1996), page 12.

> Though the call to be an apostle had reversed the direction of his life, Paul in many ways stays the same. Paul the Apostle shared many characteristics of Paul the Pharisee. One of the principal ones was that he was a zealot, fully and totally committed to the cause to which he felt called by God.

Conversion

The writer of Luke-Acts gives three accounts of Paul's conversion: Acts 9: 1–9; 22: 6–11 and 26: 9–18, the last two of which are written as if they are the words of Paul himself. Linders writes that:

The Encyclopaedia Britannica volume 25, page 463.

> Paul's conversion has often been explained psychologically as the resolution of an inner conflict... Paul's own account is much more in keeping with Old Testament callings of a prophet. Although it is impossible to state exactly what happened, the central feature was certainly his vision of Jesus in glory. It convinced him that Jesus was risen from the dead and exalted as Lord in heaven, as the Christians claimed. It was also proof that Jesus had been crucified wrongly.

See *Paul: The Mind of the Apostle* by A. N. Wilson (Sinclair Stevenson 1997), page 61.

Interestingly, A. N. Wilson has noted that the New Testament does not actually talk about Paul's religious experiences as a 'conversion'. He points out that Paul in fact continued to be a Jew, which is something that many Christians have ignored.

Paul and the Gentiles

The defining aspect of Paul's life and work once he had become a follower of Christ was his defence of the right of Gentile converts to Christianity not to have to submit to Jewish practices such as circumcision. In doing this he enabled Christianity to flourish,

> Warning. Photocopying any part of this book without permission is illegal.

rather than just survive as the Jews did, in a world where the Romans had destroyed the Jewish homeland.

Sanders argues that in spite of his concern for the Gentiles, Paul's motivation in working for their conversion should be seen in Jewish terms:

> It was the long held Jewish expectation that, in the final days, Gentiles would come to worship the God of Israel. They would come to Mount Zion bearing gifts or offerings, and they would come bringing themselves to serve God. This is the second half of a standard Jewish expectation about the end. God would first restore Israel, and then Gentiles would come in. In Romans 15 Paul quotes several passages from the Jewish Scripture which express the hope that the Gentiles will come in and worship the God of Israel. Paul saw himself as the agent of this, the second half of the divine plan. His job description was this: Apostle to the Gentiles in the Messianic era.

Paul, page 3.

The **Council of Jerusalem**, held during the first missionary journey of Paul (see *below*), saw the tension between Paul and the Jewish Christians – who believed that it was necessary for Christians to fulfil the Jewish Law – come to a head. Paul left the Council determined to continue his missionary work among the Gentiles without having to impose Jewish law upon them.

Paul went on three missionary journeys:

The missionary journeys

+ He started the first in Antioch, and took in Cyprus before travelling to the mainland of what is now Turkey. He visited places such as Perga, Salamis and Paphos before sailing back to Antioch. The Council of Jerusalem probably took place at the end of this journey

For more on the Council of Jerusalem, see the *Edexcel AS Guide*, pages 66–67.

+ The second missionary journey saw the founding of many important churches, such as those in Philippi, Thessalonica and Beroea. Paul went to Athens, but was unable to establish a church there. He did however manage to found a church at Corinth, another city in Greece. From Corinth Paul returned to Antioch via Ephesus, Caesarea and Jerusalem

+ The third journey saw Paul settling at Ephesus for three years, after which he visited and founded churches at Colossae, Hierapolis and Laodicea. From Ephesus he wrote to Corinth, and then visited the church there. He then returned to Ephesus, and later visited Macedonia in preparation for another visit to Corinth. While at Corinth he wrote to the Christians in Rome.

Paul's journey to Rome began after he exercised his right as a Roman citizen to appeal to the emperor after Governor Festus attempted to have him tried in Jerusalem. Acts does not say what happened to Paul, but it is traditionally held that he was imprisoned in Rome, and beheaded c.65 CE on account of his Christian faith.

Arrest and imprisonment

Lindars sees Paul's contribution as crucial in terms of the later development of Christianity. He comments that:

Assessments of Paul

> Paul's lasting monument is the worldwide Christian Church. Though he was not the first to preach to the Gentiles, his resolute stand against the Judaizing party was decisive for further progress. It can be justly claimed that it was due to Paul more than anyone else that

The Encyclopaedia Britannica volume 25, page 466.

The Theology of Paul the Apostle, page 2.

> **Further study**
>
> Visit a library or a large bookshop and see what is available on Paul. Is it easy to tell the difference between material written to encourage Christian devotion and material meant to help academic study? Which academic books can you find which might be useful to read?

The *The Theology of the First Letter to the Corinthians* by Victor Paul Furnish (Cambridge University Press 1999), page 29.

Christianity grew from being a small sect within Judaism to become a world religion.

Dunn also sees Paul as immensely important:

> Paul was the first and greatest Christian theologian. From the perspective of subsequent generations, Paul is undoubtedly the *first* Christian theologian… Paul belongs to that group of Christians who have seen it was part of their calling to articulate their faith in writing and to instruct others in their common faith, and who have devoted a considerable portion of their lives to so doing.

The issues concerning the early Church at Corinth as reflected in 1 Corinthians

This subject area needs to be treated with some caution. The only source we have for it is the Corinthian letters themselves. Victor Paul Furnish comments:

> It is an open question how fully or precisely Paul himself understood the situation that he obtained in his Corinthian congregation. There is no way either to determine what he had learned about developments since he had been in Corinth or to assess the accuracy of what he had learned. One can do no more than draw certain inferences about his own perception of what was going on there.

The following are the major issues which appear in 1 Corinthians:

- The existence of **partisan groups** within the church: 'one of you says that "I belong to Paul", or "I belong to Apollos", or "I belong to Cephas", or "I belong to Christ"' (1: 12)

- **Immorality**: 'It is actually reported that there is immorality among you, and of a kind that is not found even among pagans; for a man is living with his father's wife' (5: 1)

- The Corinthian Christians were **taking each other to civil courts**: 'Can it be that there is no man among you wise enough to decide between members of the brotherhood, but brother goes to law against brother, and that before unbelievers?' (6: 5–6)

- The eating of food that had been offered to **pagan idols**: 'But some, through being hitherto accustomed to idols, eat food as really offered to an idol; and their conscience, being weak, is defiled' (8: 7)

- Eating together was exposing **social divisions** rather than acting as a memorial of the Last Supper: 'For in eating, each one goes ahead with his own meal, and one is hungry and another drunk' (11: 21)

- Worship had become **chaotic**: 'If any speak in a tongue, let there be only two or at most three, and each in turn' (14: 27).

Victor Paul Furnish, *The Theology of the First Letter to the Corinthians*, page 2.

Corinth had 'an ethnically, culturally and religiously very diverse population'. In these circumstances it was not surprising that those who joined the church brought some of their old pagan beliefs with them and that, in an age in which there was much religious frenzy, meetings got out of hand. Another point to consider is that, according to Furnish, 'what most controlled the city's life and defined its moral character was not sexual decadence, but a relentless competition for social status, honour, wealth and power'. Hence the danger that eating in the church became an occasion for snobbery, with those who could afford it enjoying their feasts while poorer Christians watched them.

Dunn puts the matter into a broader perspective, examining the possibility that there were Gnostic elements in the Corinthian church. He writes: 'The licentiousness of the conduct indicated in chapters five and six makes some sense on the assumption of Gnostic licence and liberty: since the material body counts for nothing it could be indulged without effect on the spirit. Likewise, the asceticism reflected in chapter seven could make sense against a Gnostic background: since the material body counts for nothing it should be dealt with harshly and should not be indulged.' In effect, then, these two arguments cancel each other out.

For more on Gnosticism see page 47.

See *1 Corinthians* by James D. G. Dunn (Sheffield Academic Press 1995), page 39.

Paul's teaching in 1 Corinthians

In 1 Corinthians 12 Paul describes the 'varieties' of gifts from the Spirit (12: 4), and lists nine specific gifts, including 'faith', 'healing' and 'tongues' (12: 8–11). The Church is the body of Christ and God has given different gifts to different people to build it up (12: 27–31). The church in Corinth should 'earnestly desire' spiritual gifts (14: 1), most especially that of 'prophesy'. Spiritual gifts should be exercised in a helpful rather than a disruptive way (14: 26–33). Importantly, however, the best way to establish the church is through love and not through spiritual gifts (12: 31–13: 13).

Spiritual gifts

Dunn comments:

> Paul did not turn away from the thought of the Spirit as the experienced Spirit. It was too fundamental to his own and his churches' spirituality. The existential reality of 'receiving the Spirit' was too central to his understanding of the crucial transition to Christian discipleship. However, he was wise (or experienced) enough to hedge the experiential dimension around with critical tests and to insist on Christ and the remembered character of Christ as the fundamental norm by which all claims to experience the Spirit should be measured.

The Theology of the Apostle Paul, page 434.

Paul wishes to remind the church at Corinth that he has experienced at first hand the truth of the message he has given to them (15: 1). So he states that Christ 'died for our sins... was buried and was raised on the third day in accordance with the scriptures' (15: 3–4). He then lists the appearances of the resurrected Jesus, finishing with Jesus' appearance to him (15: 4–11). He says that the value of Christianity depends on the Resurrection (15: 12–19), which is the 'first fruits' of the coming kingdom of God that will destroy every evil power (15: 20–28). Spiritual bodies will come into existence as the resurrected form of the physical body (15: 35–50). For some the change to the resurrected body will happen before they have physically died. At this last moment, a trumpet will sound, the mortal will become immortal and death itself will die (15: 51–57).

Resurrection

Furnish comments of Paul's teaching about resurrection:

> The apostle's primary aim is to demonstrate both the necessity and plausibility of believing in the resurrection of the dead. He develops an argument for the necessity of this belief, mainly on the basis of the Church's tradition... He supports his argument that it is plausible to believe in the resurrection of the dead with analogies from nature as

The Theology of the First Letter to the Corinthians, page 109. See pages 108–121 for Furnish's section on the importance of the Resurrection in Paul's teaching.

Sexual relations and marriage

Further study

Look at the way Paul distinguishes when he is speaking on his own authority: 1 Cor 7: 10, 12 and 25. To what extent do you think Paul is trying to show that he is offering human advice rather than divine laws?

The Theology of the Apostle Paul, pages 690–1. See pages 689–698 for all of Dunn's analysis of Paul's teaching on this point.

Worship and the Lord's Supper

Further study

Find out more about Paul's teaching in 1 Corinthians in the context of the early Church in general. You might find the following helpful:

- Sections on 'Assemblies for Worship', and 'The Eucharist', in *The Primitive Church* by Maurice Goguel (Allen and Unwin 1964).
- *The Social Setting of Pauline Christianity: Essays on Corinth* by Ger Theissen (T&T Clark 1995).

See *The Theology of the Apostle Paul*, page 623. Dunn's analysis of Paul's teaching on worship and the Lord's Supper in 1 Corinthians is on pages 599–623.

For a very good introduction to Paul's thought see *The Theology of Paul the Apostle* by James D. G. Dunn (T&T Clark 1997). A helpful commentary is *The Epistle to the Romans* by Leon Morris (IVP 1988).

---

well as an appeal to scripture. Finally, however, the rhetoric of argument gives way to expressions of wonder and praise.

Paul is concerned with some aspects of the behaviour of members of the church in Corinth. In 5: 1 he states that 'a man is living with his father's wife' and that this is a degree of immorality which 'is not found even among pagans'. In his instructions and advice on sexual issues Paul says that the ideal is for a man not to touch a woman (7: 1), but given that sex is so tempting, men and women should be married and be sexually active within this framework. However it is better not to be married, unless marriage is the only thing that can save you from burning with desire (7: 2–9). The married are to stay married and even those who are married to unbelievers should not divorce them. But if the unbelieving partner wants a divorce then the Christian partner should agree to it (7: 10–16). Paul repeats his advice that people should ideally stay single if they are single and married if they are married, before concluding that being unmarried is better as there are then no distractions from serving God (7: 32–35; see also 7: 5). A widow can remarry, but, of course, Paul thinks that it would be better if she remained single (7: 39–40).

Dunn remarks of Paul's teaching about sexual relations and marriage:

> Sexual rules were generally much more relaxed in the Hellenistic world. However, Paul, in deliberate contrast, stood foursquare within the Jewish tradition... the question naturally arises why he should have held on so firmly to Jewish tradition at this point when he qualified and abandoned it at so many others which equally affected human relationships... The answer presumably is that Paul retained from his Jewish upbringing a sharp sense of uncontrolled... legitimate desire which can all too quickly be corrupted into lust.

On this matter Paul again condemns practices that were common in the Corinthian church. Paul criticises the Christians in Corinth for turning the Lord's Supper into an orgy of eating and drinking: 'When you meet together it is not the Lord's Supper that you eat. For in eating, each one goes ahead with his own mean, and one is hungry and another is drunk' (11: 20–21). Paul gives his version of what Jesus said about and did with the bread and wine during the Last Supper (11: 23–25). He also says that self-examination is an important part of the ritual of the Lord's Supper and that death can result from taking part with the wrong attitude (11: 27–32). In fact, worship in the Corinthian church seems chaotic (14: 26–33), and Paul concludes that 'all things should be done decently and in order' (14: 40).

Dunn says of Paul's teaching on the Lord's Supper that:

> In linking the Lord's Supper with judgment as well as spiritual food, with Christ's coming again as well as his death, Paul underlines the extent to which celebration of the Lord's Supper does indeed proclaim the whole Gospel and provide instruction as well as sustenance during the long slog from the already to the not yet.

Paul's teachings on the relations with the authorities in Romans 13

In Romans 1–11 Paul puts forward his belief that a Christian has been put right with God by faith. This, Paul believes, has been achieved by the death and resurrection of Jesus rather than by doing good works in an effort to please God. The rest of Romans is mostly concerned with the way a Christian should live in response to being saved by faith. Romans 13: 1–7 concerns how Christians should behave in relation to political authority:

> There is some doubt as to whether 13: 1–7 was originally part of Romans: see the essay by James Kallas in *New Testament Studies* vol. XI.

✦ Christians should be subject to these authorities as they have been appointed by God and can punish those who do not obey them (13: 1–4)

✦ Christians should therefore pay taxes and respect those in authority (13: 5–7).

Morris comments of these verses:

> This understanding of the state has been strongly criticised on the grounds that it justifies every tyrant and compels the believer to obey him. It is this that is behind [the] remark that no passage has caused more unhappiness and misery than this one. But it must be borne in mind that Paul is writing in general terms to meet the need of the Romans and not legislating for every conceivable situation in which the Christian might find himself.

The Epistle to the Romans by Leon Morris, page 459.

Indeed, Dunn suggests that we must consider the context in which Paul was writing:

> We have to recognise the political realities within which these first Christian churches had to exist. There was no possibility for them to exercise political power such as the democracies of the 20th century take for granted. The responsibilities of ancient government were exercised by right of birth, connection, wealth, or ruthless self-advancement. For the rest, the great majority, there was political power and no realistic hope of wielding it. It was hardly even thinkable for Paul, then, that his Roman readership could or should try to change social and political structures.

The Theology of Paul the Apostle by James D. G. Dunn, page 680.

Certainly the teaching of Romans 13: 1–7 has frequently been used by leaders to justify political repression. But it could be argued that Morris and Dunn are taking a rather lenient view of Paul's teaching as there were groups, such as the Zealots, who were prepared to make sacrifices and even to die to 'change social and political structures'.

Test yourself

1. What does Romans 13: 1–7 teach about attitude to political authority? Is this teaching justified considering the political culture of that time?

2. What did Paul teach about TWO of the following in 1 Corinthians: spiritual gifts, resurrection, sexual relations and marriage, worship and the Lord's Supper? What was Paul trying to achieve in his teaching on these issues?

3. According to Acts, what did Paul achieve and how did he achieve it?

4. To what extent can we say that the problems the Corinthian church was experiencing were due to its pagan environment?

Christianity

The Reformation in England

Influences on the development of the Reformation in England 1603–1702

Christian England vol 2 by D. L. Edwards (Collins 1981) is easy to read, covers all the topics on the specification and makes some stimulating judgements.

Before the Reformation there had been very close links between the Church and the State. The Pope had influenced and sometimes controlled the government of European countries. One of the important factors in the early Reformation was the desire of many people to practise their religion in a way that was free from politically motivated religious control. They wanted Church and State to be separate, and this pressure to divide the two strengthened during the later Reformation.

The relationship between the Church and State

The 'early Reformation' refers to the 16th century, specifically 1517–1603, while the 'later Reformation' concerns the 17th century, 1603–1702.

An example of this increasing divide is provided by Oldridge. He argues that the Church in England in the early 17th century can be seen as either an **evangelical** body (which means that it believed that its authority came directly from God), or as an **institutional** body (which means that its authority was tied up with the authority of the State). As the Reformation progressed, there was increasing pressure for the Church to operate as an evangelical rather than an institutional body, and so weaken its ties with government.

Religion and Society in Early Stuart England by Darren Oldridge (Ashgate 1998).

William Laud (1573–1645) was a key figure in the Church's efforts to resist the more extreme Protestant attempts to undermine its links with the State. He taught that the king had the ultimate say in affairs of state, and the power to convene the governing body of the Church and put into practice its decisions. However Laud did not comment on what would happen if the king disagreed with the Church's governing body.

For more on Laud's teaching see pages 93–97 of *The Anglicanism of William Laud* by E. C. E. Bourne (SPCK 1947), and pages 61–62 of this guide.

It was widely believed that kings were appointed directly by God and that therefore nobody had the right to resist what they commanded.

Alongside Laud's teaching, **the Divine Right of Kings** remained an issue in 17th-century England. Miller argues that by this period the administration of a country had become so complex, and the monarch so dependent on such a range of their subjects, that the Divine Right could never work in practice, no matter how fervently monarchs, such as James II (reigned 1685–1688), believed in it.

The development of scientific and philosophical thought

The Reformation and the decline of the power of the Church meant that some Christians began to think of science and philosophy – which had previously been controlled and dominated by the Church – as areas of human study which could stand independently of the Church's teaching. During the 17th century three Englishmen in particular contributed to this development of science and philosophy:

Further study

See pages 378–397 of D. L. Edwards' *Christian England* (Collins 1981), which has an interesting discussion of these three figures together with a broader consideration of religions, magic and science.

- **Isaac Newton** (1642–1727) discovered gravity and so undermined the basic teaching of medieval science that things only move because they are, ultimately, pushed by an external supernatural force

- **Thomas Hobbes** (1588–1679) was a materialist (he believed that the nature of the world could only be explained in reference to matter, and nothing else), arguing that there was no more to humans than the physical motions of their bodies

✦ **John Locke** (1632–1704) held that none of our ideas and beliefs were innate: they all came from sense-experience.

These scientific and philosophical developments reflected and advanced the ideals of the Reformation and laid a basis for an understanding of human knowledge and society which did not depend on God.

A major response of the Church to these developments was that of the **Cambridge Platonists** who combined philosophy, reason and the Christian faith to argue that this world was in reality a changing world of appearances, but one through which the ultimate reality of God could become known.

James I (1603–1625)

James I was also James VI of Scotland, and he came to the English throne having already been King of Scotland for some years. Towards the beginning of his English reign there were two Roman Catholic plots against him and his government: the **Bye Plot** (1603) and the **Gunpowder Plot** (1605). These were a result of Catholic frustration at James' unyielding attitude to Catholicism. Catholics had been led to believe that James I would be tolerant of their religion and great bitterness ensued when he was not. James responded to the plots by passing, in 1606, two strict penal laws against Catholics. But despite these laws, during James' reign only 17 priests and five lay Catholics were executed. Norman suggests that 'the last dozen years or so years of the King's reign… were ones of repose for the Catholic community', and in fact the penal laws against Catholics were not enforced in many parts of the country.

James and Catholicism

For more on James I, see *James VI and I, King of Great Britain* by Irene Carrier (Cambridge University Press 1998). Particularly useful on Catholicism during the 17th century are pages 33–41 of *Roman Catholicism in England* by Edward Norman (Oxford University Press 1985).

Puritanism was a growing force during the reign of James I. James' reign began with Puritan requests for reforms to the Church of England. **The Millenary Petition** of 1603 asked for limited reform of the Church and in 1604 the **Hampton Court Conference** enabled leading Puritans to express their wishes to the king. Although the Puritans did not succeed in persuading James to give in to all of their demands, the Conference did result in the initiation of the composition of an English version of the Bible, an important Puritan request. This Bible, the **Authorised Bible** (also called the King James Bible) was published in 1611. Despite the production of this Bible, some scholars regard this period as something of a missed opportunity in terms of Anglican-Puritan relations. Edwards believes that the Church of England could have been broadened at this stage to accommodate more sympathetically the demands of the Puritans, a move which might have pre-empted the struggles that led to the Civil War of 1642–1647.

The development of Puritanism

The Puritans were Protestant Christians who believed in the practice of a very strict, severe and simple form of religion. They sought to impose their strict religious views through, for example, the attempt to ban sports on Sunday.

D. L. Edwards, *Christian England* vol 2 (Collins 1981).

Charles I

The reign of Charles I (1625–1649) saw the strengthening of the Puritans. They were very successful in the parliamentary elections at the start of Charles' reign, though Charles initially resisted their influence and ruled from 1629–1640 without Parliament. During this period William Laud (1573–1645) sought to remake the Church of England in the style the king wanted.

As Archbishop of Canterbury, Laud held the highest office in the

For a detailed work on Charles, see Christopher Hibbert's biography (Penguin Books 2001). Also useful is *The Causes of the English Civil War* by Ann Hughes (Palgrave 1998).

William Laud

See H. R. Trevor-Roper *William Laud* (Palgrave 1962).

Arminians followed the doctrine of the Dutch theologian Jacobus Arminius (1560–1609) who, unlike Calvin, believed that God had not pre-determined the number of those who were going to be saved. This emphasised God's grace and human free-will.

Church of England from 1633 to 1645. Laud grew up in Reading and took his degree at the University of Oxford. He became a bishop in 1621 and later as Bishop of Bath and Wells he became notorious for the measures he took against the Puritans.

Laud, like Charles, was an **Arminian**, and he believed that the Church of England was the best upholder of the Catholic faith of the universal Church. He turned communion tables back into altars and opposed the strict Puritan observance of Sundays. He also worked to remove the corruption and irreverence of the Church; for example, he removed from St Paul's in London the tradesmen and lawyers who were using the cathedral for commercial purposes.

As Archbishop Laud was well placed to act on behalf of Charles I against the more extreme Protestants. He punished those who attacked the Church of England in their preaching and put into practice reforms such as making the communion table the main feature of the church building rather than the pulpit. He insisted that clergy wear the **surplice** (a white over-robe) over their other clothes, even though to Puritans this was unscriptural and something that harked back to pre-Reformation days.

In 1640 Laud was arrested for treason after his attempt to make the Church of Scotland use the Book of Common Prayer led to public violence in England. After some years in the Tower of London Laud was beheaded in 1645 after the Puritan-dominated Parliament found him guilty of treason.

Roper comments about Laud's role in defending the Church of England:

> They [the defenders of the Church of England against the Puritans] were a defeated party, which could only secure recognition through representation and negotiation, perhaps by propaganda, but not by direct authority. By leading that party on the same basis upon which it had already been defeated, Laud lead it to another, and this time, final overthrow. (Roper 'William Laud' page 436)

Puritanism and the Civil War

But despite these reforms Charles' reign saw the strengthening of the Puritan position. The Puritans were very successful in the parliamentary elections at the start of Charles' reign, but the king resisted their influence and managed to rule from 1629–1640 without Parliament. But in 1640 Charles was forced to recall Parliament for financial reasons. This resulted in the formation of the so-called **Long Parliament**, the election of which was partly due to the increasing influence of the urban bourgeoisie. This Parliament attempted to reverse Laud's reforms and oppose the constitutional power of the king. The Puritans in particular pressed for stricter religious conduct and for the ending of Catholic influence on the English Church. Charles, a supporter of Laud, was not prepared to cede to their demands. Civil war broke out in 1642, and the Royalists (supporters of the king) were eventually defeated. The more extreme Puritans feared compromise between Parliament and the Crown, and pressed for the execution of the king, a goal they achieved in January 1649.

Further study

There has been a lot of attention given recently to the Civil War and other aspects of the Tudor and Stuart period. Try watching Simon Schama's history of this period on video or DVD.

Under the Protectorate of **Oliver Cromwell** (1599–1658) the Puritan revolution reached its apogee. Laws forbidding drunkenness and theatre were passed. In 1645 the **Directory of Public Worship** was issued to replace the Catholic-inspired Book of Common Prayer. However the Royalists were becoming increasingly active (leading to the restoration of the monarchy in 1660) and so defeat of the forces of conservatism was not possible.

Catholics had enjoyed a relatively settled religious existence during the last years of the reign of James I and this continued into the reign of Charles I. In fact there were even some moves towards an increase in their status. For instance in 1633 informal diplomatic ties with the papacy were re-established and the penal laws were employed even less than under James. The Catholic lords who fought in the Civil War were almost exclusively Royalists. Under Cromwell's rule these Royalist Catholics had their property confiscated and the penal laws were re-enacted. Yet despite this, few Catholics were put to death during the Commonwealth.

Charles II (1660–1685)

Cromwell died in 1658, leaving no obvious successor. The prospect of disjointed government and widespread disorder resulted in the **Restoration** of the monarchy: Parliament offered the throne to Prince Charles, the exiled son of Charles I, in 1660. However difficulties soon emerged with the Church, and these were precipitated by three factors in particular:

- The Anglican bishops and Puritan leaders who met at the 1661 **Savoy Conference** were unable to agree about the practice of Christianity in England. This resulted in the departure of the majority of Puritans from the Church of England

- The failure of the bishops to make the revised **Prayer Book of 1662** acceptable to the Puritans

- The enforcement of the use of the Prayer Book by the **Act of Uniformity** (1662), which further alienated the Puritans.

During the following years, a number of measures were passed to disadvantage those outside the Church of England, the 'nonconformists'. Taken together, these measures are known as the **Clarenden Code** (after one of Charles II's officials), and resulted in the persecution of Puritans. In spite of this, Puritan congregations continued to meet and their influence on the religion of the country was maintained.

Catholics had high hopes of Charles II when he came to the throne in 1660. Although he did not convert to Catholicism until 1685 when he was on his deathbed, he had been supportive of Catholics during his exile and he married a Catholic, Catherine of Braganza, in 1662. Indeed, soon after becoming king, Charles issued the **Declaration of Breda** in which he stated his desire for a country in which religious tolerance was the norm. However the Clarenden Code affected Catholics as much as Protestant extremists, and increasing anti-Catholic sentiments during the reign, specifically the fear of a 'Popish plot', led to Catholics being banned from sitting in the Lords in 1678.

See *Cromwell: Our Chief of Men* by Antonia Fraser (Phoenix 2001) for a popular biography of Cromwell.

Catholicism 1625–1660

For an excellent treatment of religion in the time of Charles II and James II, see James Spur 'Religion In Restoration England' in *The Reigns of Charles II and James VII & II* ed. Lionel K. J. Glassey (Macmillan 1997).

Further study

Try watching Michael Hoffman's 1995 film *Restoration* and think about its main themes. How is Charles II represented, and what sort of view is given of English court society?

Further study

Try reading *The Pilgrim's Progress* (1678) by John Bunyan, which was a product of the persecution of Puritans during the Restoration period. For some background on Bunyan, see *John Bunyan in Context* by Michael Mullett (Keele University Press 1996).

Catholicism under Charles II

For more details on Popish plots, see pages 449–460 of D. L. Edwards' *Christian England*.

Christianity 63

See John Miller's *James II* (Yale 2000) for a full biography.

The Duke of Monmouth was an illegitimate son of Charles II.

James II (1685–1688)

Charles II became a Roman Catholic shortly before his death, but his brother James II was a Roman Catholic when he ascended to the throne. He did not wish, however, to impose his Catholicism on the country by force. In 1685 he successfully overcame the **Monmouth Rebellion**, which aimed to place a Protestant on the throne, and in 1687 he issued a **Declaration of Indulgence** whereby he sought tolerance for both Roman Catholics and Puritans. James also passed Toleration Acts in 1687 and 1688. These actions angered many in the Church of England, who saw them as endangering Protestantism and when James' second wife, Mary, unexpectedly gave birth to a male heir, it seemed possible that England might once again become a Roman Catholic country.

Leading Protestants reacted by asking the Dutch prince William of Orange and his wife Mary to enter the country to ensure the survival of English Protestantism. James, unable to gather sufficient support for a military response, fled, and the **Glorious Revolution** of 1688 was completed. James' attempts to re-establish Roman Catholicism in England had failed.

William III (1689–1702) and Mary II (1689–1694)

The constitutional crisis caused by the Glorious Revolution and the usurpation of the throne by William III and Mary II was resolved by the passing of the Bill of Rights in 1689. This stated that only a Protestant could sit on the throne of England and that the monarch had to swear to protect the Protestant religion of England. Latourrette comments that:

Kenneth Scott Latourette *A History of Christianity* (Eyre and Spottiswoode 1954).

> The flight of James II and the coming of William and Mary were followed by the final victory of Protestantism and the permanence of many of the fruits of the Puritan revolution.

The non-jurors

> **Further study**
>
> One of the most famous of the non-jurors was William Law (1686–1781), whose spiritual writings have had a lasting impact on English Christianity. Explore his work further in *Extracts from the Writings of William Law* (Kessinger Publishing 1999).

D. L. Edwards *English Christianity*.

Some members of the Church of England refused to swear allegiance to William and Mary, and this group was known as the non-jurors, a term first used in 1691. Eight bishops, who had been appointed by James II for their loyalty, sided with the former king, and 400 clergy followed their lead. These bishops were expelled from the Church of England in February 1690, but traces of the movement continued through the bishops' practice of ordaining their own successors; the last non-juror did not die until 1805. Edwards comments: 'In an age full of cynicism [the non-jurors'] integrity led them to renounce positions, homes and incomes rather than to accept Parliament's right to dethrone James.'

Catholicism under William and Mary

William III is also known as William of Orange, since he was from the Dutch house of Orange-Nassau. William fought in Ireland to defeat the Catholics, and this resulted in the creation of the Protestant 'Orange Order' there.

William and Mary became king and queen specifically to secure Protestantism in England and consequently the position of Catholics worsened during their reign. Old penal laws were restored and new penal laws were enacted, such as that of 1689 which stated that you could be fined for being a Catholic. Although these laws were not always strictly enforced, Catholics were generally marginalised during this period.

Developments in non-conformity and sectarianism

Three important Protestant groups trace their origins to the 17th century:

> **Warning.** Photocopying any part of this book without permission is illegal.

Congregationalism was first recognised as a movement in its own right during the Civil War, when some of those who had gone abroad because of the moderation of the Church of England returned to the country. They became a distinct group when they drew away from the **Presbyterians**. The difference between the two was that Presbyterians wanted their church groups to have an overall government, whereas the Congregationalists wanted each church group to govern itself.

> Pages 816–828 of *A History of Christianity* by Kenneth Scott Latourette (Eyre and Spottiswoode 1954) are very useful on this topic. It is also worth looking at the entries on Congregationalists, Baptists and Friends in 'Protestantism' in volume 26 of the *Encyclopaedia Britannica*.

The Baptists became a movement within Reformation England when **John Smyth** (1554–1612) returned to England in 1612 having established links to a church in Rotterdam committed to baptising only adults. The Baptist movement grew very quickly from 1640–1660, with many people converting. The Baptists did suffer persecution under the Restoration monarchy, but fared better under William and Mary.

The Society of Friends (Quakers) traces its beginnings to small groups which met together during the Puritan Revolution in the 1640s. They were dissatisfied with both the Church of England and the other Puritan groups. They held meetings to 'wait upon the Lord', and their distinctive beliefs – that every person has an 'inner light' from God, and that worship best takes the form of silence and testimony – developed from these meetings. They gained thousands of converts in the following years, but soon faced opposition from the Church of England and also from some Puritan leaders.

> 'Quakers' is an alternative name for the Society of Friends. Its origin is said to lie in Fox telling magistrates that they should 'quake before the Lord'.

George Fox (1624–1691)

George Fox was born in Leicestershire to Puritan parents. He was training to be a cobbler when, aged 19, he had a deep religious experience. This led to him becoming profoundly dissatisfied with the Church of England, which he believed had turned its back on the simple Christian faith of the New Testament. He became a itinerant preacher, touring the country speaking to others about his vision of Christianity. Although he distrusted all forms of church organisation, a group of people who shared his principles and beliefs did begin to meet together. This group was originally called the 'Friends of Truth', but later became known as the Religious Society of Friends. Fox also travelled abroad, and with **William Penn** (1644–1718, the founder of Pennsylvania), succeeded in forming a Society of Friends in America. The movement grew rapidly, but was soon widely persecuted: during the reign of Charles II more than 10,000 Quakers were arrested and imprisoned. The decline of persecution of the Quakers in the 18th century led to their becoming a significant Christian denomination, particularly noted for their simplicity of worship and dedication to peace.

> See *New Light on George Fox* ed. Michael Mullett (Sessions 1991).

Test yourself

1. Briefly outline the main religious developments in England during the reign of James I. How did the Church in England benefit from his tolerance?

2. 'Charles I could do nothing to prevent the religious energies of the Puritans sweeping him from power and England into Civil War.' Do you agree?

3. What did Charles II and James II attempt to achieve for the Church in England, and to what extent did they succeed?

4. To what extent do the failures of William Laud outweigh his successes?

> Examination questions on this topic will be *either* on the Reformation throughout Europe *or* on the Reformation just in France, but not on both. If it is on the Reformation throughout Europe you can use information from the section on the Reformation in England on pages 60–65.

For a brief general summary see the section on 'Reformed Churches' in volume 12 of the *New Catholic Encyclopedia* (Gale Group 2000), pages 190–192. Also useful is Kenneth Scott Latourette's *A History of Christianity* (Eyre and Spottiswoode 1954), pages 762–775.
For more on Calvin see page 68.

These disputes were between supralapsarians – who believed that God had decided who was going to be saved before he created the world – and infralapsarians – who believed that God decided who was going to be saved after the fall of Adam.

Pages 765–769 of *A History of Christianity* by Kenneth Scott Latourette are useful here, as are pages 479–485 in the section on France in volume 19 of the *Encyclopaedia Britannica*.

> Warning. Photocopying any part of this book without permission is illegal.

The Reformation in Europe

The development of the Reformation throughout Europe

The Protestant movement was dominant in the north of **Germany** by the middle of the 16th century. Attempts were made by the Holy Roman Emperor Charles V (1500–1558) to restore Catholicism, but the **Heidelberg Catechism** of 1563 laid the basis for an expansion of Protestantism into the rest of Germany.

With the death of **Zwingli** in 1531 the Protestant advance in eastern **Switzerland** came to an end. However the success of John Calvin ensured that western Switzerland was a Protestant stronghold. Despite this, the Counter Reformation led to several of the cantons (Swiss administrative districts) becoming more securely Catholic. Two religious wars resulted from this Catholic-Protestant divide, which persisted in Switzerland until the end of 18th century.

The **Netherlands** had initially responded eagerly to the teaching of Luther, but the theology of Calvin was becoming more popular by the second half of the century. The foundation for Protestantism in the Netherlands was the creation of the **Dutch Reformed Church** in 1584, although there were disputes about its precise teachings.

The Reformed faith became mainstream in **Scotland** in August 1560, after the Scottish Parliament adopted **John Knox**'s (c.1512–1572) *Confession of Faith*. This followed a period when the country had been strongly influenced by Protestant ideas. **Andrew Melville** (1545–1622) carried forward the work of John Knox, and worked towards making Scotland a Presbyterian country. There was a rebellion in the 1660s when Charles II, failing to distinguish between Scottish and English views, sought to impose bishops on the country.

The Reformation in France

Books by Luther first began appearing in France in 1519, and there was a native Lutheran presence in the country by 1525. At first the French crown was inclined to be tolerant to the Protestants, but there was a Catholic reaction when the movement began to demonstrate anti-Catholic hostility. Henry II (reigned 1547–1559) introduced some oppressive measures.

The development of Calvinism in France gave greater impetus to the Reformation there, so that by 1562 there were about 2,000 Calvinist churches in the country. It was in this year that **The Wars of Religion** began. The most notorious event of these wars was the **St Bartholomew's Day Massacre** (23–24 August 1572), when some 3,000 **Huguenots** (French Calvinists) were massacred by the Catholic Paris mob. Fighting went on until 1594, but the 1598 **Edict of Nantes** finally guaranteed some religious freedoms for the Huguenots.

Despite the Edict, tensions continued into the 17th century, during which there were sporadic outbreaks of violence. Under **Louis XIV** (reigned 1643–1715) restrictions on the Huguenots became severe once more, until in 1685 the Edict of Nantes was revoked. Persecution led many Huguenots to flee the country leaving French Protestantism to become very much a minority movement.

Ministry and organisation of the Protestant Churches

The Lutheran Church

By 1577 there were several different Lutheran groupings. For example there were the 'Gnesio-Lutherans' who emphasised the importance of faith and the limitations of human reason. The 'Philippists' on the other hand followed the teaching of Luther's disciple **Philip Melanchthon** (1497–1560) and were more open to liberal ideas. However in 1577 a 'Formula of Concord' was agreed which allowed the coexistence of the different groups.

Calvinist Church

John Calvin brought the Calvinist Church into being in Geneva. It spread from there and began to call itself the 'Reformed Church' to distinguish it from the Lutheran Church. Chadwick describes them:

> They were agreed upon a doctrine of the Eucharist denying that the grace of the sacrament was given 'in' the bread; upon an austere simplicity of ceremonial in worship; upon a recognition of the high importance of moral disciple; and upon a driving attempt to bring the Bible into every home.

See *The Reformation* by Owen Chadwick (Penguin 1990).

The Church in Zurich

After the death of Zwingli, **Henrich Bullinger** (1504–1575) became Bishop of Zurich. It was agree that the churches in Zurich would not interfere in politics if they could continue to teach the Christian message. However the influence of the Church on day-to-day life remained very great: for example, you could not be a magistrate if you were not a member of the Church.

Similarities

Despite their failure to unite, 16th-century Lutheran and Reformed churches agreed on most doctrinal matters, and there were a matter of organisational matters which the two traditions shared:

See The Reformation, by Owen Chadwick, particularly chapter 13.

- Both the Lutheran and Reformed traditions abandoned Latin for the local vernacular in services and developed congregational singing and prayer in worship.

- Protestant churches tended to support education and literacy, believing the ability to read the Bible was essential for both priesthood and laity

- While the Council of Trent reaffirmed the celibacy of the priesthood, all protestant churches allowed priests to marry: both Luther and Hubmaier married.

Elizabeth I remained hostile to this development and opposed clerical marriages. The statute passed under Edward VI legalising clerical marriage was never in fact renewed by Elizabeth: it remained in abeyance until the reign of James I.

- The sermon became of central importance in the protestant service and thus so did the pulpit in the building of the church.

Differences

However there were some matters of theology that divided the protestant churches:

Protestant doctrinal agreement	Protestant doctrinal dispute
◆ The Bible is the only infallible source of God's revelation to man ◆ Original sin and humanity's inherent spiritual depravity ◆ Jesus Christ as the only Saviour ◆ Justification before God by faith in Christ alone ◆ God's grace bringing salvation entirely apart from man's self-will or works ◆ The spiritual priesthood of all believers.	◆ The nature of Christ's presence in Communion ◆ The absolute and immutable sovereignty of God over His creation and men's affairs ◆ Predestination ◆ The part played by good works in a Christian life

Christianity 67

In addition there were practical matters connected with the organisation of the churches which distinguished them:

Lutheran practice	Reformed practice
Lutheran church leaders tended to eliminate those things that were expressly forbidden in Scripture	Reformed leaders tended to forbid anything that wasn't explicitly sanctioned by Scripture
Lutheran pastors tended to wear long black gowns	Reformed clerical vestments were simplified or eliminated altogether in favour of doublet and breeches and churches were purged of all images and symbols other than the cross itself
Lutheran churches tended to develop under the direct control of the local head of state. Accordingly, Lutheran churches usually retained a hierarchical form of church polity governed by politically sanctioned bishops	Reformed churches adopted presbyterian and congregational forms of church government, with the laity both electing church leaders and filling significant posts
Lutherans believed members should respect the established institutions of secular society so long as they did not enforce unbiblical activity	Reformed churches believed that biblical reforms should extend beyond the sacred and clerical and members should seek to influence and reform society
Lutherans retained the altar	Reformed churches replaced it with a table
Lutherans sang hymns, many written by Luther himself, using familiar popular tunes, and Lutheran churches often included organs	The Reformed churches only allowed scriptural hymns such as the metrical psalms of Miles Coverdale and Clément Marot. Calvinist churches rarely included organs: organs were removed and sold or broken up on site
The paintings and stained glass of Catholic churches were often removed or smashed by Reformers.	Reformed churches tended to be painted white and fitted with plain glass.

John Calvin (1509–1564)

'Calvin and Calvinism' in volume 15 of the *Encyclopaedia Britannica*.

Calvin is described as 'the most important figure in the second generation of the Protestant Reformation'. He arrived in Geneva in 1536 and became involved in the Reformation there. After a three-year stay in Strasbourg he was asked to return to Geneva in 1541, where he became a virtual dictator. With the *Ecclesiastical Ordinances* Calvin established his authority and set out his ideas of how the Church in Geneva should be organised:

♦ There were to be four office bearers: pastors, teachers, elders and deacons

♦ Weekly discussions were to be held to ensure the maintenance of core beliefs

♦ There were to be quarterly meetings of ministers

This summary is taken from McNeil's *The History and Character of Calvinism*.

♦ Elders were to have authority in issues of public morality.

Institutes of Christian Religion

From his base in Geneva, Calvin taught and worked to bring into being a version of Christianity which was to prove enormously influential. Calvin was a more logical thinker than Luther and was more concerned with the detail of how Christian ideas should be put into practice. This can be clearly seen in Calvin's major work, *The Institutes of Christian Religion*, first published in 1536 and continually added to and adapted by Calvin throughout his lifetime. Perhaps the most influential work of the Protestant Reformation, the Institutes are divided into four books which deal with our knowledge of God as Creator, the role of Christ in our knowledge of God, the way in which we can gain salvation, and the ways in which God helps us. From the Institutes we can summarise the key elements of Calvin's teachings:

♦ **God.** Calvin thought that the nature of God was beyond our intellectual knowledge, but that God could be known as Creator and Saviour: 'Although our minds cannot conceive of God without worshipping him, it is not enough to believe simply that he is the only being everyone ought to worship and adore, unless we are convinced that he is the source of all goodness, and that we must seek for everything in him alone' (page 24)

A good abridged single-volume translation of the *Institutes* is that of Tony Lane and Hilary Osbourne (Hodder and Stoughton 1986). The source references here are taken from this edition.

- **Christ.** 'Christ's work as Mediator was unique: it was to restore us to divine favour and to make us sons of God, instead of sons of men; heirs of a heavenly kingdom instead of heirs of hell. Only the Son of God could do this by becoming the Son of man' (page 125)

- **The Church.** 'I will begin with the Church, the gathering of God's children, where they can be helped and fed like babies then, guided by her motherly care, grow up to manhood in maturity of faith... For those to whom God is a Father, the Church must also be a mother' (page 232)

- **The sacraments.** Calvin recognised two sacraments. Baptism is 'the sign of initiation by which we are admitted into the fellowship of the Church' (page 256), and the Eucharist is 'a spiritual feast at which Christ proclaims that he himself is the living bread on which our souls feed to receive eternal life' (page 265). Taken together, these sacraments are 'an outward sign by which the Lord assures us inwardly of his loving promises' (page 253)

- **Predestination.** This is the belief that before the world was created God had already decided that some of humankind would be saved in heaven and the rest damned in hell. Calvin writes: 'We will never be convinced as we ought, that our salvation flows from God's free mercy, until we understand eternal election. God's grace is illustrated by the fact that he does not give away salvation indiscriminately, but gives to some what he denies to others' (page 213).

See also pages 93–94.

Catholic and Counter Reformations

Catholic scholars used to think of the reforms that took place in the Catholic Church at the time of the Protestant Reformation as being purely a response to the Protestant reforms. The more modern view is that the Catholic Church would have reformed itself in any case, although of course the extent and nature of the reform was affected by the Protestant Reformation. Scholars who take this latter view prefer the term 'Catholic Reformation'. But the extent to which the process should be seen as a Catholic Reformation or a Counter Reformation remains a matter of debate.

Counter or Catholic Reformation?

An excellent guide to this topic of study is *The Catholic and Counter Reformations* by Keith Randell (Hodder and Stoughton 2000). See also *The Counter Reformation* by A. G. Dickens (Thames and Hudson 1969).

Early reforming figures include the primate of Spain, **Cardinal Ximenes** (1436–1517), who worked to reform the Spanish Franciscans, and **Gian Matteo Giberti** (1495–1543), bishop of Verona from 1524, who attempted to improve the discipline and dedication of the parish clergy.

Internal reform

The first Pope closely associated with reform is **Paul III**, who was pontiff from 1534–1549. In 1536 he set up a commission to bring about reform and it reported to him in 1537 under the heading

Warning. Photocopying any part of this book without permission is illegal.

'Consilium delectorum Cardinalium de Emenda Ecclesia'. Its main recommendation was that those who had offices in the Church should do the duties that went with them. Paul worked to put this into practice: Randell describes Paul's papacy as marking 'the change from the almost exclusively materialistic Renaissance Papacy to the spiritually dynamic Counter Reformation Papacy'.

See *The Catholic and Counter Reformations* by Keith Randell.

The Council of Trent

The Council of Trent (1545–1563) represents the Catholic Church's main response to the teachings of the Reformation. It made a number of highly important rulings:

- It was declared that it was not the responsibility of the individual Christian to interpret the teaching of the Bible, thus countering an idea that had been central to the Protestant Reformation

- The Latin version of the Bible (the Vulgate) was said to be authoritative, in response to the Protestant desire to translate the scriptures into native languages

- It confirmed that the mass was a ritual acting-out of the sacrifice of Jesus, a belief that had been abandoned by Protestants

- It rejected Luther's teaching that humankind was completely sinful and could do nothing to help bring about its own salvation.

The new orders

An 'order' is a community of monks or nuns which comes into being through the inspiration of one person and which is officially recognised by the Pope.

A sign of the increasing vitality of the Catholic Church at this time was the establishment of several new religious orders. These included:

- **The Capuchins.** This group was founded in southern Italy in 1520 and represented a reform of the Franciscans

- **The Oratories of the Divine Love.** This was a relatively small group active in Italy during the 1520s, which included both religious and lay members who met and worked together as an expression of their deep Christian commitment

- **The Ursulines.** This order (established in 1535) was active in serving others and was made up entirely of lay women until it became a religious order in 1595

- **The Jesuits.** This was the most important and most famous of the new orders.

Ignatius Loyola and the Society of Jesus

Establishment of the Jesuits

See *The First Jesuits* by John W. O'Malley (Harvard University Press 1993).

'Teach us, good Lord, to serve thee as thou deservest;
To give, and not to count the cost,
to fight, and not to heed the wounds,
to toil, and not to seek for rest,
to labour, and not to ask for any reward,
save that of knowing that we do thy will.'
Ignatius Loyola *Prayer of Generosity* (1548).

'Jesuits' is the popular term for members of the Society of Jesus. The Society was founded by Ignatius Loyola (1491–1556), a Spanish soldier, who, after being wounded in battle, had a profound religious experience. Consequently he decided to serve God, and went to study at Paris University. He founded the society with six other students in 1534 and the new religious order was approved by Pope Paul III in 1540. Ignatius was appointed the first superior general, and sent out missionaries throughout Europe and also to America and Asia to found Jesuit schools.

The Jesuits grew quickly and soon became highly influential. Their success was partly the result of Ignatius' **Spiritual Exercises**, which were used in the training of Jesuit priests. These exercises, performed under the guidance of a Jesuit teacher, consisted of a series of structured meditations on the life of Christ. They proved extremely popular and a way of winning over prominent members of society to the ideals of the Jesuits.

The Jesuits are particularly known for their work as missionaries:

Francis Xavier (1506–1552) was one of the original companions of Loyola. After finishing his studies he visited India, Malaya, Japan and China, and became known as the 'Apostle of the Indies'. Although his impact on these lands was fairly minimal, he did set an example of dedication which inspired many later Jesuits

Peter Canisius (1521–1597) was active within Europe. For 31 years he worked tirelessly to try to prevent Germany becoming Protestant. His efforts helped to ensure the continuation of Catholicism in parts of Germany, and he became known as the 'Hammer of the Protestants'.

The Jesuits also worked hard to improve Catholic **education**, the poor quality of which had been a major factor in the rapid growth and success of Protestantism. There were 46 Jesuit colleges by 1556 and 144 by 1579. This emphasis on education was reflected in the standards of Jesuit scholarship: a number of the theologians at the Council of Trent were Jesuits.

Jesuit work in the fields of evangelising and education meant that they were particularly influential in the Catholic Reformation. The *New Catholic Encyclopaedia* sums up their role as follows: 'Revivifying Catholicism spiritually and intellectually, stemming the advances of a hitherto victorious Protestantism, and even regaining vast regions lost to heresy, or seriously threatened in the Low Countries, France, and Central and Eastern Europe.' In many ways the Catholic Reformation depended upon the work of this highly visible, energetic and effective religious order.

Radical Protestant Reformation

'Anabaptists' was the name applied to certain radical Protestant sects who stood for a radical change in the way life is lived. They believed that a literal understanding of the Bible was the source of Christian teaching. This led them to conclude that it was wrong for Christians to swear oaths to a government or monarch, for example, and that the practice of infant baptism was mistaken. Indeed, 'Anabaptist' means 'to baptise again' and refers to the Anabaptist practice of rebaptising those who had been baptised as infants, on the basis that the Bible states that a commitment to Christianity can only be made by those who know what they are doing.

The earliest recognisable Anabaptist group was active in Zurich. Its first adult baptisms were carried out in 1525 under the leadership of **Conrad Grebel** (1498–1526). This group was frustrated with the pace of Zwingli's reforms in Zurich. The movement spread quickly and widely, a rapid growth resulting in large part from their ability to capitalise on the widespread religious unrest of the time.

The movement soon began to be persecuted by other religious groups; as early as 1535 the Anabaptist city of Münster was besieged by the local bishop and the Anabaptist leaders of the city ex-

Work of the Jesuits

> **Further study**
> Get hold of a copy of the Exercises, which are still used in the training of Jesuits today. Why do you think they had such an impact?

The Anabaptists
For a good summary of this topic, see 'Anabaptists' in *The Oxford Encyclopaedia of the Reformation* ed. Hans J. Hillerbrand (Oxford University Press 1996). The most recent full-length work is *The Anabaptists* by Hans Jürgen-Goertz (Routledge 1996).

The spiritual descendents of the Anabaptists are known just as 'Baptists'.

For more on Zwingli's reforms, see the *Edexcel AS Guide*.

See page 73.

ecuted. The Anabaptists splintered into several groups, with the **Mennonites** being the largest group to survive the early persecution. Named after Menno Simons (1496–1561), the Mennonites succeeded in establishing themselves in the Netherlands. Other groups included the **Amish**, who later went on to form a religious community in America.

Balthasar Hubmaier

Balthasar Hubmaier (1480–1525) was the best-educated of the Anabaptists, having attended the University of Freiburg and become professor of theology and then vice-rector at the University of Ingolstadt, before being called to be the pastor at Ratisbon Cathedral. His encounter with Zwingli on a visit to Zurich in 1523 profoundly affected his thinking.

In 1525 Hubmaier moved to Waldshut in Austria, became baptised, married, and offered the laity bread and wine at communion. These acts brought him into conflict with local bishops. When the Austrian army seized the city in December, Hubmaier returned to Zurich in search of refuge, but Zwingli, who had changed his mind about infant baptism, had him arrested.

Following his release Hubmaier continued to preach **adult baptism** before re-arrest. He and his wife were both executed.

See H. Wayne Pipkin and John H. Yoder *Balthasar Hubmaier: Theologian of Anabaptism* (Herald Press 1989). All the quotations here are taken from this book, which has a comprehensive selection of his writings and a brief biographical introduction.

- ✦ **God.** God is 'the highest good, almighty, all-wise, and all-merciful' and we recognise his omnipotence 'from the marvellous creation of the heaven and the earth, and all that is therein' (page 345)

- ✦ **Christ.** 'I believe that Jesus is the Christ, the only begotten Son of the Living God, true God and true Man, conceived of the Holy Spirit, born of Mary, the eternally chaste Virgin, who has crushed the serpent's head, and that in him all the families of the earth are blessed' (page 539)

- ✦ **Humankind.** 'After our first father Adam transgressed the commandment of God by his disobedience he lost his freedom for himself and all his descendents' (page 433). 'In the New Testament, Christ, the true doctor, mixed together both wine and oil, that is, the law and the Gospel, and made out of them a healing plaster for our souls. Thereby our souls became righteous and healthy again' (page 444)

- ✦ **Church.** 'The universal church cannot err. She is without spot, without wrinkle, is controlled by the Holy Spirit and Christ is with her until the end of the world' (page 352)

- ✦ **Baptism.** 'Whether infant baptism is forbidden in the Word of God. Answer: Yes. For baptizing believers is commanded. So by this it is already forbidden to baptize those who do not yet believe... You say: But nowhere in Scripture is there written a clear work that one should not baptise them. Answer: It is written clearly enough... or else I can baptize my dog and my donkey' (page 136)

- ✦ **The Bible.** 'For in all divisive questions and controversies, only Scripture, canonized and sanctified by God himself, should and must be the judge, no one else, or heaven and earth must fall' (page 23)

- **The Lord's Supper.** 'It is seen clearly that the Supper is nothing other than a memorial of the suffering of Christ who offered his body for our sake and shed his crimson blood on the cross for the washing away of our sins' (page 148).

Menno Simons (1496–1561) trained for the Catholic priesthood. Simons began to doubt the Catholic doctrine of transubstantiation and study of the Bible confirmed these doubts. This led him to reject the authority of the Church in favour of that of the Bible. The writings of Martin Luther confirmed this development of his thinking but the execution of an Anabaptist in 1531 caused him to question infant baptism: finding it had no scriptural authority, and was yet supported by Luther, he turned against both the Catholic Church and Luther's reforms. Yet the violence in Münster (see *above*) troubled him, even though his own brother joined the Münsterites and died in battle with them.

Menno Simons
For more on transubstantiation see page 76 of the *Edexcel AS Guide*.

Simons continued to work as a priest, but his sermons became more evangelical in tone and in 1536, he left the Roman Catholic Church and was ordained the following year as an Anabaptist bishop, becoming the leader of Dutch Anabaptism.

His followers, **Mennonites**, are the largest surviving Anabaptist group. Many fled to North America in search of religious tolerance and many settled in Philadelphia in the early 1680s.

> It is evident that the new birth, believers' baptism, discipleship and witness have a coherent existence as they find expression in the body of Christ, the Church. A formulation might be made as follows: Christ in becoming man, the second Adam, began the new creation as the Head of his own household, the church. For man in his acceptance of Christ, it is not the new birth which is crucial as detached experience, but his entrance into and life in this household.

See *Menno Simons: A Reappraisal* ed. Gerald R. Brunk (Eastern Mennonite College 1992).

Test yourself

1. Was it as good as impossible for Protestantism to have made permanent and sizable impact in France?
2. Is the spiritual renewal which occurred in the Catholic Church in this period better described as the Counter Reformation or as the Catholic Reformation?
3. To what extent should the Anabaptist movement be regarded as a distraction from the main events of the Reformation?
4. To what extent was the revival in the Catholic Church due to the personal qualities of Saint Ignatius Loyola?

Church history and Christian thought: the 19th century to the present day

The social, cultural and political context

Industrialisation and urbanisation

The **Industrial Revolution** in Britain at the end of the 18th century caused a far-reaching change in working patterns. An increasing population mostly found work in the new industries, including coal, steel, railways and cotton. As industrialisation spread, it led to a different way of looking at the world. Instead of working with nature, industrialised societies controlled and directed nature. Christianity in Europe was greatly weakened by this upheaval, which disrupted the conservative agrarian sense of community and continuity.

For a discussion of industrialisation and urbanisation see *The Secularisation of the European Mind in the Nineteenth Century* by Owen Chadwick (Cambridge University Press 1978). Hugh McCleod's *Religion and the People of Western Europe* (Oxford University Press 1997) brings the story into the 20th century, while *Religion and Change* by David L. Edwards (Hodder and Stoughton 1974) also has much useful material on this and other areas.

With industrialisation came urbanisation. During the 19th century, many towns and cities expanded as industry increased. Again, the link between humanity and nature was weakened. Christians built churches for the new urban populations, but there were many more social activities available in the towns than there had been in villages. The numbers of people going to church fell dramatically in this period.

Trade unions were an important side-effect of industrialisation and urbanisation. Workers began to group together in order to pursue better wages and working conditions. The Christian teaching on social justice meant that the Church initially played an important role in the growth of the trade-union movement. However in the 20th century trade unionism became much more of a vehicle for atheistic communism and socialism.

See *A History of British Trade Unionism* by Henry Pelling (Macmillan 1976).

The influence of scientific thinking

During the 19th century there was a quickening of the pace of scientific discovery and this weakened the intellectual domination of the Church. In particular, **Darwin's theory of evolution** challenged the Christian belief that humankind was God's special creation, and this notion was further weakened by discoveries that suggested that the earth was far older than the few thousand years postulated in the Bible. In the 20th century the progress towards a complete theory of the universe persuaded many that a traditional Christian belief in God was no longer possible.

See *The Church in an Age of Revolution* by Alec R. Vidler (Penguin 1990).

Awareness of other cultures

Frazer's *The Golden Bough* was an extremely influential account of the development of religion through agricultural myth and ritual. See the abridged version published in an Oxford's World's Classics edition.

Up to the 19th century there was generally a simple division in the minds of Christians between Christian truth and heathen error. However the Enlightenment argument that everyone has a right to their own beliefs became increasingly influential on Christianity's critics (and on Christian thought). The work of scholars such as **James George Frazer** (1854–1951), which suggested that all religions have a common, human origin, caused many to question how Christianity could claim to be the sole source of religious truth for humankind.

State responsibility for health and education

In the 19th century Christianity was an important charitable force. In Britain, Christians such as **Dr Barnardo** (1845–1905) and **Lord Shaftesbury** (1801–1885) worked to improve the health and education of the poor. However from the beginning of the 20th century the State took increasing responsibility for the welfare of the populace. Between 1906 and 1914 the Liberal government introduced a welfare state in embryonic form; by the mid-to-late

> **Warning.** Photocopying any part of this book without permission is illegal.

1940s a programme of universal education and a National Health Service had been established. Although the Churches contributed to these advances, areas of life in which they had once been prominent were increasingly dominated by secular bodies and concerns and this was sometimes reflected by Church attitudes. For instance the *Church Times* commented on the 1940s reforms that 'the Socialist State is not the same thing as the Kingdom of God'.

Further study

The Christian philosopher Keith Ward believes that the forces that weakened Christianity are now in turn losing their power. Try reading his *The Turn of the Tide: Christian Belief in Britain Today* (BBC 1986) and assess his arguments.

The ecumenical movement

There have been divisions in Christianity from the earliest times, and today the major divisions are between the Catholic, Orthodox and Protestant Churches, with the Protestants being further sub-divided into a number of small Churches. However in the 19th century there were efforts to unify the Church: these efforts were known as the 'ecumenical movement'.

A good introduction to this topic is *The Churches Search For Unity* by Barry Till (Penguin 1972). There is a brief summary of the entire history of ecumenism in volume 16 of the *Encyclopaedia Britannica*, pages 358–361.

The Church began to be seen as a human creation, with its divisions and its future perceived as being in human hands. Given the increasing pressure placed upon the position of the Church in society by nonbelievers, moves towards greater Christian unity, such as the formation of non-conformist world unions and combined missionary work, were seen by many as a way of both countering this pressure and of bringing new energy to the Church.

The first world missionary conference at Edinburgh in 1910 marked the formal beginning of modern ecumenism. Although 1,200 representatives from most of the other major world Christian denominations the Roman Catholic and the Orthodox Churches did not attend. It is not surprising that the first moves towards formal unity resulted from a missionary conference. After all, many of these Churches had cooperated in missionary work, and it was through this that they had realised how much they had in common.

The Edinburgh Conference 1910

The conference inspired future Church leaders to involve themselves in the search for unity and a **Continuation Committee** was formed to attempt to put the initiatives outlined there into practice.

In 1938 the **Faith and Order Movement** – which had worked from 1910 to bring Churches closer together – and the **Life and Work Movement** – which had been founded in Sweden in 1925 – united to form the World Council of Churches, with a headquarters in Geneva. However the Second World War meant that the first assembly of the World Council was not held until 1948, when, in Amsterdam, 147 Churches became members. The work of the Council has continued from that time.

The formation of the World Council of Churches

Further study

Have a look at the website of the World Council of Churches at http://www.wcc-coe.org for more details about its aims and activities.

The Roman Catholic Church has traditionally seen itself as the one true Church with an unbroken line of Popes, beginning with the Apostle Peter, as representatives of Christ on earth. In 1928 Pope Pius XI issued an encyclical stating that Rome was the only true focus of Christian unity. This attitude was demonstrated again when the Roman Catholics refused to join the World Council of Churches. However the Second Vatican Council (1962–1965) recognised the right of non-Catholics to call themselves Christians, and the Roman Catholic Church has been involved in a variety of

Roman Catholic and Orthodox involvement in ecumenism

An encyclical is a letter from the Pope to all Catholic bishops on a matter of significance to the Catholic Church.

Warning. Photocopying any part of this book without permission is illegal.

Christianity 75

ecumenical projects without abandoning its claim to be the sole possessor of the fullest form of Christian truth.

There were moves to involve the Orthodox Church in the ecumenical movement in the first half of the 20th century. These culminated in the representation of some of the Orthodox churches at the first Assembly of the World Council of Churches. Till writes of the 'growing participation' of the Orthodox Churches in the Council. Official links between the Churches have been strengthened by cooperation in particular communities.

See Barry Till *The Churches Search for Unity* (Penguin 1972).

The ecumenical movement in England, Wales and Ireland

The **British Council of Churches**, designed to foster the cause of Christian unity, was formed in 1942 and endured until 1990, when it was replaced by the **CTBI** (Churches Together in Britain and Ireland), which includes Roman Catholics. Other ecumenical efforts have been made, such as the discussions between Roman Catholics and Anglicans (the Anglican Roman Catholic International Commission conferences), and in ventures such as Christian Aid in which the Churches work together for international welfare. Although there have been few formal unifications of Churches in England, Wales and Ireland, ecumenical efforts throughout the 20th century did much to eliminate the distrust and hostility that existed between members of different Churches in the late 19th century. In many areas this mutual antipathy has been replaced by amity and concord, with many Churches prepared to pool resources and work together towards common Christian goals.

A History of Christianity 1920–2000 by Adrian Hastings (SCM Press 2001) includes a lot of good material on ecumenism, though the author's decade by decade approach means that this needs to be traced through the index entries for the ecumenical movement.

See page 78.

This has not however been the case in Northern Ireland, where continuing tension between Protestants and Catholics, underpinned by issued of social justice and conflicting national loyalties following partition in the 1920s, has resulted (since 1968) in frequent outbreaks of sectarian violence. Nevertheless, some ecumenical communities have attempted to create an environment in which a lasting peace might be attained.

For an excellent treatment of ecumenism in Ireland, see *Vision and Reality: A Survey of Twentieth Century Irish Inter-Church Relations* by Ian Ellis (Institute of Irish Studies 1997).

The Oxford Movement

The Oxford Movement developed out of a concern to show that the Church of England could exist independently of the state. This meant demonstrating that the Church of England's authority resulted from its being part of the Church as a whole, and led to an acceptance of the teachings and rituals of pre-Reformation Catholicism. Here are some of the main points about the Movement:

Useful general texts on this topic include volume 3 of *Christian England* by David L. Edwards (Collins 1984) and *A History of English Christianity 1920–2000* by Adrian Hastings (SCM Press 2001).

Teachings. The Oxford Movement taught that Christian truth could be traced back to the early Church, which existed without any divisions. The Church of England could be shown to be a direct descendent of that early unity, and was therefore a **catholic** Church in the same way as the Roman Catholic Church.

'Catholic' in this sense means universal.

Leaders. John Henry Newman (1801–90) was the most important of the leaders of the Oxford Movement. He did much to establish the main ideas of the Movement, but then later converted to Roman Catholicism and was in 1879 appointed a Cardinal. Other leaders of the Movement included Richard Froude (1803–1836), John Keble (1792–1866) and Edward Pusey (1800–1882).

Influence. The Movement supported Catholic practices such as the use of candles, incense and clergy vestments. Many Anglican parishes adopted these practices and some Anglican monasteries were founded. The Movement also worked to increase the concern shown by Christians for the well-being of the poor. Moreover the Movement started a debate (which continues today) about the role of the Church of England within the broader Christian Church and about its relationship to the Roman Catholic Church. In Wales, the influence of the Movement could be seen in the design of some new churches, like the parish church at Abbey Cwmhir in Radnorshire. But increased High Church influence merely heightened the resentment of the vast non-conformist movement there, and thus put increased pressure on the established Church.

The Roman Catholic Church in England and Wales

The belief that the authority of the Roman Catholic Church should lie with the Pope is called ultramontanism. This reached its fullest expression in the declaration of papal infallibility in the First Vatican Council of 1870. Newman was opposed to this, but **Henry Edward Manning** (1808–1892), the Archbishop of Westminster at the time of the Vatican Council, was a very strong supporter. Debate over ultramontanism resulted in the polarisation of English and Welsh Roman Catholics into liberal and conservative camps.

The reorganisation of the structure of the Roman Catholic Church in Britain in 1850 led to the creation of the post of **Archbishop of Westminster**. The occupant of this post is recognised as the leader of the Roman Catholic Church in Britain. Since 1850 the Archbishops of Westminster have been:

Ultramontanism

As well as the general texts already listed see *From Without the Flaminian Gate: 150 years of Roman Catholicism in England and Wales 1850–2000* ed. V. Alan McClelland and Michael Hodgetts (Darton, Longman and Todd 1999).

Leaders

Archbishop	When	Notable for
Nicholas Wiseman	1850–1865	His appointment initially caused some opposition from Protestants, but this soon abated
Henry Manning	1865–1892	See *above*
Herbert Vaughan	1893–1902	Was prominently involved in Catholic missionary work
Francis Bourne	1903–1935	During his time as Archbishop more Catholic dioceses were created and the number of Catholic converts increased
Arthur Hinsley	1935–1943	Was popular among the general English population, and was a prominent opponent of Italian and German fascism
Bernard William Griffin	1943–1956	Was active in terms of social legislation
William Godfrey	1956–1963	Was particularly interested in the training of priests
John Carmel Heenan	1963–1975	He attended the Second Vatican Council and strove to implement its decisions. He was also an outspoken opponent of abortion, contraception and euthanasia
George Basil Hume	1976–1999	A Benedictine monk, Hume gained great respect throughout Britain for his principled Christian leadership and for his efforts at maintaining harmony within the Catholic Church
Cormac Murphy-O'Connor	2000–	Has been faced with a number of pastoral crises in the church

The Roman Catholic Church in England and Wales was greatly influenced by the work of the Second Vatican Council (1962–1965). Vatican II was established to examine the spiritual renewal of the Church and to reconsider its purpose in the modern world, and was particularly innovative in its invitation to members of

The importance of Vatican II

Warning. Photocopying any part of this book without permission is illegal.

> **Further study**
>
> Visit a Roman Catholic and an Anglo-Catholic church. Find out what you can by looking at the buildings and by talking to the clergy about the two movements and their history.

Protestant and Orthodox Eastern Churches to observe. Over three years, decrees were issued that called for a liturgy in congregations' own languages, in place of the traditional Latin, an enhanced role for the laity, an emphasis on the pastoral rather than administrative duty of bishops, and recognition of the Catholic Church's relationship to other non-Christian religions – including, importantly, a declaration against anti-Semitism and a recognition of the status of Jews as 'an elected people'. For some, the continued prohibitions against artificial birth control meant that the Vatican had not gone far enough, for others, such as the French **Archbishop Lefebvre**, who eventually broke away, it had gone too far. But in an era of rapidly declining Catholic membership, attempts to revitalise the church and develop the role of the ordinary believer were important.

The Free Churches in England and Wales

19th-century expansion

While the Church of England's domination of public life was on the wane in the first half of the 19th century in England, the Free Churches expanded. This expansion was helped by evangelical revivals and meant that by 1910 Noncomformist chapels had more seatings than the Church of England.

See Kenneth Scott Latourette *Christianity in a Revolutionary Age* (Paternoster 1971).

20th-century decline

The numbers of Nonconformists peaked in the early 20th century, and have been decreasing ever since. The decline has mostly affected urban areas and particularly those in the north of England. For example, according to Hastings, the Methodists closed 493 (mostly inner-city) churches from 1971–1974. The reasons for this decline include the increasing strength of secular ideas and a reverse snowball effect, as where fewer members exist in the first place it is difficult to recruit new members.

See *A History of English Christianity 1920–2000* by Adrian Hastings (SCM Press 2001).

Influence on Christian thought

The Free Churches have had an important influence on Christian thought in England and especially Wales. Largely, their influence has been a conservative one, as some of the Free Churches have a long tradition of defending the authority of their fundamentalist interpretations of the Bible. On the other hand, some Free Church members have been important theologians and have made contributions to Church scholarship. For example the first study in English of **Friedrich Schleiermacher** (1768–1834), one of the most important 19th-century Protestant theologians and the father of liberal theology, was produced in 1913 by **William Selbie** (1862–1944), a Congregationalist minister.

The religious situation in Northern Ireland

A good general history of Northern Ireland is Thomas Hennessey's *A History of Northern Ireland 1920–1996* (Gill and Macmillan 1997).

In 1920 the government of **David Lloyd George** (1863–1945) passed the 'Government of Ireland Act', which was the first step in the partition of Ireland into the Republic in the south and Northern Ireland. The existence of a Catholic minority in the Protestant-dominated north created the potential for conflict. This was largely contained until the Catholic Civil Rights marches of 1968 led to outbreaks of paramilitary violence. Frequent violent clashes continued until 1994, when a ceasefire was declared. Despite this ceasefire, sporadic acts of violence have continued to occur.

The contribution of the Churches to peace

Although divisions within Christianity are a key factor in the conflict in Northern Ireland, there are also Christians who wish to use the teachings of their religion about love and peace to help to bring about reconciliation in the community; the ecumenical **Corrymeela** and **Cornerstone** communities have been particularly important in this area. There are also joint Roman Catholic and Protestant working groups, such as the 'Inter-Church Group on Faith and Politics', and some ministers on both sides of the divide have been active in persuading paramilitaries to give up violence. This leads Craig Seaton to conclude: 'When you examine the reconciliation movement, you find that most of the ongoing organisations are operating from a Christian perspective.'

See *Northern Ireland: The Context for Conflict and Reconciliation* by Craig Seaton (University Press of America 1998).

Key figures: Karl Barth (1886–1968)

According to Barth:

The nature of God

> God is not only unprovable and unsearchable, but also inconceivable. No attempt is made in the Bible to define God – that is, to grasp God in our concepts. In the Bible God's name is named, not as philosophers do it, as the name of a timeless being, surpassing the world, alien and supreme, but as the name of the living, acting, working Subject who makes himself known (page 38).

The Cambridge Companion to Karl Barth ed. John Webster (Cambridge University Press 2000) contains a range of interesting and useful essays. The quotations come from Barth's *Dogmatics in Outline* (SCM Press 2001).

For Barth, God is the utterly unknowable, inconceivable reality, who, through the miracle of revelation (see *below*) makes himself known as the all-powerful creator of the Universe.

Barth writes that 'The heart of the object of Christian faith is the word of the act in which God from all eternity willed to become man in Jesus Christ for our good, did become man in time for our good, and will be and remain man in eternity for our good' (page 65). He also states that 'God's revelation in the man Christ Jesus is compelling and exclusive and God's work in Him is helpful and adequate, because this man is not a being different from God, but the only Son of the Father' (page 82). Hence Barth's theology depends on the possibility of God revealing himself to humanity. This has been done, he believes, through Jesus, who, by his life, death, resurrection and ascension, has made it possible for humankind to know, love and be reconciled with God.

The person and work of Jesus

According to Barth:

Revelation

> God can be known, since it is actually true and real that He is knowable through Himself. When that happens, man becomes free, he becomes empowered, he becomes capable – a mystery to himself – of knowing God. There always remains powerless man, creaturely reason with its limitations. But in this area of the creaturely, of the inadequate, it has pleased God to reveal himself (page 24).

Barth believes that God is beyond the reach of natural human capacity. The only way God can be known is through self-revelation. By the miracle of that revelation it is the real God who is known directly by those who respond to His call by faith.

Barth says:

The Bible and the Word of God

> We must say at once, that the mere presence of the Bible and our own presence with our capacities for knowing an object does not mean the reality or even the possibility of the proof that the Bible is the Word of God (page 71).

This extract is taken from *Modern Theology* ed. E. J. Tinsley (Epworth Press 1979).

According to Barth Jesus is the revelation of God and the Bible is the witness to that revelation. We will only see the Bible in that way once we have accepted its witness.

Warning. Photocopying any part of this book without permission is illegal.

Predestination

This extract is from *Church Dogmatics: Part 2: The Doctrine of Creation* by Karl Barth (T&T Clark 2000).

Barth comments that:

> The thought of God's predestination cannot awaken in us the mixture of terror or joy which would be in order if we were confronted partly by promise and partly by threat. It can awaken only joy, pure joy... At the end of this way God's glory is revealed in the fact that He Himself removed the threat and became our salvation (page 174).

Barth refuses to accept that some people have been predestined by God to suffer eternal damnation. He does not go to the opposite extreme and state for definite that all people will be saved, but he does not limit the grace of God in this respect.

The contribution of Barth

Barth was the leading supporter of **Neo-orthodoxy**, a theological movement that made the truths of traditional Christianity dependent on miracles of faith and revelation. Consequently, some believe him to have done little more than to have reduced Christianity to wishful thinking. Indeed in some respects he can be considered to take an anti-intellectual position. For instance, he believes that human reason is useless when it comes to trying to understand the nature and mystery of God, and that God should just be accepted by faith. However others see him as a defender and expositor of the Christian faith, and as the successor to such great Christian thinkers as Augustine, Aquinas and Luther.

Dietrich Bonhoeffer (1906–1945)

The 'world come of age'

Bonhoeffer wrote in his prison paper of 8 June 1944:

> The world has become conscious of itself and the laws that govern its own existence in what seems to us to be an uncanny way... Christian apologetic has taken the most varied forms of opposition to this self-assurance. Efforts are made to prove to the world thus come of age that it cannot live without the tutelage of 'God'. Even though there has been surrender on all secular problems, there still remain the so-called 'ultimate questions' – death, guilt – to which only 'God' can give an answer, and because of which we need God and the Church and the pastor. So we live, in some degree, on these so-called ultimate questions of humanity. But what if one day they no longer exist as such, if they too can be answered 'without God'? *Letters and Papers From Prison* (SCM Press 1967), pages 178–9

See pages 86–87 of the *Edexcel AS Guide* for an introduction to Bonhoeffer. *The Cambridge Companion to Dietrich Bonhoeffer* ed. John W. de Gruchy (Cambridge University Press 1999) is an extremely useful collection of essays about Bonhoeffer's life, ideas and significance.

For Bonhoeffer, Christianity no longer has any privileged position in the world. It cannot tell non-Christians things they do not know, because in the 'world come of age' non-Christians either have their own answers or are simply not interested in the questions. Hence Christianity becomes a religion of love and service, rather than a claim to superior knowledge and understanding. In this way, Bonhoeffer's approach to Christianity can be contrasted with the theological realism of Tomists and neo-orthodox Protestants who maintain that a Christian's superior knowledge of the world was a gift of supernatural revelation received by faith.

> '[Bonhoeffer's] theology was not an amalgam of the insights of others but uniquely his own attempt to discern the significance of God's revelation in Jesus Christ in and for the world.' *The Cambridge Companion to Dietrich Bonhoeffer* ed. John W. de Gruchy (Cambridge University Press 1999), page 101.

Religionless Christianity

Bonhoeffer writes about this in a letter to Eberhard Bethge of 30 April 1944:

> God is beyond in the midst of our life. The Church stands, not at the boundaries where human powers give out, but in the middle of the village. This is how it is in the Old Testament, and in this sense we still read the New Testament far too little in the light of the Old. How this religionless Christianity looks, what form it takes, is something

> I'm thinking about a great deal... *Letters and Papers From Prison: The Enlarged Edition* (SCM Press 1971), page 282.

Bonhoeffer suggests that Christianity should not be something that strains to go beyond our ordinary human power. This is what religion has traditionally tried to do in its rites and moralities. In his *Ethics* Bonhoeffer also writes of 'that bourgeois self-satisfaction, which, by a convenient reversal of the Gospel, considered being good simply as a preliminary to being Christian'. Religion is not about being caught up in our own states of morality or relationship with a humanly constructed God, but rather it is an altruistic love for our neighbour.

See Bonhoeffer's *Ethics* (SCM Press 1955), page 184.

Bonhoeffer writes about this theme in a very condensed way in one of his prison papers, *Outline for a Book*:

Jesus, the man for others

> Encounter with Jesus Christ. The experience that a transformation of all human life is given in the fact that 'Jesus is there only for others'. His 'being there for others' is the experience of transcendence. It is only this 'being there for others', maintained till death, that is the ground of his omnipotence, omniscience, and omnipresence. *Letters and Papers From Prison*, page 381.

Religion is about **transcendence**, and for Bonhoeffer this transcendence is found not in philosophical speculation about a supreme being, but in the call to love others, giving everything for them. In this way Jesus the man for others shows us the true nature of God.

'Transcendence' is the sense that there are realities which are greater than human beings and by which we should live our lives.

Bonhoeffer writes about the sacred and the secular as follows:

The sacred and the secular

> [Man] must really live in the godless world, without attempting to gloss over or explain its ungodliness in some religious way or other. He must live a secular life and thereby share in God's sufferings... To be a Christian does not mean to be religious in some particular way, to make something of oneself (a sinner, a penitent, or a saint) on the basis of some method or another, but to be a man – not a type of man, but the man that Christ creates in us. *Letters and Papers From Prison*, page 361.

For Bonhoeffer the Christian religion has too often been a retreat from the world that God has created. Because God reveals himself in the love Jesus had for fellow human beings, the Christian should live as one fully committed to the world and not as one escaping from it.

Interpreting Bonhoeffer is challenging because his death meant that he did not leave a complete or coherent explanation of his theological views. Consequently his striking phrases about the 'world come of age' and 'religionless Christianity' have sometimes been misinterpreted. In particular Bonhoeffer is often mistakenly taken to be part of the movement that culminated in the Death of God theology of Thomas Altizer and the post-Church Christianity of those such as Don Cupitt. But in fact Bonhoeffer should be seen as continuing the Protestant tradition, which refuses humankind any concrete knowledge of God other than that brought through the revelation of Christ to the world.

Bonhoeffer in the development of Christian thinking

> 'What is so unusual about Bonhoeffer is that that his rare combination of spiritual depth, sound doctrine, and social concern has made him attractive to a broad spectrum of Christians: Protestants and Catholics, evangelicals and liberals, pietists and liberationists.' *The Modern Theologians* ed. David F. Ford (Blackwell 1989), volume 2, page 67.

Hans Küng (b.1926)

Küng is known as one of the more radical Catholic theologians. To his fellow radicals he expresses the need for Christians in

For a discussion of Küng's thinking see *Hans Küng: Breaking Through* by Hermann Haring (SCM 1998).

general and Catholics in particular to reach out into the modern world. However to the more conservative elements of the Catholic Church, he is an illustration of the dangers of contemporary culture. Here are some illustrations of his main ideas:

The nature of God. 'God is by definition that which cannot be defined, that which cannot be limited: a literally invisible, unfathomable, incomprehensible, infinite reality.' *Credo* (SCM Press 1993), page 10.

The person of Jesus. 'Christians are no less humanists than all humanists. But they see the human, the truly human, the humane; they see man and his God; see humanity, freedom, justice, life, love, peace, meaning: all these they see in the light of this Jesus who for them is the concrete criterion, the Christ.' *On Being a Christian* (Doubleday 1976), page 602.

Justification. 'Death is man's affair, resurrection can only be God's. Man is taken up, brought home, and therefore finally accepted, saved, by God into himself as the incomprehensible, comprehensive ultimate reality.' *On Being a Christian*, page 359.

Infallibility. '...no one is infallible but God himself' *Infallible?* (Collins 1971), page 196. Küng's willingness to doubt the idea of papal infallibility is one reason why his teaching licence was withdrawn by the Roman Catholic Church.

Faith and the modern world. 'By following Jesus Christ, man in the world of today can truly humanly live, act, suffer and die: in happiness and unhappiness, life and death, sustained by God and helpful to men.' *On Being a Christian*, page 602.

A brief and simple explanation of Rahner is Karen Kilby's *Karl Rahner* (Fount 1997). A useful series of extracts from Rahner is *The Heart of Rahner* (Burns and Oates 1980).

Karl Rahner (1904–1984)

Transcendence. For Rahner, everybody's ordinary experience has within it an element that suggests something beyond that experience. After reflection, this element can be thought of as 'God': 'The term of our experience of transcendence, for which we first of all have to look for a name, is always present as nameless and indefinable, as something not at our disposal.' (page 61)

Quotations in this section are taken from *The Foundations of Christian Faith* by Karl Rahner (Darton, Longman and Todd 1978).

Universal Revelation. Rahner holds that wherever and whenever there have been human beings then there have been elements in their experience which lead them to acknowledge a higher spiritual reality: 'The history of salvation and revelation takes place wherever individual and especially collective human history is taking place.' (page 145)

Anonymous Christianity. Christians believe that God can reveal himself to anyone and everyone, and that this revelation can happen even if a person has no explicit knowledge, understanding or even interest in Christianity: 'Since the transcendental self-communication of God as an offer to man's person is part of every person's life, and since it is a moment in the self-communication of God to the world which reaches its goal and climax in Jesus Christ, we can speak of "anonymous Christians".' (page 176)

Warning. Photocopying any part of this book without permission is illegal.

Modern methods. Rahner was concerned to make Catholic theology relevant in an age where explicit understanding of faith outside the Church was limited. His ideas have helped to stimulate the attempt to demonstrate that the Christian faith is not cut off from our ordinary experience and understanding of the world, but despite this they have not been universally welcomed or accepted: 'Theology is a theology that can be genuinely preached only to the extent that it succeeds in establishing contact with the total secular self-understanding which man has in a particular epoch.' (pages 7–8).

Test yourself

1. What has the ecumenical movement achieved so far and how has it achieved it?

2. Why has Bonhoeffer's teaching on 'the world come of age' and 'religionless Christianity' been influential? In your view, does it deserve the influence it has had?

3. Is it the case that religion has largely caused the problems in Northern Ireland or that religion will be a large part of their solution or are both of these propositions true?

4. Outline the key aspects of Karl Barth's Christian thinking. Was he a revolutionary or a reactionary?

Liberation Theologies

Black Theology in North America

Black Theology attempts to make sense of black experience within the context of Christian experience and thinking. In North America black experience has its origins in slavery. This gives Black Theology its theme of liberation and its sense of injustice at the hands of white Christians:

> Not only did Christianity fail to offer the Negro hope of freedom in this world, but the manner in which Christianity was communicated to him tended to degrade him. The Negro was taught that his enslavement was due to the fact that he had been cursed by God (page 120).

Black slaves were forced to be Christians by their white masters and many of them continued to worship within white communities after they had gained their freedom. However the prejudice they experienced led to the establishment of black churches. According to the National Committee of Negro Churchmen: 'The Negro Church was created as a result of the refusal to submit to the indignities of a false kind of "integration" in which all power was in the hands of white people' (page 25).

In the 1950s and 1960s Black Christians such as **Martin Luther King** (1929–1968) were heavily involved in the Civil Rights movement which brought some improvement in the status of blacks in America. However Black Theology can be seen as a criticism of this movement. **Joseph A. Johnson**, then leader of the American Methodist Church, said in 1970: 'Black men have relied too much on the goodwill and moral consciousness of white America in their fight for a better life. In doing this, they have discovered that only a small amount of progress has been "permitted" and even this at the expense of the black man's identity and true sense of worth' (page 282).

Black Power was more aggressive than the Civil Rights movement in its struggle to promote equality for Blacks. James H. Cone speaks of the difficulty he and others had in turning against the example of King, but he also writes: 'From 1966 to the present,

Experience of slavery

A key text is *Black Theology: A Documentary History 1966–1979* eds. Gayraud S. Wilmore and James H. Cone (Orbis Books 1993), from which the quotations on this topic are taken.

A key symbol for these black Christians has been the enslavement of the Israelites in Egypt and their escape to the Promised Land (see Exodus for this story). Many black spirituals, such as *Free At Last*, reflect this theme.

Encounter with Christianity

Civil Rights movement

Black Power

black theologians and preachers, both in the Church and on the streets, have been searching for new ways to confess and live our faith in God so that the Black Church would not make religion the opiate of our people. The term "Black Theology" was created in this social and religious context. It was initially understood as the theological arm of Black Power' (page 352).

Statement by the National Committee of Negro Churchmen

The National Committee of Negro Churchmen made several statements, the most famous of which was an advertisement in the *New York Times* of 31 July, 1966. Entitled 'Black Power', the statement argues that Black Power was not wrong in seeking political power for black people. It deplored the violence of riots that were taking place, but argued that it was more important to focus on the sources of the eruptions. It maintained that until the black person had a real say in their community this unrest would continue.

Joseph Washington and Albert Cleage

The publication of Joseph Washington's book *Black Religion* (1964) was seen as an important milestone on the road to black theological emancipation. It proclaimed the distinctiveness of black religion in America and called for the integration of black theological findings into mainstream Protestantism. This approach was subsumed by one more radical with the publication of Cleage's *Black Messiah*, which argued that scripture had been written by black Jews and that Jesus himself had been black, facts which Paul had hidden in order to make his message more acceptable to Europeans. Black people were called upon to rid themselves of this white theological oppression.

Liberation and community

The theme of liberation is a central motif of Black Theology, as the following statement from the National Committee shows:

> Black Theology is a theology of black liberation. It seeks to plumb the black condition in the light of God's revelation in Jesus Christ, so that the black community can see that the gospel is commensurate with the achievement of black humanity... It is the affirmation of black humanity that emancipates black people from white racism.

> For more on Black Theology teachings on God, Jesus and the Bible (as required by the specification), see the section on James H. Cone *below*.

By demanding a new 'starting-point' for theology, one that redefined the meaning and role of church and religion by rereading the Bible from the black perspective, Black Theologians hoped to bring about a liberation from white oppression. At the heart of this lies an emphasis on a distinct black community, one with a collective history of which it should be proud, and one with a responsibility to all its other members. There are obvious links between this approach and Liberation Theology, and from 1977 onwards, Black Theologians demonstrated a new awareness of liberation movements in other countries.

For a brief and useful treatment of Cone, see the chapter on him in *20th Century Theology* by Stanley J. Grenz and Roger E. Olsen (Paternoster Press 1992). Cone's key work is *A Black Theology of Liberation* (Orbis Books 1986), from which the quotations are taken.

James H. Cone

Cone, an ordained minister in the African Methodist Episcopal Church, is perhaps the most important scholar of Black Theology. Two major influences on his thinking have been:

- His experience of prejudice during his upbringing in the American Deep South

- The Bible, on which he comments, 'How could we speak about God's revelation in the Exodus, the conquest of Palestine, the

> **Warning.** Photocopying any part of this book without permission is illegal.

role of the Judges of Israel without seeing parallels in black history?' (page 48).

These influences have been important in much of Cone's works, and relate particularly to his ideas about **contextual theology**, which is the belief that theology can only make sense when we realise that it has been written in a particular context. Cone writes that: 'It was clear to me that we needed a fresh start in theology, a new way of doing it that would arise out of the black man's struggle for freedom' (page XV).

Here are Cone's ideas on some key themes:

God. Concentrating on God's deliverance of Israel from the oppression of the Egyptians, Cone argues that the God who is consistently concerned with the plight of the poor and unwanted in society in Israelite prophecy is also actively working for the deliverance of oppressed blacks in modern America. Because God identifies with and is working for blacks, he himself is described as black. 'The blackness of God is key to our knowledge of God'.

Jesus. Cone argues that Jesus is both truly man and truly God. As God incarnate, Jesus' role was to liberate the oppressed, he was God himself, coming to strike off the chains of slavery. More controversially, Cone asserted that Jesus should be seen as a black man. Black Theologians argue that it is vital for black people, especially those in the ghetto, to recognise this fact. Christ's resurrection symbolises freedom for all who are enslaved, and should provide hope for oppressed blacks – not hope for a future heavenly life (for Cone rejected this type of eschatology), but hope that will show them that their present situation need not be tolerated.

Bible. Black Theology acknowledges its scripture's central position in the Christian faith but seeks to reinterpret it in the light of black people's experience, to reread it from their perspective.

Nature of man. For Cone, human nature is not something abstract to be discovered by argument. Rather a human being becomes what he or she is through the concrete realities of life. Human nature is not something which is dictated downwards by God, but instead our understanding of God is shaped by the sometimes harsh facts of human existence. God was not incarnated as an abstract human nature but as a particular person in a set of historical circumstances, which helped determine the Christian vision of God's nature and kingdom.

African Theology

The term 'colonialism' is often used to describe the domination of one culture by another. Many countries in Africa have been controlled by colonial powers, and associated with this control is the attempt to convert natives to Christianity. Tite Tienou writes about the 'bulldozer' ethos of western Christian missions, which tend to 'level other traditions. Missions have often attacked and destroyed native religion'.

Patrick A. Kalilombe offers this insight on the relationship of traditional African culture to Christianity: 'In some cases Christianity re-

Cultural effects of colonialism

Two very useful texts are *A Reader in African Christian Theology* ed. John Parratt (SPCK 2000) and *Paths of African Theology* ed. Rosino Gilbellini (SCM Press 1994).

See *A Reader in African Christian Theology*, page 94.

Traditional African religion

See *Paths of African Theology*, page 134.

garded traditional culture and religion with suspicion [and believed that it] must be destroyed... And yet often after this destruction had been achieved, what was proposed was very much like the colonial spirituality. In other cases, Christian evangelists were able to recognise valid and positive elements in the traditional way of life.'

This has resulted in something of a reinterpretation of Christianity from the perspective of African experience. For example:

> The salvation event of Jesus Christ, the ancestor *par excellence*, remains the central religious concept which determines the manner of Christianizing tribal initiation... tribal initiation offers us a point of contact which makes clear to the believing candidate that Jesus Christ is the ancestor *par excellence*, and that he has received the salvation which God gives through Jesus Christ.' *A Reader in African Christian Theology*, page 102

Teachings of African Theology

In its early form, African Theology was primarily concerned with reconstructing an ideal of the African past before the onset of colonisation. More recently it has a need to relate Christianity to the experience of contemporary Africans, who are increasingly having to face issues such as political instability and social and economic oppression. Here are some teachings on specific themes:

- ◆ **God.** 'The Christian could learn much from the divine names and divine attributes stressed by Africans, such as friend, fecundity, fatherhood, life-giver, protector.' *A Reader in African Christian Theology*, page 61

- ◆ **Christ.** 'Christ here [in Africa] plays the role of traditional intermediary, who preserves due order in our approach to God. This concept of Christ, I submit, is very different from the classical Christian idea of mediator... Such a concept of sin is very far removed from the African understanding of God and therefore of Christ.' *A Reader in African Christian Theology*, page 67

- ◆ **The nature of man.** 'The concept of the wholeness of life is important, not just because it happens to reflect a traditional African insight, but also because it is related to some modern concerns in theology... According to the Bible, to be a creature means to be related to God... For man, to come to be and to exist mean the same thing as to be a creature of God.' *A Reader in African Christian Theology*, page 86.

South Africa has been home to many different theologies, some condoning and some condemning apartheid. Indigenous black theology emerged in the 1960s and saw greatest expression in the publication of *Black Theology: The South African Voice* in 1970, which was promptly banned. African Theology in South Africa is a theology of liberation:

> As a movement of thought and action at the same time, South African Black Theology appears on the scene as a critical review of racism as a global phenomenon historically bound up with the expansion of European capitalism. It is further inspired in the social segregation known to blacks in America and South Africa.' *Paths of African Theology*, page 22

Influences on African Theology

Despite the obvious parallels in their teachings and aims, North

American Black Theology may not have been an especially powerful influence on African Theology, perhaps because, as Archbishop **Desmond Tutu** suggests, because they have fundamentally different objectives:

> I fear that African Theology has failed to produce a sufficiently sharp cutting edge... I believe that this is where the abrasive Black Theology may have a few lessons for African Theology. It may help to recall African Theology to its vocation to be concerned for the poor and the oppressed. *A Reader in African Christian Theology*, page 43

A study of themes in Latin American Liberation Theology

Liberation Theology interprets the idea of the reign of God in a political sense, as the Old Testament did. This contrasts with the traditional Christian meaning of the idea, which holds that God will reign eternal in heaven after the destruction of the Earth. According to José Miguez Bonino:

> Biblical love is defined in its intention by God's active purpose: the establishment of his Kingdom, the sovereignty of his covenantal, humanising love...The background of this programme is the jubilee tradition and the prophetic promise of God's ultimate peace – the *shalom*. *Christians and Marxists* (Hodder 1976), page 110

The reign of God

This builds on the section on 'Liberation Theology' in the AS companion to this volume. See pages 93–96 of the *Edexcel AS Guide*. *The Cambridge Companion to Liberation Theology* ed. Christopher Rowland (Cambridge University Press 1999) contains a range of useful essays.

Liberation Theology emphasises the role of Christ as liberator of an oppressed people. It opposes the view of Christ that sets him up as a purely spiritual being looking down on earth from heaven. Gustavo Gutierrez writes of those who wish to see Christ as a purely 'spiritual' saviour:

> Those who reduce the work of salvation are indeed those who limit it to the strictly 'religious' sphere and are not aware of the universality of the process... It is those who in order to protect salvation (or to protect their interests) lift salvation from the midst of history, where men and social classes struggle to liberate themselves from the slavery and oppression to which other men and social classes have subjected them. It is those who refuse to see that the salvation of Christ is a radical liberation from all misery, all that spoils, all alienation. It is those who by trying to 'save' the work of Christ will 'lose' it. *A Theology of Liberation* (SCM Press 1974), pages 177–78

Christ the Liberator

Liberation Theology has made a considerable impact on the Church. It encouraged radical theologians to believe that progress was being made in making Christianity relevant to today's largely irreligious world. However the willingness of Liberation Theology to enter into dialogue with Marxists and to emphasise the 'Social Gospel' has led many conservative Christian thinkers to condemn it as a dangerous distraction from the Church's true mission of saving eternal souls. However as Ian Linden points out, Liberation Theology no longer occupies such a controversial role:

> For a critical period, from 1968 to the early 1990s, while it became established in the Church, Liberation Theology provided the theology and then the spirituality to underpin the Church's option for the poor. It will continue to do so, despite entrenched opposition, but it will no longer hit the headlines. *Liberation Theology: Coming of Age* (Catholic Institute for International Relations 1997)

The impact of Liberation Theology on the Church

In 1984 the Roman Catholic 'Congregation for the Doctrine of the Faith' issued an instruction on the 'Theology of Liberation' attacking those in the movement who used Marxist ideas without taking into account Christian teaching, such as the assumption

The Roman Catholic and Protestant Churches

For more on this, see 'Liberation Theology and the Roman Catholic Church' by Peter Hebblethwaite in *The Cambridge Companion to Liberation Theology*.

For an evangelical view of Liberation Theology, see *Radical Liberation Theology: an Evangelical Response* by Raymond C. Hundley (Good News Books 1990).

There is a chapter on Moltmann in *20th Century Theology* by Stanley J. Grenz and Roger E. Olsen (Paternoster Press 1992), and also in *The Modern Theologians* ed. David F. Ford (Blackwell 1989).

See also page 150. See Moltmann *The Crucified God* (SCM 2001) for his best known single work.

> **Warning.** Photocopying any part of this book without permission is illegal.

that immoral behaviour is the result of badly organised societies. This reflects the generally negative approach the Catholic Church has taken towards Liberation Theology.

Protestants are divided in their views of Liberation Theology. More liberal Protestants tend to welcome it, but evangelicals are suspicious of its emphasis on the social nature of the Gospel rather than on the salvation of the individual.

Jürgen Moltmann

Jürgen Moltmann is one of the most influential German contemporary theologians. Particularly important influences on his thinking have been:

- ✦ His experiences as a prisoner of war
- ✦ His experience of being a German in the light of the Second World War
- ✦ The Christian theology of Barth and Bonhoeffer
- ✦ The Jewish writings of Ernst Block and others.

These have framed his beliefs on a number of key issues:

Eschatology. Moltmann's work is primarily concerned with the contradiction between Jesus' death on the cross and his resurrection into heaven. The one continuity in this contradiction is that it is the same Jesus being both crucified and resurrected. This is a promise of eschatological hope: all those who occupied the same reality as the crucified Jesus can also hope for a new creation. God lovingly identifies with the godforsaken. At the end of history, God will come to rescue his creation. But this promise has effect in the present too: it shows that the world can be transformed in the direction of the new kingdom to come.

God. Moltmann's presentation of God acts as a theodicy. God's promise in the shape of Jesus' resurrection does not explain suffering, but it offers hope for God's final triumph over evil. This in turn should inspire Christians to attempt to overcome suffering in the present. God is presented as being in solidarity with those who suffer. As a triune, social God, he is three beings in one, three beings which exist in a mutual loving relationship. God genuinely suffers and feels pain when Jesus is crucified, which is important, as, in Bonhoeffer's words, 'only a suffering God can help'.

Jesus. This in turn determines how we should see Christ. Christ is also part of this mutual, social trinity, in unity with God, through the Spirit. Jesus' identity is inseparable from his relationships with God and the Spirit, as well as his relationship with humanity and the universe, where he has a healing role.

Creation. Moltmann approaches the issue of creation from an ecological perspective, calling for a renewed theological understanding of nature and humanity and their relationships to God. Humans and nature must have a mutual relationship. Moltmann stresses God's immanence in his creation. Just as the members of the divine Trinity 'dwell within' each other, so God dwells within his creation. Participation in God's glory at the end of history is the ultimate goal for nature as well as humanity.

Moltmann has been important in the development of Liberation Theology. Some have suggested that he is one of those responsible for the commitment to revolutionary change which is typical of much of Liberation Theology. This is because Moltmann tends to emphasise the role of human rights in the way that the world is to develop towards its final salvation. As Moltmann himself says, 'In Europe, the Latin American theology of liberation can awaken a new social kingdom-of-God theology'.

Jürgen Moltmann, *God For a Secular Society* (SCM Press 1999).

Test yourself

1. Compare and contrast the main themes of Black Theology and African Theology.
2. What are the main themes of Liberation Theology? Is Liberation Theology a movement whose time has already passed?
3. By centring theology on black experience, is James Cone bringing theology to life or helping it to die?
4. What are the key themes of Moltmann's theology? Does he have anything relevant to say to modern non-Christian society?

Christian belief and practice

Christian beliefs about the Trinity

The belief that God is three persons, Father, Son and Holy Spirit, each fully God but all within one God only, was defined by a process of reflection that lasted several centuries. However all three members of the Trinity are mentioned together in the New Testament, as in, for example, Matthew 28: 19: 'baptise them in the name of the Father and of the Son and of the Holy Spirit.' The Bible also presents God as Father and creator, the Son as his Word and the Holy Spirit as the power and presence of God, and these are some of the characteristics of the fully developed Trinitarian doctrine.

Biblical foundation

For a technical guide to the subject see *The Christian Trinity in History* by Bertrand de Margerie (St Bede's Publications 1982).

See *The Trinity in the New Testament* by Arthur Wainwright (SPCK 1962).

The major figures and events in the development of the doctrine of the Trinity are as follows:

Historical development

Tertullian (c.160–c.240 CE), whose major writings on the Trinity were composed between 213 and 218, was very important in the evolution of the Trinitarian language of the Church. He uses picture language to describe the Trinity; for example, he describes God the Father and God the Son as 'root and the stalk', different but nonetheless part of the same reality.

Augustine (354–430 CE), who completed his important writings on the Trinity between 400–416 CE. Augustine emphasised the role of love in the Trinity and maintained that if God is love then there must be more than one person in the Trinity. He draws an analogy between God and the human mind:

> Now just as there are two things (the mind and its love) present when it loves itself, so there are also two things present, the mind and its knowledge, when it knows itself. So there are three things – the mind, its love, and its knowledge – which are one, and when they are perfect they are equal.

This is an extract from Augustine's *De Trinitate*, in *The Christian Theology Reader* ed. Alister E. McGrath (Blackwell 2001). There is also a brief commentary on pages 187–191.

This is again an example of how what is separate can also be identical.

See 'The Filioque Clause' by Alisdair Heron in *One God in Trinity* ed. Peter Toon and James D. Spiceland (Samuel Bagster 1980), from which the following translations are taken.

The **filioque controversies** concerned two possible readings of the Nicene Creed. Roman Catholic and Protestant Christians use the Creed with a 'filioque' clause, which means that part of it reads 'And I believe in the Holy Ghost, the Lord and Giver of Life, who proceeds from the Father *and the Son*...'. However Orthodox Churches just have 'who proceeds from the Father...'. The Orthodox Church wished to emphasise that, in terms of the working of the Trinity, God the Father was the source both of the Son and of the Spirit. Catholic Christians wanted to demonstrate that the Spirit can be seen as the bond of love between the Father and the Son, so that they are equally the source of the Holy Spirit.

The **Trinitarian heresies**. There were a number of beliefs about the Trinity that the Church declared heretical:

- **Monarchism.** The belief that God the Father is superior to the Son and the Spirit
- **Subordinationism.** The belief that God the Son is inferior to God the Father. This belief is a key element of Arianism, which was a strong challenge to orthodox Christianity in the early 4th century CE
- **Tritheism.** This denies the unity of Trinity and instead believes in three separate Gods
- **Modalism.** This sees the Trinity as three ways in which the one God works, or as three attributes of the one God.

Although all of these doctrines of the Trinity were declared heretical, they were all important in terms of forcing the Church to establish an orthodox doctrine.

Modern teaching on the Trinity

Three modern theologians have been particularly influential in their teaching on the Trinity: Karl Barth, John Macquarrie and Karl Rahner.

For more on Karl Barth and Karl Rahner, see pages 79 and 82.

Barth argued that theology starts with God's self-revelation as Trinity. As Father he is inscrutable, as Son he reveals himself to us, and as Spirit he comes to us. God is one, there is only one divine 'I'. To avoid the idea that the Trinity is three different beings, he refers to Father, Son and Holy Spirit as three 'ways of being' of the one God, which his critics took to be a form of modalism. Our understanding of the Trinity should come from Scripture and attempts to rationalise it should be avoided.

Macquarrie approached Christianity in an existentialist way, which means that he saw Christianity as giving individuals ways of finding meaning in their own lives. Following this, he divided the Trinity into three states of existence:

- God the Father is **primordial Being**, by which Macquarrie means that God encompasses the mystery of existence
- God the Son is **expressive Being**, which expresses the way in which primordial Being becomes the world of structure and meaning
- God the Spirit is **unitive Being**, which is the search of expressive Being to find its meaning and purpose in relation to the totality of being.

For Macquarrie these categories give us the means to live an authentic life using Christian ideas without being limited by their logical impossibility.

Rahner wishes to move the focus from intellectual speculation about the Trinity to the experience of the Trinity in the life of the believer. He famously claimed that 'the Immanent Trinity is the Economic Trinity and vice versa'. By this he meant that the God we experience in creation and in history is the same as the external, transcendent God (Eastern Orthodox Christianity posits that there is more to the eternal God than we can know).

See chapter 9 of Macquarrie's *Principles of Christian Theology* (SCM Press 1977).

> **Further study**
>
> See pages 55–62 of *The Catechism of the Catholic Church* (Geoffrey Chapman 1994) for a traditional explanation of the nature and importance of the Trinity. Compare it with the more modern views expressed by Barth, Macquarrie and Rahner.

Modern teaching about the divine presence of Jesus

Barth holds that Jesus, as the Son of God, is with his followers through their faith in him. This is possible because of the miracle of the self-revelation of God in Jesus:

> Faith in Jesus is to feel and comprehend the unheard of love of God, to do the ever scandalous and outrageous will of God, to call upon God in his incomprehensibility and hiddeness. To believe in Jesus is the most hazardous of all hazards.

For more detail on Barth's views on this topic, see his *Dogmatics in Outline* (SCM Press 2001).

Wolfhart Pannenberg saw the presence of Jesus in people's lives as a function of his role as Son of God: 'The new man lives on the basis of the community with God as the Father that was opened up through Jesus... Through the Spirit of Sonship, the Son of God wants to become the person-building, existence-integrating power in all men.' Through the Resurrection Jesus has the power to bring the reality of his life as the Son of God into the lives of those individuals who have faith in him.

Quoted in *Jesus* ed. David F. Ford and Mike Higton (Oxford University Press 2002), page 416.

See *Jesus: God and Man* by Wolfhart Pannenberg (SCM Press 2002).

For **Jürgen Moltmann** Jesus most fully revealed the nature of God when he was crucified. As a result of that utter humiliation of God we can know the presence of Jesus, as God, in our lives: 'The incarnate God is present, and can be experienced, in the humanity of every man... No one need dissemble and appear other than he is to perceive the fellowship of the human God with him. Rather, he can lay aside all dissembling and sham and become what he truly is in this human God.'

The Crucified God by Jürgen Moltmann (SCM Press 2001), pages 276–77. For more on Moltmann in general, see page 88 of this guide.

Rahner wishes to see the presence of Jesus in believers' lives in a phenomenological way. In other words, the content of the experience should be accepted in its own terms: 'In this relationship to Jesus Christ a person grasps the absolute saviour in Jesus and makes him the mediation of his immediacy to God in his own self, and when it is actualised and understood adequately it contains in itself its own validation.' In other words, it is part of the Christian's experience that he is aware of God through Jesus as the Saviour and this awareness does not have to be proved in any other way.

Foundations of the Christian Faith by Karl Rahner (Darton, Longman and Todd 1978), page 206.

Hans Küng states that 'Jesus acts now through the Spirit, in the Spirit, as Spirit'. He goes on to say 'The Spirit of God and of Jesus Christ is essentially a Spirit of freedom: in the last resort freedom from guilt, law, death; freedom and courage to act, to love, to live in peace, justice, joy, hope and gratitude'. Thus in experiencing the power of the Spirit in their lives, Christians are experiencing the presence of Jesus.

On Being a Christian by Hans Küng (Doubleday 1976), pages 470–471.

The Scottish theologian **Donald M. Baillie** (1887–1954) avoided talking about the direct presence of Jesus in the life of the believer. Instead he was concerned with the effects of the life, death and resurrection of Jesus in the life of the believer, without being concerned about how these are subjectively known: 'The Christian message tells us that God was incarnate in Jesus, and that his sin-bearing was incarnate in the Passion of Jesus... For that story, with the Christian interpretation of it, makes us willing to bring our sins to God, to see them in His light, and to accept from Him the forgiveness we could never earn. That brings release and a new beginning.'

Donald M. Baillie *God Was In Christ* (Faber and Faber 1956), page 201.

'Thomist' refers to St Thomas Aquinas (1033–1109), a medieval Catholic theologian.

Eric Mascall (1905–1993) was a theologian in the Tomist tradition. He spoke of the presence of Christ in the life of the believer through the Eucharist: 'far from Eucharistic worship being a matter merely of the sanctuary and the sacristy, it is of direct relevance to the world in which Christians live and work and love and die. For the Body which appears in its sacramental form upon our altars is the same Body which in its mystical form is at work in the world and of which we are members.'

Christ, the Christian and the Church by Eric Mascall (Longmans, Green 1955), page 162.

Christian beliefs about atonement and salvation

The work of Christ

There is a debate in Christian thought over the exact nature of the relationship between the person of Jesus and the work of Christ. This focuses on the relationship between Christian beliefs about who Jesus was and what Jesus did to save humanity. If salvation is seen as something psychological (ie we are 'saved' when we find meaning in life) and if belief in Jesus gives us this, then who Jesus really is or was is not essential to salvation. This contrasts with a traditional view that holds that Jesus is able to save us only because of who he was.

For more on this, see *Christian Theology: An Introduction* by Alister E. McGrath (Blackwell 2001), pages 345–47.

Atonement

Theories of atonement form part of **soteriology**, which examines the belief that the death of Jesus somehow mended the broken relationship between God and humanity. Christians have developed a number of theories about how atonement works, the most important are:

- **Substitution.** Jesus died for us in a sacrificial offering on the cross, taking responsibility for our sins and dying in our place
- **Victory.** By dying and rising from the dead, Jesus overcame the evil that held humanity in its grip
- **Example.** By dying Jesus showed us how to live fulfilled lives committed to good, which will give us peace with God.

For more on atonement see *Christian Theology: An Introduction*, pages 410–430.

Sin and grace

The word 'sin' comes from the old English for 'falling short'. In modern Christian theology sin is seen as a moral failing that destroys humanity's relationship with God (old treatments tended to regard sins as criminal offences and divine justice as a complex legal code full of fixed penalties). Sin is so deeply embedded in human nature that it is like a hereditary disease, or a prison from which we cannot escape. Sin has also made us liable to the judgement of a just and righteous God. Grace, on the other hand, has the sense of 'undeserved favour'. It is a term used to describe the willingness of God to bring salvation to a fallen humanity that does not deserve salvation and that cannot save itself.

See *Christian Theology: An Introduction*, pages 440–475 for more on sin and grace.

In Christian theology **merit** is the achievement of something that makes individuals worthwhile and acceptable to God. Both Protestants and Catholics are clear that human beings can do nothing to merit God's forgiveness. Hence the *Catechism of the Roman Catholic Church* states that: 'Since the initiative belongs to God in the order of grace, no one can merit the initial grace of forgiveness and justification, at the beginning of conversion. Moved by the Holy Spirit and charity, we can then merit for ourselves and for others the graces needed for our sanctification, for the increase of grace and charity.'

The Catechism of the Roman Catholic Church (Geoffrey Chapman 1994), page 436. The Catechism is a useful source for a traditional/Catholic expression of all the Christian beliefs and practices covered in this section.

Justification by faith

A number of views about the concept of justification by faith were developed during the Reformation in the 16th century. The most important of these were held by the Protestant reformers Luther and Calvin, and by the Catholic theologians at the Council of Trent.

Martin Luther (1483–1546) believed that he had rediscovered in Pauline theology the doctrine of justification by faith as it is found in the Bible. The Roman Catholic Church, he believed, had developed a false theology of earning salvation by doing good works. Humankind, Luther maintained, was too sinful to earn salvation in this way. Instead the only way to be saved was by believing that the death of Jesus gave you salvation. Seeing this faith, God would consider you to be righteous and you would be united with Christ. Luther said: 'Faith does not merely mean that the soul realises that the divine world is full of grace, free and holy; it also unites the soul with Christ as a bride is united with her bridegroom.'

See page 420 of *A Reader in Christian Theology* ed. Alister McGrath (Blackwell 2001) for this quotation in context, along with a brief commentary. Also see pages 428–30 of this book for more on the views of Calvin and the Catholic reformers at Trent.

John Calvin (1509–1564) drew a distinction between the act of justification by which forgiveness was given by God and the process of sanctification, by which the Christian grows in holiness. However Calvin believed that, despite justification or salvation, nobody can become good through their own efforts. Any righteousness we do have is 'imputed' to us by Christ. In other words, righteousness comes to us from the outside.

See also page 68.

The Council of Trent. This Council (1545–1563) was strongly opposed to Calvin's ideas about justification. The Catholic theologians (in the *Decree on Justification*) held that that justification brings about a change for the better in the human personality.

See also page 70.

Predestination

Traditional Christians believe God to be omnipotent, which means that nothing can happen without God willing it. Consequently, it must be God who decides who in the end will be saved, so the scope of salvation is pre-determined. This idea is called predestination. However Christians have also always believed in human free will. The paradox between predestination and free will bothers some Christians but not others.

Augustine believed that it is entirely up to God to decide who goes to heaven and who goes to hell, and that human minds are too limited to understand why some are chosen and others are not. It is only by God's grace that anyone at all is saved.

See pages 465–474 of *A Reader in Christian Theology* ed. Alister McGrath (Blackwell 2001) for more on these theologians and their ideas about predestination.

Calvin worked out the specific implications of predestination. In particular, he taught **double predestination**, by which he meant that as a result of God's decision there are people destined for hell as well as heaven.

Warning. Photocopying any part of this book without permission is illegal.

Barth reinterprets the ideas of Calvin. Barth holds that it is only Jesus who is predestined to know the judgement of God. No human being is predestined to hell. This leaves open the possibility that all human beings will be saved.

Modern teaching on Atonement

See page 20 of *Christus Victor* by Gustaf Aulen (SPCK 1970). This book is seen as one of the masterpieces of 20th century theology.

Gustaf Aulen (1879–1977) by contrast worked with Luther's ideas and was a strong advocate of what he saw as the classic Christian teaching of the Atonement, which he called the 'dramatic' theory: 'Christ – Christus Victor – fights against and triumphs over the evil powers of the world, the "tyrants", under which mankind is in bondage and suffering, and in Him (Jesus) God reconciles the world to Himself.'

Colin Gunton wishes to guard against the many metaphors Christians use to talk about the death of Jesus and against seeing Jesus' atonement as somehow imaginary or fictional. He argues that, in theology, metaphorical language can be about realities that we have experienced, are experiencing now and will experience in the future: 'Accordingly, when the New Testament speaks of the life, and particularly the death of Jesus as a sacrifice, a victory and the justification of the sinner, may it not be that we encounter not "mere" metaphors but linguistic usages which demand a new way of thinking about and living in the world. Here is *real* sacrifice, victory and justice.'

See pages 51–52 of *The Actuality of Atonement* by Colin E. Gunton (T&T Clark 1988).

Christian beliefs about death and eternal life

The theological implications of the resurrection of Jesus

- ◆ **The person of Jesus.** Belief in the resurrection of Jesus means belief in him as the one God risen from the dead. For some Christians this is proof of Jesus' divinity

- ◆ **Sin, death and salvation.** The resurrection is seen as a victory over sin and death, and central to the salvation of humanity

- ◆ **Eternal life.** Christians believe that the resurrection brings the possibility of a different sort of life to human beings, a life which is characterised by joy rather than defeat and despair. This is 'eternal life', which some Christians believe comes about after death, some see it as happening in the present, and others as occurring both during this life and after death.

See pages 397–404 of *Christian Theology: An Introduction* by Alister McGrath (Blackwell 2001) for a good discussion of the Resurrection, while pages 145–50 of *The Catechism of the Catholic Church* (Geoffrey Chapman 2000) clearly express traditional Christian teaching on the subject.

Eschatology in Christian teaching

Eschatology – teaching about what is going to happen at the end of life and the world – was first presented in the **New Testament**, but in two different ways. One set of teachings sees eschatology as concerned with the future – futurist eschatology – and the other sees the realities of eschatology as something that can be experienced in the present. This is called realised eschatology.

See 1 Corinthians 15 for an example of futurist eschatology, and John 3: 17–18 for an example of realised eschatology.

Later the early-Church theologian **Augustine** introduced the concept of 'two cities'. One of these is the 'city of the world', which is our ordinary day-to-day life, and the other is the 'city of God' (Civitas Dei), which is the eternal presence and reality of God. For Augustine, the purpose of life is to find our way from the city of the world to the city of God.

See pages 556–57 of *Christian Theology: A Reader* ed. Alister McGrath (Blackwell 2001) for a quote from Augustine and a brief commentary on this issue.

For a traditional Christian expression of belief in Heaven and Hell see *The Catechism of the Catholic Church* (Geoffrey Chapman 2000), pages 233–40.

In traditional Christian belief **heaven** is the place where the saved will go at the end of time or after death to be eternally happy in the presence of God. Modern liberal Christians have tended to see heaven as a symbol for a life lived unselfishly and not as a post-death reality. **Hell**, on the other hand, is viewed by traditional Christians as the place where the unsaved will go at the end of time to be punished for all eternity. Some modern Christians see hell as symbolic of a life lived in an egotistical and selfish way. Some Christians reject the possibility of hell entirely; they are called 'Universalists' because they believe in universal salvation. Reinhold Niebuhr (1892–1971) criticised this optimistic belief thus:

> A God without wrath brought men without sin into a Kingdom without judgement through the ministrations of a Christ without cross. *The Kingdom of God in America*

See also exclusivism, inclusivism and pluralism, page 96.

Eschatology played an important role in the thought of several modern theologians, most notably that of Albert Schweitzer and Jürgen Moltmann. Schweitzer (1875–1965) thought that Jesus, like any other Jew of his time, believed that the end of time was close at hand and that God was going to establish his Kingdom on Earth. Schweitzer thought that Christianity should abandon this idea and see eschatology as meaning the coming of the Kingdom of God into our lives in the present: 'In the thought of Paul the supernatural Kingdom is beginning to become the ethical kingdom and with this to change from the Kingdom to be expected into something which has to be realised. It is for us to take the road which this prospect opens up.'

See page 183 of *The Kingdom of God and Primitive Christianity* by Albert Schweitzer (Adam & Charles Black 1968).

On the other hand **Moltmann** represents a return to a more traditional understanding of eschatology. He sees it as the hope of salvation for the whole of the cosmos: 'Out of the resurrection of Christ, joy throws open cosmic and eschatological perspectives that reach forward to the redemption of the whole cosmos. A redemption for what? In the feast of eternal joy all created beings and the whole community of God's creation are destined to sing their hymns and songs of praise.'

See pages 88–89. See also *The Coming of God* by Jürgen Moltmann (SCM Press 1996), page 338.

Rudolf Bultmann's programme of 'demythologisation' was intended to remove the mythical elements of Christianity, which he believed did not fit into a modern scientific view of the world, while leaving behind the existential meaning of Christianity. Hence Bultmann believed in realised eschatology, and he saw elements of this idea in the New Testament and especially in John's Gospel: 'The Gospel of John describes the mission of Jesus as eschatological. His work is "to give life" and "to judge". But these do not refer to the "last judgment"… as a vivid cosmic event which is to come sooner or later. The eschatological event is already being consummated.'

Demythologisation

See *Faith and Understanding* by Rudolf Bultmann (Fortress Press 1969), page 165.

Christian teachings on work and leisure

Christians have placed a high value on work. Work was to be part of Adam and Eve's experience of paradise, and is seen as the opportunity to share God's creative activity and to transform the world for good. However because of the Fall (Genesis 3: 17–18), work is not always constructive and enjoyable. But despite this a Christian should always aim to work for the Glory of God.

Work

Very useful on this subject is *Work and Leisure in Christian Perspective* by Leland Ryken (IVP 1990).

The **Protestant Work Ethic** was a term coined by the sociologist Max Weber. He identified particular attitudes to work which had their origins in the Protestant theology of John Calvin and which he thought had come to characterise Protestant societies. In particular these attitudes held that:

◆ Leading a successful life is pleasing to God

◆ The discipline required by hard work helps to control the constant temptation to sin

◆ The life lived in the ordinary world can be just as pleasing to God as an ascetic life lived in a monastery.

See *The Protestant Ethic and the Spirit of Capitalism* by Max Weber (Routledge 2001).

The Protestant Work Ethic has contributed to the success of the western way of life, but with work-related stress levels reaching an all-time high and with the ecology of the planet under threat from excessive western economics some argue that its value has run its course.

The use of leisure time

Christianity takes its lead on this issue from the Jewish institution of the Sabbath, the day on which God rested after making the world. It is a Christian duty to set time aside for leisure, to ensure that the body and mind created by God finds its recreation in positive and enjoyable ways. Issues for a Christian include the question of when leisure becomes laziness and whether some leisure activities, such as frequent heavy drinking, are healthy for the individual or for society.

Challenges presented by modern society

The nature of modern life has begun to challenge these Christian viewpoints on work and leisure:

◆ Can work that is boring, repetitive and underpaid remain unchallenged by Christians?

◆ Can the Churches help to create a situation in which unemployment is an opportunity rather than a catastrophe?

◆ Have Christians anything constructive to say about leisure activities which, at best, do not always promote Christian values: eg watching most television programmes?

Christian relations with other religions

Increasing knowledge of non-western societies and non-Christian religions posed a challenge to theologians. Were all these people damned through ignorance or could they find their way to God? Christianity has rarely allowed for any route to God other than faith in Jesus (see Jn 14: 1–14), but how is widespread perdition to be reconciled with ideas of divine love? Three different responses can be seen:

Exclusivism

See *A Christian Theology of Religions* by John Hick (Westminster John Knox Press 1995), page 84.

Exclusivism is the belief that only Christians can be saved and go to heaven. It is a belief characteristic of a strongly evangelical Christianity. John Hick quotes William Lane Craig as saying: 'If we take scripture seriously, we must admit that the vast majority of persons in the world are condemned and will be forever lost.' An exclusivist might defend this position in terms of the claim that God is known to be a God of love and grace, and so the punishment of hell cannot contradict this, although our limited human minds find it hard to understand. The exclusivist claim is in effect to know the absolute truth which is hidden from others. Exclusivism is not a widely held position and tends to be found only in tightly-knit, often Calvinist sects.

Inclusivism is the belief that Christianity is the one true religion, but that God has means of saving those who are not confessing Christians. This view is particularly associated with Karl Rahner. His teaching about 'anonymous Christians' maintained that the mystery of God is present in all human experience of the world. Those who respond to that mystery in good faith have received the grace of God without necessarily knowing who God is. Rahner's critics see the concept of 'anonymous Christians' as neo-colonialist. Nevertheless, inclusivism is now probably the attitude most likely to be encountered in churches of any mainstream denomination.

Inclusivism

Pluralism is the belief that no one religion can claim to be the only truth. **John Hick** holds that there is one ultimate reality which is known in different ways by different religions: 'My reason to assume that the different world religions are referring, through their specific concepts of the Gods and Absolutes, to the same ultimate Reality is the striking similarity of the transformed human state described within the different traditions as saved, redeemed, enlightened, wise, awakened, liberated.' Hick moves the focus away from Christ to God and stresses the doctrine of God's love for humanity. Hick's critics regard this shift as an abandonment of Christianity, since it is precisely the revelations in Jesus' life and death that make Christianity possible.

Pluralism

See *A Christian Theology of World Religions* by John Hick, page 69.

Test yourself

1. What is the traditional Christian teaching about the Trinity? To what extent should Christians be prepared to reinterpret this teaching for today's world?

2. 'It's not who Jesus is but what he is believed to have done for us that matters.' Comment on this interpretation of Christian belief in Jesus.

3. Are beliefs about what happens when we die and what will happen at the end of the world any longer a necessary part of Christianity?

4. What do Christians believe about work and leisure? Do Christians have any useful to say about these topics in today's society?

5. 'Only Christians can be saved'. Discuss the rival claims of exclusivism, inclusivism and pluralism.

World religions

Buddhism

The expansion of Buddhism

The Buddha told his followers to travel and to spread his doctrines: from its very beginnings Buddhism has been a missionary religion. The most notable example of the spread of Buddhism occurred during the reign of **Ashoka**, emperor of India from c.269–232 BCE. His empire covered most of modern-day India, the largest until the sub-continent's conquest by the British.

Ashoka converted to Buddhism in c.260 BC, but it took the effects of a series of bloody battles the following year in the Kalinga region for his newfound faith to have direct political consequences. He issued an edict after the conquest stating his great remorse at the destruction he had caused and expressing his aim to govern in accordance with Dharma, to improve the quality of his subjects' lives so as to provide a sound basis for their moral and spiritual development. He introduced a series of reforms based upon Buddhist principles, such as the introduction of free medicine, public works such as wells and rest-houses, and a fairer system of justice. He appointed special servants to see that the new approach was adopted by everybody. In line with the Buddhist concept of ahimsa or non-injury, Ashoka abandoned conquest, hunting and promoted vegetarianism. As Peter Harvey has neatly put it, 'Asoka gave Buddhism a central place in his empire, just as the Roman emperor Constantine did for Christianity'. He was also concerned with the spread of Buddhism elsewhere, and promoted missionary activity, sending monks out to border regions and emissaries to other countries, to spread the ideals he was attempting to foster within his own empire. Although he did not achieve the lasting conversion of India to Buddhism for which he had striven, his influence on the development of India was enormous. He helped to make India a much more peaceful society and was instrumental in creating a Buddhist dominance of India that was to last for several centuries.

Due to the arrival of foreign merchants from central Asia, Buddhism has been present in China since the 1st century CE. However real progress was not made until after the decline and break-up of the Han dynasty. Buddhism had failed to find a place in Chinese society before then due to the strength of **Taoism** and **Confucianism**. The Buddhist emphasis on the metaphysical did not sit well with traditional Chinese pragmatism, while the stress on individual development and monasticism clashed with the Confucian emphasis on family ties. As people lost faith in Confucianism after the break-up of the Han dynasty, Buddhism was able to fully establish itself. A number of different schools emerged from the 5th century CE.

T'ien-t'ai and Hua-yen. Both originating in China, T'ien-tai and Hua-yen were heavily based on a synthesis of teachings of different texts: the T'ien-tai school, founded by Chih-i (c.539–597) placed the *Lotus Sutra* and the *Parinirvana Sutra* at the forefront of its teaching, while the Hua-yen school, founded by Tu-shun (557–

Ashoka

There are many good secondary texts on Ashoka, including articles in the *Encyclopaedia of Religion* (Macmillan 1987) and the *Encyclopaedia Britannica*. See also *The Legend of King Asoka* by John S. Strong (Princeton University Press 1983). Note that the name Ashoka is frequently transliterated as 'Asoka'. When researching him you should look for material under both names.

'In the annals of kingship, there is scarcely any record comparable to that of Asoka, both as a man and as a ruler... In his efforts to establish a kingdom of righteousness after the highest ideals of a theocracy, he has been likened to David and Solomon of Israel; in his patronage of Buddhism, which helped to transform a local into a world religion, he has been compared to Constantine in relation to Christianity, in philosophy and piety he recalls Marcus Aurelius; he was a Charlemagne in the extent of his empire'. Radhakumud Mookerji *Asoka* (Motilal Barnarsidass 1962).

China

There is useful information on developments in China and Japan in the following texts: *A Concise History of Buddhism* by Andrew Skelton (Windhorse Publications 1994); *Buddhism in China: A Historical Survey* by Kenneth Cohen (Princeton University Press 1964); *Buddhism in Japan* by E. Dale Saunders (University of Philadelphia Press 1964).

Taoism was a religious and philosophical system founded by (the perhaps mythical) Lao-tzu, who is said to have been born in 604 BCE. Confucianism, the dominant ideology of Chinese society, was founded on the teachings of K'ung Fu-tzu (or Confucius) 551–497 BCE.

640) emphasised the importance of the *Avatamsaka Sutra*. Both schools saw ultimate reality as inherent in the nature of all things.

Pure Land. The most popular form of Buddhism in China soon became the Pure Land school. Central to this school was the idea that the Buddha, or **Amitabha**, lived in a paradise or Pure Land. He had taken a vow, stating that if he reached enlightenment, he would ensure that anyone who called to him in faith would be reborn in this paradise. This has been viewed as a distinct move away from the traditional Buddhist concept that liberation is a solely individual responsibility, towards the idea that it could be reached through faith and grace. It is important to remember however that the Pure Land school never equated rebirth in Amitabha's paradise with the attainment of nirvana: a Buddhist reborn there would still have to find enlightenment for themselves. In China, this school was led by various patriarchs until the 9th century: T'an-luan (476–542), Tao-ch'o (562–645) and Shan-tao (613–681).

Ch'an. The Indian monk **Bodhidharma** (c.470–520 CE) established the Ch'an school. Ch'an Buddhists claim that their school goes back to the Buddha himself, to the occasion when instead of speaking a sermon, he silently showed the crowd a flower. One of the crowd, Mahakasyapa, realised the importance of the direct experience of enlightenment without obstruction from thought, and this became the essence of Ch'an. The single-minded emphasis on meditation came from the idea that the Buddha-nature is inherent within us, within our minds. To find our Buddha-nature, and thus become enlightened, we have to concentrate on gaining insight into this. Study, good works and devotion are seen as distractions from this process and discouraged: indeed, early Ch'an masters were known for spitting on or burning images of the Buddha. Ch'an monasteries developed in China, particularly after Shen-Hsiu (600–706 CE) became the sixth patriarch of the school.

> You may see this school described as the Zen school. Technically, Zen is the Japanese term for this school. The word Ch'an comes from a word for meditation.

Buddhism arrived in Japan in the 6th century CE, after a Korean king sent Buddhist ambassadors there. It became popular, initially especially so at court and among the Japanese elite, and was made the state religion of Japan by the prince Shotoku (573–622). While the Tendai (the Chinese T'ien-tai school) and Shingon schools flourished at court, devotion to Amitabha and **Avalokitesvara** spread among the people. Many Japanese Buddhist schools developed.

Japan

> Avalokitesvara is an important figure in Mahayana Buddhism: he vowed not to become a Buddha until all beings had been saved from suffering. He is seen as the very embodiment of compassion.

Pure Land. Pure Land Buddhism arose at a time of pessimism and insecurity. The Tendai monk Honen (1133–1212) came to view the traditional path to enlightenment as too difficult, as the world was too degenerate to allow direct entry into nirvana, and humans were too helpless and ignorant. He taught that simple faith in **Amida** (the Japanese name for Amitabha) was enough, and that the Pure Land would act as a platform for reaching nirvana. He was banished from Kyoto by the Tendai authorities, and continued to spread his teaching in the countryside. He accumulated a number of followers, out of whom a Pure Land school developed: the first Buddhist school independent of state power. Like its Chinese counterpart, this school was controversial in placing emphasis on salvation by faith, and not through good works.

Zen Buddhism. Zen Buddhism was brought to Japan from China in its **Rinzai** form by the monk Eisai (1133–1212). Its emphasis on discipline and indifference to death ensured that it became very popular among the samurai. Rinzai meditation stresses the importance of the **koan** in attaining enlightenment; enlightenment is seen as happening very suddenly. Another Zen school, **Soto**, which developed around the monk Dogen (1200–1253) had a more popular appeal. He advocated enlightenment through following the same practice as the Buddha himself: he stressed the importance of 'sitting' meditation (zazen). He also argued that this practice was not technically a means of attaining enlightenment, but enlightenment itself: we all have an innate Buddha-nature, and our task is to meditate upon it, forgetting the self.

> A koan is a subject for meditation, usually the sayings of a great Zen master of the past.

Key Buddhist concepts

The original teachings of the Buddha are scattered among a large range of discourses or 'suttas'. Buddhism has a much freer tradition of interpretation than Christianity or Islam, for example. This means that modern teachers are seen as being able to communicate the full truth of Buddhism. One of most widely recognised of these modern interpretations is *What the Buddha Taught* by Walpola Rahula (Oneworld 1997).

> A single volume containing some of the most important suttas is *The Middle Length Discourses of the Buddha* tr. Bhikkhu Nanamoli (Wisdom 1995). Compilations of his teachings are also available, such as *The Teachings of the Buddha* ed. Jack Kornfield Shambhala 1996).

Dukkha

The word dukkha generally translates as suffering, although it can have many shades of meaning, including pain, discomfort and disease. The basic concept is that suffering cannot be separated from life. The conditions that bring about birth are identical to those that bring about suffering. Whereas most people would see this as hopelessly negative and would want to reduce suffering if only by not thinking about it, someone attracted to Buddhism finds that awareness of suffering is part of the fabric of their life, that they wish suffering to be completely overcome and want to know how this can be achieved.

> For more on the Four Noble Truths, see the *Edexcel AS Guide*.
>
> 'It was the problem of dukkha, rather than abstract questions like "Who made the world?" that shocked the Buddha into his own spiritual quest.' John Snelling, *The Elements of Buddhism* (Element 1996).

Anatta

Anatta means 'no-self'. The Buddha taught that the personality of all living things is made up of five factors: rupa (physical form), vedana (feelings), sanna (cognition), sankhara (disposition) and vinnana (consciousness). He could find no evidence to support the belief that we have a 'self' or soul, an idea particularly potent at that time. The Buddha recognised that there may be some continuity of character from rebirth to rebirth, but argued that this was due to the continued existence of various 'mindsets' which in themselves did not constitute a self, and though long-lasting, were subject to change. There is no 'I': and so the expressions 'I am hungry' or 'I am sad' are false.

> 'The Buddha's teaching on Anatta, no-Soul, or no-Self, should not be considered negative or nihilistic. Like Nirvana, it is Truth, Reality; and Reality cannot be negative. It is the false belief in a non-existing imaginary self that is negative.' Walpola Rahula *What the Buddha Taught* (Oneworld 1997).

Anicca

Dukkha and anatta are two of the three fundamental marks of existence. The third is anicca: impermanence. Everything that *is* is subject to change and is impermanent. Suffering arises out of our insistence on seeing ourselves as permanent, fixed points in a world which constantly collides and interferes with us. If we could realise that we and the world are part of a constantly changing flux then we would learn to live without being intimidated by the fact that it is impossible to find permanence in life. This process of realisation happens through meditation.

> 'The key feature here is the tendency people have to grasp at things, hoping that they will be a permanent source of comfort or pleasure... Anicca is a radical reminder that all such grasping is unsatisfactory, because the desired object, however good in itself, is also impermanent.' Mel Thompson *101 Key Ideas of Buddhism* (Teach Yourself 2000).

Buddhists have always aimed for a final state of being undisturbed by the suffering that is experienced when the truths of dukkha, anatta and anicca have not been realised. This state is known as 'nirvana', which translates as 'the flame has been put out': the end to all cravings. Theravada Buddhists see nirvana as only realisable at the end of a long series of rebirths, whereas Mahayana Buddhists believe that it can be achieved in the here and now. The Buddha argued that speculation as to the exact nature of nirvana was redundant, and argued that we should focus less on what nirvana *is* and more on attaining it. The early sources tend to define it in terms of what it *isn't*, as the 'absence of desire' the 'cessation' or 'blowing out'. There are some references to nirvana as 'the further shore' and passages that suggest that it is a transcendendant reality which is 'unborn, unoriginated, uncreated and unformed', but these are generally difficult to interpret.

Nirvana

'Nirvana is the *summum bonum* of Buddhism – the final and highest good. It is both a concept and an experience. As a concept it offers a particular vision of human fulfilment and gives contour and shape to the ideal life. As an experience it becomes incarnate over the course of time in the person who seeks it.' Damien Keown, *Buddhism: A Very Short Introduction* (Oxford University Press 1996).

The Mahayana tradition places great emphasis on working to save others. This idea finds expression in the ideal of the Bodhisattva, who takes a vow to work tirelessly over countless lifetimes to lead others to Nirvana. A Bodhisattva helps others by reducing their suffering in practical ways, by encouraging and helping them and by teaching them the path to liberation. Central to the Bodhisattva's practice are the six virtues known as the six perfections (paramitas). These are generosity, morality, patience, energy, meditation and wisdom.

Bodhisattva

'My happiness is incomplete as long as there is a single unhappy being in the world.' Bodhisattva vow, Mahayana scriptures.

Bodhisattvas are popular figures in Buddhist art, appearing in richly symbolic paintings. They are recognised as exceptionally powerful beings, indeed, as Keown has pointed out, the line between a Buddha and an advanced Bodhisattva is not always clear. Certain individual Bodhisattvas are regarded as particularly significant and are worshipped and celebrated: Avalokitesvara is the most notable of these. His name means 'The Lord who looks down in compassion' and he is frequently depicted as having many arms, with which to reach out universally in compassion. The Tibetan **Dalai Lamas** are believed to be incarnations of Avalokitesvara. Another such Bodhisattva is Manjusri, whose name translates as 'gentle glory'. In Buddhist iconography Manjusri is depicted with the sword of wisdom, to cut through ignorance.

Set texts

There are many ways of interpreting Buddhist scriptures, but here are some key themes and teachings you may wish to consider when approaching the Questions of King Milinda:

The Questions of King Milinda

The chariot. The chariot that features here is a simile for an important Buddhist theme. Just as a chariot can be broken down into its component parts to show that, ultimately, no chariot exists, so the self can be broken down into its component parts to show that it does not exist as a fixed and permanent reality.

See the section on anatta above.

Rebirth and the self. Death is followed by rebirth and the person who is reborn is both the same as and different from the person whose life gave rise to that rebirth, as when one candle is lit from another, the new flame is both the same as and different from the flame from which it arose. This teaching is not logical in the

Warning. Photocopying any part of this book without permission is illegal.

> These texts are taken from *Buddhist Scriptures* ed. Edward Conze (Penguin 1979).

modern western sense, but Buddhists see logic as a poor way of approaching spiritual truths.

Five virtues. This text presents five significant Buddhist virtues that must be cultivated if one is to attain enlightenment and reach nirvana:

- Wisdom: to recognise the futile and harmful nature of one's cravings
- Morality: through compassion for others, which in turn purifies the mind
- Faith: confidence that you are on the path that led the Buddha to truth
- Vigour: determination to keep to the teachings of the Buddha
- Mindfulness: continuous attention to the freedom-giving Buddhist truth, or dharma.

Nirvana. This is gained by freeing the self from attachment to objects perceived by the senses. Nirvana is presented here as sharing qualities with the lotus flower, with water, with space, with medicine, with a jewel and with a mountain peak. Nirvana is as pure as a lotus, removes thirst (craving) like water, is free from birth, aging and death like space, ends sickness like medicine, brings joy like a jewel, and is unshakable like a mountain peak. Like the wind, nirvana cannot be seen but we are certain of its existence.

Saints. Those who have reached the stage whereby they will no longer be reborn are presented as having minds like giant trees, unmoved by winds which bend and snap the branches of weaker trees. Their minds are untouched by the things that disturb others.

The Deer Park Sermon

In the Buddha narrative, the Deer Park Sermon is the first teaching the Buddha gives after he finds enlightenment. It is also called 'Setting the Wheel of Dharma in Motion'. The sermon was heard by five men who had been followers of the Buddha in his ascetic stage. Upon hearing it, all five instantly became Buddhists.

Your prescribed extract from the Sermon is perhaps the most important piece of all Buddhist scriptures, in that it contains the Buddha's Four Noble (or Holy) Truths. These are presented here as:

- 'The holy truth of ill': suffering cannot be separated from life
- 'The holy truth of the origination of ill': Buddhists think that we suffer unnecessarily because of our anger, hatred and lust. Whenever we give into these thirsts or cravings then we are fostering a very strong sense of self and so suffer more than we need to when the inevitable pains and disappointments of life happen
- 'The holy truth of the stopping of ill': Buddhists believe that the process which leads to suffering can be reversed. As we meditate on and become more aware of our experience we will begin to see that our pain and pleasure arises from a combination of factors: it isn't *ours* in the same way as a pair of shoes is ours. As we become more detached from such things, they are sup-

planted by the peace and joy which, for Buddhists, is at the deepest level of our personalities

◆ 'The steps that lead to the stopping of ill': These steps to enlightenment make up the **Eightfold Path**. Some Buddhists take the path as a detailed instruction manual, whereas others interpret it as more general guidance as to how life should be lived.

For more on the components of the Eightfold Path, see the *Edexcel AS Guide*.

The Lotus Sutra

Mahayana Buddhists believe that their approach to enlightenment is the one 'great vehicle' to salvation, as distinguished from the other 'lesser vehicles', or Hinayana. This belief is based on the idea that their emphasis on compassion via the figure of the bodhisattva, the profound wisdom of Mahayana teachings and the ultimate goal of attaining Buddha-status are the true elements of Buddhism. Around 200 AD, a sutra known as the 'Lotus of the true Dharma' or Lotus Sutra was developed that built on this idea. Chapter 2, your prescribed text, is particularly important here as it incorporates the key Mahayana concept of **skilful means**, the idea that the Buddha adapted his teachings to match the perception and temperament of his audience.

In chapter 2 of the Lotus Sutra, it is argued that the Buddha employed different levels of teaching (depending on his audience) that might initially appear conflicting, as the 'higher' levels involved a revision of some of the more basic, over-simplified original teachings. The Buddha's key message is that all beings should become Buddhas themselves. But this is simply too incredible for those at an early stage of Buddhist development to accept, and so the Buddha first teaches the Four Noble Truths, which set out the Buddhist goal as the attainment of nirvana through becoming an **Arhat**, someone who has become enlightened and escaped the cycle of rebirths. But for those prepared to listen further, the Buddha teaches that in leaving the unenlightened to fend for themselves, the Arhat possesses a subtle pride. True enlightenment is aimed at Buddhahood.

'In these scriptures he never tells them directly that they also ought to become Buddhas in this world. And why did he not do so? Because the Saviour speaks only after he has paid attention to the proper time for doing so, and when he had perceived that the right moment has come.' *Buddhist Scriptures*, page 201.

This idea is put forward in the Lotus Sutra in terms of vehicles. The Buddha originally offered three vehicles whereby one might reach enlightenment:

◆ Vehicle of the disciple. Those who 'prefer to hearken to the authoritative voice of a teacher, and by a thorough understanding of the four holy truths, hope to win final nirvana for themselves'

◆ Vehicle of the pratyekabuddhas. Those who 'prefer to strive for a cognition which brings self-discipline and calm, owes nothing to a teacher and by a thorough understanding of causes and conditions, hope to win final nirvana for themselves'

◆ Vehicle of the bodhisattva. Those who 'want to strive for the understanding of the all-knowing... to win final nirvana for all beings'.

In chapter 2 of the Lotus Sutra, it is explained that it is actually only the third of these vehicles that truly leads to enlightenment. The author uses the parable of a father who sees his house burning down with his young sons inside. He calls to them to leave the burning building, but they do not understand him, and continue to play inside. So he promises them their favourite toys, their deer,

Warning. Photocopying any part of this book without permission is illegal.

goat and ox carts, pretending they are waiting outside the house. The boys rush out to find that the carts are not there, but the father, overjoyed that his children are safe, buys them more ox carts, the best and fastest type of cart. The author explains that the father represents the Buddha and his sons all beings, caught up in the flames of craving and ignorance. The Buddha recognised that beings will not leave this world of suffering for the infinite happiness of Buddhahood, as they cannot see its importance. Like the kind father, he offers three vehicles to enlightenment, promising 'the delight of the cardinal virtues, the powers, the limbs of enlightenment, the trances, emancipations and Transic attainments, and you shall find much happiness and joy!' Once we act on these incentives, and are sufficiently detached from samsara, it can be revealed to us that actually only the vehicle of the Bodhisattva is the true path.

Test yourself

1. Outline and assess the achievements of Ashoka.
2. Compare and contrast the early development of Buddhism in China to that of its early development in Japan.
3. Explain how in Buddhist thought dukkha, anatta, anicca and nirvana relate to each other. To what extent do these concepts represent an attempt to escape from the realities of life?
4. What is the significance of Bodhisattvas to those Buddhists who believe in them?
5. What can be learnt about Buddhist teachings from the Questions of King Milinda?

Hinduism

The modern development of Hinduism

Ramakrishna

For more on Ramakrishna, there is a useful article in volume 9 of the *Encyclopaedia Britannica*. For a fuller treatment, see *Ramakrishna as we saw him* ed. Swami Chetanananda (Vedanta Society of St. Louis 1990).

Ramakrishna (1836–1886) was born to a poverty-stricken family in Bengal as Gadadhar Chatterji and is arguably the most notable Hindu saint of the 19th century. In 1852 he became a priest in Calcutta. He began to have a series of mystical visions of the goddess Kali. He became an ascetic and explored the mystical traditions of other religions, which led him to his key teaching that all religions are based on the experience of one ultimate reality. All religions are true, as they are all paths to the One eternal being. This belief can be seen as a form of Hindu self-assertion in the face of imperial Christian powers like Britain.

> 'Sri Ramakrishna's message to the modern world was, "Do not care for doctrines; do not care for dogmas or sects or churches or temples. They count for little compared with the essence of existence in each man, which is spirituality".' Swami Chetanananda, *Ramakrishna As We Saw Him*.

Ramakrishna attracted some followers who kept his message alive after his own death, and from this grew the Ramakrishna Order. The Order has over one hundred centres in India which, through teaching and works of compassion, carry forward the work of Ramakrishna. His life can be seen in the context of an Indian people increasingly dominated by the British. He arose as a symbol of their own self-consciousness. Ramakrishna brought vitality to the Hindu attempt to express religious ideals.

Gandhi

There are many books on Gandhi: two good, recent ones are *Gandhi: A Very Short Introduction* by Bhikhu Parekh (OUP 2001) and *Gandhi* by David Arnold (Longman 2001).

Mohandas Karamchand Gandhi (1869–1948) was undoubtedly the most famous Indian of the 20th century. He led the movement that resulted in India gaining its independence from Britain in 1947. He trained as a lawyer and was politically active in South Africa for some years before returning to India and taking up the struggle there.

Gandhi believed in a simple Hindu religion based on doing what is right irrespective of the consequences. He lived as a poor man and spun the cloth with which to make his own clothes. His support for Indian independence was based on the belief that the traditional Hindu way of life was adequate and did not need foreign supplementation.

Gandhi taught and lived according to the demands of non-violence (**satyagraha**). He saw this principle as being deeply embedded in the Hindu teaching of **ahisma** or harmlessness. Gandhi was a man of tremendous spiritual striving, but saw taking an active role in politics as a key way of expressing this striving. He has been hugely influential in both spheres.

> **Further study**
> Watch *Gandhi* starring Ben Kingsley (Columbia Tri-Star Home Video: DVD (CDR10135), VHS (C9065163)). Compare the treatment of people and ideas with that given in Gandhi's autobiographical *The Story of my Experiments with Truth* (Public Affairs Press 1948).

Dayananda Sarasvati (1824–1883) founded the Arya Samaj, a group of Hindus who wished to return Indian society to its vedic roots. As a boy growing up in India Dayananda came to dislike the use of idols and offerings, and he turned to the practice of yoga instead. He moved around India and earned a reputation for his defence of the authority of the Vedas. This dependence on the Vedas ensured that he stood in opposition to some of the later practices of Hinduism, such as child marriage and the practice of suttee, and he supported the emancipation of untouchables, as the vedic authorities did not prescribe their lower status. The vedas were also the source of an Indian nationalism that could be taken on board by those unhappy with British rule. Dayananda made it possible for Indians to return to a common scripture and culture, to replace the feuding that had been going on between different Hindu groups.

Dayananda Saravati

For a good biography see *Dayananda Sarasvati: His Life and Ideas* by J. T. F. Jordens (OUP 1978).

> Suttee or *sati* refers to the process whereby Hindu widows would throw themselves on to their husband's funeral pyres.

Radhakrishnan (1888–1975) was president of India from 1962–1967. He was married at the age of sixteen to a distant cousin and he spent the early part of his marriage working his way through college and into university. He gained professorships in philosophy at Mysore and then Calcutta. He moved on to Oxford before returning to academic life in India. Politically, he was an Indian delegate to the United Nations and ambassador to the Soviet Union before becoming vice president and then president.

Radhakrishnan was committed to a view of Hinduism that permitted politics to run its course without interference from religion. He can be seen as a moderating influence on a Hindu extremism that suggests the world can only be run effectively along Hindu lines. He is described as having been a socialist politically and a modernising influence on traditionalist Indian politics.

Sri Radhakrishnan

For information on Radhakrishnan's philosophical thought, see *Thinkers of the Twentieth Century* ed. Ronald Turner (St James Press 1987) pages 633–4. For a full biography see *Radhakrishnan: A Biography* by Sarvepalli Gopal (OUP 1992).

As a philosopher, Radhakrishnan believed that there was something special in the human way of being aware of the world: we see life as having an ultimate value. This led him to conclude that all people have an inherent religious tendency and that everyone seeks a spiritual life and spiritual truth. Humankind has one religion that expresses itself in different ways. Radhakrishnan was able to quote western sources such as Spinoza to support his philosophical views, and this shows a broadening of Hindu thought beyond its traditional sources.

> 'In his own country Radhakrishan is still important, for he brought together two powerful and living forces – pride in the past and faith in the future... but he was primarily a philosopher of the whole world.' Sarvepalli Gopal *Radhakrishnan*.

> **Warning.** Photocopying any part of this book without permission is illegal.

Key Hindu concepts

For Hindus the depth of human consciousness is a great mystery, and that is the mystery of Atman, the self. We need to recognise that the mystery at the heart of our selves is identical with the mystery at the heart of all reality, the mystery of Brahman. God is transcendent (above and beyond all things) and God is immanent (within all things). Hindus aim to realise this identity as the way of finding peace, joy and contentment. The relationship between atman and Brahman is not always easily realised, as Klaus Klostermaier has pointed out:

Atman and Brahman
The term 'atman' has its roots in the Sanskrit for breath and movement, which emphasises its closeness to the source of human life. 'Brahman' has its root meaning in 'growth' or 'development'.

Klaus Klostermaier, *A Survey of Hinduism* (University of New York Press 1994).

> The Upanisadic atman is not simply and unequivocally identical with the Brahman under all circumstances, only in "turiya" (real consciousness)… which is not easily accessible. Only persistent effort opens up the depths of the self.

'The two aspects [atman and Brahman] may be likened to the individual waves of the ocean: the senses perceive their distinction, the mind their identity.' *A Dictionary of Hinduism*.

There is an illustration from the Chandogya Upanishad about how Brahman can be in everything but visible nowhere. A child asks his father how this is possible, and the father asks his child to dissolve some salt into some water. 'Can you see the salt?' asks the father. 'No,' says the child. The child then drinks and discovers that the salt is everywhere.

Samsara and moksha

Samsara translates directly as 'wandering'. It suggests a person going through a long series of reincarnations, always looking for peace and happiness but never finding it. Hindus have a basically positive attitude to life, but they believe that samsara ensures that we cannot find ultimate peace of mind and happiness. We are kept in the cycle of endless births and rebirths by our bad **karma**: when we act in ways motivated by lust, greed or anger we increase the illusion that we are the truth at the centre of reality. This illusion must corrected by accumulating good karma.

For more on karma in Hindu thought, see page 118 of the *Edexcel A2 Guide*.

The word moksha comes from the Sanskrit term meaning 'to free oneself'. It is a state of unity with Brahman in which all illusions are gone and there is perfect oneness with what is eternal and true. Hindus expect to reach moksha after living through a huge number of rebirths, gradually lessening the hold that this world has on them. Although moksha is often used in the sense of being liberated from samsara or the cycle of rebirths, it is also *any* moment when a person grasps the eternal truth that atman is Brahman. Moksha does not describe the final state (partly because it cannot be described) but the process of achieving it. There is some disagreement between groups of vedic scholars as to whether moksha is alleviated through the knowledge that there is no 'self', or selfless devotion to God and his loving grace.

Dharma

Dharma comes from the Sanskrit word for 'hold', in the sense of providing a base or foundation for something. In Hindu belief the individual, the community and the universe are related to each other and it is dharma that ensures that this relationship is harmonious. The dharma of the individual, and thus of the community, is to live out the teachings of the faith. This means to live a moral life and to keep to the rules of worship. Specifically, this is manifest in the concept of varnashrama dharma, which holds that the duties and obligations a person performs are to be done in accordance with their social class and stage of life. The moral aspect of

'Dharma… is its own justification: it is inherent in nature and does not allow modifications. Dharma guarantees the continued existence of India; the avatars appear in order to rescue dharma from corruption and thus restore the country. In the strictest and fullest sense, dharma coincides with Hinduism.' Klaus Klostermaier, *A Survey of Hinduism*.

dharma developed in later Hinduism, as originally it was purely to do with the sacrificial system.

Hindus do not think of their religion as 'Hinduism': rather they think of it as 'dharma', that is, the truth about the world and our part in it. Keeping to dharma benefits others as well as oneself.

Set texts

The Katha Upanishad is one of the most famous Hindu texts. It is popular because of the way in which it expresses simply the basic truths of Hinduism.

1:1. The Upanishad begins with Gautam Vajshravas giving away his possessions for religious reasons. He offers his son Nachiketa to Yamraj, the god of death. Surprised at the offering, Yamraj gives Nachiketa three wishes. He wishes first to return to his father, and uses the second two to wish for spiritual knowledge.

1:2. Yamraj teaches Nachiketa that the eternal in us, the atman, can never be found in that which is limited by time and space: 'The atman is unborn, eternal, ancient… the subtlest of the subtle and greater than the greatest and is hidden in the deep-seated cavity of the human heart… In spite of the fact that atman is without body, all-pervading and supreme, it dwells in perishable, impermanent bodies. Knowing this, the wise do not grieve.' The atman cannot be realised through studying the scriptures, or through the intellectual mind. The atman is revealed to 'the one who chooses It alone'. To find the atman, one needs to be moral, able to meditate and able to control one's mind.

1:3. The one who is to realise atman needs also to be spiritual, or else they will be lost in samsara: 'He who is impure, thoughtless and devoid of intellectual discrimination can never realise the atman, and is ever stuck in the cycles of birth and death.' The person who realises the atman within '…having known That is released from the jaws of death.'

2:1. In chapter 2, Yamraj's teaching continues. In order to realise the Atman within, attention needs to be turned inwards instead of always chasing what is shown to us by the five senses. Once the Atman has been realised, the ultimate unity of all things will be recognised and rebirth will be no longer needed. 'As the pure water poured into pure water stays the same, similarly, the one who knows of this unity and the Atman in practical life, becomes one with the self.'

2:2. Yamraj goes on to describe Brahman: 'He pervades and permeates all truth. He is omnipresent in the sky. He is born in the water. He is born on the earth. He is born in sacrifice and in the truth. He is born on the mountains. He is the highest truth and the greatest of all.' Salvation is found in realising that the Brahman lies inside the human personality at the Atman: [Brahman] is the only eternal Truth among the transitory non-eternal; the consciousness in all that is conscious; the only One who fulfils innumerable desires. The wise who realize Him within themselves obtain eternal peace: the others do not.'

2:3. In order to achieve this realisation, the practice of yoga is

Katha Upanishad

See *Katha Upanishad* by Ambikanandra Saraswati (Frances Lincoln 2001) for a translation and explanation of this text.

needed: 'The firm control of the senses… is called yoga. After this control, the Yogi becomes free from the intoxications of what pollutes the mind.' The Upanishad warns that this control can be achieved and then lost again, but it concludes: 'Nachiketa having been so instructed by Yamraj in this knowledge of the whole process of yoga, became free of what controls us from outside, from impurities and death.'

Bhagavad Gita

There are a range of editions of the Bhagavad Gita available. See, for example, the Penguin Classic edition (tr. Juan Mascaro), which is frequently reissued.

The Bhagavad Gita (which means 'The Song of the Lord') is part of the great Indian epic called the *Mahabharata*. The Gita is seen as one of the great spiritual classics and was, for example, the constant source of inspiration for Mahatma Gandhi.

Chapter 1. The story of the Gita begins with two opposing armies on a battlefield. The leader of one of the armies, Arjuna, feels unable to fight as there are many of his relatives on the opposing side. At the same time, he feels unable to give up the fight. In despair he calls to the god Krishna to come and resolve the problem. Arjuna is caught between the key Hindu principles of non-violence (ahimsa), and the need to do his duty (dharma) as a warrior. His situation is seen as symbolic of the individual struggling to find spiritual truth. They do not know the way forward but they cannot bear to go back.

Chapter 2. Krishna teaches Arjuna that as a human being he is both material and spiritual, body and soul. He reassures Arjuna that the spiritual element in those whom he fights will not die, as it cannot. Instead 'As a man leaves an old garment and puts on one that is new, the Spirit leaves his mortal body and wanders on to one that is new.' The person with awareness knows this: 'In the dark night of all beings awakes to Light the tranquil man.'

For more on yoga, and karma yoga in particular, see the Edexcel AS Guide, pages 114–115.

Chapter 3. The second argument Krishna employs concerns duty, and it is this that eventually convinces Arjuna to fight. Krishna tells Arjuna that he must live in accordance with the truth of karma yoga. All humans are compelled by their senses to act. There is little point in repressing this, instead, one must focus on controlling the senses and engaging in acts of devotion. The way to do this is simply to perform one's prescribed duty.

Chapter 4. Krishna expounds upon the theme of transcendental knowledge. He tells Arjuna that he has no attachment to the results of his actions, and he is not bound by karma. Anyone who, while performing their duty, can be equally detached from the 'fruits' of their actions, and who possesses knowledge of nature of the Lord can be liberated.

A theophany is a moment when a god chooses to manifest himself to a person.

Chapter 11. Chapter 11 represents a **theophany**, as Arjuna asks Krishna to reveal his cosmic form. Krishna gives Arjuna a divine eye, allowing him to see Krishna as creator and destroyer of all things, comprised of the entire universe and all its creatures, colours, scents and gods. Arjuna is completely overcome by this, saying 'I see the splendour of an infinite beauty which illuminates the whole universe. It is thee! with thy crown and sceptre and circle. How difficult thou art to see! But I see thee: as fire, as the sun, blinding, incomprehensible!'

Warning. Photocopying any part of this book without permission is illegal.

Chapter 18. In the final chapter of the Bhagavad Gita, Arjuna asks Krishna to help him understand renunciation and the sannyasa stage of life. Krishna explains that acts of charity, sacrifice and penance should be performed with no thought as to their consequences. This will lead one to the 'supreme perfectional stage'. But no one should renounce their prescribed duties. This is the central theme of the Bhagavad Gita, that dharma and renunciation are compatible, and lead to liberation.

For more on the stages of life in Hindu thought, see the *Edexcel AS Guide*, pages 118–119

Test yourself

1. Can Ramakrishna be fairly described as a Hindu saint?
2. 'It is easier to overestimate Gandhi's contribution to Hinduism than to underestimate it.' Discuss.
3. Explain the Hindu concepts of samsara and moksha.
4. What can we learn from the Katha Upanishad about Hindu spirituality?
5. What do the set texts from the Bhagavad Gita teach about karma and dharma? How might these beliefs help a Hindu make sense of this life?

Islam

The development of Islam

The title 'Rightly Guided Caliph' is given to the first four leaders of Islam after the death of Muhammad in 632 CE. They are called 'Rightly Guided' as Muslims believe that Islam could only have become established as a religion after the death of Muhammad through the inspiration of Allah.

A useful book for this section is *The Concise Encyclopaedia of Islam* ed. Cyril Glasse (Stacey International 1989).

The Rightly Guided Caliphs

History contains many caliphs, but after the first four these are usually best understood as kings, although many did also have a religious function.

Abu Bakr. After the death of Muhammad in 632 CE, there was uncertainty as to who was going to take over the leadership of the fledgling Muslim community. Abu Bakr, Muhammad's father-in-law, had been one of the first to respond to Muhammad's message. He emerged as the Caliph. Following the death of Muhammad there were rebellions in some of the newly conquered territories, and Abu Bakr ended these. This, along with the continuation of the unity of Islam, is seen as his main achievement.

Omar. Omar (sometimes written as 'Umar') was appointed Caliph by Abu Bakr in 634. He had originally opposed Muhammad and had even planned to assassinate him. However he converted to Islam, and turned out to be one of its greatest leaders. The Muslim community expanded further under Omar and he led the Muslim army which captured Jerusalem in 637. He also declared that the Muslim calendar should begin with the year in which Muhammad travelled to Medina. He made whipping a judicial punishment for some offences and ensured that the economic gains of conquest were handed out with some measure of fairness between the Arab people. Omar was later assassinated in 644.

Uthman. Uthman was appointed Caliph in 644 by a group especially chosen by Omar to do so. He was an early convert to Islam, whose caliphate was not without its problems. After a peaceful few years there were rebellions against Islam in both Iraq and Egypt and fighting broke out between those who had been closely associated with Muhammad. Uthman was guilty of putting his own relations into positions of power. On the positive side, it was Uthman

Warning. Photocopying any part of this book without permission is illegal.

> **Further study**
>
> For a view of the Rightly Guided Caliphs in the context of Muslim history in general, see *Islam: A Short History* by Karen Armstrong (Phoenix 2001).

Sunni and Shi'i Islam

See the chapter on deminations and sects in *Islam: A Concise Introduction* by Neal Robinson (Curzon 1999).

'Messianic' refers to the religious belief that at some time in the future God will send a saviour. All three monotheistic religions (Christianity, Islam, Judaism) have messianic elements.

Islam in one modern country: Iran

See *Islamic Iran* by Asaf Hussain (Frances Pinter 1985), or for a briefer treatment see under 'Iran' in *Encyclopaedia Britannica* Vol 15.

> **Further study**
>
> Find out what you can about the controversy raised by Rushdie's book *The Satanic Verses*, and consider why Muslims may have found the work offensive.

> **Warning.** Photocopying any part of this book without permission is illegal.

who was responsible for the first edition of the Qur'an. He was assassinated in 656 by one of the enemies he made.

Ali. Ali (made Caliph in 656) was both cousin and son-in-law of the Prophet. Ali was an early convert to Islam, and was famous for his success in defending Islam during its initial growth. There were members of the Islamic community who believed that Ali was Muhammad's original choice of successor and that the first three Caliphs had had no right to that role. This sense of injustice to Ali led to the major split in Islam between Shi'i and Sunni Muslims, and it was these events that overshadowed his caliphate.

Shi'i Islam. The term 'Shi'i' comes from the Arabic for 'party', and Shi'i Muslims are those who belong to the party of Ali, the fourth of the Rightly Guided Caliphs. Some Muslims believed that Ali should have been the first Caliph, and that the caliphate should have passed from him to his sons. When Ali was assassinated in 661 his son Hasan gave up the caliphate to those who opposed his father. Hasan's brother **Husayn** tried to take the caliphate by force after his brother's death, and was killed. Those who revered Husayn as a martyr formed a party within Islam. The defining characteristic of Shi'a Islam is the belief in the authority of the **Imams**, spiritual leaders of whom Ali was the first. The most prominent Shi'a group, the 'Twelvers', charts a chain of twelve Imams through the early centuries of Islam. The Twelfth Imam is held to have disappeared, to return in the future to save the world. This belief has become messianic in nature.

Sunni Islam. Sunni Muslims make up about 90 per cent of the world's Islamic population. The name derives from the Arabic for 'custom' and is used because Sunnis believe that they follow the customs of Muhammad. Being a Sunni Muslim centres around practice rather than theological allegiance: adherence to one of the four schools of **law** authorised by the community as a true implementation of the customs of Muhammad. These customs, recorded in the hadith (sayings of Muhammad) and passed down among generations of Muslims, are held as the perfect example of the Islamic way of life. From this – and the Qur'an – jurists developed **Shari'a** law, which governs all aspects of Muslim life.

Historical context. Iran is a Shi'i state that has been Muslim since the early days of Muslim conquest. It used to be a tolerant Islamic state under the Shahs, but in 1979 there was a revolution, and **Ayatollah Khomeini**, believed to be the Twelfth Imam, became the leader of a radical Muslim state. There was an attempt to run the country according to strict Muslim rule, and a great deal of hatred was directed towards America, which had supported the Shah. The **fatwah** against Salman Rushdie in the late 1990s was a sign of continuing extremism. However there were reforming elements in the Iranian government and they achieved some success.

Islam in Iranian society. Since the revolution there have been a number of developments that have affected the practice of Islam:

♦ Islam's military background was used as support for martyrdom

♦ The Shi'ite tradition that absolute law could be made by decree by religious leaders was used to create the revolutionary state

- A secular education was transformed into an Islamic education
- Women were made to wear the **hijab** (veiling) as a symbol of the successful introduction of fundamentalist Muslim principles.

Paradoxically, the fundamentalist Iranian government was unable or perhaps even unwilling to introduce radical Islamisation to all aspects of life. Fariba Adelkhah has noted examples of where certain Muslim practices are becoming less religious and more social in significance, rather than the other way round. She points to the social aspect of Friday prayers of contrition, and the social role of funerals: 'Through speculation in cemeteries, preparation by a restaurant or a caterer of the funeral meal, the sums charged for funeral services... death is now part of the "commercialised" world to which the middle classes belong and more and more Iranians want to belong.' She has also noted how the fundamentalist state uses apparently rational arguments to support itself, and the ordinary believer copies this, hence 'polygamy is considered harmful in the light of the teachings of western psychology; a woman who is a victim of polygamy has every chance of being a bad mother and not being able to perform her role in society well.'

Fariba Adelkhah, *Being Modern in Iran* (C. Hurst 1999).

Since Khomeini's death in 1989, it has been argued that 'the quietist tendency in Shi'ism' is re-emerging, with the landslide 'anti-establishment' victory of Muhammad Khatami in 1997, though it is worth noting the brutal suppression of pro-democracy demonstrations by clerically-controlled militias in 1999.

Malise Ruthven, *Islam: A Very Short Introduction* (Oxford University Press 2000).

Continued unrest

Key Islamic concepts

'Allah' is the usual Muslim term for the supreme being. Belief in Allah is the basis of the Muslim understanding of life. To become a Muslim you must declare that 'There is no God but Allah, and Muhammad is His Prophet'. The declaration that there is no God but Allah is made in all of the five daily Muslim prayers, and is customarily the first thing said to a newly born Muslim and the last words heard by a dying Muslim.

Allah

Muslims believe that Allah is a unity and without equal. The oneness of Allah is referred to as **tawhid** and this is probably the most fundamental of all Islamic concepts. It reflects Islam's early history, acting as a challenge to the Arabian paganism, Christian concepts of the incarnation and Zoroastrian dualism that existed at that time. The response to this supremacy of Allah is to be 'Muslim', which means to be wholly submitted to him.

> 'God, there is none but He, the alive, the ever real. He does not slumber or sleep, Everything in the heavens and earth is His, and who - without his permission – will say prayers to him on behalf of someone else? He knows everything that mankind have presently in hand and everything about them which is yet to be. Sura 2: 255.

Other Muslim beliefs about Allah include:

- That Allah is the creator of the universe. Several parts of the Qur'an use the Design Argument to emphasis this divine creativity
- Allah determines all that happens, although humans do have free will to disobey him
- Allah is the supreme judge who will give a perfect judgement on every life after this world has been brought to an end
- Allah is merciful. This is shown in the way in which nature is ordered to allow life to be lived. It is also shown by the way

Islam thus means 'submission', but it also translates as 'peace', which is the state of mind and society created by being Muslim. The sin of believing that Allah has an equal or rival is known as 'shirk'.

Warning. Photocopying any part of this book without permission is illegal.

World religions 111

Allah gives his message to humankind through the prophets, and in the way in which He shows mercy to those who seek forgiveness for their sins.

✦ By keeping Allah at the heart of their lives, Muslims should experience **taqwah**, the constant awareness of the presence of Allah, a constant fear that will guide them in their moral choices.

Revelation and the Qur'an

Islam as a religion is based on the idea of revelation. Human beings are too weak and limited to discover much, if anything at all, about Allah, who transcends them in every way. However Allah can choose to show or reveal himself to human beings.

Discovering the Qur'an by Neal Robinson (SCM 1996) approaches the Qur'an from a number of Muslim and non-Muslim perspectives and makes for a comprehensive and interesting treatment of the subject.

Muslims believe that Allah has sent thousands of prophets to humankind with the message that Allah is unique and that human beings should be submitted to him. These prophets have been largely ignored or persecuted. The greatest and last of the prophets was Muhammad, the 'Seal of the Prophets', as he completed the work of all his predecessors. Muhammad is distinct because Allah revealed the words of the Qur'an through him, which for Muslims, as the Word of God, expresses the final and absolute truth about Allah, the world and how human beings should live: 'This is a blessed Book which We [Allah] have given from above. Follow it in due fear of Allah' (Surah 6: 155). It is complete and without contradiction, and, unlike for example the Torah, the Qur'an was not written specifically for any one religious group, it is universal.

> **Further study**
>
> As Muslims are not permitted to make images of human beings, calligraphy has become a major form of religious expression. If you can, try to visit the Islamic artefacts room of the British Museum to explore this and other aspects of the Muslim faith.

Muslims see the Qur'an as miraculous in nature, as they believe that no one living in Muhammad's time could have produced such a masterpiece without the help of Allah. Muslims believe that the Qur'an is untranslatable, and that another language can only be an interpretation of the Qur'an. It is used every day in worship and the body of the book is treated with the greatest respect.

Sufism

There is an excellent article in Volume 14 of *The Encyclopaedia of Religion* (Macmillan 1987). For a full-length work, see *Sufism: A Short Introduction* by William C. Chittick (Oneworld 2000).

Those who practice Sufism are known as Sufis, a word which probably comes from the Arabic for 'wool', after the simple clothes worn by early Sufis. Sufism is the mystical tradition of Islam. As we have seen, Muslims have a strong sense of the transcendence of Allah, and Sufism can be regarded as balancing this with a sense that the reality of Allah can be directly and deeply known in personal experience. The roots of Islamic mysticism can be found in the Qur'an, which for example says that 'Allah is closer to you than your jugular vein'. As a wider movement Sufism can trace its beginnings to part of the Muslim reaction to the Umayyad rulers of Islam, who from 661–750 CE were more concerned with political power and enjoyment of the privileges of power than with keeping to the spiritual truths of Islam. **Al-Ghazzili** (1058–1111) was a medieval Muslim theologian who showed that Islam and the mystical aspect of religion were not incompatible. The great poet of Sufism is **Rumi** (1207–1273).

From the Middle Ages, different orders of Sufism established themselves. For example:

✦ **Mawlawiyah** Sufis tend to concentrate on the importance of beauty, both in terms of ritual and of language, in their approach to Allah.

- ✦ **Bektashiyah** Sufis emphasise the unity of all religions in their attempt to experience the divine
- ✦ **Rifaiyah** Sufis concentrate on religious meetings and services, which make a huge impact on those who attend. Fire-eating and hand piercing are two aspects of these
- ✦ **Shadhiliyah** Sufis are known for the wisdom of their teaching on Sufi topics.

The extracts below demonstrate some key Sufi teachings:

- ✦ **Sufism on God**: 'For thirty years I sought God. But when I looked carefully I found that in reality God was the seeker and I the sought.' Bayazid Bistami.
- ✦ **Sufism on purity**: 'Your heart is like a polished mirror. You must wipe it clean of the veil of dust that has gathered upon it, because it is destined to reflect the light of divine secrets.' Al-Ghazzali.
- ✦ **Sufism on love**: 'Leave everything and cleave to love! Turn your heart from all else; feel love in your whole being! Take love as your guide to the land of being so that you may reach the True Beloved, enter into the Paradise of God's essence, behold the beauty of the Friend, gather the rose of the garden of Union.' Sheikh Muzaffer.

These quotations are taken from *Essential Sufism* eds. James Fadiman and Robert Frager (HarperSanFrancisco 1997).

Further study

Read some of Rumi's devotional poetry – see, for example, *The Essential Rumi* ed. Coleman Barks (Penguin 1999) – for a sense of what Sufism is about. A visit to your local library should tell you if there are any Sufi groups in your area to whom you may be able to talk.

Set texts

'Al Fatiha' or 'The Opening' is the most famous of the suras. It is recited in all Muslim formal prayers and can be said at any time by Muslims who feel a need to be reassured or reminded of their faith. Within it:

- ✦ God's name is revealed as Allah (Qur'an 1: 1). By establishing Allah's name, the concept of tawhid is also established: 'God' could refer to any number of deities, and Islam is strictly monotheistic
- ✦ God's compassion and forgiveness (Qur'an 1: 1) will be most clearly experienced at the Day of Judgement (Qur'an 1: 4)
- ✦ Allah is sole creator of the physical universe (Qur'an 1: 2). He is also praised for his role in sustaining the world, and bringing good to individual lives
- ✦ All worship is to be directed to Allah alone (Qur'an 1: 2)
- ✦ The concept of the 'straight path' is introduced, a phrase found throughout the Qur'an. Muslims believe that life in this world is ultimately a test of faith. Those who know the 'straight way' of Islam will not be distracted and fail that test.

Sura 1

A useful edition of the Qur'an for this purpose is *The Holy Qur'an: Text, Translation and Commentary* by Abdullah Yusuf Ali (IPCI Islamic Vision 1999).

'Al Baqarah' (The Cow) is the longest sura in the Qur'an. The first 29 verses are essentially a warning to those people who appear to accept the message of Allah, but do not really listen to it in their hearts. The next ten chapters document the creation of human beings by Allah and their disobedience to him. Verses 40–86 deal with the story of the covenant Allah made with Israel, and his faithfulness to Israel; chapters 87–103 with the fact that Moses had

Sura 2

Warning. Photocopying any part of this book without permission is illegal.

been given a book by Allah – the Torah (Tawrat) – but the people rejected that book. The sura goes on (verses 104–141) to state that the people should believe the messages that Allah sends to them. If they do believe then they will be rewarded. Muhammad is not responsible for the response of Jews and Christians. Abraham worshipped as Allah wished and Abraham's religion continues in Islam. It is established that the Ka'ba stone in Mecca is the central shrine of Islam (141–167) and that Muslims are all part of the same religious family and so should keep to set ways of acting towards each other (168–242). The stories of Saul and David are introduced to demonstrate that struggle for righteousness is needed (243–253). The final chapters remind believers that the way of the Muslim, in response to the greatness of Allah, should be a path of truth and obedience.

Sura 96 'Al-Alaq' (The Blood Clot) is recognised as the first sura to have been given to Muhammad to recite. The title is taken from the first two lines: 'Recite: In the Name of your Lord who created, created man from clots of blood'. It is Muhammad who is being told to recite, and he is being reminded of his insignificance: like all living creatures he is created from 'clots of blood'. Muslim tradition is that Muhammad was illiterate, and this tradition safeguards the Qur'an from any 'interference' from Muhammad's mind. However as a merchant, it was very likely that Muhammad could read and write. This need not threaten the authenticity, from the Muslim point of view, of the revelation of the Qur'an to him.

The sura continues: 'Recite: And your Lord is the Most Generous, He who taught by the pen, taught man what he did not know.' The giving of the Qur'an was an act of generosity by Allah; without the Qur'an humankind would have been lost and without guidance.

The rest of the Surah speaks of a master who attempts to prevent his servant saying his prayers. This is seen as an example of the persecution the early Muslims faced in Mecca, when active attempts were made to stop them following their religion. Muhammad is assured that such a master will be punished.

Sura 112 'Al-Ikhlas' (Sincerity) runs, in full, as follows:

> Say: 'He is Allah, Absolute Oneness,
> Allah, the Everlasting Sustainer of all.
> He has not given birth and was not born.
> And no one compares to Him'.

This short sura is an expression of the central Muslim belief in tawhid, the complete uniqueness of Allah. Abdullah Yusuf Ali has commented:

Abdullah Yusuf Ali, *The Holy Qur'an* (IPCI Islamic Vision 1991).

> The nature of Allah is here indicated to us in a few words, such as we can understand... Here we are specially taught to avoid the pitfalls into which men and nations have fallen at various times in trying to understand Allah. The first thing that we have to note is that His nature is so sublime, so far beyond our limited conceptions, that the best way we can realise Him to feel that He is a Personality, He, and not a mere abstract conception of philosophy. He is near us, He cares for us, we owe our existence to Him.

Test yourself

1. 'Sunni and Shi'a Muslims have much more in common than they have that which divides them'. Discuss.
2. To what extent was the revolution in Iran and the state to which it gave rise genuinely Muslim?
3. What impact does belief in Allah and Quranic revelation have on the lives of Muslims?
4. Outline the main teachings of Sufism. Is Sufism a part of Islam or in opposition to Islam?
5. What can we learn about Islam from Sura 2 'The Cow'?

Judaism

The development of Judaism

Moses Mendelssohn (1729–1786) lived in Germany. He made his own contribution to the philosophy of the **Enlightenment** and became one of the most famous Jews of his day. When challenged in 1769 by the Christian Johann Lavater to refute Christianity or convert to it, Mendelssohn replied that he saw himself as a traditional Jew, but that this was not incompatible with modern ideas on rationality.

Mendelssohn was active in trying to emancipate Jews from the restrictions they faced in European society – Jews had lived in Europe for many centuries, but had frequently been the target of discrimination. He was an enthusiastic supporter of religious toleration, from which the Jews could only benefit. In order to help modernise Judaism he made a translation of the Pentateuch into German. He is often referred to as the first modern Jew, thanks to his attempts to combine participation in new European intellectual currents with traditional Jewish concepts.

David Friedlander (1750–1834) was a follower of Moses Mendelssohn. He was a successful businessman who used his position of influence to help to establish a Jewish school that did not require fees. He ran this school for two decades, and was also involved in running a printing press and bookshop that produced and sold Jewish works. He wrote textbooks and translated works in traditional Jewish languages into Hebrew.

Abraham Geiger (1810–1874) became the leader of Reform Judaism in 19th-century Germany. He made a lot of liturgical and ritual changes to Judaism, which he felt had become outdated in some of its beliefs and practices. Or as *The Oxford Dictionary of the Jewish Religion* puts it: 'The outstanding intellectual of figure among the early Reformers, he was animated by the desire to liberate Judaism from its ceremonialism, to link it with European traditions, to organise it on modern scientific lines, and to interpret it in the light of the ethical universality based on the prophets.'

Hirsch (1808–1888) is regarded as the founder of the Neo-Orthodox movement in Judaism. This movement was an attempt to combine a traditional understanding of the Torah as the absolute word of God (something which Reform Jews rejected) with a genuine engagement in contemporary society, something which he believed that Orthodox Jews was failing to achieve).

Moses Mendelssohn

The Enlightenment was the period of time in European intellectual history, usually seen as spanning the 18th and 19th centuries, when the concept of relying on one's own powers of thought rather than the authority of religion gained force, and democracy as a modern political idea came into being.

David Friedlander and Abraham Geiger

Samson Raphael Hirsch

Further study

Read about these figures in the context of Jewish history as a whole. See *A History of the Jews* by Paul Johnson (Phoenix 2001).

Zionism and Israel

For more detail on this see *History of Zionism: A Handbook and Dictionary* by Abraham J Edelhelt (Westview 2000).

Renamed the World Zionist Organisation in 1960, it is still active.

The Balfour Declaration is contained in a letter from Arthur Balfour, Britain's foreign secretary, to Lord Rothschild. The text of the letter can be found on several websites

The Holocaust

There are numerous books available on this topic. Particularly useful is *A Holocaust Reader: Responses to the Nazi Extermination* ed. Michael L. Morgan (Oxford University Press 2001), which features a wide ranging collection of Jewish theological responses.

Warning. Photocopying any part of this book without permission is illegal.

Hirsch was a rabbi who put forward his ideas through public speaking, teaching and writing. He argued that it was part of the law of God that Jews should develop their humanity to the full, and that this could only be done if contemporary resources of scientific knowledge and culture were made part of Jewish life.

Zion was initially the name of a hill in Jerusalem, and Zionism came to symbolise the desire of the Jews to have a homeland of their own. The Jews lost their homeland when the Romans destroyed Jerusalem in the 2nd century CE, and from that time they lived in communities spread around various countries. Towards the end of the 19th century, some Jews began to assert that the Jewish state should be recreated in Palestine, the original 'Promised Land' of the Jews. These ideas are particularly associated with **Theodor Herzl**, who wanted a Jewish state as a protection against anti-Semitism and also as a way of helping Jews to become a modern political entity. He founded the Zionist Organisation in 1897 at the First Zionist Congress in Basle.

Jews began to emigrate to Palestine and set up communities there. In 1917 Britain committed itself to establishing a Jewish state in the **Balfour Declaration**. The Holocaust (see *below*) did much to end opposition to the establishment of an Israeli state, not least by ending the lives of many of the Orthodox Jews who saw political attempts to establish a Jewish state as an attempt to achieve by human means what could actually only be achieved through God's decision to establish the messianic age. In 1948 Israel declared itself to be an independent state, a declaration recognised by many major governments around the world.

Zionism continues to be a source of great controversy. For some Jews it demonstrates that their religion has come of age in a secular world. Other Jews remain hostile to the idea, and for some in the non-Jewish world, Zionism has become the banner under which Jews perpetuate racist oppression of the very kind they themselves suffered fromso greatly in the 20th century.

In Jewish scripture, a holocaust was a sacrifice that was consumed by fire, and this idea of a complete sacrifice has been applied to the deaths of the six million Jews who were killed under National Socialist rule in Germany. The Holocaust is often seen by Jews as the culmination of a European anti-Semitism that had its roots in the belief that in killing Christ the Jews committed deicide, and so forfeited their human rights.

The bleak conclusion of some commentators was that Hitler could claim more of a posthumous victory over Judaism than he achieved in his lifetime. There was a widespread loss of faith among Jews who could find no **theodicy** (justification of the goodness of an almighty and all-knowing God in the face of such evil) with which to reconstruct their faith. The sheer scale and darkness of events restates the problem of evil in an overwhelmingly powerful way. Conversely, others would point to the Tenakh, the Psalms (such as 126: 6) and Job, which wrestle with humanity's finite nature and frustration at having to trust in the goodness of God in the face of the seemingly futile suffering of the innocent. Hans Jonas argues that the Holocaust has ensured that the traditional beliefs about

God must go. Instead, God must be seen as a limited and suffering God, and a new religious consciousness must be forged from this basic belief.

Other writers have seen such apocalyptic events as galvanising Jewish identity and faith. Like the burning bush which was engulfed in fire but not consumed, God has brought Israel out from the Holocaust as he brought it out of Egypt. Eliezer Berkovits believes that God could be found in the concentration camps, and that this experience is part of developing Judaism (he also argues that the Jews need no help from Christians or secular thinkers to understand the Holocaust). Emil Fackenheim believes that the message of the Holocaust is that a new commandment exists for Jews today: to survive whatever forces are against them. In contrast, Menahem Hartom asserted that the Holocaust was a punishment for the Jews for failing to live up to the demands of the Torah.

See the essay on the Holocaust in *The Oxford Dictionary of the Jewish Religion* for more on these Jewish writers and their ideas.

Further study

If you can, visit the permanent Holocaust exhibition at the Imperial War Museum in London.

Key Jewish concepts

Jews frequently link the concepts of Law and authority with the Hebrew word 'Torah', a word of several different meanings. Here are some of the connections between Law and Torah:

✦ In the Pentateuch, laws about one subject are referred to as the 'Torah' of that subject

✦ Torah refers to the first five books of the Jewish scriptures in which the most important collection of Law is found

✦ Torah refers to laws that originate specifically in the Jewish scriptures as a whole, as opposed to the work of the rabbis

✦ Torah refers to the Written Law as opposed to the Oral Law (law passed down by word of mouth)

✦ Torah can also be used to refer to the entirety of Jewish Law in whatever form it takes.

For Orthodox Jews both the Written and Oral Torahs were given by God to Moses on Mount Sinai. The 8th of the Thirteen Principles of Maimonides includes the statement that 'the entire Torah in our hands was given to our master, Moses'. A tradition developed that the Torah given to Moses existed in heaven before the world was made and that it was through the Torah that the world was created. See, for example, Proverbs 8: 22: 'The Lord made me [Wisdom, interpreted as Torah] as the beginning of his way, the first work of old.'

According to Orthodox Jews, the Oral Torah was passed on by word of mouth from Moses until it began to be written down (from about 200 CE) in the works of the **Mishnah** and the **Talmud**. Orthodox Rabbis have the authority to interpret the Written and Oral Torahs and so to make rulings which are binding on the Jews in the broadest sense of 'Torah' but obviously not in the sense of being Written or Oral Torahs themselves. The rules for Jewish life and conduct that come out of the Torah are known as **Halakhah**.

Reform Jews hold that each generation of the faith has the right and duty to interpret the Torah in a way which is fitting to their times.

Law and authority

See the articles on 'Torah' in *The Encyclopaedia of Judaism* and 'Torah' and 'Oral Law' in *The Oxford Dictionary of the Jewish Religion*. For a recent consideration of how Orthodox Rabbis use their authority in interpreting the Law see *Rabbinic Authority and Personal Autonomy* ed. Moshe Z. Sokoi (Jason Aronson 1992).

See page 120.

Warning. Photocopying any part of this book without permission is illegal.

For Reform or 'Progressive' Jews the Torah was not revealed in one single moment to Moses. They argue that God's revelation has always been a progressive *human* process. Modern scholarship on the Pentateuch suggests that it evolved over a great period of time and contains traditions going back to Moses and earlier. If this is the case, Torah is still a fundamental idea in Judaism but the process of establishing Law is an ongoing one. Torah, halakhah and the teaching of the rabbis are to be used to inspire, but Reform Jews argue that God's will can never be fully known and so every new situation requires a modified reasoned response.

Covenant people of God

> For an interesting modern treatment of the idea, with a clear general background to the topic, see *Covenant and Community in Modern Judaism* by S. Daniel Breulauer (Greenwood Press 1989).

A covenant is a solemn and binding agreement between two parties. In terms of the Jewish religion, it is the agreement that was made between God and his people on Mount Sinai during the 40 years of travelling from Egypt to the Promised Land. The covenant stated that Israel would be God's chosen people if they kept his laws. Later on in the Jewish scriptures the development of another covenant tradition is documented, an unconditional covenant made by God to his people. It stated that the messiah, a descendent of King David, would at some time arise to overcome the enemies of Israel and to bring a thousand-reign peace on earth.

> See, for example, Ps 132. Later writers read 2 Sam 7 in messianic terms.

The idea of covenant has dominated Jewish life for probably three millennia. Out of the covenant comes the observance of the Jewish Law and the determination that even in its minute details life should be lived according to the will of God. The great Jewish festivals celebrate various aspects of the covenant relationship and through them the Jews of every generation become, symbolically, part of the original covenant people in the wilderness. It is through being the covenant people of God that the Jews have survived in spite of the persecutions they have suffered.

One modern Jewish scholar writes this about covenant:

> [In the Torah] the Israelites, brought before God, listen to some stipulations [rules] some of them to do with religion, some ethical, some civil, and accept them. They gain from this a national identity and they become a 'holy' people, while each individual gains an identity. Throughout the Torah the personal identity established by obedience to the obligations of the covenant is as important as the communal one: covenant leads to the expectation of meaning in personal life. This is 'selfhood'. S. Daniel Breslauer *Covenant and Community in Modern Judaism*.

The Chasidim

> You will often see this written as 'Hasidim' when studying this topic. See the relevant articles in the encyclopedias listed *above*, or for a detailed guide to Chasidic thought see *The Religious Thought of Hasidism: Text and Commentary* by Norman Lamm (Yeshiva University Press 1999).

Chasidism began as a movement which aimed to put new energy into Judaism. It originated in Poland in the mid-18th century under **Ba'al Shem Tov**, as a reaction to two contemporary forms of Judaism that had lost their appeal to ordinary Jews. These were the Judaism of the interpretation of the Law, which had become very technical and legalistic, and the mystical Judaism of the **kabbalah**, which had also become obscure and difficult for ordinary Jews to follow.

Knowledge of the life of Ba'al Shem Tov is limited. His basic beliefs are summarised in the following passage:

> He taught of a God who was present throughout the universe, even, and perhaps especially, in the most unlikely of places. A person only needed to train his awareness to see everywhere the sparks of divine light that in each moment seek out the Jew to redeem them. The Jew's

> **Warning.** Photocopying any part of this book without permission is illegal.

task is not to turn away from the world but to embrace all that surrounds him and encompass it in his devotional life. *The Oxford Dictionary of the Jewish Religion*.

Chasidism tends to be dynastic in its leadership. Among many groups, the largest is **Habid** or Lubavitcher Chasidism, founded by Rabbi Schneur Zalman (1745–1812), a disciple of Baal Shem Tov. The movement is still active from its base in New York. The Habid Chasidim teach that only God possesses real existence, and that everything else, including the existence of humans as separate entities, is just an illusion. The purpose of the spiritual life is to allow Jews to realise this, intellectually, spiritually and ethically. A key figure in the development of Chasidism was the founder's son DovBev of Lubavitch (1773–1827). He was responsible for followers of the Chasidim going around the Jewish communities of Poland, challenging the rich and the comfortable with the Hasidic message.

You will sometimes see 'habid' written 'Chabad'.

A second grouping is **Satmar** Chasidism, a 20th-century movement which developed in Transylvania around the teacher **Yo'el Teitelbaum** (1887–1979). Satmar Chasidism is an attempt to assert Jewish identity in an area of the world in which the Jews had come under considerable pressure. It is notable for its anti-Zionist policy.

Set texts

Exodus 21–22. Exodus 20: 22–23: 33 forms what is known as 'The Covenant Code'. This is a group of laws that would play a significant role in an agricultural society. Modern critical opinion holds that this law code evolved as the Israelites settled into (or emerged out of) the various tribal groups who lived in Canaan before Israel became a united monarchy under David. The laws in chapters 21 and 22 concern: the treatment of slaves (21: 1–11), violent conduct (21: 12–27), injury to and by animals (21: 28–36), theft (22: 1–3), accidental damage and loss (22: 4–15) and laws regarding various matters of morality and the cult (22: 16–31).

Jewish scriptures

This section of the Code includes the famous **lex talonis**: 'If any harm follows, then you shall give life for life, eye for eye, tooth for tooth, hand for hand, foot for foot, burn for burn, wound for wound, stripe for stripe' (21: 23–4). This rule 'was a first step toward making violence a concern of the entire society. Violence between private persons became a public crime, to be punished by the state.' This is one example of how 'The Book of the Covenant' expresses and facilitates the move from an unregulated primitive society to civil society as we know it today.

Goran Larsson *Bound For Freedom* (Hendrickson 1999).

Leviticus 19. This is part of 'The Holiness Code' that spans Leviticus 17: 1–26: 46. The Code contains laws that emerged at different times in the history of the Israelite religion. It is believed to have reached its present form around the 6th century BCE.

The Holiness Code is named thus because its main theme is that Israel is to be holy (pure and set apart) because her God is holy (see 19: 1–2). This theme is clearly reflected in Chapter 19, which contains a range of commandments, some of outstanding importance. These include laws about leaving unreaped crops for the poor (9–10), treating foreigners with kindness (33–34) and a com-

Warning. Photocopying any part of this book without permission is illegal.

mand for basic justice and fairness (15). Five of the Ten Commandments are also present in this section. Hence the chapter represents the core of the Jewish Law: it is a call for a moral response to the fact of being part of God's chosen people, recognising that all are equal in God's sight.

The most famous law here is 'You shall love your neighbour as yourself' (18). This has been a problem for Jewish interpreters. Leibowitz quotes one Jewish source as saying: 'To fulfil such a command to the letter, man would have to grieve for his fellow's sorrows just as he grieves for his own. This would be intolerable, since scarcely a moment passes without hearing of someone's misfortune. Hillel therefore correctly interpreted this passage in a negative manner. At least do nothing to your neighbour which you would not like to be done to yourself.'

Nehama Leibowitz *Studies in Vayikra (Leviticus)* (The World Zionist Organisation 1980).

The Ethics of the Fathers

For an introduction and translation see *Scriptures of the Oral Torah* by Jacob Neusner (Scholars Press 1990), as well as articles under 'Avot' in the encyclopaedias listed above.

'The Ethics [or as they are more usually referred to in English, 'The Sayings'] of the Fathers' are known in Jewish scholarship as the **Avot**. They are part of the Mishnah and are thought to have originated in about 250 CE. This is the only section of the Mishnah that contains no rules for living, but is instead a collection of sayings from Jewish scholars from around the period 300 BCE to 200 CE.

The sayings cover a wide range of topics, but some themes can be identified. These include the crucial importance of Torah study, the observance of commandments, freedom of choice, divine providence, justice, reward and punishment.

These are some sayings from the Avot which are central to the concerns of Judaism:

- 'Rabbi Simeon ben Gamiliel says, "On three things does the world stand: on justice, on truth and on peace"' (1: 18)
- 'Rabban Yohanan ben Zakki... would say, "If you have learnt much Torah, do not puff yourself up on that account, for it was for that purpose that you were created"' (2: 8)
- 'Rabbi Tarfon says: "The day is short, the work formidable, the workers lazy, the wages high, the employer impatient"' (2: 15). This is a picture of life lived with a sense of the urgency that Judaism brings to it
- 'In any loving relationship which depends upon something, when that thing is gone, the love is gone. But any which does not depend upon something will never come to an end.' (5: 16)

Further study

'The position of the authorship of Avot on the issue of process – the relationship of the oral Torah to the written Torah – is stated implicitly. Specifically, the authorship of the tractate [Avot] listed as its authorities Moses, Joshua, prophets, and onward, in a chain of tradition... the Mishnah's rules derive from authorities who stand in a direct line to Sinai. Then the Mishnah enjoys the standing and authority of God's revelation to Moses at Sinai and forms part of the Torah of Sinai.' Jacob Neusner, *Scriptures of the Oral Torah*. What does this reveal about the significance of the Avot for Jews?

The Avot has become an important part of Judaism. It plays a part in many Jewish prayer books and many Jews read it at home and in the synagogue as part of their liturgy. It has been reproduced in many languages.

Thirteen Principles of Faith

The Thirteen Principles were composed by Maimonides as part of his commentary on the Mishnah. Although they usually only appear in summary form, he in fact wrote a commentary on each one. The translation featured here is taken from the chapter 'The Thirteen Articles of Faith' in *The Credo of Maimonides* by Carol Klein (Philosophical Library 1958). Some of the comments below are also based on material in that chapter.

Warning. Photocopying any part of this book without permission is illegal.

Maimonides' Principle	Comments
1. 'I believe with perfect faith that the Creator, blessed be His name, is the Author and guide of everything that has been created, and that He alone has made, does make, and will make, all things.'	God exists. God has created all other things that exist not because God needs them, but because it has suited God's perfect will to make them.
2. 'I believe with perfect faith that the Creator, blessed be His name, is a unity, and that there is no unity in any manner like unto His, and that He alone is our God, Who was, is and will be.'	God is a unity, unlike anything that has been created. What is created is compound, but God is simply God with no other agent or essence present.
3. 'I believe with perfect faith that the Creator, blessed be His name, is not a body, and that He is free from all the accidents of matter, and has not form whatsoever.'	God has no body. 'Accident' here is meant in its Aristotelian sense of a quality something has just because it happens to be the way it is.
4. 'I believe with perfect faith that the Creator, blessed be His name, is the first and the last.'	God is eternal. To ask 'Who or what made God?' is to ask a nonsensical question as God is by definition a being with no creator.
5. 'I believe with perfect faith that to the Creator, blessed be His name, and to Him alone, it is right to pray, and it is not right to pray to any being besides Him.'	This article protects Jews from idolatry, which is confusing what is created with what is uncreated. God is the only being who is able to listen and respond to prayer.
6. 'I believe with perfect faith that all the words of the prophets are true.'	God has used the prophets to speak his message to the world and so their words are to be trusted.
7. 'I believe with perfect faith that the prophecy of Moses our teacher, peace be unto him, was true, and that he was the chief of the prophets, both of those who preceded him and followed him.'	As Moses received the Torah on Mount Sinai and this was the most important of God's messages to the Jews, then Moses is the greatest of the prophets.
8. 'I believe with perfect faith that the whole Law, now in our possession, is the same that was given to Moses our teacher, peace be unto him.'	Both the Written and the Oral Law possessed by the Jewish people are as they were when given to Moses on Mount Sinai.
9. 'I believe with perfect faith that this Law will not be changed, and that there will never be any other law from the Creator, blessed be His name.'	The Torah is the revelation of the will of God to the Jews and as such it cannot be bettered or replaced.
10. 'I believe with perfect faith that the Creator, blessed be His name, knows every deed of the children of men, and all their thoughts, as it is said, "It is He that fashioneth the hearts of them all, that giveth heed to all their deeds".'	As our Creator, God knows everything that is in our thoughts.
11. 'I believe with perfect faith that the Creator, blessed be His name, rewards those that keep His commandments, and punishes those that transgress them.'	Jews believe in a judgement whereby the actions of each person are judged according to whether or not they have kept the Law.
12. 'I believe with perfect faith in the coming of the Messiah, and though he waits, I will wait daily for his coming.'	Jews look forward to a time when the messiah will arise among the Jewish people and lead them and the rest of the world to peace.
13. 'I believe with perfect faith that there will be a resurrection of the dead at the time when it shall please the Creator, blessed be His name, and exalted be the remembrance of Him for ever and ever.'	This belief developed within Judaism under the influence of near eastern apocalyptic belief. Orthodox Jews accept this straightforward picture of life after death.

Test yourself

1. What did Moses Mendelssohn contribute to Jewish development?
2. Give a brief account of Zionism. Has Zionism saved the Jews?
3. 'Reform Jews do not take the authority of the Law seriously enough.' Assess this claim.
4. Outline and evaluate some of the ways in which the concept of 'covenant' has an impact on the life of modern Jews.
5. What do we learn about Jewish religion from the set texts taken from the Jewish scriptures?

Issues in Religion

Introduction

Synoptic, as students who have studied the Gospels will know, means 'seeing together'.

Issues in Religion is the compulsory synoptic module, for which there is one 1½-hour examination. It is worth a maximum of 20% of your final A-level mark, 5% more than either of the examinations for any of modules 7–11. In the examination you have to answer ONE question out of a choice of 32.

See pages 6–8.

The Issues in Religion examination has, like the other A2 examinations, 60% of marks available for AO1 and 40% for AO2. AO1 and AO2 for Issues in Religion are the same as for the rest of the A2 modules, apart from each adding a sentence about relating different parts of the course together, which is what Issues in Religion is all about.

A synoptic module is a requirement in many A-level subjects. For Edexcel Religious Studies, the synoptic requirement is met in Module 12, Issues in Religion, by giving a choice of question on every possible *combination* of modules. This has to be qualified slightly as those modules which give students a further option of deciding which section to do from within the module are not treated in the same way:

- ✦ Religious Ethics and Old Testament are treated as two separate modules as far as Issues in Religion is concerned
- ✦ New Testament, Christianity and World Religions (modules 4, 5, 6, 9, 10 and 11) are dealt with so that there are the same questions in the Issues in Religion examination whatever sections within the modules you may have studied.

What about your combination of modules?

Assuming, as is almost certainly the case, that you are doing the same modules for A2 you did at AS, then you have no choice as to which combination of modules you will study for Issues in Religion.

This is important, because the combinations of modules in this module vary enormously in what we might call their 'user friendliness'. Some combinations are areas of study that are of obvious significance and interest, and that are the focus of scholarly work. However some other modules combine rather awkwardly and few would think about linking them if it were not for the demands of the synoptic unit. But it is not at all the case that if you are studying one of the more natural combinations then you are bound to get a high mark in the examination nor that if you are studying one of the more difficult ones that you will necessarily get a low mark. Whatever the question, if you offer a well researched and argued answer that demonstrates that there is little or no connection between the two modules you have studied, then you should get just as good marks as someone who, dealing with another combination, is able to outline and discuss a great deal of common ground between the two areas. The important thing is to understand what sort of combination you have.

Approaches to Module 12

The Module 12 specification works on three levels:

- ✦ There are 14 headings representing the various combinations of modules, eg Philosophy of Religion and Religious Ethics; Christianity and World Religions

✦ These 14 areas are divided into 32 more specific areas. Most combinations have two of these more specific areas, but the ones involving Christianity have three

✦ Each of these 32 areas has so far (August 2003) had three examination questions set on it (one in the specimen examination booklet, one in the 2002 A2 examination, and one in the 2003 examination), and this further narrows down the area about which questions will be asked.

This three-storied structure means that Module 12 can be studied at the most general level of one of the 14 combinations, on the level of the 32 areas, or on the level of the examination questions. Of course, these levels of study may also be combined.

Studying one of the 32 areas

The most obvious level on which to work is that of the 32 areas that divide the 14 subject combinations. You could just study one of these 32 areas. This could be quite a high-risk strategy, but it is probably worth adopting it if:

✦ You are absolutely clear about what the area expects from you in terms of knowledge and understanding. This is more likely to be the case if there is some scholarship available on that area

There is detail about the scholarship available on each of these areas on pages 125–138.

✦ You are confident of being able to answer the questions on your chosen area both in the specimen examination booklet and in the past examination papers, and that there is little chance that you will get a question in the examination that will ask about aspects of the area that you have not covered.

These warnings are necessary as it is not always easy to see how the specimen and real examination questions link in with the 32 area headings or what exactly the questions are asking for. This is especially the case with those questions that have to bring together two badly matched modules or sections within modules.

Studying two of the 32 areas

Generally, each of the module combinations has two of the 32 subject-area headings. Studying the material under both of the headings for your module combination could make a lot of sense as this will mean that you have a choice of two questions in the examination. It is also quite possible that the two headings will overlap and reinforce one another. The drawback is that you will effectively have to remember twice as much material in order to put yourself in a position to write for an hour and a half on either of the two subject areas.

Preparing for the rogue question

In the examination you may be faced with a question that you are not sure how to answer. The key to dealing with this sort of question is to have a knowledge and understanding of your subject area that is based on first principles. If, for example, you are studying area number 3, 'A study of religious and ethical language' then you would need to know what the mainstream academic views on this are. You can find this out by looking at authoritative textbooks, encyclopaedias and other works of reference, many of which are listed in this book and in the *Edexcel AS Guide*.

Warning. Photocopying any part of this book without permission is illegal.

Remember that what you write should be 60% knowledge and understanding (AO1) and 40% argument and evaluation (AO2).

You should aim to be able to write about the core issues of your subject area for about 30–45 minutes from the point of view of each of your modules. So for area 3 you should be able to write for 30–45 minutes on religious language and then for the same amount of time on ethical language. If you can do this then whatever question you get in the examination you should be able to approach it in a way which is based on a thorough knowledge and understanding of the topics involved.

Preparing for the predictable question

You may feel confident that you can predict the general area that the question in the examination will cover. If that is the case then you can prepare an answer to the question using any relevant scholarship. But even if you do this, a more general awareness of the issues as suggested *above* would be very useful.

General points

There are some general things you can do to help improve your performance for Module 12:

- Make sure you are aware of **critical thinking techniques**. This involves being clear about things like the assumptions and conclusions of your arguments, as well as different sorts of evidence and argument

- A well-known way of expanding and structuring thinking about a large topic is to develop a **mind map**. This involves writing the central theme of what you are studying in the middle of a blank piece of paper and then writing down connecting ideas around it. Further subsidiary points can be added until the topic has been covered. Putting the two topics you are covering for this module together on a mind map would be an important and interesting way of exploring the connections between them

- If you are being taught in a **group** then it will almost certainly be the case that your colleagues will be facing the same question in the A2 examination. Discussing different ideas with people and assessing their good and bad points could be very useful for this module. Ask your teacher to provide some examination answers from previous candidates (these are now recoverable from Edexcel under certain conditions) and consider these with your group

- It might help you to realise that the question and mark schemes for this module are **generic**. This means that they are not designed to cover just one possible issue out of the range covered by your module combination. They are designed to allow flexibility of approach. However remember that your task is to answer the question directly and in a relevant manner, so a balance must be found between writing generally about the topics under consideration and answering the specific question asked.

Additional note on Christianity

If you are studying Christianity then you will have three subject-area headings under each module combination, apart from 'Christianity and World Religions', which has two. In each case where there is a choice of three, one heading seems to me to be very difficult and worth avoiding. These headings are:

- Under 'Christianity and Philosophy of Religion', I would avoid number 9: 'An investigation into the religious experience of a significant person/group'. This approach simply is not taken in Philosophy of Religion and it is hard to see how an essay on it could be kept within the realms of proper philosophical study

✦ Under 'Christianity and the Old Testament/Jewish Bible', I would avoid number 16: 'A study of the relationship between the state and religion in the Old Testament and Christianity'. The role of the state and religion in the Jewish Bible/Old Testament is a very specialised topic and not ideally suited to A-level

✦ Under 'Christianity and Religious Ethics', I would avoid number 23: 'A study of law and state and the religious/ethical implications'. There is some interesting material here, but this area is far harder than the other two subject areas in this module combination.

Sample combinations

Philosophy of religion and Old Testament/Jewish Bible

Some key texts for this include:

✦ Genesis 1: the story of creation, God as creator of the world

✦ Genesis 3: the Garden of Eden, Evil comes into the world

✦ Exodus 3: Moses and the Burning Bush, the experience of God's mystery

✦ Exodus 14: the parting of the Red Sea, God the miracle worker.

One approach would be to analyse these texts in the light of standard discussions in the philosophy of religion relating to the **Cosmological Argument**, the problem of evil, religious experience and miracles. There would probably be no need to go beyond the standard textbooks on these issues. Have a look at the notes and references in the philosophy of religion section of the *Edexcel AS Guide* and on pages 12–21 of this guide.

A different approach would be to compare a more general philosophical description of God with a description of the presentation of God in the Old Testament. See:

✦ The first chapter of John Hick's *Philosophy of Religion* (Prentice Hall 1990) for a philosophical description of God

✦ Keith Ward's *The Concept of God* (Blackwell 1974) presents a philosophically traditional view of God in an accessible fashion. His more recent *God: A Guide for the Perplexed* (Oneworld 2003) is lively, entertaining and learned

✦ *The Faith of Israel* by H. H. Rowley (Xpress Reprints 1994) for a good treatment of the way in which God is presented in the Jewish Bible

✦ *Biblical Faith and Natural Theology* by James Barr (Clarendon 1993) is also very useful for this section.

Some questions to raise in this topic are:

✦ What types of language are used in the Jewish Bible?

✦ In the light of modern philosophy, can myth, symbol and metaphor in the Old Testament convey philosophical truth?

The nature of God in the Old Testament and in the philosophy of religion

Religious language in the Old Testament/Jewish Bible

Warning. Photocopying any part of this book without permission is illegal.

Traditionally the language of philosophy has been about the intellect discovering and expressing timeless truths. A sharp distinction was drawn between the philosophical language and the religious language found in the Old Testament: because the latter was myth, symbol and poetry it could not be philosophically true. However the work of **Nietzsche** and **Wittgenstein** made it possible to see such language as a way of expressing philosophical truth. Indeed, much of the philosophy of the 20th century was concerned with language.

> See pages 18–21 in this guide for more on this. For a very useful discussion of the language of the Jewish Bible see *Language and Imagery in the Old Testament* by J. C. L. Gibson (SPCK 1998).

Philosophy of religion and religious ethics

Religious and ethical language

Language was the main concern of much 20th-century philosophy, and there was consequently a great deal of philosophical debate about the nature and function of religious and ethical language. In ethics, the concern with language is called meta-ethics, as opposed to, for example, normative ethics, which relates to behaviour.

One approach to this subject is to compare and contrast the philosophical work done on religious language to that done on ethical language. Good sources for doing this are:

- *The Philosophy of Religious Language* by Dan R. Stiver (Blackwell 1996). Stiver gives a clear history of the development of the interest in religious language in 20th-century philosophy

- *Ethical Theory* ed. Hugh LaFollette (Blackwell 2000) has a section on meta-ethics that introduces some of the main themes.

There are books that deal with religious and ethical language in a related way and that can be usefully discussed. Here are some examples:

> For more on Ayer's arguments, see page 20 and also page 33. See pages 138–141 for a sample essay in this area.

- *Language, Truth and Logic* by A. J. Ayer (Penguin 2001) argues that religious and ethical language is meaningless

- *An Empiricist's View of the Nature of Religious Belief* by R. B. Braithwaite (Cambridge University Press, 1955) suggests that religious language cannot tell us truths about the world, but that someone who makes religious statements is expressing their intention to live a moral life.

A philosophical study of applied ethics

Good sources for tackling this are:

> For more on Emotivism and Intuitionism, see page 33.

- A. J. Ayer's *Language, Truth and Logic* (Penguin 2001). Ayer puts forward his theory of Emotivism in the context of epistemology (he says that we can only know what our senses tell us) and metaphysics (he says that only the world which we can perceive by our senses exists). Ethical theories such as Emotivism, Intuitionism and Utilitarianism are probably best related to euthanasia or abortion, as there is a lot of material available on these topics

- *Ethics in Practice* ed. Hugh LaFollette (Blackwell 2001). This has a range of essays on these issues, including a particularly good one on 'Rule Utilitarianism and Euthanasia'

- *Catechism of the Catholic Church* (Geoffrey Chapman 1994). This would prove useful if you approached this topic by examining a religious approach to abortion or euthanasia. You could then contrast this approach with a Utilitarian point of view.

> **Warning.** Photocopying any part of this book without permission is illegal.

Philosophy of religion and New Testament

Key texts you should look at include:

+ Matthew 28, Mark 16, Luke 24 and John 20, which contain the stories of the Resurrection of Jesus

+ 1 Corinthians 15, which is Paul's treatment of the Resurrection.

You should think about what sort of writing the Resurrection narratives are and also whether they record events that could actually have happened.

For a theological discussion of the resurrection stories with an awareness of philosophical issues see:

+ *God's Action in the World* by Maurice Wiles (Xpress Reprints 1993), pages 91–94. This combines a theological discussion of the Resurrection narratives with an awareness of the main philosophical issues

+ *Reason and Religious Belief* by Michael Peterson and others (OUP 2003). This provides a useful philosophical treatment of the Resurrection

+ *Death and Eternal Life* by John Hick (Macmillan 1985). The relevant chapters in this discuss the Resurrection in the context of a wide-ranging consideration of the issues surrounding life after death.

A philosophical study of life after death in the New Testament

For this topic you should read the introduction and the material on the miracles themselves in a good Gospel commentary. See for example:

+ Matthew 8: 5–13; 8: 23–27; 9: 35; 12: 10–13; 14: 14; 20: 34

+ Mark 4: 2–12; 35–41; 6: 34–44

+ Luke 7: 1–10, 22; 8: 22–25, 43–48; 11: 20; 13: 11–15; 14: 2–5

+ John 2: 1–11; 4: 46–54; 5: 1–18; 6: 1–14; 6 16–21 and 26; 9: 1–41; 11: 1–44.

Also useful are the notes and references under miracles and signs in Luke and John in the *Edexcel AS Guide*.

Once you are familiar with the miracle stories, you can begin to compare and contrast them. A distinction between, for example, nature miracles (the calming of the storm, Mk 4: 35–41) and miracles of healing (the healing of the man with a withered arm, Mk 3: 1–6) might raise slightly different philosophical points. You can then compare your ideas with those of philosophers. See the relevant chapters in:

+ *The Puzzle of God* by Peter Vardy (Fount 1999)

+ *Reason and Religious Belief* by Michael Peterson and others (Oxford University Press 2003)

+ *God, Miracle and the Church of England* by David E. Jenkins (SCM Press 1987).

The nature and significance of miracles in the New Testament and philosophy of religion

> Warning. Photocopying any part of this book without permission is illegal.

Philosophy of religion and Christianity

A philosophical investigation of Christian beliefs about the nature of God

A good starting point for this section would be to look at some expressions of the Christian understanding of God. For example:

- See the relevant section of *The Catechism of the Catholic Church* (Geoffrey Chapman 1994)

- There are also relevant readings under the heading 'God' in *The Christian Theology Reader* ed. Alister McGrath (Blackwell 2000). The relevant chapter in *Christian Theology: An Introduction* by Alister McGrath (Blackwell 2001) is also a useful source.

These sources can then be compared with more philosophical discussions concerning the nature of God. See for example material that deals with God's attributes in:

- *The Puzzle of God* by Peter Vardy (Fount 1999)

- *Reason and Religious Belief* ed. Michael Peterson and others (Oxford University Press 2003)

See page 124.

- *The Concept of God* by Keith Ward (Blackwell 1974).

A particularly interesting issue to think about is whether the language that Christian theology uses regarding God lacks philosophical precision. If you think it does, does this reflect badly on Christian theology or on philosophy? Another way of looking at this question is to ask whether a God who can be precisely defined and described in philosophical terms could possibly be something in which people could believe.

A philosophical study of Christian attitudes to life after death

Key areas of concern include:

- Whether the Christian idea of resurrection of the body can make sense given that our personal identity seems to be completely tied up with our existence within the present world

- Whether the claim that we have souls as well as bodies can be philosophically justified.

Good sources for tackling this area are:

- *Death and Eternal Life* by John Hick (Macmillan 1985). An excellent source, Hick provides a detailed summary of various aspects of Christian treatment of the topic before setting out his own philosophical views

See pages 15–18 for more on life after death.

- *Reason and Religious Belief* ed. Michael Peterson and others (Oxford University Press 2003). Another good discussion of life after death from a philosophical perspective

- *The Catechism of the Catholic Church* (Geoffrey Chapman 1994). Some very clear statements of traditional Christian belief

- *The Christian Theology Reader* ed. Alister McGrath (Blackwell 2001). Plenty of examples of mainstream Christian approaches

- *Christian Theology: An Introduction* Alister McGrath (Blackwell 2000). Also useful

- *Reforming Christianity* Don Cupitt (SCM Press 2001). Puts forward a radical Christian rejection of the reality of life after death.

Several of the individuals who formed part of your Church history studies would need further attention here, particularly those who had a profound change of views. It is worth examining the thinking of some prominent theologians about religious experiences. Particularly worth looking at are Karl Barth, Hans Küng, Jürgen Moltmann and Karl Rahner. You could try:

◆ *Foundations of Christian Faith* by Karl Rahner (Darton, Longman and Todd 1976). Rahner argues that human experience always includes within it the infinite, the mysterious and the unknowable, and he links this to our knowledge of God. The first chapter, 'The Hearer of the Message', is particularly useful

◆ *The Puzzle of God* by Peter Vardy (Fount 1999). An account of religious experience that contrasts with Rahner

◆ *Reason and Religious Belief* by Michael Peterson (Oxford University Press 2003).

An investigation of the religious experience of a person/significant group

See the references to these thinkers on pages 79–83 and page 88.

Philosophy of religion and world religions

Religions often have different schools of thought and philosophical traditions that you could contrast. The best sources for this area are those books that take a philosophical view of the world religion that is being studied. Some useful books in this respect are:

◆ *The Central Philosophy of Buddhism* by T. V. R. Murti (Unwin Paperbacks 1980). This is a classic work on the subject

◆ *Indian Philosophy: An Introduction to Hindu and Buddhist Thought* by Richard King (Edinburgh University Press 1999)

◆ *The Philosophy of Religion and the Advaita Vedanta* by Arvaita Sharma (Pennsylvania State University Press 1995). A comprehensive and precise treatment

◆ *The Philosophy of Islam* by Muhammad Hosayni Behisti (Islamic Publications 1988). More a statement of, rather than an argument for, Muslim philosophy. See also *A Short Introduction to Islamic Philosophy, Theology and Mysticism* by Majid Fakhry (Oneworld 1997)

◆ *God in Search of Man: A Philosophy of Judaism* by Abraham J. Heschel (John Calder 1956). This is a comprehensive treatment of the subject

◆ *Medieval Jewish Philosophy: An Introduction* by Dan Cohn-Sherbok (Curzon 1996).

Issues to look out for include questions of how the religion under consideration articulates and defends its view of what transcends humanity, and how we can know that this transcendence is real.

Philosophical arguments in one religion

Buddhism. Many books on Buddhism include discussion on the issue of life after death. See for example chapter 2 of *An Introduction to Buddhism* by Peter Harvey (Cambridge University Press 1990)

Hinduism. Reincarnation is a key aspect of Hindu teaching. See the relevant extracts from *The Essential Teachings of Hinduism* ed. Kerry Brown (Arrow 1990)

Islam. Belief in life after death has always been a key aspect of

Attitudes to life after death in one world religion

Warning. Photocopying any part of this book without permission is illegal.

Islam, but not one that has engaged the attention of Muslims in the same way as, for example, Muslim law and society. Hence there are just short sections on life after death in introductions to Islam. See pages 129–132 of *An Introduction to Islam* by David Waines (Cambridge University Press 1995), and relevant pages in *Islam: The Straight Path* by John L. Esposito (Oxford University Press 1998)

Judaism. Judaism has arguably always been the most 'this worldly' of the major religions and this is reflected in the fact that the very large *Contemporary Jewish Religious Thought* ed. Arthur A. Cohen and Paul R. Mendes-Flohr (Free Press 1988) has only one chapter on the topic 'The Resurrection of the Dead'.

The chapter on life after death in *Reason and Religious Belief* ed. Michael Peterson and others (Oxford University Press 2003) gives an outline of the main concerns of philosophers on this issue, particularly:

- Do the ideas of religions about life after death make philosophical sense?
- Can concepts of life after death be shown to be true, or, at least, shown not to be false?
- What exactly is it that survives or comes back to life after death?

Old Testament/Jewish Bible and New Testament

Moral and social teaching in the Old Testament/Jewish Bible and New Testament

The simplistic view of the issue is generally that the Jewish Bible/Old Testament presents a morality that does not get beyond 'an eye for an eye and a tooth for a tooth' whereas the New Testament teaches a lofty ideal of love and tolerance. The reality is rather more complex, with the Old Testament having some very developed and complex moral and social ideas, including 'Love your neighbour as yourself' (Lev 19: 18), while some New Testament writers use the language of violence and spite against those of whom they do not approve.

The following themes need to be explored: Law, obedience, love, righteousness, reward and punishment. These should be tracked down as they appear in the Old Testament and the New Testament. A concordance (which lists every appearance of a given word in the Bible) can be a useful tool here. See also:

A good concordance on the Internet is www.searchgodsword.org.

- *Toward Old Testament Ethics* by Walter C. Kaiser (Zondervan 1992)
- *The Faith of Israel* by H. H. Rowley (Xpress Reprints 1994)
- *The Ethics of the New Testament* by Wolfgang Schrage (T&T Clark 1996).

Many general books on the Old Testament and New Testament will have sections on ethical teaching.

The nature of God as found in the Old and New Testaments

The basic issue here tends to be whether the simplistic view that the God of the Jewish Bible is a vengeful God whereas the God of the New Testament is a loving/forgiving God can be justified. To approach this you should explore the following themes in the Old Testament: God as creator, sustainer, covenant, special relationship, law and obedience; and the nature of love, atonement, forgiveness and salvation in the New Testament.

Useful works to look at include:

- *The Faith of Israel* by H. H. Rowley (Xpress Reprints 1994)
- *God in the New Testament* by Neil Richardson (Epworth 1999).

Old Testament/Jewish Bible and Christianity

This could be approached through the teachings on a just society found for example in Amos (see pages 28–29) and the other prophets. You could then compare these teachings to practice in various periods of Church history:

- Social injustice as a cause of both the European and English Reformations
- Social injustice and how the Church in England tackled it in the 19th and 20th centuries
- Social injustice and the inspiration of the Jewish Prophets on Liberation Theology
- Social injustice and Black Theology
- Social injustice and African Theology.

The basic problem for the Church has really been the same in all the five areas listed here. This has been the tension between those who are deeply moved by social injustice and the idealistic teaching of the Old Testament and those who see the Church's task as being the maintenance of the status quo and the support of the power structures as they exist in society.

To write on this topic you will need a good understanding of how God is presented in the Jewish Bible. Most introductions and guides will cover this, but particularly useful are:

- *The Faith of Israel* by H. H. Rowley (Xpress Reprints 1994)
- *The Faith of the Old Testament* by Werner H. Schmidt (Blackwell 1983).

You will then have to choose which particular aspect of Christian teaching about God you want to look at. This will probably depend on which Christian period you have studied.

European Reformation. You should look particularly at Calvin and Luther for this. See *The European Reformation Sourcebook* by Carter Lindburg (Blackwell 2000) and *The Theology of Martin Luther* by Paul Althaus (Philadelphia: Fortress Press 1966).

English Reformation. Thomas Cramner is the most important thinker to consider.

20th-century Europe. Bonhoeffer is a good thinker to examine. See *The Cambridge Companion to Dietrich Bonhoeffer* by John W. de Gruchy (Cambridge University Press 1999). See also *below*.

19th- and 20th-century Europe. Look particularly at Barth, Küng and Rahner. Consult the *Cambridge Companion to Christian Doctrine* ed. Colin E. Gunton (Cambridge University Press 1997), which is useful both in itself and for its concise reading lists.

Black and African Theology. James H. Cone is a key figure. See *Black Theology and Black Power* by James H. Cone (Orbis Books 1997).

The application of Old Testament teaching on moral and social issues within Christianity

The first three topics are covered in the *Edexcel AS Guide*. For the Reformation, see pages 72–84; for England in the 19th and 20th centuries, see pages 89–92; for Liberation Theology see pages 93–96. For Black Theology and African Theology see pages 83–87.

The presentation and nature of God in the Old Testament and Christianity

It would be particularly useful to look at the section on 'Christian belief and practice' in this guide, pages 89–97. See also the *Edexcel AS Guide*, pages 96–102. These cover aspects of belief in God that would be suitable for work under this heading.

The relationship between the state and religion in the Old Testament and Christianity

See *The Psalms: A Form-Critical Introduction* Hermann Gunkel (Fortress 1967).

The relationship between the state and religion in the Old Testament is a rather specialised area of study. *Sacrifice in the Old Testament* by George Buchanan Gray (Clarendon 1925) has a couple of chapters on the political role of the priesthood. You could also find out more about the Israelite monarchy. You might find it helpful to investigate the psalms that form critic Hermann Gunkel called the 'Royal Psalms', which support the monarchy, and the dispute between Samuel and Saul (Samuel and Kings). You can read Gunkel in English translation. A more recent book, looking at Gunkel's approach, is *Court Oracles in the Psalms: The So-Called Royal Psalms in their Ancient Near Eastern Context* by Scott R. A. Starbuck (Scholars Press 1999). You could also focus on the emphasis given to social justice by certain Old Testament prophets. See page 22.

On the relationship between the state and religion in Christianity, a good deal is already covered on the specification. Dietrich Bonhoeffer is an obvious point of study. See:

- *The Cambridge Companion to Dietrich Bonhoeffer* by John W. de Gruchy (Cambridge University Press 1999)
- *Bonhoeffer: The Man and his Work* by Rene Marle, tr. R. Sheed, (Geoffrey Chapman, 1965)
- *The Cost of Discipleship* by Dietrich Bonhoeffer (SCM 2001)
- *Secularization* by Arnold E. Loen (SCM 1967)
- 'Friday's Child' by W. H. Auden (a poem in various collections).

Church of England. In Britain, the Church of England published a report in 1984 called *Faith in the City*. This report drew attention to the problems being faced by those in inner cities who lived deprived lives, and called for the Church to take action. It criticised Margaret Thatcher's government for not doing enough to lessen social inequality and identified 'Urban Priority Areas' in which the Church of England concentrated its efforts to care for the deprived. See:

- *Faith in the City: A Report of the Archbishop's Council On Urban Regeneration* (Church of England 1985). This report was followed by another called *Faith in the Country*.

Latin American Liberation Theology. Gustavo Gutiérrez is a writer of particular influence. A useful introduction to this topic is *Liberation Theology* by Phillip Berryman (Tauris 1987)

The Stuarts during the later English Reformation would be good to study, as this was a period of considerable upheaval. Christopher Hill, a Marxist historian, has written several useful (and controversial, so find later, contrasting views) books on this topic.

Old Testament/Jewish Bible and World Religion

Significant concepts in the Old Testament and one world religion

See pages 106–133 of the *Edexcel AS Guide*, and 98–121 of this book.

A particularly good area to pursue for this topic would be **worship**. Most general works on the Jewish Bible contain information and comment on worship. *Offerings, Sacrifices and Worship in the Old Testament* by J. H. Kurtz (Hendrickson 1998) is helpful here.

Once you have looked at Old Testament worship, then you can compare practices with a modern world religion. There is plenty of material here in this guide and the *Edexcel AS Guide*. Good introductory books are:

- *An Introduction to Buddhism* by Peter Harvey (Cambridge University Press 1990)
- *An Introduction to Hinduism* by Gavin Flood (Cambridge University Press 1996)
- *To Pray As A Jew* by Hayim Halevy Donin (Basic Books 1991)
- *Muslims: Their Religious Beliefs and Practices* by Andrew Rippin (Routledge 2001).

One particularly interesting area to examine is the development of the concept of sacrifice. For instance animal sacrifice, a key aspect of worship in the Old Testament, develops into a symbolic sacrifice of all that matters most to the religious believer as a sign of obedience to God.

Moses is probably the best figure for working with here, because he is the central theological figure of the Old Testament. It is Moses who provides the link between God and the chosen people. In the Book of Exodus we follow his life as a chosen baby, through to his religious calling, his battle with Pharaoh to free the Israelites, and his leadership of his people during the 40 years in the wilderness.

The contributions of significant people in the Old Testament and one world religion

For more details on Moses see page 36 in the *Edexcel AS Guide*. See pages 142–144 for a sample essay.

There are plenty of figures within the world religions with whom you can compare and contrast these aspects of the life of Moses. Perhaps particularly interesting would be comparisons with the Buddha, Gandhi, Maimonides and Muhammad. Look at the other individuals discussed in the chapters of this guide and see which one particularly catches your interest.

Religious ethics and New Testament

For this you need to show that you know about the ethical values of the New Testament and that you have considered to what extent the existence of these values depends on religion. Important areas to look at are law, forgiveness, righteousness, love, obedience, trust and faith, which are some of the ethical themes that run through the New Testament. A useful book to look at is *The Ethics of the New Testament* by Wolfgang Schrage (T&T Clark 1996).

The relationship between religion and morality

Once the themes have been identified, areas to consider might be:

- That ethics does depend on religion because the New Testament shows ethics to be the revealed will of God for humanity. This is the Divine Command Theory
- That the New Testament shows that ethics must depend on religion as it is only in a religious context that human life has a value
- That ethics cannot depend on religion because the promise of reward is at the heart of the ethical values of the New Testament and this promise is a corruption of ethics.

In order to write on this topic you need to have a really good grasp of one of the central ethical theories: Utilitarianism, situation ethics, deontological ethics, Emotivism, Intuitionism and natural moral law.

Ethical concepts in the New Testament

See the references to these theories on pages 41–45 of the *Edexcel AS Guide* and pages 33–35 of this book.

You will also need to be aware of the central ethical themes of the New Testament: love for others, non-violence, concern for the poor and needy, rejection of wealth, marriage, divorce, theft and murder. In the examination you may well be asked to apply one of the ethical theories to one of these New Testament ethical issues.

By using a book such as *The Ethics of the New Testament* by Wolfgang Schrage (T&T Clark 1996) it should be possible to identify the ethical teaching of the New Testament on the given issue and then to analyse them in terms of the major ethical theories.

Some more specific books that you might find helpful are:

◆ *The Puzzle of Sex* by Peter Vardy (Fount 1997) on the relationship of natural moral law to marriage

◆ *Situation Ethics* by Joseph Fletcher (Westminster John Knox Press 1997) on the relationship of situation ethics to murder.

Religious ethics and Christianity

Ethical theory and ethics in Christianity

See the references to these theories on pages 41–45 of the *Edexcel AS Guide* and pages 33–35 of this book.

In order to write on this topic you need to have a really good grasp of one of the central ethical theories: Utilitarianism, situation ethics, deontological ethics, Emotivism, Intuitionism and natural moral law.

The following would be interesting areas to study:

◆ Liberation or Black or African Theology from the point of view of situation ethics or Utilitarianism

◆ The role of duty (deontology) in the life and teachings of Dietrich Bonhoeffer

◆ Natural moral law and sexual ethics

◆ Emotivism and Christian attitudes to work and leisure.

Applied ethics in Christianity

The specification lists several topics that appear as being part of applied ethics in the ethics sections of Units 1–11. These are 'conscience and freedom, war and peace, authority, justice, law and punishment'. A problem in recommending suitable sources here is that only one of these topics would be recognised as being part of applied ethics in a straightforward way and that is 'war and peace'.

This leads to the question of how 'war and peace' as a topic relates to the specification areas on Christianity. The best link is with 19th- and 20th-century Christianity. There is a connection here as Liberation or African or Black Theology can be analysed in terms of the 'Just War' criteria as they are found under the topic of war and peace. Following the notes and references to Just War and Liberation or African or Black Theology should give a basis for this study. A search on the Internet should reveal some useful material.

Ethical concepts in the New Testament

The New Testament contains a good deal of ethical debate. Among the ethical issues to be found there are: concerns for the poor and attitudes to wealth and the wealthy; marriage and divorce; theft, murder and other issues of violence. You could make links between the treatment given to these issues by New Testament authors and the way they are handled by Utilitarian, Situation Ethics or Natural Law philosophers. You may find useful *The Cambridge Companion to Christian Ethics* ed. Robin Gill (Cambridge University Press 2000). It contains a range of essays but also a lot of bibliographical information for possible further reading.

The two most interesting areas in the specification on this are conscience and war and peace.

You could look at, for example, the role that conscience played for those people involved in the Reformation. Martin Luther is probably the most suitable individual to study in terms of the European Reformation, and Thomas More ideal for the English Reformation.

Good topics to analyse in terms of war and peace are Liberation Theology, African Theology and Black Theology. These can be looked at from the perspective of the Just War. Following the notes and references to these areas in the AS Guide and in this book should give a basis for this topic. A search on the Internet should reveal some useful material.

Religious ethics and world religions

Possible areas to look at here include:

- **Buddhism as a pacifist religion.** There is a detailed and useful chapter on this in *An Introduction to Buddhist Ethics* by Peter Harvey (Cambridge University Press 2000)

- **Hinduism, issues of autonomy and the value of life.** There are relevant chapters in *Dilemmas of Life and Death: Hindu Ethics in a North American Context* by S. Cromwell Crawford (University of New York Press 1994)

- **Crime and punishment in Islam.** See *The Different Aspects of Islamic Culture* ed. A. Bouhdiba and M. Ma'ruf al-Dawalibi (Unesco Publications 1998)

- **Jewish perspectives on relationships.** See *Contemporary Jewish Ethics and Morality: A Reader* ed. Elliot N. Dorff and Louis E. Newman (Oxford University Press 1995).

The relevant chapters in all these books will give an outline and discussion of how the particular ethical issue under consideration is treated in that religion. Many general books on each world religion will also give these topics some consideration. It might also be worth contacting local or national congregations for further information and discussion.

A good starting point for work on this topic is a summary of the ethics of the particular religion you have been studying. Good books are:

- *An Introduction to Buddhist Ethics* by Peter Harvey (Cambridge University Press 2000)

- *Christian and Hindu Ethics* by Shivesh Chandra Thakur (Allen and Unwin 1969). The sections on Hindu ethics are very clearly written

- *Social Justice in Islam* by Sayyid Qutb (Islamic Publications International 2000)

- *Contemporary Jewish Ethics and Morality: A Reader* ed. Elliot N. Dorff and Louis E. Newman (Oxford University Press 1995).

The relationship between the law and the state and their ethical/religious implications in a period of Church history

See the *Edexcel AS guide* pages 76–77 and page 80.

Applied ethics in one world religion

Ethical concepts in one world religion

Warning. Photocopying any part of this book without permission is illegal.

Once you are aware of the basic ethical principles of the religion that you are studying, you should address these principles from the point of view of an ethical theory. For instance you could question how utilitarian Hindu attitudes to marriage are, or the extent to which deontological principles affect Islamic beliefs about charitable giving.

New Testament and Christianity

The application of the teachings of the New Testament concerning moral and social issues within Christianity

Christians have often applied the teachings of the New Testament to social and moral issues, and as a result this topic can be studied from a number of perspectives and during several historical periods. For example:

The Reformation. It would be interesting to examine the significance of the teachings of Romans 13: 1–7 in the light of the Reformers' willingness to challenge political authority

The 19th and 20th centuries. What is the significance of the teachings of Romans 13: 1–7 in the light of the revolutionary aspects of Liberation Theology, African Theology and Black Theology?

Christian belief and practice. You might like to consider the extent to which Christians apply New Testament teaching on sexual relationships today. A helpful book on this is *Dirt, Greed and Sex: Sexual Ethics in the New Testament and Their Implications Today* by L. William Countryman (SCM Press 2001).

The differing views on the person and work of Christ in the New Testament and the Christian Church

Many books on the New Testament will include material on the teaching and work of Christ. Very helpful is *New Testament Theology* by Donald Guthrie (IVP 1981), which has over a hundred clearly written pages on the issue. As far as the person and work of Christ in the Church is concerned, two good books are:

✦ *The Christian Theology Reader* ed. Alister McGrath (Blackwell 2001). This contains a wide-ranging selection of readings from Christian theologians on the person of Christ

✦ *Christian Theology: An Introduction* by Alister McGrath (Blackwell 2000). This presents a clear introduction to Christian thinking about Christ.

This topic can be approached in a number of ways. One possibility is to look at the way that ideas like atonement developed in Christian thinking. Another area to look at might be the relationship between the Christology of the New Testament and that of later Christian theology.

The contributions of significant people in the New Testament and Christianity

Probably the best New Testament figure to examine is Paul. We know a lot about Paul's life and thought through his writings, and there is also plenty of secondary material available on him. Some good books to look at would be:

✦ *Paul* by E. P. Sanders (Oxford University Press 1991)

✦ *Paul and his Converts* by Ernest Best (T&T Clark 1988)

✦ *1 Corinthians* by Leon Morris (IVP 1997)

Paul could be compared with:

Luther. There are interesting points of comparison in the theology of Paul and Luther, and you could also look at how both Paul and Luther acted to shape radical versions of Christianity that could prosper in a changing world.

William Laud. Laud could be contrasted with Paul on the basis that the former was a conservative reformer who would have disliked the radical approach of Paul.

Bonhoeffer. There are points of comparison in terms of their theology: is Bonhoeffer's 'religionless Christianity' what Paul meant all along? Also, if we accept that Paul was a martyr then comparisons can be made between the reasons for and significance of his death and that of Bonhoeffer.

New Testament and world religions

Probably the best area to look at is ethics, as this is good for investigating similarities and differences. Concepts of love and forgiveness, law and authority can be brought into this too. For New Testament ethics, see *The Ethics of the New Testament* by Wolfgang Schrage (T&T Clark 1996). The following books are useful for the ethics of the various world religions:

Significant concepts in the New Testament and one world religion

- *An Introduction to Buddhist Ethics* by Peter Harvey (Cambridge University Press 2000)
- *Christian and Hindu Ethics* by Shivesh Chandra Thakur (Allen and Unwin 1969). The sections on Hindu ethics are very clearly written
- *Social Justice in Islam* by Sayyid Qutb (Islamic Publications International 1999)
- *Contemporary Jewish Ethics and Morality: A Reader* ed. Elliot N. Dorff and Louis E. Newman (Oxford University Press 1995).

One approach to this area would be to compare, for example, the contribution of Christ to Christianity with that of the Buddha, Muhammed or Moses to their respective faiths. You could also compare Christ as the Son of God with Krishna as an avatar (manifestation) of God. Donald Guthrie's *New Testament Theology* (IVP 1981) is helpful on the figure of Christ.

The contributions of significant people in the New Testament and one world religion

Points you might like to explore in comparisons are:

- The similarities and differences between Christ's teaching and that of the Buddha. How does the baptism/transfiguration/resurrection of Christ compare with the Buddha's enlightenment?
- In what ways do Hindus regard Krishna and Christ as equivalent incarnations of God? Does what is being missed out from a Christian perspective matter?
- What are the explicit and implicit comparisons made in the Gospels between the figure of Christ and the figure of Moses?
- Was the mission of Christ and the mission of Muhammad essentially the same: to warn people to give up idolatry and to follow the way of the one true God?

Significant beliefs in Christianity and one world religion

Christianity and world religions

Try comparing the role of scripture in the Reformation with the role of scriptures in the world religion you have studied. A useful book for the importance of scripture during the Reformation is *The Reading and the Preaching of the Scriptures in the Worship of the Christian Church: The Age of Reformation* by Hughes Oliphant Old (Eerdmans 2002)

If you have studied 19th- and 20th-century Christianity, you could examine how Bonhoeffer's teachings on the nature of religion relate to that of the world religion you have studied

Alternatively, look at how Christian beliefs about the nature of God compare with those of the world religion you have studied. If you have studied Buddhism then you might need to consider whether it is atheistic religion. See *The Emptying God* eds. John B. Cobb Jr. and Christopher Ives (Orbis Books 1990).

The contributions of significant people in Christianity and one world religion

Particularly relevant to this topic are the Reformation and 19th- and 20th-century Christianity. You might want to try comparing Luther, Calvin or Cranmer with a reforming figure in a major world religion. Possibilities might be King Asoka for Buddhism, Ramakrishna for Hinduism, Moses Mendelssohn for Judaism and Muhammad for Islam. For the 19th and 20th centuries, Bonhoeffer would be interesting to compare with any of the reforming figures from the world religions. For an excellent historical outline, see:

◆ *A History of Religion East and West* by Trevor Ling (Macmillan 1968).

Sample essay with comments: 1

Here is an example of how to tackle an Issues in Religion essay. This answer was written on the basis of 15 minutes planning and 75 minutes writing, and is of average length at about 1,500 words. It would gain an A grade in an exam.

Combination: Philosophy of Religion and Religious Ethics

Compare and contrast the distinctive features of religious and ethical language.

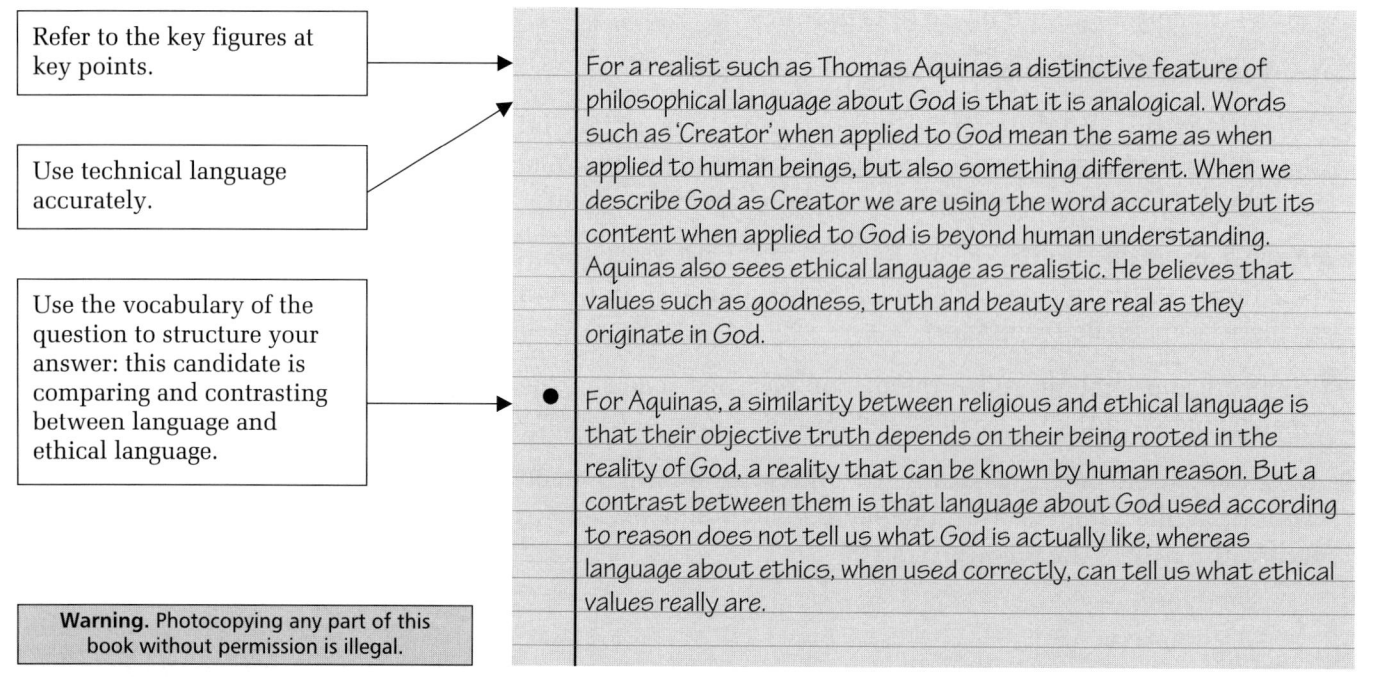

Refer to the key figures at key points.

Use technical language accurately.

> For a realist such as Thomas Aquinas a distinctive feature of philosophical language about God is that it is analogical. Words such as 'Creator' when applied to God mean the same as when applied to human beings, but also something different. When we describe God as Creator we are using the word accurately but its content when applied to God is beyond human understanding. Aquinas also sees ethical language as realistic. He believes that values such as goodness, truth and beauty are real as they originate in God.

Use the vocabulary of the question to structure your answer: this candidate is comparing and contrasting between language and ethical language.

> • For Aquinas, a similarity between religious and ethical language is that their objective truth depends on their being rooted in the reality of God, a reality that can be known by human reason. But a contrast between them is that language about God used according to reason does not tell us what God is actually like, whereas language about ethics, when used correctly, can tell us what ethical values really are.

Warning. Photocopying any part of this book without permission is illegal.

- A different basis for the realistic truth of religious language is found in Reformed Epistemology. The argument is that the truth of language about God is foundational: it must be assumed to be true for any other truths to be known. For Reformed Epistemology a distinctive feature of religious language is that the language of revelation (found for example in the Christian Bible) can be based in reality. This compares with the Divine Command Theory, which holds that a distinctive feature of ethical language is that objective ethical principles can be found in what has been revealed by God (again, for example, in the Christian Bible).

> Show awareness of the diversity of opinion within any given tradition and cite contrasting and opposing views.

One implication that the ideas of Aquinas and Reformed Epistemology have for language about God is that in the life of the ordinary believer, symbol, metaphor and myth are going to have an important function in enabling a sense of the 'reality' of God to be constructed. Abstract language is either extremely limited (Aquinas) or useless (Reformed Epistemology). It can be argued that Nietzsche did the same for ethical language when he dismissed conventional philosophy and replaced it with stories about 'superman', the 'will to power' and 'eternal recurrence'.

> Refer to the key figures at key points and bring out differences of opinion.

- For Kant, a distinctive feature of language about God is that it cannot be known to be true. Kant argued that we could only know the world on which we impose categories such as space and time (the phenomenal world) and not the world as it really exists (the noumenal world). Hence we can never know what exists independently of us, and that ignorance includes God. In contrast, for Kant a distinctive feature of ethical language is that its truth is based on the Categorical Imperative, and is therefore objective for any rational being. For Kant, a second distinctive feature of language about God is that the reality of God is a necessary assumption based on the rationality of the Categorical Imperative.

- As a logical positivist, Ayer believed that a proposition only has meaning if it makes a difference to the world as it is perceived through the five senses. This 'verification principle' means that metaphysical language is meaningless. For Ayer a distinctive feature of ethical language was that it expressed people's emotions rather than give information about the world ('Emotivism'). In a similar way he thought that language about God was not factual, and his attack was taken further by Flew and his idea of 'falsification'. Flew held that those who use language about God are unable to say what difference it would make to the world if this language was false, and thus such language is effectively meaningless.

> Show how the points you are making answer the question. This answer makes regular reference to 'distinctive features' of religious and ethical language and makes its comparisons and contrasts as explicit as possible. This way you can score marks for material that is very different from that which is in the examiner's mark-scheme.

Ayer was much more concerned with explaining why people made meaningless ethical statements than explaining why people made

Issues in Religion 139

meaningless statements about God. In a sense, then, Ayer sees religious language as less important than ethical language.

For Braithwaite, a distinctive feature of religious language is that it is really ethical language in disguise. He argued that when, for example, a Christian says the Creed he or she is really stating their intention to live a morally good life. In this respect, religious and ethical language become identical.

Indeed Wittgenstein also saw religious and ethical language as identical. He held that they are both 'language games'; this means that they have certain features in common. Religion and ethics both come from basic ways in which human beings think and act: they are both 'forms of life' in Wittgenstein's terms. As language games, the truth of religious and ethical language depends on a particular word being used correctly in relation to the other words in the language game, in the same way that the move of a chess piece is only correct in relation to the rules of the game as a whole.

Wittgenstein would have accepted that there is an overlap between the religious and ethical language games. For example the Ten Commandments is both a religious and ethical piece of writing. He would also have seen the potential of religious and ethical language to give rise to philosophical confusion. If we use religious and ethical language as though it was scientific language then we are trying to get factual information from it, but this in fact cannot be done. Wittgenstein was quite clear that ethical language is a type of aesthetics: we think that things are good because they are to our taste. Some Christian philosophers have seized on his work on religious language, as a way of showing that language about God can be true even in a world dominated by science and secularism.

In evaluating the above ideas, it is possible to argue that there is a core validity to ethical language which has basically remained unchanged, whereas there is more uncertainty about whether religious language can any longer be thought of as meaningful.

In order to begin to defend this position we will note that the Christian philosophers referred to conclude above all that the basic Christian ethic of love for one's neighbour remains the same whatever theoretical ethical position is taken. Aquinas is well known for his detailed working out of the practical implications of this basic Christian teaching, while Reformed Epistemology upholds the Biblical revelation of the teaching of love in full force. Furthermore Kant's various formulations of the Categorical Imperative can all be seen as variations on the command of Jesus 'to love your neighbour as yourself', and Braithwaite sees all of Christian language as basically ethical. So our examples of Christian philosophy all support the ethic of love for your neighbour.

We note a similarity of view in Utilitarianism. Part of Mill's defence of Utilitarianism is that its language is nothing more than the familiar teaching of Christianity and other religions on the theme of love for one's neighbour.

Margin notes:

Beware of citing too many authorities: this candidate has clearly read extensively around the subject but this argument is in danger of being obscured rather than advanced by so many names being dropped. Note that they continually refer back to the terms of the question in order to keep their answer under control.

Keep a clear distinction between knowledge and understanding (AO1) and evaluation (AO2), and signal when you change from AO1 to AO2.

This question does not ask for critical evaluation directly, but you must be able to identify a single viewpoint on a critical issue related to the subject matter of the answer. Use this as an anchor for the AO2 part of your answer, going on to either challenge or support it with other arguments.

Don't abandon a key figure once you've mentioned them: they can be brought into your argument more than once. This helps make clear that you really are discussing them, not just dropping names.

Even those who explicitly reject the defence of ethical values on the basis of Christian philosophy are at least open to the possibility that life should be lived in accord with Christian morality. The exception to this might seem to be Nietzsche, with his ethical language of domination and superiority. However we could interpret Nietzsche as saying that the superior person is one who can choose his own way of life regardless of the actions of the herd. In this case, Nietzsche would accept that a Christian morality might be chosen providing it is for one's own reasons and not in mindless conformity.

Ayer's Emotivism also gives freedom for us to choose what morality we like. Mackie's response to this freedom to 'invent right and wrong', to make the words of ethical language mean what we want them to mean, is to suggest that most people would invent something instantly recognisable as a form of Christian morality. Similarly Wittgenstein is well known for his plea that 'philosophy leaves everything as it is' and he would include Christian morality in this assessment.

- Thus there seems to be a validity about ethical language based on love of one's neighbour which cannot be denied by the language of ethical theory, and perhaps in places is supported by it.

The situation is rather different for religious language. The realism of someone like Aquinas and the supporters of Reformed Epistemology has been undermined by the attacks of verification and falsification to the point that many philosophers accept that religious language cannot be about realities that exist beyond the language used to describe them.

- The non-realists such as Braithwaite, Moore and Phillips, with their talk of the need to understand 'God' in grammatical terms, seem not to understand the real force of religious language as it exists in the Bible.

Those who turn to the idea of religious language as myth, metaphor, story and symbol seem at least to do justice to the power of religious language, and it is easy to see how that language can have a truth for those who accept it as such. However the philosopher might well ask why stories about God and a burning bush are accepted as symbolic and in some way to be accepted by the believer as true, whereas stories about, for example, Sisyphus in Hades rolling the rock up the hill every day are accepted as symbolic but false.

Hence there seem to be problems with the 'truth' of religious language that those who seek to defend its truth on philosophical grounds cannot answer. However there appears to be a truth in certain types of ethical language that is not subject to the same criticisms. Perhaps ethical language is something which nearly all of us at some deep level think and feel has to be true, whereas there seems to be something much more optional about religious language.

> In the final paragraph give a specific answer to the question and give your reasons for it. If, as here, the question simply asks you to 'Compare and contrast', you need to not only summarise the similarities and differences, but also come to a conclusion on any evaluation you have done.

This question has been taken from the *Specimen Papers with Mark Schemes* and covers subject area 3, 'A study of religious and ethical language'.

Combination: Old Testament and World Religions

Sample essay with comments: 2

Explain and consider critically the importance of one or more persons of the Old Testament with the status of one or more figures in the world religion you have studied.

> [Establish straight away what the subject of your essay is and justify your choice.]

Many would claim that Moses should be seen as the founder of Judaism, although the question is complicated. Claims could be also be made for Abraham and for Ezra in this regard. The claim for Moses is based on his role as the one who spoke with God 'face to face'. Tradition recorded in Jewish scripture states that in his encounter with God on Mount Sinai Moses was given the heart of the Jewish Law, the Ten Commandments, as well as nearly all of the other 613 which can be found in the Torah, meaning, in this sense, the Five Books of Moses. It was also through Moses that the Sinaitic Covenant was made. As the Law and the Covenant are the two foundations of the Jewish faith, we can see that the claim of Moses to be the founder of the religion is strong.

> [Avoid scene-setting and begin the process of comparing and contrasting your two chosen figures straight away.]

> [Use technical vocabulary accurately and appropriately.]

There has never been any question about the role of the Buddha as the founder of Buddhism, and so of his uniquely high status within that religion. The teaching and the example of the Buddha are crucial to Theravada Buddhists' own quests to reach the state of being an Arhant: one who is ready to pass into the state of paranirvana after death and so to freedom from the round of rebirths, which is Samara. Mahayana Buddhists to some extent play down the importance of the single life of the Buddha, believing rather that we are all Buddha, and that the Buddha is a universal cosmic principle as well as the life of the historical Buddha. Having said that, the influence of the historical Buddha on the Mahayana is still immense.

> [Here the candidate has chosen iconography as an interesting way of bringing out a contrast. This makes for a more varied discussion and reflects wider study.]

An interesting comparison between the status of Moses and the Buddha in their respective religions can be found in their artistic representation. Judaism is a religion of the word rather than of the visual. Hence representations of Moses have no religious significance at all, and, although he is seen as a hero of the Jewish faith, his importance lies much more in being the human channel of the words of the law and the covenant which God is believed to have revealed through him. This is in great contrast with the Buddha. For Buddhists his personal example is a mainspring of their own religious life and his image is to be found in great numbers wherever there are Buddhists. Statues of the Buddha come in a variety of poses each with their own significance. For example, in some the Buddha has his hand raised as a symbol of courage and in others he is touching the earth as a witness to his Enlightenment. Many Buddhists worship the reality of the Buddha as made present in this religious art, which shows his supreme status, and, of course, Jews would never dream of worshipping Moses in any form.

> [Give specific example to illustrate your point.]

> [Flag up clearly each time you move on to a new point.]

There is also an interesting comparison between the two in terms of how the traditions about them are treated as history. Both have life stories found in their respective scriptures and both life stories have been subjected to a great deal of criticism in terms of their historical reliability. For Reform and Progressive Jews,

142 Issues in Religion

and for Buddhists, this criticism need not detract at all from the religious truth and value of their life stories. For Orthodox Jews the situation is rather different. Doubting the historical reliability of the story of Moses would, for them, mean doubting the essential truth of their faith. This shows the importance of the written word in religions which have what may be broadly categorised as 'fundamentalist' elements. Moses is important mostly because he was a channel whereas the supreme status of the Buddha for Buddhists depends more on who he is, and he is a teacher in his own right rather than a channel for revelation. Both these aspects come out in the scriptures which are written about them irrespective of their historical reliability.

One aspect of the importance of Moses and the status of the Buddha can be seen by turning to the life stories themselves. We note an interesting similarity as both men are portrayed as being

> Remember that each religious tradition contains different schools and conflicting points of view.

> When comparing and contrasting two individuals or traditions, remember that similarities can be as revealing and as worthy of comment as differences.

brought up by royalty, and how this comes about and the effect it has on the two men tells them something about how they are regarded in their respective religions. For Moses the royal connection means the Egyptian court after he was found by the Pharaoh's daughter in the bulrushes, having been put there by his mother in defiance of the ruling that all Hebrew children should be killed. The Buddha, on the other hand, is a prince by right of birth. How they came to leave this royal upbringing is also an interesting contrast. Moses has to flee after having killed an Egyptian who had in turn killed one of Moses' fellow Hebrews. The Buddha, in contrast, leaves after he has seen the four signs of ill, old, dying and ascetic seeker.

Jews would point to these, and other aspects, of the life of Moses and suggest that his religious genius sits alongside his very ordinary human nature. This is an important truth for Jews: our humanity and spirituality are not in total contrast to each other, but rather, complement each other. This is an element in the importance Moses has for them.

On the other hand, for Buddhists, the story of his early years is an ideal, and symbolises a need to turn away from our humanity when, as is inevitable, we are caught up in its bodily and mental pleasures. The Buddha's willingness to renounce the conditions of his luxurious upbringing is another reason why he has such a high status for Buddhists.

This comparison continues when we consider the points in their lives when they have their personal encounters with spiritual reality. Moses encounters Yahweh in the Burning Bush and this is the start of what we might call his religious career which culminates in seeing the back of God when receiving the commandments on Mount Sinai. The religious runs alongside the political as Moses leads the people of Israel out of Egypt, and we see Moses as a doubting and fearful man as well as the inspired leader of his nation. The story of the Burning Bush in which the name of Yahweh is revealed to Moses shows that he is very important to Jews but other aspects of his life are also significant in their own right.

In contrast the Enlightenment experience of the Buddha is undoubtedly the culmination of his spiritual journey rather than its beginning, and it is because of this enlightenment experience that the Buddha has supreme status for Buddhists. Moses is inspired by Yahweh so that he can go on and do other things, whereas the Enlightenment of the Buddha is the point and purpose of his being on earth.

> *Refer to a range of scholarly opinion.*

Von Rad makes the following point about Moses: 'The figure of Moses everywhere stands at the centre of the historical events from the Exodus down to the end of the wandering in the wilderness… he is everywhere the representative of Israel to whom the words and actions of God are expressed.' There would be a great deal of critical agreement about this assessment of the role of Moses. According to McKeating, Moses is the ideal of both the priestly and prophetic: he represents the people of Israel at Mount Sinai and speaks out the message of God to them. Again, there is wide spread critical agreement on this point.

Peter Harvey concentrates on the significance of the Enlightenment experience of the Buddha: 'We might suggest that Siddharta now finally saw through his "I" or ego, saw that in an ultimate sense it was an illusion, a creation of thought rather than anything with a more solid existence.' Again this is representative of the emphasis Buddhist scholars put on this central experience.

Hence we find scholarly confirmation of our basic points about the

> *Make sure that at the end you reach a conclusion that pulls your different points together.*

importance of the figure of Moses to Jews who brought the Jews their most important revelation from God and led them in the key event of their history, and the status of the Buddha as the individual who found enlightenment.

BUILDING SMALL BOILERS

BY
ALEX WEISS

TECHNICAL CONSULTANT
KEVIN WALTON

© 2013 ALEX WEISS

All rights reserved. No part of this publication may be reproduced, stored in a retrieval system, or transmitted in any form or by any means, electronic, mechanical, photocopying, recording or otherwise without prior permission in writing from the publishers.

Alex Weiss asserts the moral right as author of this work.

British Library Cataloguing-in-Publication-Data: a catalogue record of this book is held by the British Library.

First printing 2013

ISBN 978-1909358-03-4
CAMDEN MINIATURE STEAM SERVICES
Barrow Farm, Rode, Frome, Somerset, BA11 6PS
www.camdenmin.co.uk

Camden stock one one of the widest selections of engineering, technical and transportation books to be found; contact them at the above address for a copy of their latest free Booklist, or see their website.

Layout design by Camden Studios

Printed by Symposium Design & Print, Cowbridge, South Glamorgan

---

WARNING

Making even small boilers is potentially hazardous. The author and publisher are merely passing on information and whilst every care has been taken in the presentation of this information, they cannot be held responsible for any damage or injury, howsoever caused, that may arise during boiler making or subsequent use of a boiler. Use your common sense, think of the hazards and remember at all times: **YOUR SAFETY, AND THAT OF OTHERS, IS YOUR RESPONSIBILITY**

CONTENTS

	PAGE
ACKNOWLEDGMENTS	v
INTRODUCTION	**1**
About small boilers	2
Boiler types	4
Tools and equipment	9
Safety precautions	10
About this book	11
CHAPTER 1: MATERIALS AND PARTS	**13**
Introduction	13
Boiler barrels	13
End-plate forms	14
Flanged end plates	15
Stays and spacers	20
Flues and fire tubes	21
Water tubes	22
Domes and threaded bushes	24
Pickles	24
Cladding and banding	25
Smoke boxes	26
Fireboxes	28
Chimneys	29
Burners	30
Boiler fittings	30
Boiler identification	31
Paint, varnish and adhesives	31
CHAPTER 2: SILVER SOLDERING	**33**
What is needed	33
Silver soldering the boiler	37
Other silver-soldering tasks	40
Safety	42
CHAPTER 3: BOILER TESTING	**43**
Inspection	43
Testing	44

Certification	46
Boiler water	46
Maintenance	47
Boilers that will not be steamed in public	47

CHAPTER 4: FITTINGS FOR THE BOILER — 49
Threaded bushes	49
Screw-in fittings	49
Other fittings	51
Sealing joints	52
Boiler feed pumps	53
Automatic boiler controls	53
Lubricators	54

CHAPTER 5: HEAT SOURCES — 55
Liquefied petroleum gas	55
Burners	55
Gas containers	58
Pipework and valves	59

CHAPTER 6: VERTICAL-BOILER DESIGNS — 61
Overview	61
108 mm (4¼") vertical boiler	62
4" (102 mm) vertical boiler	68
3½" (89 mm) vertical boiler	72
Optional baseplates	76
Conclusions	78

CHAPTER 7: HORIZONTAL-BOILER DESIGNS — 79
Overview	79
3" (76 mm) horizontal boiler	80
54 mm (2^1/$_8$") horizontal boiler	90
42 mm (1^2/$_3$") horizontal boiler	96
Conclusions	102

CHAPTER 8: OPERATING BOILERS — 103
Installing the boiler	103
Lubrication	104
Oil separators	104
Steaming the boiler	106

APPENDIX — 111
Introduction	111
Safety calculations	111
Burner heat output	115
Boiler steam production	117
List of useful addresses	119

INDEX — 121

ACKNOWLEDGEMENTS

I could not have written this book without the help of a technical consultant. Kevin Walton has provided this role and was involved in designing and building all the boilers described in this book, and the selection of their burners. His long experience of full-size steam and hot-water boilers has been applied to their design. He has provided continuous support during the research, building and testing phases. He has allowed me to take numerous pictures in his workshop. He has answered many technical questions and often come up with improvements that have been incorporated into the designs. He has also shown his expertise at problem solving when boiler performance has initially been lower than expected.

Three companies have provided the vast majority of the materials and fittings for the boilers. I would particularly like to thank Andy and Jane Clarke of Polly Models for their help with fittings for the boilers. Howard and Sarah Proffitt of College Engineering have been exceptionally patient and helpful in the provision of the metal used to make the various parts of the boilers. Phil and Dee Handcock of Forest Classics have supported our use of ceramic burners, while Tony Wood of Walker Midgley Insurance Brokers has been patient in explaining the kind of insurance needed for small boilers. I have much appreciated the personal help and time they have given. Their organisations are listed in the Appendix with their contact details and web-site addresses. I would also like to thank Simon Bowditch who has edited the book and suggested a number of significant improvements.

There are a few photographs in this book of boiler models and parts taken at model-engineering exhibitions. I would like to thank all of the builders and suppliers for providing me with the opportunity to feature these various items.

My dear wife has had put up with my obsessiveness in building boilers in my workshop, and sitting at my computer for many hours, working to complete this book. This is something to which she has become very accustomed and I am extremely fortunate that she has been very philosophical about it.

The Author

The Technical Consultant

Six boilers after silver soldering. Clockwise from top left, the 108 mm (4¼") vertical, the 4" (102 mm) vertical, the 3½" (89 mm) vertical, the 54 mm (2¹/₈") horizontal, the 42 mm (1²/₃") horizontal, and the 3" (76 mm) horizontal. The boilers have been silver soldered and are ready for hydraulic testing.

INTRODUCTION

Comparing the number of static steam engines exhibited at model engineering shows with the number of boilers on display suggests that many modellers feel unable to build a suitable boiler. There are a few stand-alone vertical boilers to be seen, mostly coal fired, and rather more complete steam plants, particularly fitted in boats. Many model ships employ commercially built boilers. It is also clear that quite a lot of people who build

Photo 1. Some of the vertical and horizontal boilers described in this book.

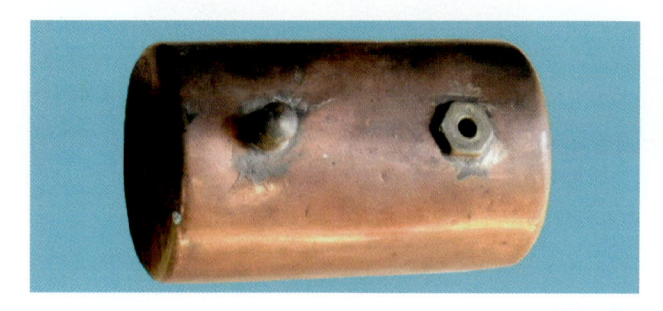

Photo 2. A simple pot boiler will have a very low steam-production rate.

steam locomotives, lorries and traction engines get their boilers professionally built, at some considerable expense. This lack of home-built boilers may be because no new book on the subject has been published since Martin Evans' *Model Locomotive and Marine Boilers* and Alex Farmer's *Model Locomotive Boiler Making* appeared a quarter of a century ago. Also they dealt almost entirely with large, complex boilers that needed rigorous independent testing.

This book gives construction details and shows how to build six different, but simple, boilers; three vertical fire-tube boilers, one horizontal water-tube boiler and two single-flue boilers. They all require independent testing if they are to be steamed in any public place. Every one is ideal for home building and can be silver soldered in a single session. All are designed to be heated by natural gas and provide excellent steaming.

These boilers are aimed at those who have built or are making a single- or twin-cylinder model steam engine. The engine may be for static use, or to install in a model boat, lorry or one of the smaller-gauge locomotives. The book aims to show model engineers that it is relatively simple to build a small boiler from copper tube. This will provide an adequate source of steam for their engine, with construction that is straightforward.

The book does not cover basic model-engineering skills. It assumes the reader can work from drawings to make parts from bronze or brass bar stock using a lathe or milling machine. It provides the dimensions of each component but does not go into detail of how to build these parts. It assumes confidence and experience in drilling, turning, facing and milling.

While buying a small ready-finished cylindrical model boiler is a relatively costly proposition, building one is a great deal less expensive. It is also much less difficult than might be thought. It is a project easily achieved by the average model engineer for about the same cost as making a simple single-cylinder slide-valve engine from castings. Despite this, it seems that many people, who cannot afford to buy a professionally built boiler, are scared by the thought of making one and then getting it independently tested. Less stringent rules apply to small

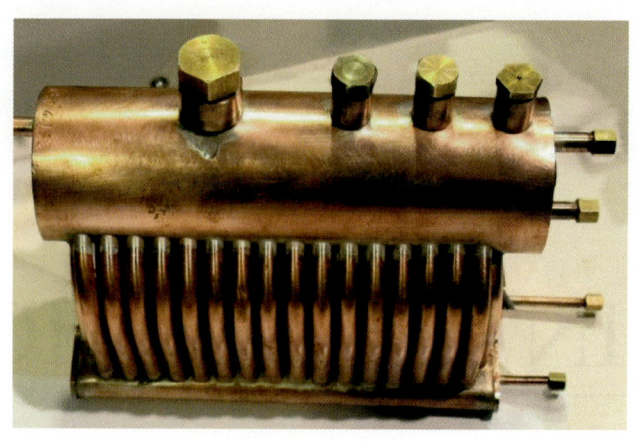

Photo 3. A small Yarrow three-drum marine boiler. With 66 water tubes it is designed to operate at 100 psi (6.9 bar). It is not easy to build!

boilers with a capacity of less than 3 bar/litres than to larger boilers. Hopefully, this book will help to overcome any fear and will benefit those who enjoy operating small steam engines in a realistic manner.

ABOUT SMALL BOILERS

The small boilers, made from copper tube, described in Chapters 6 and 7 are relatively simple to construct. Such boilers do not hold large amounts of water, but the water volume multiplied by the steam pressure must not exceed three bar-litres (77.6 psi-pints) if the most rigorous rules of independent testing are to be avoided. Thus operating at a pressure of 5 bar (73 psi) allows capacity of 600 ml (1 pint) of water, while at 4 bar (58 psi) pressure the capacity can be up to 750 ml ($1^{1}/_{3}$ pints). Since even these small copper boilers run at a relatively high temperature, silver soldering is an essential part of their construction. However, they need the use of only a single-melting-temperature silver solder.

POT BOILERS
The pot boiler is a simple pressure vessel formed from a single cylindrical sealed copper tube heated from below. It has a minimum surface area where water is exposed to heat so it is a very inefficient steamer. It is only suitable for powering the smallest unloaded engines. There are simple ways of increasing the heating area using either fire or water tubes. These will enable the boiler to heat up more rapidly than an equivalent-size pot boiler and to produce a much increased rate of steam generation.

COMPLEX BOILERS
A single soldering session with just one type of silver solder means that it is not possible to build locomotive,

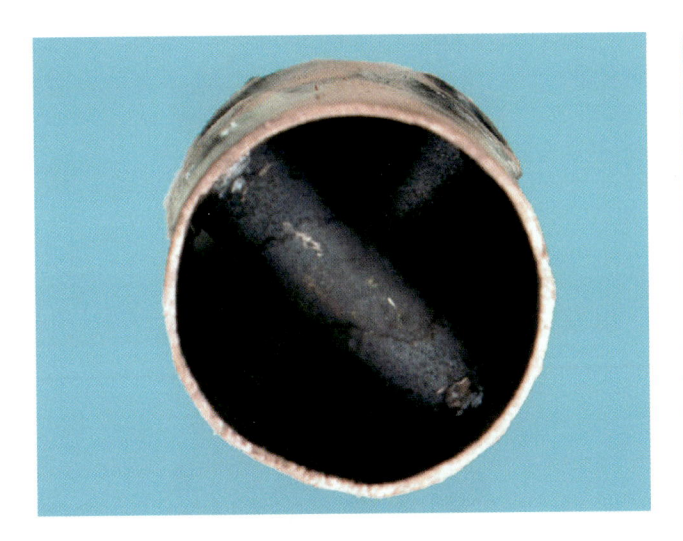

Photo 4. Galloway tubes soldered into a flue with a high-temperature silver solder.

Photo 5. A pair of flanged end plates, made from circles of flat copper sheet, which are ready to be drilled for a set of fire tubes.

traction-engine or lorry boilers with stayed fireboxes, or Babcock, Scotch and Yarrow boilers. Photo 3 indicates some of the complexities of a small Yarrow boiler. Although within the 3 bar-litre limit, building it required two different melting-temperature solders as well as a number of jigs to hold the parts in position during the soldering process. Using Galloway tubes is also not feasible. Photo 4 shows Galloway tubes across a sectioned flue. The Galloway tubes were silver soldered with a high-temperature solder and lie in two directions at 90° across the flue. The flue is then fixed in the boiler with normal-melting-temperature silver solder. The same problems apply to more complex designs, such as those for 2½" gauge and larger locomotives or 1" scale and bigger steam lorries and traction engines.

MATERIALS

The basic materials that are needed to build a small boiler include copper tube of appropriate length, diameter and wall thickness, copper rod and sheet of the required thicknesses as well as bronze rod and lagging materials. Detailed information is provided about how to flange copper end plates over home-made wooden forms. All the necessary calculations have been completed for the boiler designs illustrated to ensure that the materials recommended have sufficient strength. These can be found in the Appendix. Two materials are not recommended for making small-boiler pressure vessels. Steel is hard to work and its strength is not needed for small boilers, while its tendency to rust makes it an unattractive material. Brass should never be employed as part of the pressure vessel, even dezincification-resistant (DZR) brass. With time, in the presence of hot water, dezincification will selectively remove zinc from the alloy, leaving a porous, copper-rich structure with little mechanical strength. This is not what is needed in a boiler. However, brass sheet and strip may safely be used for making fire and smoke boxes and there is information about when to use these materials. Dimensions are also given for boiler bushes and steam domes that can be readily turned from bronze but never from brass.

COST AND PERFORMANCE OF BOILERS

As an example of the cost of making a boiler, the price of the materials needed to build a typical 4" (102 mm) diameter vertical copper boiler without fittings is about the same as that for a set of un-machined castings for a single-cylinder slide- or piston-valve steam engine.

With a maximum length between its end flanges of say 5" (127 mm) and 23 fire tubes of 8 mm ($^5/_{16}$"), it will have a capacity of 810 ml (1.44 pints) and thus may be run at a maximum pressure of 3.7 bar (53 psi); sufficient for most requirements. The steam capacity of such a boiler, fitted with a 2¾" (70 mm) diameter circular ceramic burner, is sufficient to run a twin-cylinder slide- or piston-valve engine with a bore and stroke of ¾" (19 mm), such as the Stuart Double Ten. Alternatively it will readily run a single-cylinder engine with a bore of 1" (25 mm) and a stroke of 2" (51 mm) such as the Stuart Beam Engine.

Simple tubed boilers will run single- and twin-cylinder static steam engines as well as twin-cylinder engines that are fitted to small steam lorries and boats up to 2 metres (78") long.

BOILERS TO BUILD

There are many different types of small boiler. This book shows how to build the following six boilers:

- Three vertical boilers fitted with fire tubes; 108 mm (4¼"), 4" (102 mm) and 3½" (89 mm) diameter.
- A 3" (76 mm) horizontal boiler with external water tubes heated from below.
- Two single-flue horizontal boilers with 54 mm (2$^1/_8$") and 42 mm (1$^2/_3$") diameters.

4 INTRODUCTION

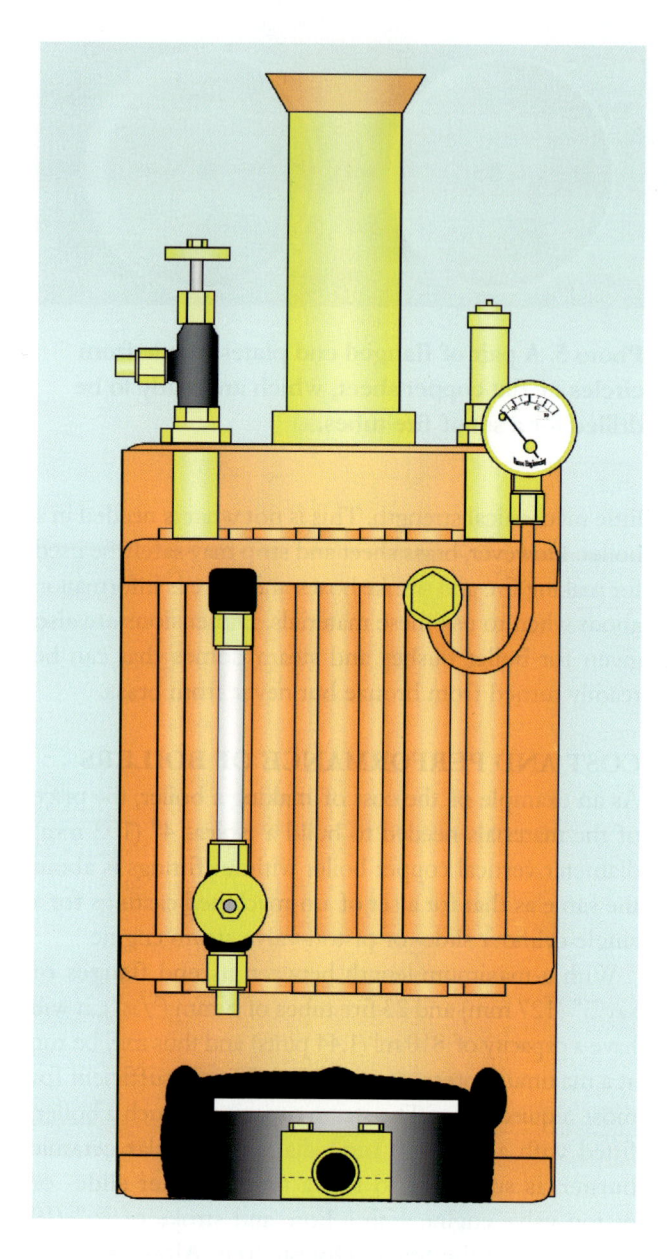

Drawing 1. The cross-section of a small fire-tube vertical boiler with a ceramic burner.

The choice of which boiler to build will depend on its final application. The largest vertical boilers will provide the most steam, albeit not at the highest pressure. The smaller ones are ideal for single-cylinder and low capacity twin-cylinder engines. The largest horizontal one is primarily designed for boat use but is also suitable for powering static engines. The two smallest horizontal ones have been designed for static applications as well as for Gauge 1 and 32 mm narrow-gauge locomotives.

BOILER TYPES

There are many different possible boiler layouts that can potentially be built. However, for boilers that are

Photo 6. The vertical-boiler fire tubes and tube plate assembly prior to a test fit in the boiler shell.

simple to construct and that avoid some of the most serious aspects of independent testing, all the boilers described have a relatively small water capacity. All meet the three bar-litre limit. Every one is based on a simple copper-tube barrel and all can be built with a single melting-temperature silver solder. Thus, just one soldering session is sufficient to complete each boiler even though it has to be turned over during soldering to give access to every part.

When choosing what to build, it is essential not to build too small a boiler for the engine it is to power. Too large a boiler, on the other hand, will have some spare capacity. This is not a bad thing as the burner can always be turned down a little.

Many boilers fail to perform satisfactorily either because they have insufficient area exposed to the heat from the burner or because the burner itself gives an inadequate heat output. The majority of the boilers described in this book have plenty of area exposed to hot gases and are heated by ceramic gas burners. The exceptions are the two smallest horizontal ones that rely on powerful gas torches. All the boilers have been tested running steam engines and have shown a satisfactory performance in relation to their physical size.

FIRE-TUBE BOILERS

One method of enlarging the heating area of a pot boiler is to run fire tubes, a flue or both through a vertical boiler. The heat will travel through the flue and fire tubes that are in contact with the water in the boiler. A flue is not necessary if a sufficient number of fire tubes is fitted. The use of fire tubes involves cutting sets of

Drawing 2. The cross-section of a horizontal boiler with three water tubes and a ceramic burner.

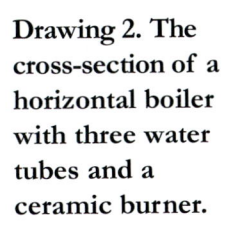

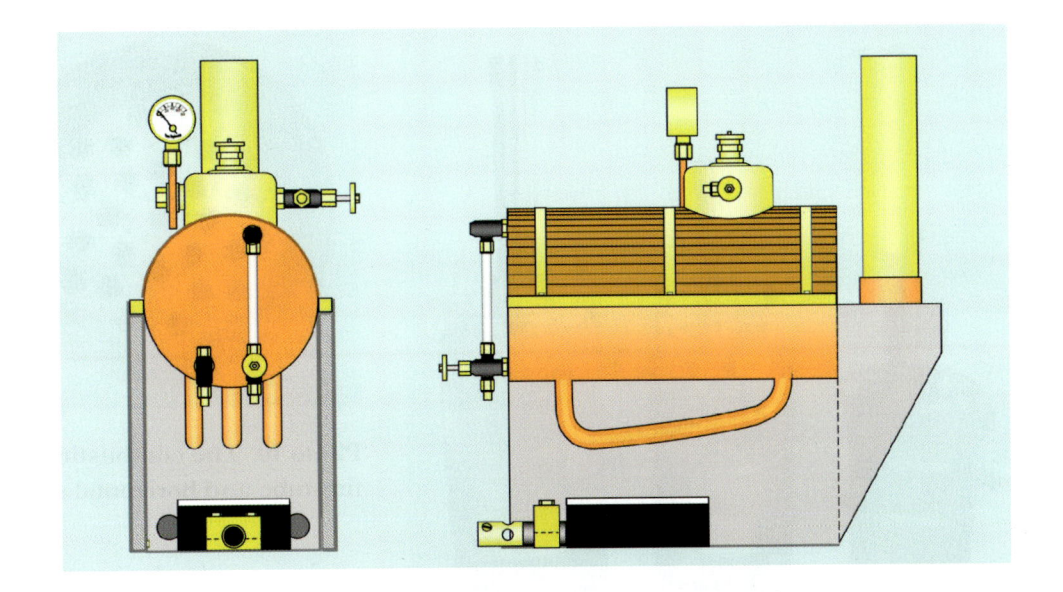

holes in the two boiler end plates but fortunately fitting fire tubes will generally negate any need for stays.

A good size for fire tubes in boilers of 89 mm - 108 mm (3½" - 4¼") diameter is 8 mm (5/16") diameter copper tube. Fire tubes do reduce the internal water capacity of the boiler, but for the 108 mm and 4" ones, this is helpful in keeping the capacity within the 3 bar-litre limit at a higher working pressure than if the tubes were not fitted.

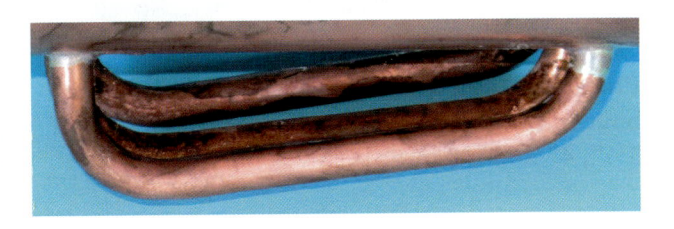

Photo 7. Water tubes under the body of a boiler.

WATER-TUBE BOILERS

Another method of augmenting the heating area is to fit external water tubes beneath a horizontal boiler, which are also exposed to heat from the burner. These tubes should slope upwards from the burner end of the boiler towards the chimney end and towards the steam dome. For a boiler of 3" (76 mm) diameter, water tubes of 8 mm diameter copper tube can readily be bent to the required shape. When calculating its water capacity, the internal volume of the water tubes has to be added to the capacity of the boiler shell itself to ensure it stays within the 3 bar-litre limit. Photo 7 shows three water tubes silver soldered in place beneath a 3" boiler shell.

SINGLE-FLUE BOILERS

Horizontal boilers with a single flue down their length are ideal where a small diameter unit is needed. The flue tube fitted to the two smallest horizontal boilers is 15 mm diameter. The flue does reduce the internal water capacity of the boiler but also negates the need for stays. A gas torch feeds its heat along the flue to a smoke box at the other end where the gases are turned through 90° to exhaust up the chimney.

VERTICAL BOILERS

An upright boiler has many attractions for the modeller. It looks very attractive when completed. It is readily built with an integral firebox and with a number of fire tubes.

Drawing 3. A simple single-flue boiler suitable for a small locomotive.

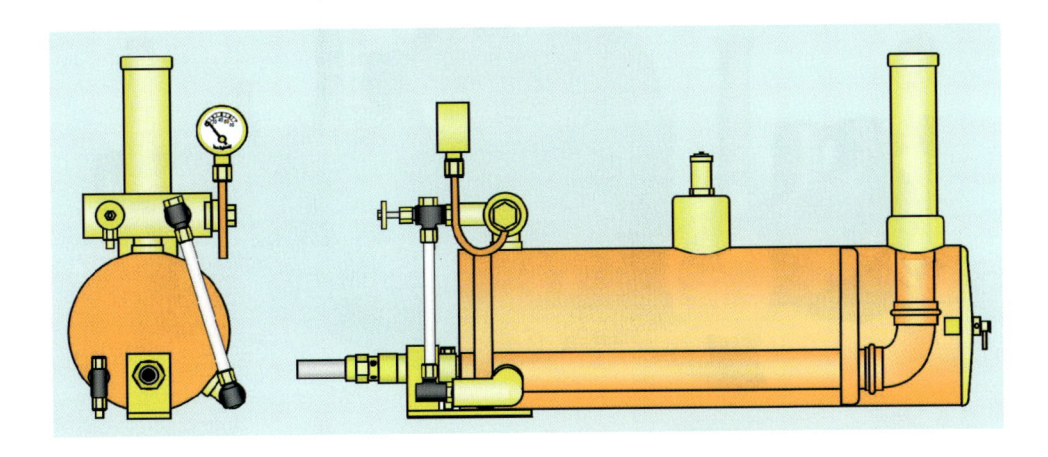

6 INTRODUCTION

Photo 8. Three wood-lagged vertical fire-tube boilers; from left to right, they have diameters of 3½", 4" and 108 mm.

It will be very effective at producing steam. Its main limitation is in applications like conventional steam locomotives and some model boats where a horizontal boiler is often preferred. A simple fire-tube vertical boiler is not difficult to make though it does require carefully drilled end plates.

HORIZONTAL BOILERS
Apart from a very few locomotives with vertical boilers, 32 mm narrow-gauge and Gauge 1 locomotives may

Photo 10. The combustion chambers of vertical fire-tube and horizontal single-flue boilers.

employ a stay-less horizontal boiler with an internal flue tube. Some model boats require boilers to fit below the decks or need the complete model to have a low centre of gravity for stability reasons. These horizontal boilers may use water tubes or a single flue. Both types will need a steam dome or manifold to avoid priming of the engine. Apart from designs fired with a gas torch in the flue, horizontal water-tube boilers need a firebox to support the boiler and house a ceramic burner.

COMBUSTION CHAMBERS
A simple vertical boiler can have the firebox located within the boiler shell below the bottom tube plate. It can equally have a separate short length of tube as a firebox; particularly useful if the length of copper tube available is too short for an all-in-one boiler shell and firebox. Both types of firebox will need adequate air holes drilled. Horizontal boilers can have the burner in the

Photo 9. Three horizontal boilers; from left to right a 54 mm single-flue boiler, a 3" water-tube one and a 42 mm single-flue boiler.

Photo 11. A pair of locomotives with a 42 mm and 54 mm boiler respectively.

form of a gas torch, installed in a flue, but water-tube boilers will need a separate firebox below the boiler. This is relatively easy to make from sheet metal bent to shape with a slot for air and a simple door for access to a ceramic burner. In all cases, it is essential to provide access to the burner and allow sufficient air to enter the combustion chamber so that the gas can burn efficiently.

FLUES

The flue provides a means of flowing the products of combustion through the boiler and out to the atmosphere. It is important there is a clear flow path for the burned gases up the boiler chimney. The vertical boilers in this book use the fire tubes to feed the gases to a smoke box at the top and up a chimney without the need for a flue. The small horizontal boilers have a direct connection from the centre flue to the chimney while the water-tube boiler uses the shape of one end of the combustion chamber to feed the gases into the chimney.

STEAM CAPACITIES

The steam capacity required by any steam engine will depend on the type of engine, the number and bore of the cylinders, the stroke of the engine, the maximum speed and load at which it operates. Also important are variations in the load on and the speed of the engine. While in theory the consumption also depends on the valve cut-off timing, this may be ignored due to other more significant losses in small engines.

The steam capacity available from any boiler will depend on the surface area of the water exposed to heating, the amount of heat the burner is producing, the conductivity of the boiler metal (usually copper) and the pressure at which the boiler can continuously operate. The Appendix gives details of practical steam tests.

WORKING PRESSURES

The working pressure of all the steam boilers described in this book is limited to a maximum of 60 psi or 4 bar, or less if the water capacity exceeds 750 ml ($1^1/_3$ pints). Inevitably, the required pressure will depend on the engine to be powered. Almost every engine suited to one of these boilers will run well at 40 psi ($2^3/_4$ bar) or even less. Thus, while this book quotes the highest design working pressure for each of the boilers described, safety

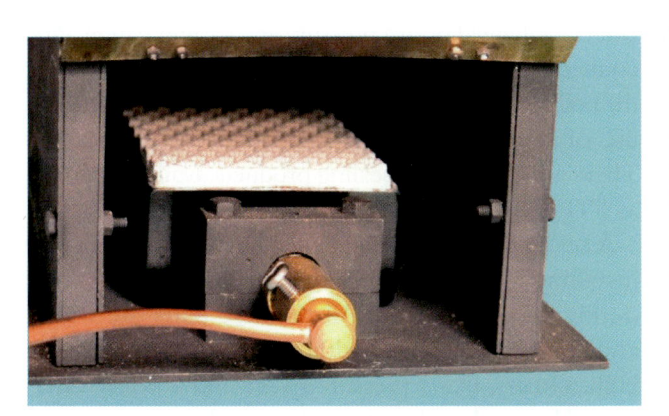

Photo 12. The combustion chamber of a horizontal water-tube boiler, with the access door open.

Photo 13. The 3" horizontal boiler test powering a three-cylinder oscillating engine fitted with an aircraft propeller.

Photo 14. The 108 mm boiler provides more than enough steam to drive the Stuart mill engine at its maximum speed. A lubricator and permanent pipe work are yet to be fitted.

Photo 16. A selection of basic steam fittings. From left to right, two pressure gauges and a siphon, a water gauge, a steam valve, a check valve, three safety valves and bottom a spare glass that can be cut to length for a water gauge.

valves will normally be set to a maximum of 45 psi or 3 bar. This requires the boiler to be hydraulically tested to twice the working pressure before it is used to generate steam. Regardless, all the boilers described have been hydraulically tested to 120 psi (8.3 bar).

HEATING SMALL BOILERS

By far the most practical source of heat is a mixture of natural gases, conveniently available in relatively small disposable cans. These contain a mix of propane and butane, often also including some isopropane. The gas may feed a circular or rectangular ceramic burner or a small gas-torch burner, depending on the configuration of the boiler and its flue. All the vertical boilers and the one horizontal water-tube boiler described in Chapters 6 and 7 are heated by ceramic burners. The other two horizontal boilers employ a gas-torch burner.

For those who wish to operate their boilers in radio-controlled boats without a boiler feed pump, it is essential that the gas capacity is exhausted before the water in the boiler reaches the low safe limit; about one quarter full. Small refillable gas tanks are available for this purpose. Although not recommended, such tanks are sometimes home-made but, in this case, serious independent testing to 24 bar (350 psi) is essential.

None of the boilers described in this book have been designed either for heating with a methylated-spirits burner or with a coal fire.

BOILER FITTINGS

The fittings for model boilers include blow-down, bypass, check and clack valves, globe, regulator, steam-stop and union valves as well as safety valves. The last are particularly important; they must be of sufficient capacity and correctly set to avoid exceeding the 3 bar/litre limit. Boilers will need both a pressure and a water gauge. Pipe connectors, elbows and tees will be required to connect the boiler to the engine it will power. This will involve the use of copper tube, olives, nuts and copper washers. There are also several sealing products available, as well as PTFE tape, for making fittings steam tight.

A set of fittings is an additional cost and will involve installing a number of bronze bushes on the boiler during its construction. All of these parts are widely available from suppliers although some can be home built. Others, like a pressure gauge and a safety valve, should be purchased ready-made. In addition, it is normal practice to lag small boilers to reduce heat losses and to improve the appearance of the boiler.

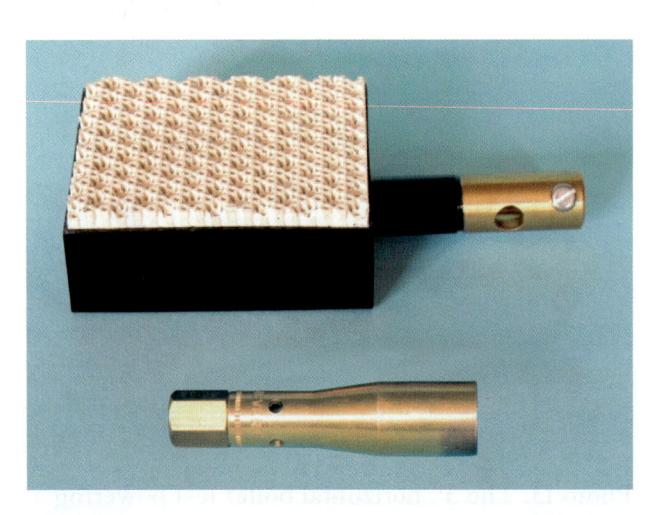

Photo 15. A rectangular ceramic burner and a small gas torch.

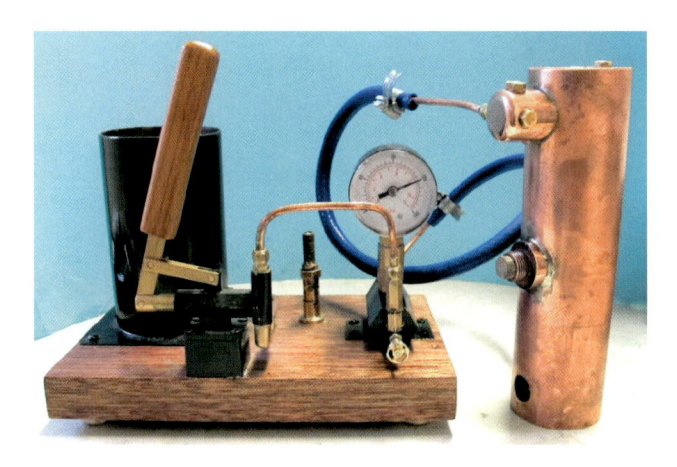

Photo 17. Hydraulically testing a 54 mm horizontal boiler at 120 psi (just over 8 bar).

Photo 18. A Sentinel steam lorry powered by a 3½" vertical boiler and a twin-cylinder oscillating engine.

TESTING

The rules in *The Examination & Testing of Miniature Steam Boilers (Revised Edition 2012)* state that boilers below 3 bar-litres require independent testing and certification but are exempt from many of the requirements of the code. All the boilers described in this book meet that combined capacity/pressure criteria. Running within an organised club always requires independent testing and certification for safety and insurance reasons. Examples include the Association of 16 mm Narrow Gauge Modellers and the Model Power Boat Association.

A boiler that is solely used for home running does not require independent testing, just initial and subsequent hydraulic testing as well as annual steam testing and correctly setting the safety valve. It is in the interests of any builder to meet the rules for *The Examination & Testing of Miniature Steam Boilers* even if the boiler is only steamed at home and never operated in public.

Getting a boiler tested is not a particularly difficult task but must be carried out by an authorised independent tester; a person found in most model-engineering clubs. Photo 17 shows a boiler under hydraulic test. There is a full description of how the necessary tests are carried out and how they are documented in Chapter 3.

OPERATING SMALL BOILERS

Installing a boiler, whether on a static base plate to drive a stationary engine or in a vehicle, locomotive or boat requires care as does connecting the boiler output, via a lubricator to the engine. Carrying out these tasks is not difficult. They include discovering how to fire up and steam a boiler to obtain best performance and to maximise the life of both the boiler and its associated steam engine. Chapter 8 shows a number of the boilers operating a range of different steam engines. It also gives detailed information on how to build an oil separator; an essential ancillary item in many installations.

TOOLS AND EQUIPMENT

Most of the tools needed to make small boilers will be found in the average model-engineer's workshop. The key items include a lathe, a pillar drill, a metal-working vice, a hide-faced hammer and the normal selection of other workshop tools. A milling machine and a rotary table will make working on boiler plates much easier but this task can also be carried out on a pillar drill. In both cases, a special copper-drilling bit is desirable. Making a water-tube boiler requires a tube-bending tool but these are surprisingly inexpensive as are steam-pipe bending tools needed for all boiler installations. Neither

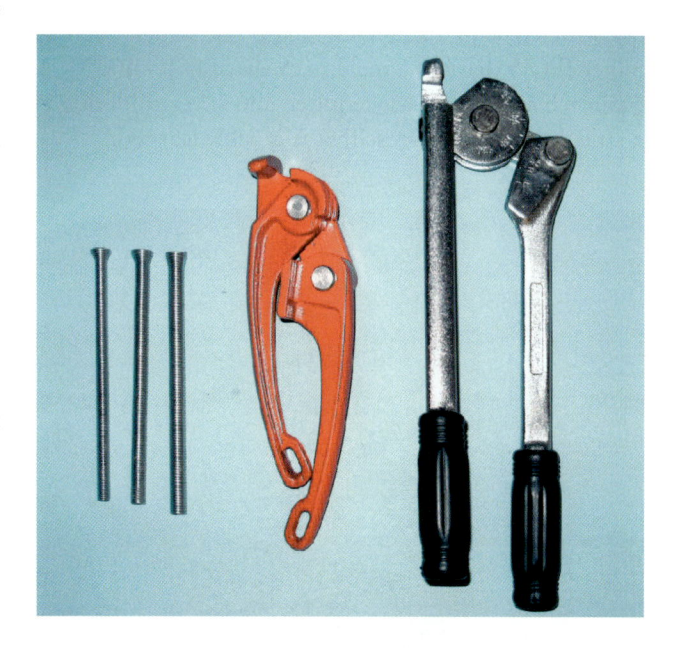

Photo 19. Three bending tools, from left to right, a set of bending springs, a small pipe bending tool and an 8 mm (5/16") pipe-bending tool.

Photo 20. A Sievert liquefied-petroleum-gas torch.

the lathe nor the milling machine need to be large. The biggest smoke-box cover that has its perimeter turned is less than 120 mm (4¾") in diameter and will thus fit on any but the smallest lathe.

In addition, a brazing torch and a relatively small hearth are needed. Tongs are used for turning over hot boilers and a pair of pliers are ideal for picking up hot pieces of metal and dunking them in cold water. An acid pickle is used to clean parts both before and after soldering a boiler. This can be done with citric acid, which is relatively harmless, or carefully with dilute sulphuric acid.

Anyone who has built a small static steam engine, such a a Stuart H10 or V10, should have no problems building any of the boilers shown in this book.

SILVER SOLDERING SMALL BOILERS

Small copper boilers run at a relatively high temperature, 144° C at 4 bar (58 psi) pressure. Thus no soft solders, even high-temperature ones, can ever provide sufficient strength. Silver soldering that takes place at over 600° C is essential. Fortunately, all the boilers are designed to be constructed with a single-melting-point solder, such as Silver-flo 55 that has a melting range of 630 - 660°C. A gas torch and hearth are required and silver soldering is a straightforward process that is quickly learned.

Photo 21. Silver soldering a boiler in a low-cost hearth made from five thermalite blocks.

Photo 22. An excellent pair of leather protective gloves for use when silver soldering.

Gas torches

A gas torch that runs on propane is a must for silver soldering. A range of torches is widely available from DIY stores and model-engineering suppliers. What is needed is a complete torch, a suitably sized burner and a couple of metres (yards) of hose. The Sievert PMPX kit is a complete solution as is the much less expensive Clarke PC108 gas torch, available from Machine Mart. Both will run well from an 11 kg propane cylinder.

Domestic DIY blowlamps that come with disposable gas cartridges are not suitable for work on even small boilers as they do not produce sufficient heat. They are, however, useful for soldering smaller items such as olives on steam pipes.

Hearths

There are several approaches to making a small hearth. Fire bricks, thermalite blocks or Skamolex insulating bricks and board, made from asbestos-free Vermiculite insulation, are all suitable for making brazing hearths. The latter two can be sawn to size. Most builder's merchants, DIY stores and fire-place shops offer a range of suitable materials. For brazing the boilers described in this book, a hearth that measures 300 x 150 mm (12" x 6") is sufficient.

SAFETY PRECAUTIONS

Several areas of boiler building involve potential dangers. These include brazing flames, hot metal, liquefied petroleum gas (LPG), acid pickles and boiler pressure.

A little forethought, a dose of common sense and a first-aid kit are all requirements for safe working.

BURNS

Care is needed when handling gas torches and silver soldering hot metal. Always wear protective leather gloves, which must not include any plastic linings. Use tongs to turn boilers and dunk parts being annealed. When steamed, boilers themselves get very hot and can cause burns, as can steam when operating an engine.

LIQUEFIED PETROLEUM GAS

The use of gas torches, ceramic burners and gas cylinders requires care. Pipes and connectors must be correctly fitted and regularly checked. As the gas is heavier than air, any leaking gas can pool on the floor of a workshop, in the hull of a model boat or the body of a car or van carrying a model with a working boiler. Always refill gas tanks out of doors and remove disposable gas cans after use. A single spark is all that is needed to explode a pool of gas. Do make sure all the gas valves are always securely turned off after use.

ACID

Using acid pickles is another area of potential danger. Always work in a well-ventilated area, add acid to water to dilute it, and NEVER add water to acid. Wear protective clothing and goggles. If a splash of acid hit your body, wash it off with copious amounts of water. The same applies to clothing as acid quickly causes holes.

BOILER PRESSURE

After they have been built, boilers must undergo hydraulic and steam testing. Independent testing is almost always required. Safety valves must be set so the working pressure is never exceeded by more than 10%. A check of the boiler condition and a steam test must be carried out once a year; a hydraulic test every four years.

ABOUT THIS BOOK

This book starts by looking at the choice of materials, and their thicknesses, used to build any boiler. All the ones in this book employ seamless copper tube for the boiler barrel. It shows how flanged plates are shaped over suitable home-made wooden forms. Appropriately sized fire or water tubes and threaded bushes are needed, as are internal flues and stays on some horizontal boilers. There are several other components and parts that are fully described. Any boiler should be lagged to reduce heat losses. For the majority of boilers described in this book, the use of wooden planking will produce an attractive finish, but some applications require lagging beneath a metal cladding.

Silver soldering is an essential skill for copper boiler construction and many model engineers will be familiar with the process. It requires a suitable torch and gas cylinder, as well as a simple hearth to hold the boiler during assembly. Recommendations are made of suitable solders and fluxes, with cadmium-based solders no longer available. The boiler will need to be cleaned and set up prior to soldering the whole assembly, and then cleaned once again after the soldering is completed.

Any boiler must be tested before use. If it is to be operated in public or at a club, it will need independent examination, testing and certification; not too difficult for 'small boilers.' For home use only, a suitable pressure gauge, but not a model-sized one, and a boiler feed pump are essential for hydraulic testing. Once the initial test is done, fitting out of the boiler can be finished ready for the second hydraulic and steam tests.

There is a wide range of ready-made fittings available for use on small model boilers. The minimum required for a practical model boiler are a safety valve, pressure and water gauges, a steam valve and, preferably, a clack valve for filling with water. A boiler feed pump of some sort is a desirable option and automatic boiler control may be chosen for certain installations. A displacement or mechanical lubricator should be fitted to the steam line and filled with a quality steam oil. For model boats, an oil separator on the engine exhaust is usually essential and is highly desirable for many other installations.

Heat to produce steam is an integral part of any boiler and can be done with liquefied petroleum gas. There are several types of gas and a mix is recommended. The gas can feed a ceramic burner, of which there are a number of sizes and shapes, or a small gas-torch. The gas must be safely stored and filler nozzles, jets, pipe work and gas valves provided, as well as a suitable igniter.

Chapters 6 and 7 contain a large amount of detailed information showing how to build six different vertical and horizontal boilers. These consist of three vertical boilers with diameters of 108 mm, 4" and 3½". The 108 mm boiler has a separate firebox due to the availability of materials used during construction. The other two have integral fireboxes. The three horizontal boilers comprise a 3" water-tube boiler with a separate firebox, together with 54 mm and 42 mm single-flue boilers. Dimensioned drawings of the various parts are provided, as well as copious photographs showing the various stages of construction.

The last chapter covers boiler operation; installation, connecting an engine, filling, steaming and occasionally cleaning the boiler. It includes details and plans showing how to build an oil separator.

The Appendix provides stress calculations for all the boilers and details of burner tests. There is a list of useful suppliers and also a comprehensive index.

METRICATION

Finally, a word on metrication. Much of the UK still deals with both imperial and metric units. When building a boiler, some manufacturers and suppliers will quote imperial sizes for equipment and materials whereas others will offer metric standards. While imperial material sizes were traditionally used in model engineering, many items are becoming more and more restricted to metric equivalents. The use of metric sizes for copper tube is increasingly found in the selection of the boiler shells. This metric standard is usually more readily available and is often significantly cheaper. It is a trend that is increasingly also applying to many other items. Where materials and fitting are sold to imperial dimensions, these are quoted first but are often followed by metric equivalents. Sometimes there is no direct metric counterpart as, for example, fittings in the UK with only an imperial $1/4"$ ME thread. To avoid tedious repetition, individual equivalents are not continuously repeated throughout the book. It is clear that metrication is likely to become even more prevalent as the years roll on.

Table 1 gives metric equivalents of imperial sizes in $1/64"$ intervals up to 1". The use of a calculator to divide millimetres by 25.4 gives the answer in inches. Multiplying inches by 25.4 converts them to millimetres.

For those with imperial number and letter drills, the following metric equivalents may prove useful for drilling tapping and clearance holes in various boiler fittings:

Size	Tapping	Major diameter
4BA	3.1 mm or No 31	3.6 mm or 0.142"
5BA	2.7 mm or No 36	3.2 mm or 0.126"
6BA	2.3 mm or No 42	2.8 mm or 0.110"
7BA	2.1 mm or No 45	2.5 mm or 0.098"
8BA	1.8 mm or No 50	2.2 mm or 0.087"
$3/16"$ ME	4.2 mm or No 19	4.8 mm or $3/16"$
$1/4"$ ME	5.8 mm or No 1	6.35 mm or $1/4"$
$5/16"$ ME	7.2 mm or Letter K	8 mm or $5/16"$

inch fraction	decimal	mm	inch fraction	decimal	mm	inch fraction	decimal	mm	inch fraction	decimal	mm
1/64	0.016	0.40	17/64	0.266	6.75	33/64	0.516	13.10	49/64	0.766	19.45
1/32	0.031	0.79	9/32	0.281	7.14	17/32	0.531	13.49	25/32	0.781	19.84
3/64	0.047	1.19	19/64	0.297	7.54	35/64	0.547	13.89	51/64	0.797	20.24
1/16	0.063	1.59	5/16	0.313	7.94	9/16	0.563	14.29	13/16	0.813	20.64
5/64	0.078	1.98	21/64	0.328	8.33	37/64	0.578	14.68	53/64	0.828	21.03
3/32	0.094	2.38	11/32	0.344	8.73	19/32	0.594	15.08	27/32	0.844	21.43
7/64	0.109	2.78	23/64	0.359	9.13	39/64	0.609	15.48	55/64	0.859	21.83
1/8	0.125	3.18	3/8	0.375	9.53	5/8	0.625	15.88	7/8	0.875	22.23
9/64	0.141	3.57	25/64	0.391	9.92	25/64	0.641	16.27	57/64	0.891	22.62
5/32	0.156	3.97	13/32	0.406	10.32	41/32	0.656	16.67	29/32	0.906	23.02
11/64	0.172	4.37	27/64	0.422	10.72	21/64	0.672	17.07	59/64	0.922	23.42
3/16	0.188	4.76	7/16	0.438	11.11	11/16	0.688	17.46	15/16	0.938	23.81
13/64	0.203	5.16	29/64	0.453	11.51	45/64	0.703	17.86	61/64	0.953	24.21
7/32	0.219	5.56	15/32	0.469	11.91	23/32	0.719	18.26	31/32	0.969	24.61
15/64	0.234	5.95	31/64	0.484	12.30	47/64	0.734	18.65	63/64	0.984	25.00
1/4	0.250	6.35	1/2	0.500	12.70	3/4	0.750	19.05	1	1.000	25.40

Table 1. Imperial to metric conversion table.

1: MATERIALS AND PARTS

INTRODUCTION

The main metals used for building the boilers in this book are copper, bronze, gunmetal and brass. Copper is ideal for the boiler shell, end plates, flues, fire tubes and water tubes. Bronze or gunmetal are the only materials suitable for the various threaded bushes and steam domes that are an integral part of the boiler pressure vessel. Brass must not be used for these parts.

However, brass is suitable for removable smoke-box covers, fireboxes, cladding on horizontal boilers and for metal bands around wooden lagging. Hard wood is required to make wooden forms for producing boiler end plates. A decorative wood like mahogany or teak is ideal for lagging.

Steel is neither desirable nor needed when making the pressure vessel for small boilers. Its major advantages are its strength, roughly twice that of copper of the same dimensions, and its relative cheapness. The strength is unnecessary and it rusts in the presence of moisture in the air, which weakens its structure over time. It is also much harder to work steel, for example to form flanged plates, which becomes a blacksmithing job. Thus it not an ideal material for making small boilers.

Photo 1. Copper tube comes in all sorts of sizes and wall thicknesses.

MATERIAL THICKNESSES

The copper used in the boilers described in this book is mostly 16 gauge (1.6 mm/0.064"); C106 tube or C101 plate. The exceptions are the 20 gauge (0.9 mm/0.036") fire tubes and water tubes, the spacing tubes, and the 18 gauge 1.2 mm/0.048") thick boiler shells and 22 gauge (0.7 mm/0.03") flue tubes for the two small single-flue horizontal boilers. Both should be to EN 1057 - Type X (previously BS 2871 Table X), which is sold by plumbing suppliers and will be marked on lengths of the tube.

The bronze fittings can all be made from round or hexagonal bar. CZ108 common brass plate, used for smoke-box covers, is also 16 gauge but the brass boiler banding is 20 gauge. The brass sheet for the horizontal water-tube boiler firebox is also 20 gauge.

BOILER BARRELS

Without exception, all the boilers described in this book use round copper tube for the boiler barrels. C106 hard-drawn copper is available from a number of model engineering suppliers. The Appendix shows that 16 gauge copper tube will meet the strength requirements for all the vertical and the largest horizontal boiler in this book. The two smaller horizontal boilers use 18 gauge plumbing tubes and similar calculations are given in the Appendix. It is essential that the boiler shell of the required diameter is cut to the right length and that the ends are square. Most suppliers will automatically do this when the tube is ordered but the odd burr may need to be cleaned off.

The boiler shell will need drilling for any bushes required to mount fittings or other components to the boiler barrel. In addition, air holes must be drilled in the firebox of vertical boilers and a cut out made for the ceramic-burner nozzle. The boiler shell can be clamped to a drilling or milling machine table with two flanged

Photo 2. Drilling a boiler shell with a special copper drill bit. The flanged plates have been fitted in the boiler shell beneath the retaining strap to avoid distorting the shell.

end plates fitted inside, to avoid distorting the tube when clamped. This is shown in Photo 2, with a strip of rubber protecting the copper from the clamping bar. The horizontal water-tube boiler needs holes for these tubes milled in the boiler shell so that they can be fitted parallel to each other. One easy way to hold the boiler shell is to attach it to a rotary table swivelled though 90° so the shell is parallel to the milling table. A disc of wood holds the bottom end central and a similar disc, part turned just to fit inside the boiler shell with the other part of a greater diameter, supports the other end. (These blocks are made in a similar way to end-plate forms). Both are centre drilled and the whole assembly held in place with threaded rod, a nut and washer. This is shown in Photo 3, where the free end of the shell is supported by V-blocks with small protective strips of rubber and held down with a length of steel bar. The six holes for the water tubes are cut with an 8 mm ($^5/_{16}$") slot mill at around 1,200 rpm, moving the milling table to position the holes. The shell is then rotated

Photo 3. Milling holes in a horizontal-boiler shell for its water tubes. Stepped blocks give extra support.

Photo 4. Seven wooden forms, the larger five for fire-tube boilers have a central hole, the smaller two for horizontal boilers have no central hole.

through 180° on the rotary table and a 12 mm or a ½" slot drill, turning at 1,000 rpm, used to form the hole for the steam dome.

END-PLATE FORMS

In order to flange an end plate, a hard wood or medium-density fibreboard (MDF) cylindrical form should be made. The form must be the boiler's internal diameter less twice the end-plate thickness. For 16 gauge metal, this amounts to 3.2 mm ($^1/_8$"). Ideally, the form should be made on a wood-working lathe but, as Photo 6 shows, the work can readily be done on a metal-turning one although the sawdust does make quite a mess. Metal-working tools cut the wood easily and the final finish can be achieved with strips of sandpaper held carefully to the wooden surface while the lathe is turning. The sharp corner of one end of the wooden form should be chamfered to give a gentle curve from the end plate to its flange.

For a vertical fire-tube boiler, the form should have a hole, the same diameter as the fire tubes, drilled through its centre so the plate can be bolted to the form to hold it centrally and securely when the rim is being flanged and later turned. For horizontal boilers, one or more holes can be drilled or milled for any flues or stays by clamping the plate to the table, attached to its form.

A flat wooden or metal disc of the same diameter as the form is also needed to hold the copper disc flat when the flange is being formed by hammering its edge. When the flanging is complete, the end plate can be re-fitted and bolted on its form, then returned to the lathe so that the rim can be turned to size. The form can normally be held in the chuck's external jaws but for those who only have a small lathe, there are two alternatives. Either a smaller spigot can be glued in the centre of one end of the wooden block or, if the block has been centre drilled, a stud can be passed through the hole, held in place with a pair of nuts and the stud held in the chuck.

The smallest two boilers described in this book can have their rims turned in the lathe by pressing them onto the form with a short length of wood or metal pushed against the plate with a rotating centre in the tailstock.

FLANGED END PLATES

Making a flanged plate from copper or brass appears to be much more difficult than it is in practice. Providing the metal is regularly annealed, even the first-time boiler maker should have no difficulties.

Flanged end plates are made from circular discs of copper sheet. First cut a circle of the correct diameter of copper from 16 gauge sheet. This disc should be about an 1" (25 mm) larger in diameter than the end plate itself to allow for a $^3/_8$" (9.5 mm) flange with a bit to spare. The material will need the circle marked on it, either scribed with a pair of dividers into engineer's blue or, after covering one side of the sheet with masking tape, drawn on with a pencil in a pair of compasses. The disc can then be cut out with a bandsaw or by hand with a piercing saw fitted with a suitable blade. Clean up the cut edges with a file, emery cloth or a power sanding machine.

Copper sheet as supplied will be relatively stiff as the metal hardens with time and it also work hardens. Before work starts on flanging end plates, the copper must be softened by annealing it; a relatively simple process requiring a propane gas torch (see Chapter 2 for details) and a hearth or a firebrick on which to heat the copper disc. To anneal the copper, heat it with a gas torch until

Photo 6. Wooden forms can be turned on a metal-working lathe with a metal-cutting tool but a lot of sawdust will need to be cleaned off afterwards.

it is red hot. Then carefully pick up the disc with a pair of tongs or water-pump pliers and plunge the red-hot disc into a bowl of clean cold water. The copper will now be soft and once dried, a start can be made to be forming the flanges. It will need regular re-annealing and cleaning between each flanging session to keep the copper soft each time it work hardens.

For vertical fire-tube boilers, the centre hole drilled through the copper plate can be used to hold it in place on the form. For a flanged smoke box cover, the same technique can be applied to a circle of brass sheet. For horizontal boilers where there is no central hole in the end plate, carefully place the disc of copper centrally between the form and its associated wooden or metal disc. As the sandwich of wooden form, copper and supporting disc is rotated in the vice during flanging, take care that their relative positions do not change. After the first flanging session, the slightly dished copper will automatically fit centrally on the form.

Photo 5. The annealing process; heating a slightly dished disc, the red-hot disc and dunking it in water.

Photo 7. An annealed flat copper disc and form clamped in a vice ready to start shaping the flange. A length of 8 mm ($5/16$") tube holds it centrally.

Photo 9. After a second re-annealing the third shaping session is about to start. The wooden disc on top of the flange holds it flat.

FLANGING PLATES

Photos 7 - 13 illustrate the work needed to flange copper tube plates for a 4" boiler. Clamp the form, the annealed copper plate and the wooden or metal disc between the jaws of a vice and start gentle tapping with a hide-faced hammer as shown in Figure 7. Do not use a metal hammer but a small wooden mallet is a reasonable alternative. The copper initially will bend easily but will quickly work harden. After bending the top third of the disc, loosen the vice, rotate the whole assembly and re-tighten to continue bending the plate around its whole circumference. The aim should be to achieve a small but even amount of bend around the perimeter of the plate after each annealing to avoid any buckling. Figure 8 shows the bending achieved in the first session; further forming of the re-annealed disc has just started.

By the end of the fourth session, the flange is forming correctly and this can be seen in Photo 11. Do not get concerned if there is slight unevenness in the flange. Keep re-annealing the metal and gently tapping any parts that are not as far bent as the rest of the flange. Should a serious crease start to form on the perimeter, anneal the copper again and gently tap inside the flange at the appropriate point with the round head of a ball-pein hammer against a steel surface to reduce the distortion. Once the fifth session is complete or when the flange is

Photo 8. The disc had been re-annealed after the first shaping session and the second is just starting.

Photo 10. The fourth session is about to start. The copper is starting to curve to form the flange.

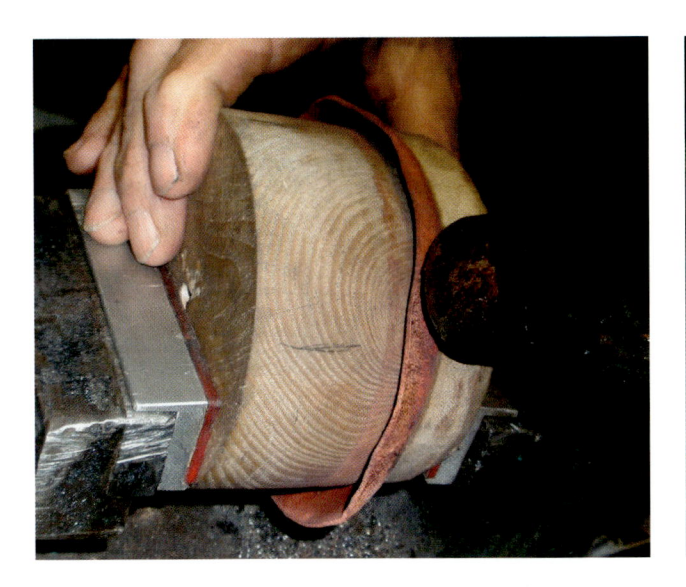

Photo 11. The fifth shaping session is about to start with the flange already developing well. There is no sign of creasing.

Photo 13. The sixth shaping session has the flange and form reversed so the worker has a better view of how close the flange is to the form.

approaching 90° turn the form and flange round so that it easier to see the distance between the flange and the form. This is illustrated in Photo 13. After six or seven sessions of re-annealing and further bending, the flange is completely formed, as shown in Photo 14. The plate can now be removed from the form for checking.

Photo 15 shows a pair of smaller flanged end plates made using similar techniques. This pair is for a 3" horizontal water-tube boiler. In this case, however, the flanges have no centre hole and the form is centred first visually and then, as the flange starts to form, by feel as well.

Exactly the same technique can be used to flange brass sheet for smoke box or oil separator covers. This metal

Photo 14. After the seventh session the flanging is complete and the plate removed from the form.

Photo 12. Should a serious crease start to form, use the round end of a ball-pein hammer to reduce it.

Photo 15. End plates for a horizontal boiler.

Photo 16. A flanged brass smokebox cover showing how it looks after the second session of hammering. It is now ready for further annealing.

Photo 17. The flanged smokebox cover showing how it looks at the end of the last session.

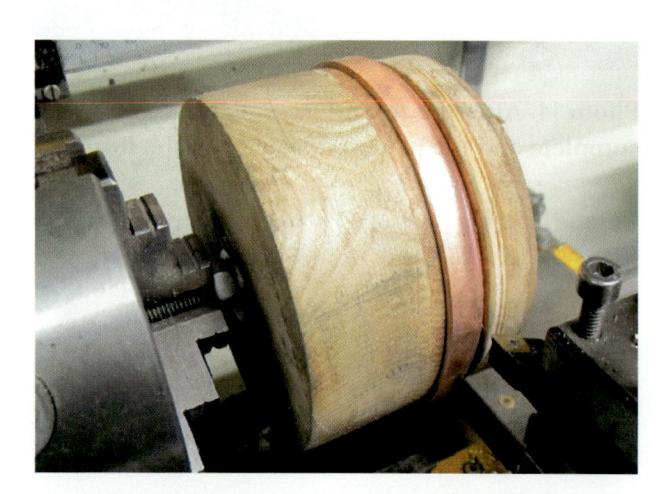

Photo 18. A finished flanged plate is fitted back on the form and its edge turned to size.

Photo 19. Checking that the boiler tube will fit over the flanged plate.

is a little harder than copper but it flanges just as easily with regular annealing.

Once the copper plates are successfully flanged, they will need to have their rims turned so that they fit inside the boiler shell with 0.1 mm to 0.15 mm (0.004" - 0.006") clearance all round for silver soldering. Re-fit the flanged plate to the form and mount in the lathe chuck. The flange can then be turned to the right diameter in the lathe. This is shown in Photo 18 for a tube plate with a centre hole. Turning should continue until the boiler shell just fits over the flange with a slight clearance as illustrated in Photo 19. For horizontal boiler plates other holes may be used as shown in Photo 20. Flanged brass discs should be held in external jaws so the internal side of the flange can be turned to allow the copper boiler tube to fit inside it.

Photo 20. A small flanged plate, screwed to the wooden form, has its flange trimmed to size.

Photo 21. A twist drill designed for use on copper.

DRILLING END PLATES FOR FIRE TUBES

For any tube plate that requires a number of holes to be drilled for the fire tubes, it is well worth investing in a drill designed for use on copper. As Photo 21 shows, this has a centre point and two outer points reminiscent of a wood drill.

The holes for a vertical boiler are on three different radius circles. Cut a wooden disc to fit inside the flanged tube plate from 12 mm chipboard and centre drill 8 mm ($^5/_{16}$"). Mount one flanged plate, with the second one back-to-back, on the wooden form on a rotary table fixed to a milling table ready for drilling. The use of a laser

Photo 23. The set up for drilling the fire-tube holes in a pair of tube plates for a vertical boiler.

centre finder helps to position the rotary table exactly under the centre of the head of the milling machine; adjustments being made with the X and Y axes handles. The bolt screwed into the centre of the rotary table has its head centre-drilled in the lathe in a 3-jaw chuck. Bolt down the tube plates and set the rotary table at zero degrees, lock it and, using the milling table to locate it accurately, drill the first hole right through both plates. Photo 23 shows a scrap length of fire tube though this hole and a second hole as added security. Unlock the rotary table and rotate to the required angle, re-lock and drill the remaining holes on that diameter. Move the milling-machine table to a new radius and drill the next set of holes. Continue drilling all holes, including the three small ones for the spacer-tube rods, but not the two for steam and safety valves. Carefully remove the top plate, re-tighten the bottom one in the same angular position and drill the final two holes. Their positions are indicated in red in Chapter 6 Tables 2, 3 and 4.

Photo 22. Using a laser centre finder on a rotary table mounted on a milling machine. The bolt in the rotary table was centre marked in a lathe.

Photo 24. A pair of plates with all the fire-tube holes drilled.

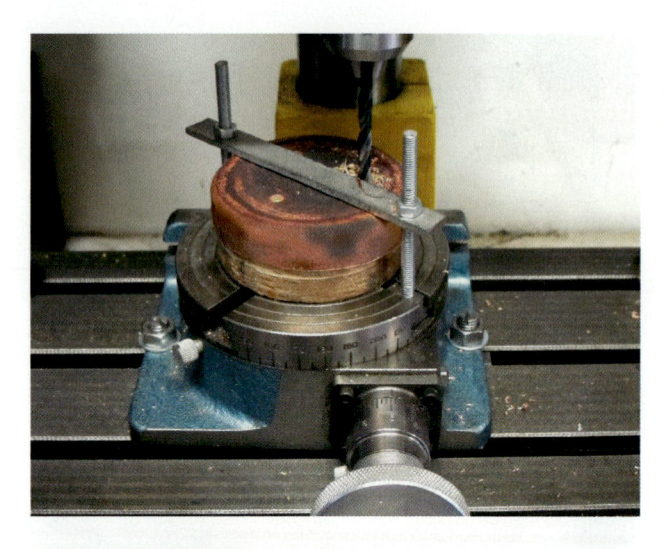

Photo 25. Drilling one clamped end plate for the 3" horizontal boiler.

For those without a milling machine, a vertical drilling machine can do the job, although changing the radius will have to be done manually.

DRILLING END PLATES FOR STAYS AND FITTINGS

The 3" horizontal water-tube boiler requires both the flanged end plates to be drilled for three stays. One of the end plates also needs three further holes for the threaded bushes for the water gauge and a clack valve.

The flanged copper discs should be mounted in turn on a rotary table, with their wooden form inside, and held in place with a steel strip over the top. Aim a laser mounted in the chuck at the edge of the disk, which is rotated to ensure that it is correctly centred. Move the milling table the distance from the edge of the plate to the required radius for the stays and then remove the laser from the chuck.

Drill three holes for the stays at 120° intervals at this radius. Then, on one end plate only, drill the one $^5/_{16}$" (8 mm) and two $^3/_8$" (9.5 mm) holes for the three threaded bushes. The setup is shown in Photo 25. Then screw

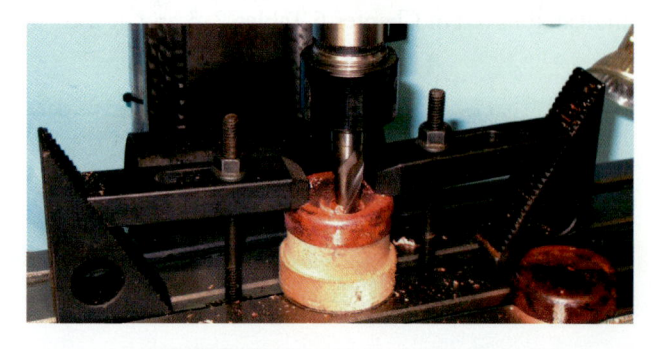

Photo 26. Cutting the flue hole in the end plate of the 54 mm boiler with a 15 mm slot mill.

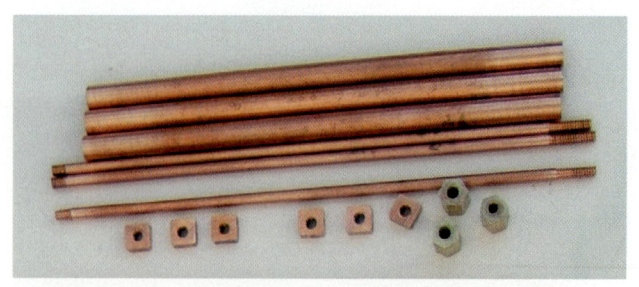

Photo 27. A set of threaded rods, spacer tubes, square copper nuts and three brass spacer nuts.

each flanged plate to the form and hold with outside jaws in a 3-jaw chuck to trim the flanges to size.

DRILLING END PLATES FOR FLUES

Two horizontal boilers, the 54 mm and 42 mm, need holes to accommodate their flue tubes.

Having formed the flanged end plates, now cut a hole of the appropriate size in the right place to fit the flue tube. Mark its position on the plate with the perimeter of the hole 5 mm ($^3/_{16}$") in from the edge of the flange along a radius.

In turn mount each flanged plate on its wooden form and clamp it to the milling-machine table, as shown in Photo 26. Carefully cut the flue hole with a 15 mm slot mill. For those who prefer, there is no reason why the 15 mm holes cannot be drilled but that requires a 15 mm drill, preferably suitable for use on copper, whereas a 15 mm slot drill is a fairly standard item and more likely to be found in the average workshop.

STAYS AND SPACERS

The boilers with fire tubes do not require any further stays as the tubes themselves act in this role. The same is true of the flues of the 54 mm and 42 mm boilers. The 3" horizontal boiler is the only one where stays are essential and these are made from $^3/_{16}$" (5 mm) bronze rod that is threaded at each end and fitted with circular threaded nuts; circular rather than hexagonal as they look better when the boiler is finished. The stays fit inside lengths of $^5/_{16}$" (8 mm) copper tube that act as spacers for the end plates when building and soldering the boiler.

To simplify assembly of the boilers for silver soldering in a single session with a single-melting-point solder, all the fire-tube boilers use thin copper spacing tubes $^3/_{16}$" (5 mm) x 22 gauge with $^1/_8$" (3 mm) rods threaded 6BA or M3 at the end and held in place with home-made copper or bronze nuts. These are not a part of the structural strength of the boiler and thus their size is not inherently important.

Photo 28. Threaded bronze stays, nuts and copper spacer tubes for a horizontal boiler.

FLUES AND FIRE TUBES

The flues on the two smallest horizontal boilers are lengths of 15 mm diameter 0.7 mm (22 gauge) EN 1057 - Type X copper pipe used for plumbing. All the fire and water tubes for the other boilers are made from 8 mm ($^5/_{16}$") 20 gauge copper tube.

FLUES

The flues are lengths of 15 mm copper pipe, which run the length of the boiler and contain the burner flame. Each flue has two copper olives fitted to space the flanged end plates correctly so their outside edges are the right distance apart. Fit the first olive in place by using a straight plumbing compression fitting to squeeze it firmly in place. However, before trying to fit the second olive, the nut on the compression joint must be partially sawed through so that once the second fitting is firmly in place, the rest of the nut can be carefully sawed through and removed. Photo 29 shows the component parts and a flue with one olive fitted near each end.

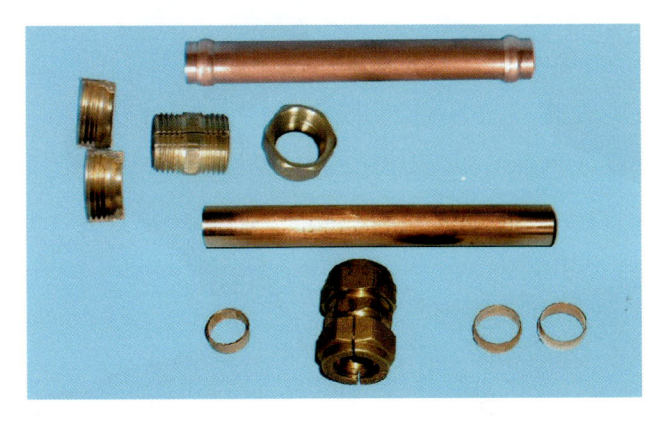

Photo 29. Above, the flue tube with olives fitted and one split and one normal compression nut. Below, the flue tube, spacer ring, compression fitting with partly sawn-through nut and two olives.

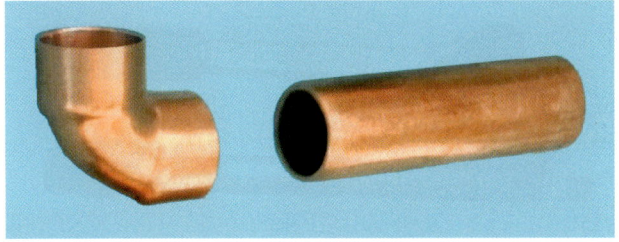

Photo 30. The elbow and 15 mm tube used to connects the flue to the funnel of the 54 mm boiler.

These boilers use an additional short length of 15 mm tube and an elbow to connect the flue to the chimney. However, these parts are installed after the boiler has been pressure tested. They are held in place with ceramic high-temperature caulking, sealant and adhesive rather than being silver soldered.

FIRE TUBES

The fire tubes needs to be slightly longer than the distance between the tube plates so that they can be safely silver soldered in place. They also need to be flared out at one end. This is readily done by holding the tube vertically on a piece of wood and gently hammering a fixed lathe centre into the hole at its top with a copper hammer until it is splayed out sufficiently not to pass through the holes in the tube plate. Fortunately, copper tube is normally soft enough for this to be done without annealing the tube. No damage will be done to the lathe centre as it is hardened steel working relatively soft copper with the copper end of a hide-faced hammer. The alternative is to use a small commercial flaring tool.

Photo 31. A fixed lathe centre may be used to flare one end of the tube.

Photo 32. A set of 8 mm ($^5/_{16}$") fire tubes, each with one end splayed.

22 MATERIAL AND PARTS

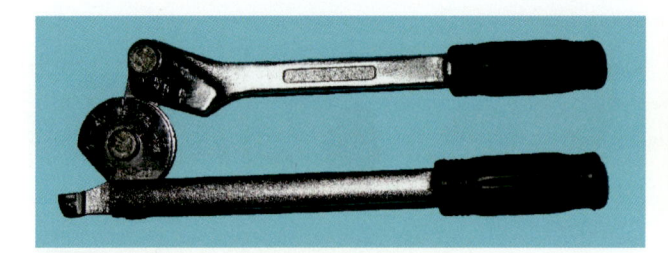

Photo 33. This HBM $^5/_{16}$" (8 mm) tube bender is an inexpensive tool to acquire.

WATER TUBES

The water tubes fitted beneath the shell of the 3" horizontal boiler are made from 8 mm ($^5/_{16}$") tube. They

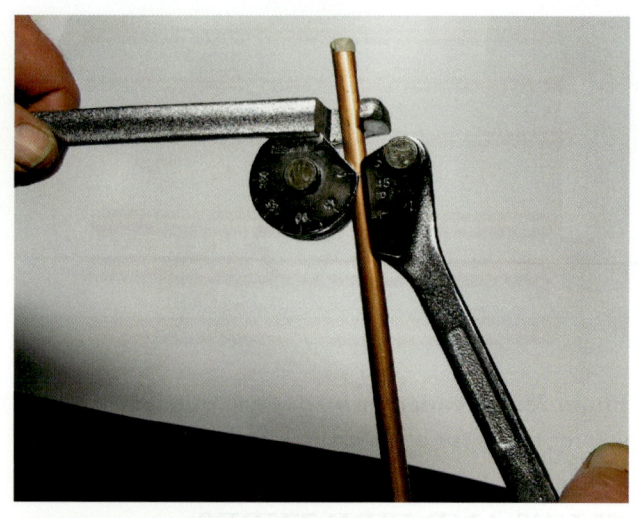

Photo 35. A copper water tube ready for making the first bend.

do, however, need bending to the right shape. A simple proprietary pipe bender, such as the one in Photo 33, is very economically priced and will suffice. Larger, more flexible and more expensive tube benders can also be used to do the job.

Cut three lengths of tube 9" (230 mm) long. Before bending the tubes, fill them with fine dry (bird) sand so that the tube does not flatten or kink when it is bent. Seal one end with a small piece of masking tape. Roll a small funnel from paper and tape it to the other end. Pour sand into the funnel and tap the tube until it is

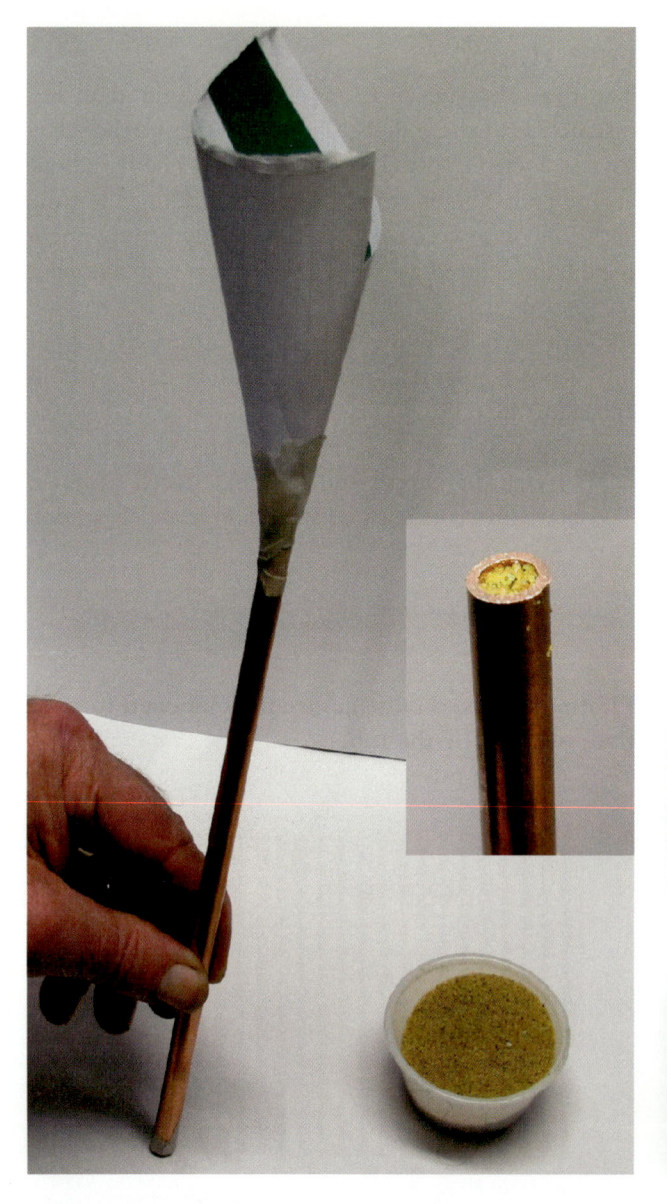

Photo 34. A copper water tube ready to be filled with sand and, inset, full of sand.

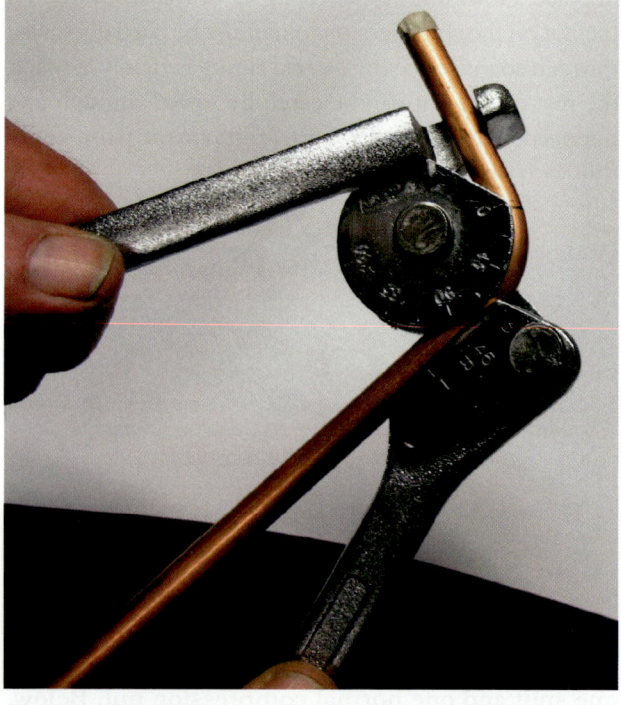

Photo 36. The first bend in the tube of 80° is just about complete.

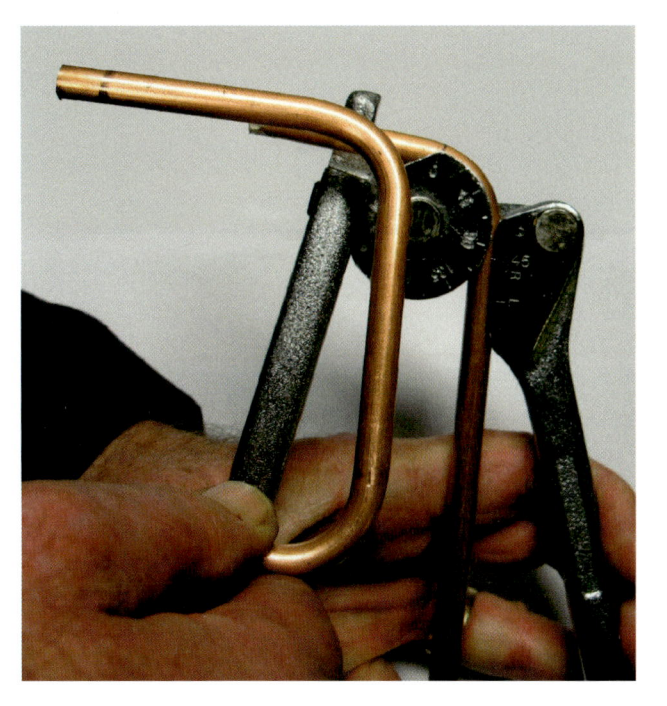

Photo 37. Comparing the bend angle of the first tube with the second one.

full. Remove the paper funnel and tape over the top end. Make a pair of pencil marks 2" (54 mm) and 5⁷/₈" (149 mm) from one end. Then, with the first mark against the zero reference on the tool, bend the tube through 80°. As Photo 37 shows, it is important to compare the bend angles on all the tubes to ensure they are the same. Then move the tube to the second mark and, ensuring the second bend will be parallel to the first one, make

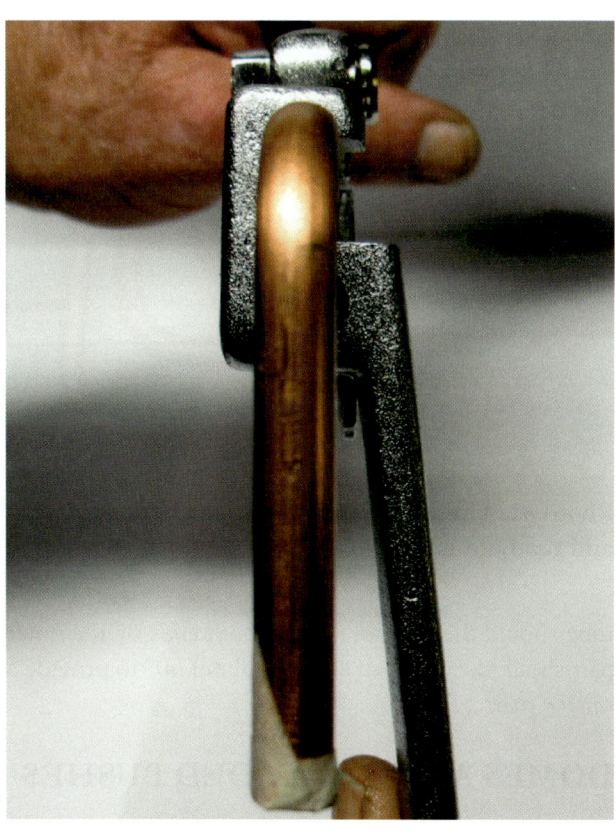

Photo 39. Before making the second bend, ensure the first bend is parallel to the side of bender.

the second bend through 100°. With care, three identical water tubes will result with 4" (102 mm) between the centres of the verticals. Take care to get the bends in exactly the right places, the correct angles and that the bent ends are in line. Empty the tubes of sand and cut their ends to length, noting that the outer tubes have longer ends than the centre one. The ends of the centre

Photo 38. The tube has been moved up ready for the second bend.

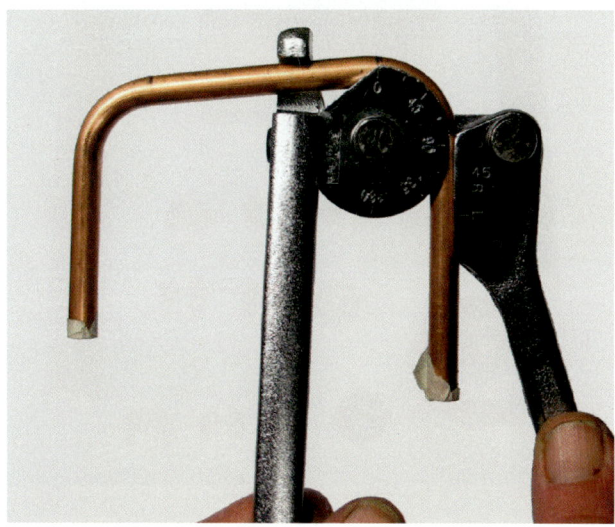

Photo 40. Making the second bend in the tube of 100°.

24 MATERIAL AND PARTS

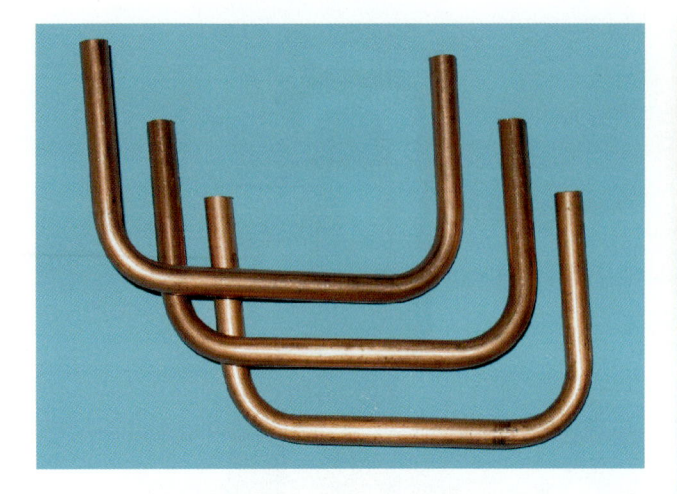

Photo 41. Three copper water tubes bent to shape and ready to be cut to length.

tube should then be cut square. Both ends of the outer pair should be cut at an angle of about 30° to provide a mirror pair.

DOMES AND THREADED BUSHES

Several horizontal boilers need steam domes or similar parts for housing the safety valve. These, and any bush silver soldered into a boiler, must be made from one of the bronzes, of which gunmetal is very popular. Either round or hexagonal bar of the required diameter is readily available. Making threaded bushes is a straightforward turning and drilling job, followed by tapping to cut the desired thread to hold the fitting; usually $^3/_{16}$", $^1/_4$" or $^5/_{16}$". Alternatively, ready-made bushes can be purchased.

Photo 42. Bronze bars with steam domes and threaded bushes made from them. The hexagonal rod will be used for steam outlets.

Photo 43. Above, twisted galvanised wire holding threaded bushes in place for soldering. Below an alternative of two thin home-made jubilee clips.

Never use brass for bushes or steam domes as this metal will deteriorate as the zinc leaches out with continued boiling and will eventually cause the boiler to fail.

RETAINING BRONZE PARTS IN PLACE

To hold threaded bushes and steam domes when soldering them in place, use thin galvanised steel wire with the ends twisted to hold the bushes in place. As an alternative use thin home-made jubilee clips. These involve measured lengths of thin steel strip; bending and drilling holes in the ends. In both cases, make sure all the components are held firmly in place after they have been fluxed.

PICKLES

Before a boiler is silver soldered, its parts need to be thoroughly cleaned. The same is true after the soldering has been completed. This cleaning process is best done in a dilute-acid pickle in a well-ventilated area. The safest approach is to use a 3% solution of citric acid. This is available in powdered form from many chemists and wine-making shops. It readily dissolves in water.

An alternative and a faster-acting pickle is dilute sulphuric acid, which some modellers carefully obtain from old car or leisure batteries. Unfortunately, its speedier cleaning action also makes it more dangerous to use. Common sense is needed in its handling as it will slowly burn flesh and clothing. It should be safely stored in a plastic container with a screw-top lid, preferably a child-proof one. In both cases, a plastic box into which the boiler will fit, is an ideal container for the cleaning

BUILDING SMALL BOILERS

Photo 44. An old ice-cream container being used to pickle; left a boiler shell and tube plates, right a 3" horizontal boiler after silver soldering.

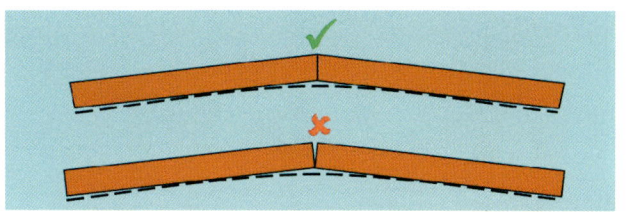

Drawing 1. Planks should have their edges slightly chamfered to fit the curve of the boiler.

process. Photo 44 show a 2 litre ice-cream container that is suitable for all the boilers described in this book.

CLADDING AND BANDING

Lagging a boiler, after it has been hydraulically tested, will help to minimise heat loss and to improve its looks.

Hardwood planks are popular for lagging, glued in place and fitted with brass boiler-bands. Many model and craft shops sell 1.5 mm ($^1/_{16}$") thick sheets of mahogany and teak which are 36" x 3" or their metric equivalents 1,000 x 75 mm. The wood should be cut into planks about 6 mm (¼") wide using a bandsaw, a plank cutter or a craft knife and a steel ruler. Some shops sell pre-cut narrow planks but these tend to be more expensive. Clean up the edges with fine sandpaper and then slightly chamfer them to fit the curve of the boiler, as shown in Drawing 1.

Start by cutting the first plank to length and checking its fit. Place a thin line of glue on the copper boiler, preferably a gel variant that is easier to control, and then press the plank firmly down. Repeat for each plank. Use sandpaper bent over a length of appropriately sized rod to make curved areas to fit around any threaded bushes or other parts soldered to the boiler shell. When all the planks have been fitted to the boiler, they need sanding to give a smooth finish before painting with three coats of varnish. Lightly sand between coats. An eggshell finish will give a more realistic finish than a glossy varnish. Photo 45 shows a 108 mm boiler being planked and also the tools used, including a razor saw, craft knife, sanding tool and lengths of different diameter brass tube.

Photo 45. Planks of mahogany, cut to width on a bandsaw, being fitted to a boiler shell. Tools used include a cutting board, scalpel and razor saw, a sanding tool and sandpaper that can be wrapped around different diameters of tube and a bottle of gel superglue.

Photo 46. Mahogany planking is attractive. Top, a boiler band with ends folded at 90° and clearance holes for the bolt. Below, blocks soldered to the bands; one drilled clearance and the other tapped.

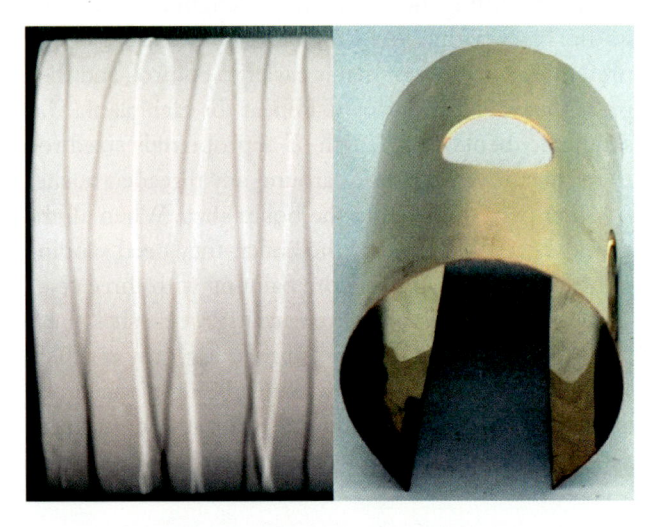

Photo 47. Left, a PTFE-wrapped locomotive boiler prior to fitting the brass cladding, right.

Boiler-banding brass strip 6 mm (¼") wide and 20 gauge (0.9 mm) is normally fitted over the planks or cladding. Carefully measure the length around the boiler and then add an additional ¾" (19 mm) to allow a ¼"

Photo 48. Insulation cut to size to fit one side of a 3" horizontal boiler firebox.

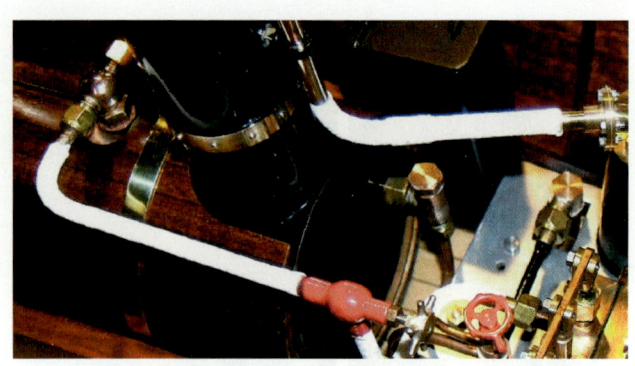

Photo 49. Nicely lagged steam and exhaust pipes.

(6 mm) flap to be bent up at each end with a little to spare. Drill clearance hole 8BA or 2 mm centrally in the ends so that the bands can be held in place with brass nuts and bolts. The alternative is to silver solder a ½" (12.5 mm) length of ¼" (6 mm) square brass rod, centre drilled and tapped 8BA or 2 mm to a correctly cut length of banding. Then cut the brass rod in half and drill one of the existing holes to clear a bolt. Chapter 2 Page 41 shows how this is done.

The two smaller boilers may be fitted into steam locomotives, in which case, cladding of brass sheet may be preferred to planking. If so, the boiler can be wrapped with PTFE tape under the cladding.

High temperature ceramic matting 6 mm (¼") thick is an excellent material for insulating the firebox of horizontal boilers and it is used on the 3" water-tube boiler. It is readily cut to size and shape with scissors and fitted between the twin brass walls of the firebox.

As well as heat emitted by the boiler, heat is also lost from copper steam pipes. These too should be lagged. Bind string tidily around the pipe, holding it in place with cyano superglue. Then paint the string with several coats of matt white enamel to simulate the look of asbestos that was used to lag full-size pipes in the steam-engine era.

SMOKE BOXES

Smoke-box covers for vertical boilers can be made from flanged copper on the same form and the same size as the tube plates. Alternatively, the cover can fit outside the boiler shell and be made from brass or copper. This will require a second and slightly larger form, though if the cover is made first, the form can then be turned down slightly in size to make the tube plates. The big advantage of an external smoke-box cover is that it also forms a solid edge for any planking fitted around the boiler. The covers on all the vertical boilers are held in place by the steam outlet nuts.

BUILDING SMALL BOILERS 27

Photo 50. A painted copper smokebox cover that fits inside the boiler shell.

Photo 52. The 108 mm vertical boiler smokebox cover. Its chimney mount is silver soldered in place.

Photo 51 shows a brass smoke-box cover for a 108 mm boiler, which has just had a centre hole cut out with a 2 mm ($^5/_{64}$") slot drill. The flanged cover has been fitted to the form that has had insulating tape wrapped round the lower part of the form until it is the same diameter as the cover. The cover is held in place on the form with a large jubilee clip. A zinc-plated clip 90 - 120 mm (3½" - 4¾") is ideal for the larger boilers, while one 85 - 100 mm (3¼" - 4") is useful for the smaller ones. However, if the finished cover will have other holes in it, drill these first and then screw the cover to its form for milling. Then mount the cover screwed to its form in the lathe and trim its outside edge. Silver solder in place a tapered chimney mount, made of brass or bronze, to support the chimney and allows its easy removal.

For the two smallest horizontal boilers, a 15 mm elbow and short length of 15 mm copper pipe connect the flue to the chimney and are held in place with ceramic adhesive. The brass smoke-box cover, a disc of 16 gauge brass, is formed in a simple steel two-part forming tool.

Photo 51. Left, the centre section of a smoke box flanged brass plate has been removed by milling prior to drilling small holes where the steam pipes will pass though. The plate is held in place by a large jubilee clip. Right, finishing the rim of the smokebox cover, which has been attached to the wooden disc via the two holes drilled in the cover.

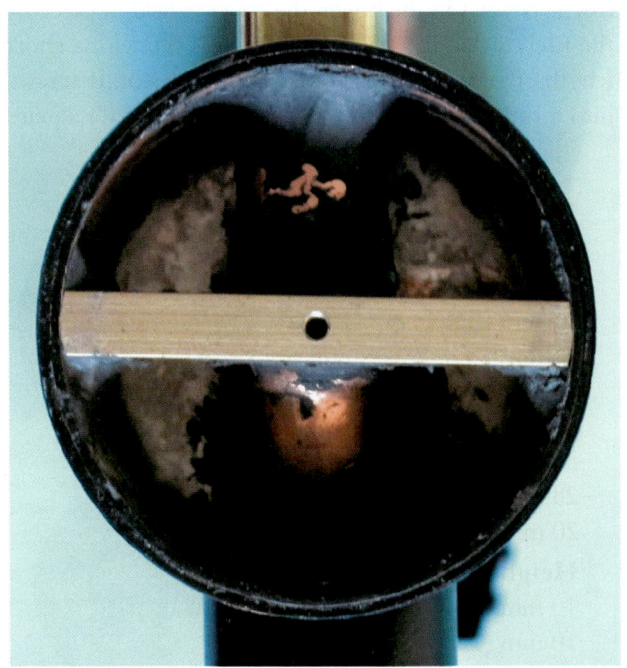

Photo 53. The 54 mm horizontal boiler smokebox showing the brass strip for mounting the cover. The parts are held in place with ceramic adhesive.

28 MATERIAL AND PARTS

Photo 54. The form tool used to shape the brass smoke-box cover for the 54 mm horizontal boiler, the retaining handles and the cover.

Photo 55. Trimming the formed smoke-box cover for one of the small horizontal boilers.

This is carefully turned in the lathe from two short lengths of round steel bar to give the right profile. Place the annealed brass plate inside the female form, fit the male part inside female form and press the two parts of the form together in a vice to produce the curved centre portion and the line of the smoke-box door. This will replicate the front of a locomotive smoke box. After forming, the cover has a small hole drilled through its centre. It is then turned down to the boiler diameter. It may either be screwed to or held in place with a live centre on a wooden form, recessed to match the curve of the cover. On the boiler, the cover is held in place by the firebox handle. This is a threaded bolt, with a short length of brass wire silver soldered in its slot. It screws into a drilled and tapped length of 6 mm (¼") square brass fixed to the sides of the smoke box. The other handle is a nut, also with wire soldered to it.

FIREBOXES

The firebox for the 108 mm vertical boiler is a separate item that bolts onto the bottom of the boiler shell and is shown in Photo 56. The brass top of the firebox has a much larger hole than the smoke-box cover. This is cut out with a small slot mill and silver soldered to the copper firebox. The removed portion of brass may well be suitable for making an oil-separator cover.

The firebox has a series of air holes drilled around it as well as a cut-out for the burner nozzle. The other two

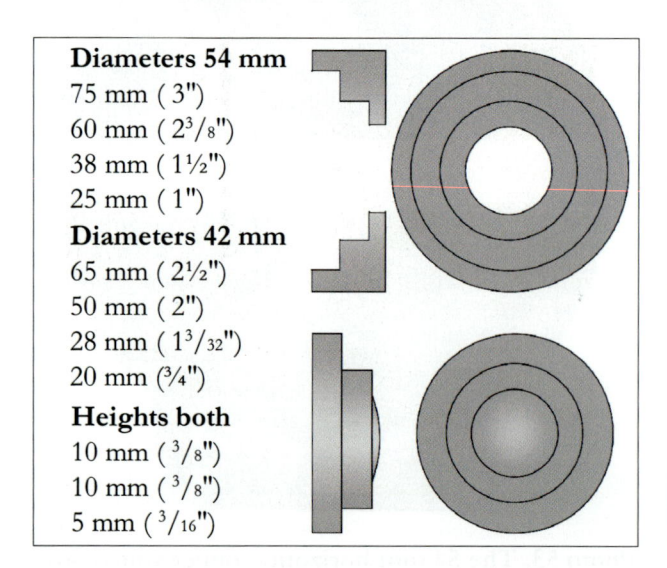

Diameters 54 mm
75 mm (3")
60 mm (2³⁄₈")
38 mm (1½")
25 mm (1")
Diameters 42 mm
65 mm (2½")
50 mm (2")
28 mm (1³⁄₃₂")
20 mm (¾")
Heights both
10 mm (³⁄₈")
10 mm (³⁄₈")
5 mm (³⁄₁₆")

Drawing 2. Form tool dimensions for the 54 mm and 42 mm horizontal-boiler smoke-box covers.

Photo 56. The separate firebox of the 108 mm boiler has 11 air holes and a slot for the burner nozzle.

Photo 57. The inside of a vertical boiler firebox showing the fire tubes, air holes and cut out for the burner nozzle.

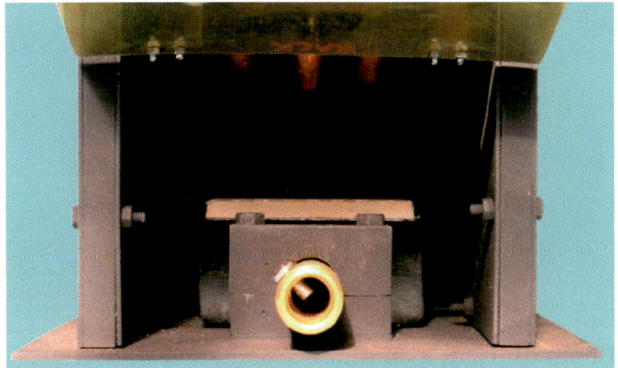

Photo 59. The 3" horizontal boiler firebox with the door open showing the ceramic burner.

vertical boilers have very similar fireboxes but these are an integral part of the boiler shell. Both types of firebox need to be mounted on a baseplate to hold the ceramic burner used in these vertical boilers and several types are shown at the end of Chapter 6.

The firebox and the smoke box for the 3" (76 mm) horizontal boiler form a single structure, which is made from 20 gauge brass sheet and brass strip. Although mild steel could be used, brass makes it easier to cut the pieces to size and bend them accurately to shape. A vice-mounted bending tool was used to form the various parts and Photo 58 shows the bender forming the tabs on the small front piece of the combined firebox/smoke box. The side walls of the firebox are double skinned with a layer of ¼" (6 mm) ceramic insulation cut to fit between the pair of plates. The brass plates and strips are all drilled and bolted together with 8BA or M2 nuts and bolts. Suitably sized hinges are needed for the fire door as well as a chimney mount for the top of the smoke box. Construction details are given in Chapter 7.

Neither of the two smallest boilers have a separate firebox as the burner feeds directly into an internal flue that runs almost the complete length of the boiler.

CHIMNEYS

The tube for a chimney for any boiler can be made of thin-wall brass, copper or stainless-steel tube. It may also be turned to shape from a length of brass or bronze. It can be adorned with a splayed out top of a different metal; bronze, copper or brass.

On vertical boilers the chimney should be readily removable to allow the burner to be lit from the top of

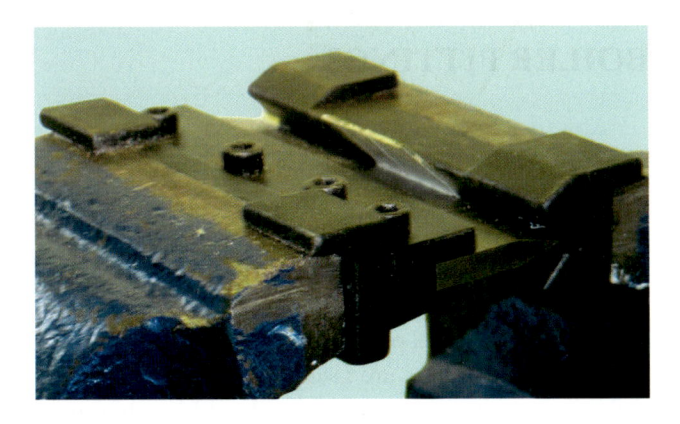

Photo 58. A Warco vice brake being used to form a tab on a piece of brass sheet.

Photo 60. Four chimneys; from the left one with a turned bronze tapered top silver soldered to brass pipe, a smaller brass one with a flared copper top made from a short length of central-heating pipe, a plain stainless steel one and a turned bronze one.

30 MATERIAL AND PARTS

Photo 61. Left, a chimney mount, and right a chimney top, both turned from bronze.

the boiler. These chimneys should be a push fit into a bronze or brass mount.

For horizontal boilers, it may be preferable to have the chimney removable but this is rarely essential. The 3" horizontal boiler has a stainless-steel chimney that is a push fit into a brass mount on the smoke box. Both the smallest two horizontal boilers have a chimney turned from bronze with its bottom fly cut. As an alternative for the 54 mm boiler, a short length of annealed thin-wall brass tube can have its top splayed out and the bottom curved before it is secured to a length of 15 mm copper tube sticking out of the smoke box. The 42 mm boiler has its chimney silver soldered to the boiler shell.

BURNERS

Four of the boilers use a ceramic burner powered by a propane/butane mixture. Although not cheap, these burners produce an amazing amount of heat. They are available in a range of sizes of which the circular 2" (51

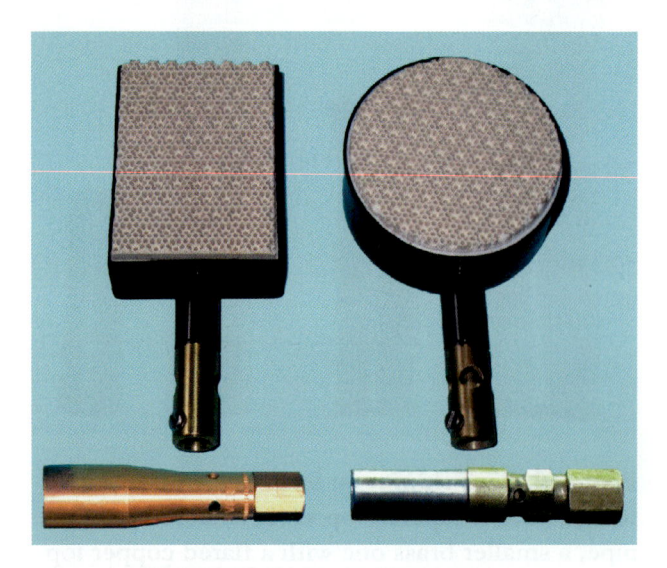

Photo 62. A rectangular and a circular ceramic burner, with two small blow-torch burners.

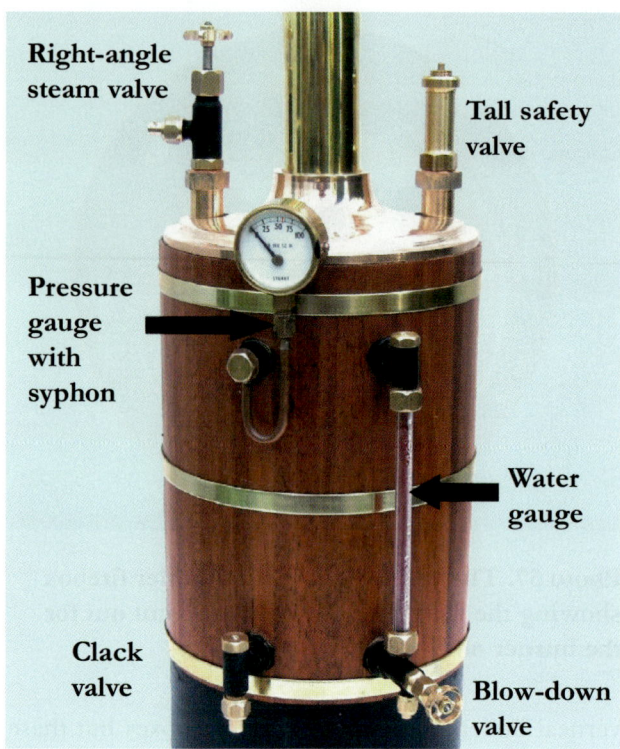

Photo 63. A selection of ready made fittings on a vertical boiler, including a tall safety valve, a 1" (25 mm) pressure gauge and a water gauge.

mm) and 2¾" (70 mm) ones are used for the vertical boilers. A 2¾" x 2" (70 x 51 mm) rectangular one fits the 3" horizontal water-tube boiler. The large round burner uses a No 10 gas jet; other two are fitted with No 8 jets.

The smallest two horizontal boilers use a blow torch; a Sievert 8720 on the larger and a Sievert 8842 for smaller, with a simple modification to its steel casing. It is unscrewed and slightly shortened to spread the flame.

Ceramic burners can be fixed to the boiler baseplate while blow torches need to be held in place at the entrance to the boiler flue. Full details of the burners and their mounts are given in Chapter 5.

BOILER FITTINGS

Very few boiler builders will consider it a worthwhile task to make their own pressure gauges, water gauges, safety valves, steam valves, clack valves or blow-down valves. These parts can all be purchased ready-made. A selection of fittings attached to a boiler are shown in Photo 63. Most model pressure gauges read in psi though ones that read in bars are also available. The diameter and pressure range of the gauge should be chosen to suit the size and pressure rating of the boiler. A water gauge is installed in a pair of threaded bushes. The glass

Photo 64. Three different-thickness copper washers that help seal fittings to threaded bushes.

for the water gauge, which may be clear or with a red line for easier reading, has to be cut to length with care using a resin-bonded cutting disc in a small hand-held electric drill. A decision is needed on whether to fit a gauge with a blow-down valve as well.

Safety valves come in a range of different shapes and sizes. All are adjustable so the blow-off pressure can be set to suit the boiler and the engine it is to power. An accurate valve with the capacity to stop boiler pressure rising more than 10% is essential.

The boiler fittings screw into the threaded bushes and other parts of the boiler with copper washers to provide a seal. The washers come in a range of thicknesses and sizes to fit the item being screwed into a boiler boss and to allow its angular orientation to be set vertical, at an angle or horizontal as needed.

To ensure that the fittings are leak-proof once they are installed, thin strips of PTFE tape may be cut and wrapped around the thread of the fitting. Alternatively, apply Heldite or a similar jointing compound to the thread.

The various fittings are described in much more detail in Chapter 4.

BOILER IDENTIFICATION

Every boiler should have a unique identification. This will typically include the diameter, builder's initials and month and year of completion of construction. This is signified by successful hydraulic test. The details can be punched into the firebox, or a small brass plate, engraved or marked with Letraset and then etched in copper chloride, can be bolted to the firebox. It is essential that

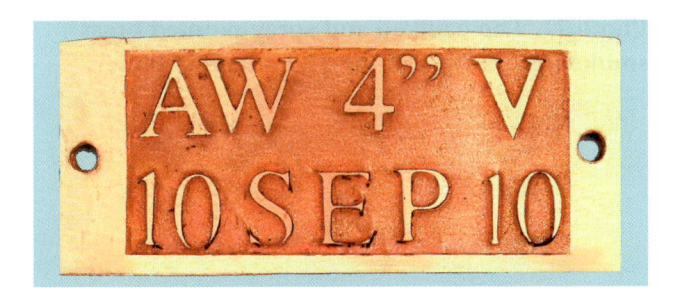

Photo 65. A brass boiler-identification plate etched in brass with ferric chloride.

Photo 66. Two different heat-resistant paints; one for brushing and one for spraying.

the structure of the boiler itself is not compromised when this is done. Photo 65 shows an example of a bolt-on plate for a 4" vertical boiler that had its first hydraulic test on 10 September 2010.

PAINT, VARNISH AND ADHESIVES

Wooden lagging on any boiler needs to be varnished to protect it from the effects of oil and water. Three coats of an exterior-quality varnish, lightly sanded between coats, give the best results. The varnish may either be satin or gloss to choice, though satin will make the wood look more like that of full-size boiler lagging.

The fireboxes of most model boilers and the smoke boxes of some are painted black, so it is important to use a high-temperature paint for this job. Otherwise, the paint will discolour, blister or start melting. Several paints exist for coating wood-burning stoves, fireplaces and barbecues. Most will withstand temperatures up to 600°C and are available in tins though some also come in aerosols. The most widely used colour is matt black and

Photo 67. The wooden lagging has received three coats of varnish. The firebox has been painted with two coats of Blackfriar heat-resistant paint.

32 MATERIAL AND PARTS

Photo 68. The sand-blasted fire box of the 3" horizontal boiler masked and ready to be sprayed with Hammerite barbecue paint.

Photo 70. The brass frame of this version of the 42 mm boiler has been etch primed and painted with matt black enamel.

a spray can or small 125 ml or 250 ml tin will suffice. These can be painted or sprayed directly onto copper. However, brass requires a different approach.

Unfortunately, a heat-resistant acid-etch primer, such as Metcote or SEM, is only heat resistant up to 220°C and is not designed for use on brass. For the brass firebox of the 3" horizontal boiler, the best solution is to mask and then sandblast the surfaces to be painted. As an alternative, cleaning it in an acid pickle will provide a good key for the paint. Etch primer will not survive the high temperatures and should not be tried for fireboxes.

A high-temperature ceramic filler glue, such as Ceramix TC, is needed for the assembly of some of the boilers. It is a black-colour, high-temperature caulking, sealant and adhesive compound that will withstand temperatures up to 1250°C. The boilers that will need to use this sealant are the 108 mm vertical and all three of the horizontal boilers. It is water soluble before it cures.

Brass parts not exposed to high temperatures, like the supporting frame for the two smallest horizontal boilers, may have etch primer sprayed or brushed on them. They can then be coated with normal enamel paint in a colour to suit the builder.

High-temperature paint and ceramic adhesive filler can be obtained from fireplace shops and DIY stores. Etch primer is available from many DIY stores and model railway suppliers.

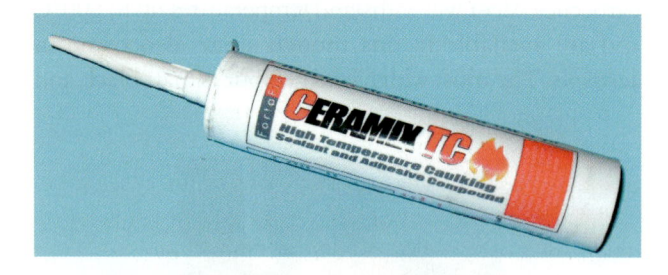

Photo 69. Ceramix is a ceramic high-temperature caulking, sealant and adhesive.

Photo 71. The caulked and spray-painted brass smokebox/firebox on the 3" horizontal boiler.

2: SILVER SOLDERING

The ability to silver solder is an essential skill for boiler making and some readers will already be familiar with the technique. For those who have never tried to silver solder, it is not difficult to become proficient. The essential criteria are:

1. All the materials to be soldered are really clean.
2. The right silver solder and flux are used.
3. There is an adequate, but not an excessive source of heat so the solder can readily melt and flow.

For all the boilers described, a single propane-powered torch with an adequately sized nozzle will suffice to heat the boiler in a suitable hearth. There are other silver soldering tasks involved before steaming a boiler, such as soldering nipples onto copper tube. These are best carried out with a self-contained blowlamp or a small hand-held torch.

The use of an oxy-acetylene torch for silver soldering is not necessary for small boilers. It provides very high temperatures concentrated over a small area that can readily melt small bronze components.

WHAT IS NEEDED

Natural gas, also known as liquefied petroleum gas (LPG) is commonly found in at least five different forms. These are methane, ethane, propane, butane and pentane. Of these, propane alone or a propane and butane mixture are the only ones that are useful for boiler building; the former for gas torches, the latter for small self-contained blowlamps. Both gases are widely available from DIY stores in a range of cylinder sizes.

LPG is dangerous if basic safety precautions are not observed. It is heavier than air and will pool on the ground if there is a leak with the potential to cause an explosion. Therefore it is recommended, for safety reasons, that silver soldering boilers is not carried out in an enclosed workshop but out of doors. Always turn off the gas both at the torch and the gas cylinder after use. Since all LPG is odourless, Mercaptan is added, before the gas is bottled, to give it an unpleasant smell and thus reduce the risk of an undetected leak.

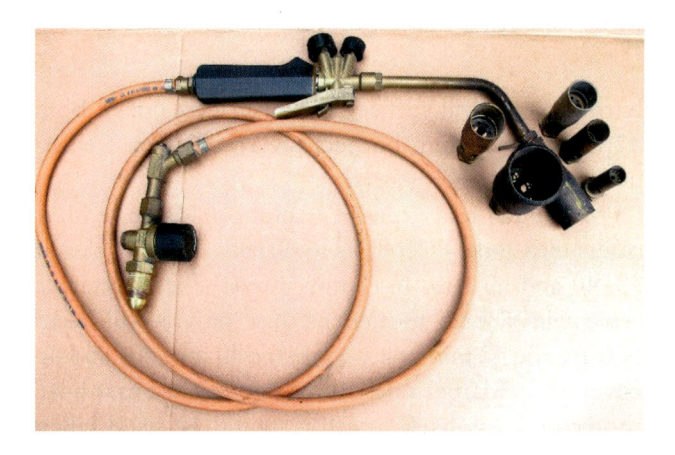

Photo 1. Sievert's economiser gas torch with five spare nozzles, regulator and hose-failure fitting.

GAS TORCHES AND CYLINDERS

A propane-powered gas torch is essential for boiler making as a fair amount of heat is required, even for small boilers. The Sievert range of torches is a market leader and is widely available from model-engineering suppliers like CuP Alloys, Shesto and Reeves 2000 as well as many DIY stores. What is needed is a handle with a regulating valve and preferably an economising valve as well, a bent-neck tube, a selection of burners from 35 mm to 22 mm diameter, a 1 - 4 bar regulator with a hose-failure fitting and 2 metres (6 feet) of hose to connect the torch to a propane cylinder.

The Sievert Pro 88/86 torches are excellent or there is the Sievert PMPX kit, which uses the Pro 86 torch and is a complete solution supplied with 3 metres of hose and a 0.35 - 4 bar adjustable regulator, 3486 Handle, 3511 Neck Tube and a 2941 Burner. It only has a 28 mm

34 SILVER SOLDERING

Photo 2. Machine Mart's gas torch comes with three nozzles and a regulator.

burner, which will suffice for the smallest boiler. Both 32 mm and 35 mm burners are readily fitted when dealing with larger boilers.

For a much less expensive solution, Machine Mart offers the Clarke PC108 gas torch with three nozzles of 25, 40 and 50 mm. A 17 mm nozzle is also available separately. The 25 mm nozzle may provide sufficient heat for the 42 mm boiler while the 40 mm one should cover all the larger ones. In both cases, a burst-hose protector/flash-back arrestor should be used when connecting the torch to the gas cylinder.

The popular size of gas cylinder holds 13 kg of propane when full and is painted red. It can deliver 3.8

Photo 4. The size of propane cylinder needed for silver soldering most of the boilers in this book.

kg per hour at 20°C but only 1.6 kg at 0°C. The half-size cylinder with 6 kg of propane suits smaller burners but is not large enough to continuously run a 28 mm burner.

Propane should always be used for silver soldering a boiler. The pressure of butane tends to reduce much more rapidly as the tank temperature falls near to or below freezing. A mixture of propane and butane is normally used with small portable gas blowlamps like the one illustrated in Photo 3.

When the liquid petroleum gas (LPG) turns from a liquid to a gas, the liquid cools. This reduces the pressure in the container. When larger burners are used for a reasonable length of time, a suitably large container is needed to allow the burner to work at full power

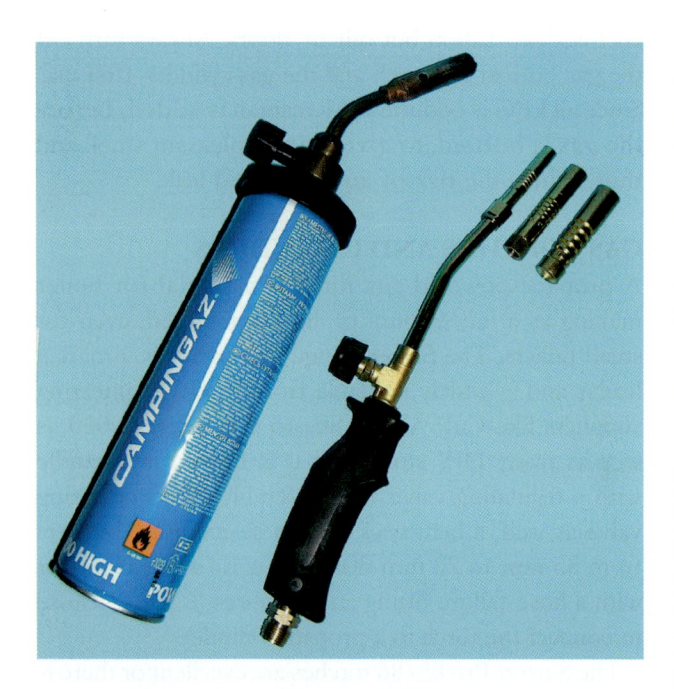

Photo 3. Left, a portable gas blowlamp that runs on a propane/butane mix from an easily replaced cartridge. Right, the small Silverline soldering and brazing torch with 10, 14 and 17 mm nozzles.

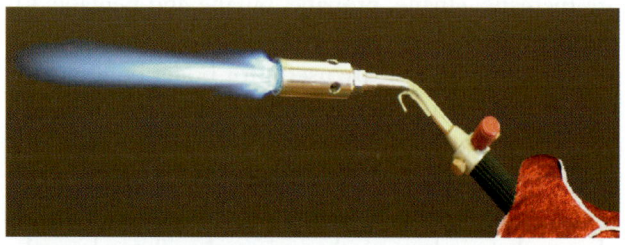

Photo 5. The flame produced by a reasonably sized nozzle will easily silver solder the largest boilers described in Chapters 6 and 7.

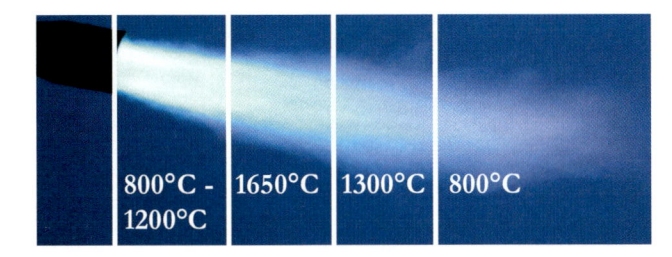

Photo 6. The flame temperature varies. The hottest part is bright-blue coloured.

without the gas pressure falling due to its temperature drop. The table below shows the gas consumption and heat output of burners of different sizes.

Burner diameter	28 mm	32 mm	35 mm
Gas used per hour	0.6 kg	2.0 kg	3.35 kg
Heat output	7.7 kW	26 kW	43.5 kW
Boiler size mm	42	54 - 76	89 - 108
Boiler size inches	$1^{2}/_{3}$	$2^{1}/_{8}$ - 3	$3^{1}/_{2}$ - $4^{1}/_{4}$

For the 42 mm boiler, a 28 mm torch nozzle was used. For the 54 mm and the 3" one, the size was 32 mm and for all the other boilers described in this book, a 35 mm burner was ideal. A 17 or 22 mm nozzle is a useful add-on for smaller silver-soldering tasks.

Domestic DIY blowlamps that come with disposable gas cartridges are not suitable for work on even small boilers as they do not produce sufficient heat. They are still very useful for smaller tasks such as silver soldering nipples onto steam pipes.

Photo 8. A hearth made from three Thermalite blocks, one of which has been sawn in half.

HEARTHS

For brazing the boilers described in this book, a hearth that measures 300 x 150 x 200 mm (12" x 6" x 8") will suffice. There are several alternative ways of making one. Fire bricks or Thermalite blocks can be used to make a hearth. Photo 7 shows a hearth built from an old oil can cut to shape with fire bricks fitted inside. Photo 8 illustrates a hearth made from Thermalite blocks that have been sawed to size. The same can be done with Vermiculite board. Most builder's merchants, DIY stores and fire-place shops offer a range of suitable materials.

PROTECTIVE GAUNTLETS

When dealing with hot boilers, a pair of protective gauntlets is essential. It is all too easy to accidently touch a very hot part of the boiler or hearth. Heat-resistant gloves, which must not have any parts made of plastic, are widely available for use when welding or with barbecues and wood-burning stoves. The best are made

Photo 7. A small hearth made from four fire bricks sitting in an old five gallon (10 litre) tin.

Photo 9. A small hearth from three blocks and one plate of Vermiculite and some insulation.

Photo 10. Removing a hot chimney, with groove-joint pliers, after soldering a flared top onto it. Note the use of protective gauntlets

from heat-resistant leather with a cotton liner and are quite affordable if not already owned.

SOLDERS AND FLUXES

Historically, Easy-flo 2 solder was the modeller's first choice. However, it contained cadmium, a metal that is poisonous if hot fumes from it are inhaled. Effectively, all cadmium-based brazing materials were therefore prohibited from being placed on the market in all EU member states from December 2011. Therefore, Easy-flo 2 is no longer available for sale in the UK. There are, however, several cadmium-free alternatives. They perform well but as they contain a higher percentage of silver they tend to be a bit more expensive.

For the boilers described here, as step soldering is not required, a single type of silver solder is used. One that does not have too high a melting temperature, and which flows well into the joints being made, is preferred. Silver-flo 55 (also referred to as AG103), which has replaced Easy-flo 2, has a melting range of 630 - 660°C. It is certainly the best cadmium-free solution for the boilers described in this book, as it provides good flow and moderately sized fillets. It comprises 55% silver, 21% copper, 22% zinc and 2% tin. Silver solder can be bought as 500 mm (19½") long rods in a range of diameters, of which 1 mm and 1.5 mm (40 and 60 thou) are well suited to small boiler construction. 0.5 mm (20 thou) wire is useful for soldering nipples to copper tube.

Flux is essential if the silver solder is to flow correctly and form an effective joint. Easy-flo flux is ideal for use with Silver-flo 55 solder. It is available as a powder or a ready-mixed paste. Flux not only cleans the surface of the metals being joined, it also protects them to prevent further oxidisation when hot. The flux powder needs to be mixed with water and one drop of washing-up liquid

Photo 12. Easy-flo flux by Johnson Matthey is perfect for use on small boilers.

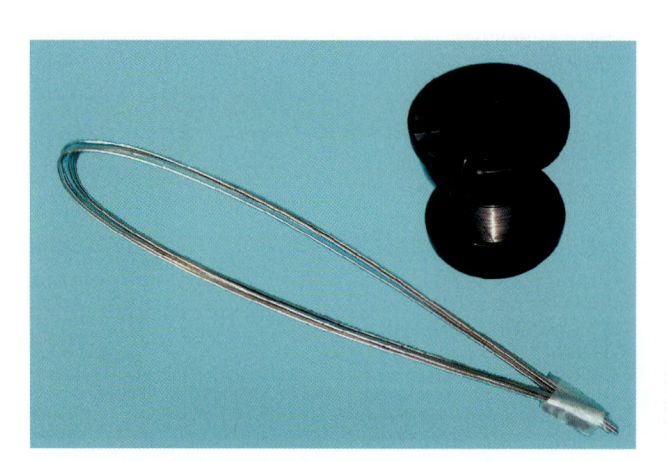

Photo 11. Silver-flo 55 silver solder is ideal for single-step work. It is available as rods or wire.

Photo 13. Cleaning a pair of formed and drilled tube plates prior to assembly for silver soldering.

Photo 14. The fire tube and plate are clean and fluxed ready for soldering.

to form a thick paste, or the ready-made paste can be used. It is best applied with a small clean artist's-type paint brush. The powder adheres well to a warm silver-solder rod allowing additional flux to be transferred to the joint area via the rod.

The flux powder has a working range of 550 - 800°C (575 - 825°C for the paste). It is very fluid at its lower working temperatures providing excellent flux spread. This ensures that the surfaces to be joined are protected early from oxidation. The fluidity of the flux also helps to minimise flux voids and its low viscosity aids its displacement by the silver solder from the joint gap. It is suitable for use with silver-brazing filler metals that melt below 750°C. Both the powder and paste come in 250 g and 500 g packs.

SILVER SOLDERING THE BOILER

There are some key tasks to carry out before soldering a boiler is complete.

PREPARING THE BOILER

Cleanliness is the first essential. All the surface scale, oxides, grease, oil and any other dirt must be removed. This includes finger marks, which are greasy. Any parts, such as flanged plates, which have been heated to anneal them, will first need to be cleaned in pickle and rinsed in clean water. Then scrub these and all other parts with wire wool to ensure they are scrupulously clean.

For silver solder to make good joints, it is essential to have a small gap of around 0.05 - 0.15 mm (0.002" - 0.006"). The solder will flow by capillary action into the joints and will also provide small fillets if the gaps are not too large. The parts should be prepared for soldering by painting the adjoining parts with flux and assembling in the order described in Chapters 6 and 7 for each

Photo 15. A fire-tube boiler ready for soldering with wire holding the threaded bushes in place.

particular boiler. Secure threaded bushes and steam domes with twisted galvanised-steel wire or thin home-made jubilee clips. Rings of silver solder may be placed around the edge of the tube plates, fire tubes or flues as shown in Photo 16. As both the flux and the solder will flow fairly extensively, it is possible to limit the flow, for example around threaded bushes, by coating the surroundings with a thin line of correcting fluid, sold in small bottles with built-in brush, under names such

Photo 16. Rings of solder around the end plate and flue of the 54 mm horizontal boiler.

Vertical boilers should be stood upright in the hearth with the flared ends of the fire tubes at the top so they may be soldered in place before the boiler is turned upside down for access to the other end. Horizontal boilers can also be soldered vertically. For the water-tube boiler, the brass support strips can be held in place with galvanised wire. The water tubes themselves must be secured with a jig as shown in Photo 17. The boiler is also supported on offcuts of Skamolex.

As any boiler will be turned over, the hearth itself needs to be kept relatively clean. Don't forget to check that everything needed for soldering is to hand; silver solder, flux, tongs and heat-resisting gloves. Photo 18 shows blanking plugs in the steam dome to avoid thread damage by overheating. Care is also needed with small bronze components to avoid starting to melt them.

Photo 17. The fluxed 3" horizontal boiler with the brass support strips located with steel cross strips. All the parts are held in place with 1 mm wire and a Scamolex former for the water tubes. Skamolex is an asbestos-free Vermiculite insulation board,

as Tipp-ex and Snopake. The end plates are held in the correct position by the spacers, by the stays or by the flue, depending on the layout of the particular boiler.

THE SOLDERING PROCESS

Make sure there is plenty of gas in the cylinder before starting. For the bigger boilers in this book, a significant amount of heat is needed. Fit the correct size of nozzle to the gas torch, light it and start heating up one end of the boiler. Use the bright-blue part of the flame to give maximum heating. Keep the flame moving across the metal to avoid overheating any particular area. Keep evenly heating the end of the boiler to be soldered until it reaches the solder melting temperature. The flux can act as a temperature guide. It becomes clear or opaque as it approaches the right temperature for soldering. A ring of silver solder placed in the area to be soldered will indicate the right temperature has been reached by melting. If blackening of the flux occurs this can be a sign of insufficient flux or overheating of the flux. Touching a silver solder rod, already warmed in the flame and then dipped in the flux powder, to a joint in the boiler should result in immediate melting and flow around the joint. If it does not, the metal is insufficiently hot. Avoid applying the flame onto the solder rod as its heat will melt the solder even though the boiler is insufficiently hot. It is a good idea to form a ring of silver solder around, for example, a flue tube, fire tubes or an end plate prior to applying the heat.

Silver is expensive and so is silver solder. Yet using too little is a mistake. Each joint needs a small fillet around it. This should happen automatically on small joints such as fire tubes and threaded bushes. However, soldering larger items like the tube plates in place will require a degree of patience, particularly in working right round the inside of the boiler shell while applying most of the heat from the outside. The silver solder will try to flow towards the hottest part of the boiler. If in doubt, remember that using too much silver solder merely wastes a little money. Using an insufficient amount can result in

Photo 18. Using a 32 mm burner nozzle to heat up the 54 mm boiler ready for soldering. Note the rings of solder around the end plate and flue.

Photo 19. Silver soldering the 108 mm firebox onto the brass flanged plate.

a leaking boiler that may take a lot of work to rectify. In addition, the silver solder will not normally show once the boiler is finished. Should any small blob of solder occur, it is easily removed later with a file and emery cloth.

For a vertical boiler, quickly touch each fire-tube joint, checking the solder runs right round. Then repeat this process on the joint between the end plate and the boiler shell before applying silver solder to the top bushes on the side of the boiler. With your hands still protected by heat-proof gloves, remove the heat and quickly turn the boiler over using tongs. Re-apply the heat and repeat the process for the fire tubes, end plate and bushes at the other end.

In the case of a horizontal water-tube boiler, it may be propped up vertically. As Photo 21 shows, this 3" horizontal boiler is stood on strips of Skamolex in a Thermalite block hearth. Start at one end working on the flanged plate, the stay nuts and the threaded bushes. Then deal with that end of the water tubes. Turn over the boiler to work on the other end of the water tubes and the other end plate and stays, as well as the steam dome.

Photo 20. Soldering the top boiler-tube plate of a vertical fire-tube boiler.

Photo 21. Soldering the end plate of a water-tube boiler.

Rectifying leaks

The main reasons for faulty joints are insufficient flux or solder and under-heating or over-heating the parts to be joined. Should one or more silver-soldered joints leak, rectification will be required. First, identify where the leak or leaks occur and mark the position. Next, clean the boiler in an acid pickle and wash in clean water. Flux all the joints, good and bad, and then re-heat and re-solder

Photo 22. The soldered 42 mm boiler sits on a disc of metal with a 25 mm (1") hole for the flue.

Photo 23. How <u>not</u> to silver solder. The torch should not be played on the solder stick. Here, the heat should be applied from outside the shell.

the leaky joints. Note that a higher temperature is needed to re-melt the solder than is required to melt any new solder added to a joint.

CLEANING THE BOILER

Once the silver soldering is complete, and the boiler has cooled down, it will be in a well-annealed state and must be handled carefully to avoid distorting any part of it. Fortunately it will harden to a fair degree over a period of time without any further action being taken.

Any flux residues left at the end of the soldering session are corrosive and must be removed. The residues of Easy-flo flux powder are easily got rid of by soaking in hot water for around half an hour. Any remaining residue can then be brushed off in running water. To

Photo 24. A 108 mm vertical boiler is given a final soak in pickle after silver soldering.

Photo 25. A chimney boss being silver soldered to a smokebox cover.

remove any flux inside the boiler, soak well in acid pickle and then thoroughly rinse.

Once the boiler is clean, inspect the joints to check that they are all well made before any testing starts. It is also well worthwhile running a tap through all the threaded fittings to clean their threads.

OTHER SILVER-SOLDERING TASKS

There are a few other items that do not form part of the boiler shell that also need silver soldering. These include the 108 mm boiler's firebox, its smoke-box cover and its chimney mount. These can be soldered with the gas torch used for the boiler. Smaller items, like the parts attached to the base plates for all the vertical boilers and the oil separator base and top cover need a smaller nozzle or a self-contained gas torch. Some of these are shown being silver soldered in Photos 26 and 27.

BOILER BANDS

Although the two ends of boiler bands can be bent at right angles and drilled for a nut and bolt, a very neat solution is to use a short length of ¼" square brass block

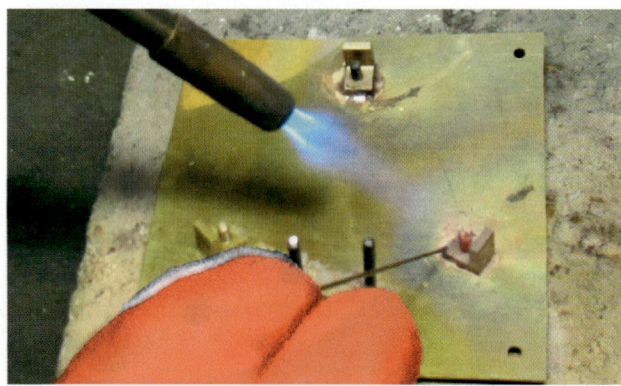

Photo 26. Soldering one of the attachment points on the base plate for the 4" vertical boiler.

BUILDING SMALL BOILERS

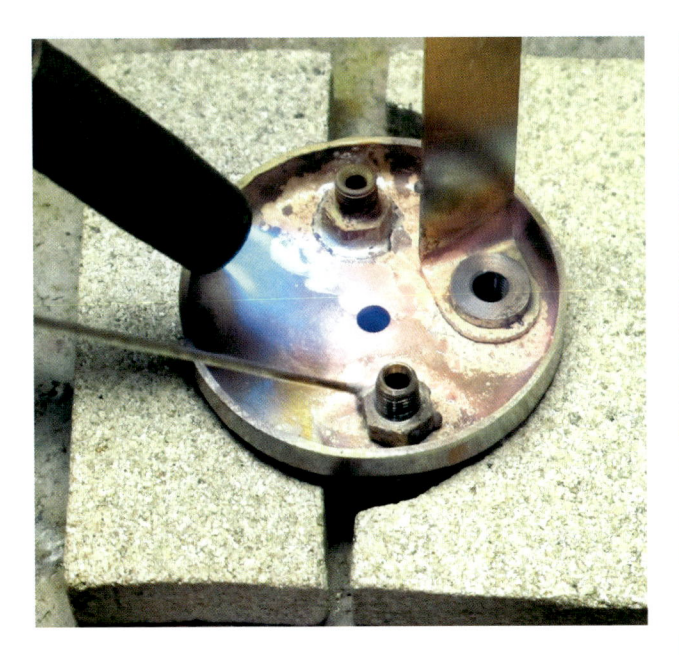

Photo 27. Soldering the fittings to the top cover of an oil separator with a hand-held torch.

½" (12.5 mm) long. This should be centre drilled and tapped 8BA or M2 along its length, and two small V grooves made with a triangular file along what will be the underside.

Drawing 1 shows a jig of Skamolex insulating board, an asbestos-free Vermiculite product, which will hold the parts in position for soldering. The ply and Skamolex are glued together with PVA white glue. The slot for the boiler band is easily filed.

Measure around the planked boiler and cut each band exactly to length. Square the ends and use a G-clamp to hold each end in the slot in the jig, so both ends are touching. Clean the visible ends of the bands for about $^5/_{16}$" (8 mm), flux and, with the under-surface of the block also cleaned and fluxed, clamp it in the jig so it is centred over the join. Heat with a small torch and apply

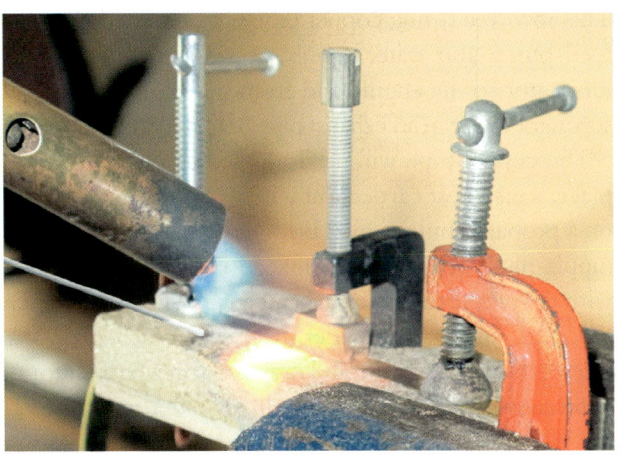

Photo 28. Soldering a brass block onto a boiler band.

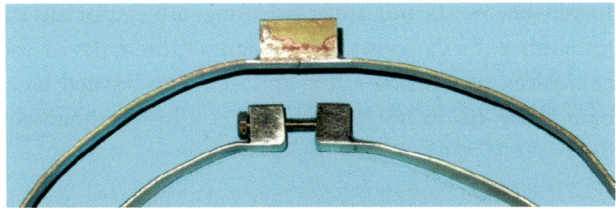

Photo 29. The block before and after cutting.

silver solder to each end. Clean in pickle, carefully hold the block in a vice and saw in half. Clean the sawn ends and camber the underside so it will slide over the planks. Drill one half of the block to clear the joining bolt then polish the block and the outside of the band. Ensure the banding flows in a smooth curve all the ways round, bolt in place on the boiler and tighten to hold the planks in place.

COPPER PIPE AND NIPPLES

Once building and testing the boiler is complete, it is time to connect it to the engine and various other parts.

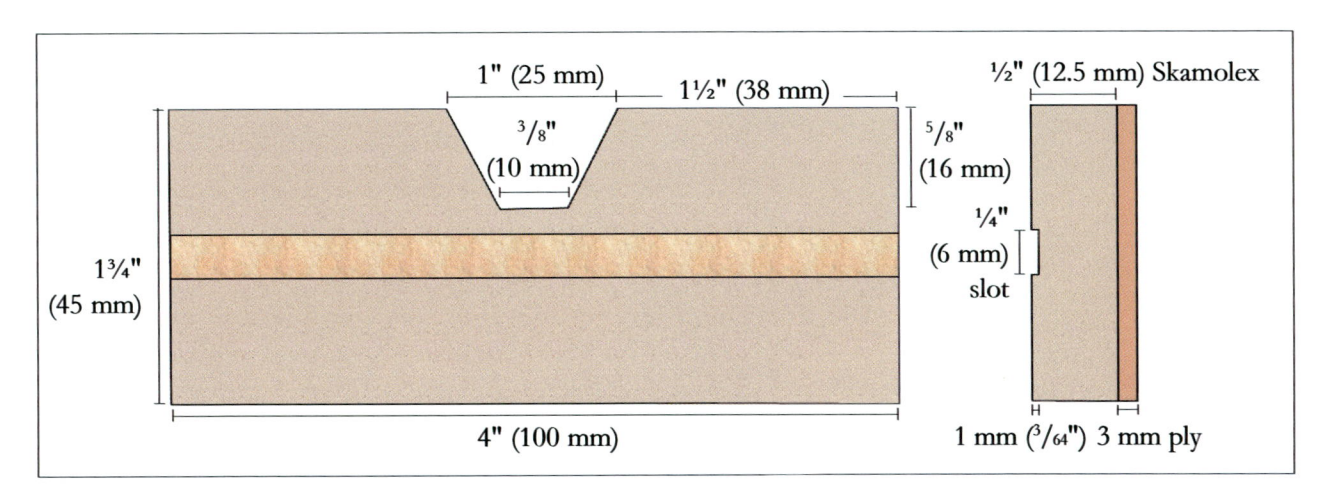

Drawing 1. A jig made of a Skamolex/ply laminate for soldering brass blocks onto boiler bands.

This involves fitting copper pipe between the boiler, its feed pump and water supply, as well as steam via its lubricator to the engine and from the engine via an oil separator either to an exhaust pipe or to the boiler chimney.

The copper pipe will need nipples silver soldering in place; a task best carried out with a hand-held torch run on a propane/butane mix. Both the copper pipe and the nipple must be clean and fluxed. The end of the pipe with the nipple on it is then heated and will rapidly reach red heat when silver solder, if briefly touched on the intersection of the pipe and nipple, form a perfect joint. Alternatively, place a ring of silver-solder wire around the pipe adjacent to the nipple and heat until it melts.

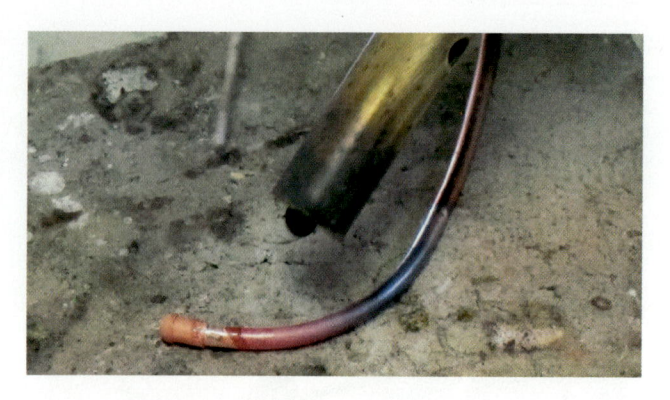

Photo 30. Soldering a nipple onto a length of copper pipe.

SAFETY

Finally before starting silver soldering, it is important to remember the various areas of danger; the risks of an explosion, of causing a fire, and of being burned by a bare flame or on hot metal. LPG is a heavier-than-air gas and a leak of the gas can cause an explosive mixture with air to form. The dangers of causing a fire with a lit burner are obvious. Touching hot boiler parts with bare flesh during silver soldering will cause nasty and painful burns. It is sensible to undertake boiler soldering out of doors, wear protective gloves and to ensure that all valves are tightly closed once the soldering is completed.

3: BOILER TESTING

The UK 'bible' of boiler testing is *The Examination & Testing of Miniature Steam Boilers (Revised Edition 2012)*, known as the Green Book. From 1st January 2013, new rules mean all the boilers in this book need independent testing if they are to be operated in a public place. Boilers under 3 bar/litre capacity must meet the requirements of Section 14; somewhat less extensive than the rules for higher bar/litre-capacity boilers. Model engineering clubs can usually provide their members with access to a qualified independent inspector, who will examine and test the boiler. It is well worth talking to the club inspector ahead of the testing session. The initial hydraulic test is at twice working pressure, without any cladding or fittings on the boiler. If this test is successful further hydraulic testing is recommended every four years, but at only one-and-a-half times the operating pressure.

An additional hydraulic test, at one-and-a-half times working pressure, is required after installing any cladding and the fittings, excluding the safety valve. First of all, the pressure gauge and its red line are checked for accuracy. This is done before the first steam test of the boiler. There is also a visual examination of the fittings and pipe work.

The steam test is carried out immediately after this hydraulic test and then every twelve months. The boiler is steamed with the burner turned up to give its maximum output and sustained for sufficient time to satisfy the inspector that stable conditions have been attained. The safety valve is checked to ensure that it operates at the specified working pressure of the boiler. The correct operation of the water-level gauge is verified, as well as the boiler feed pump if fitted.

On satisfactory completion of the test a Certificate of Examination is issued to the boiler owner. This certificate is essential if the boiler is operated in any public place and is to be covered by the model engineering club's insurance.

INSPECTION

Section 7 of the regulations covers examination of home-built new boilers. Inspectors will assess as much of the boiler as possible, both internally and externally, to determine its general condition and that there is no sign of collapsed fire tubes. Due to the ductility of annealed copper in a new boiler, minor distortion or slight bulging may be acceptable. They will check the materials used are of the correct thickness and specification and that the boiler construction is in accordance with the design in Chapters 6 and 7 of this book. They will also assess soldering procedures to ensure that the joints are sound, with particular attention to the penetration of silver solder. They will inspect threaded bushes to ensure screw threads are not burnt or scorched and the threads of fittings and their mounts are of adequate depth to maintain sufficient strength. The faces of mounts for

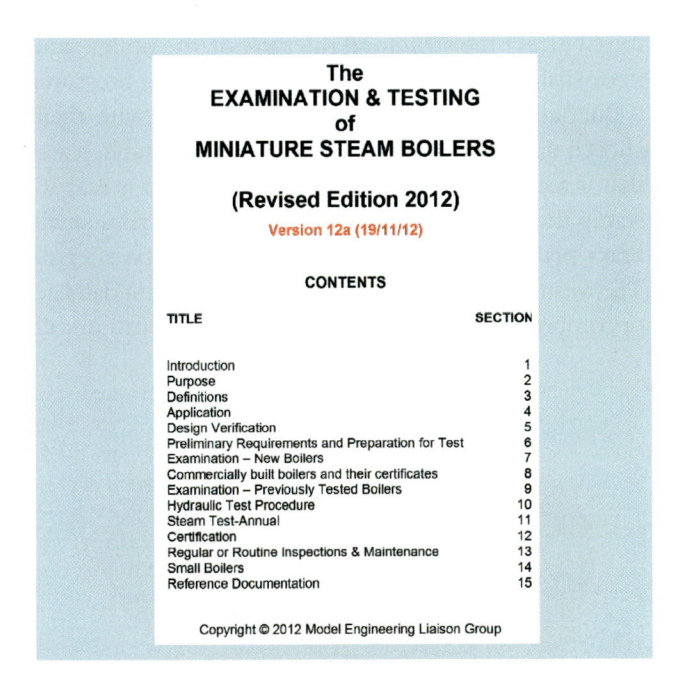

Photo 1. Boiler test rules are contained in *The Examination & Testing of Miniature Steam Boilers*, which can be found on the Internet.

Photo 2. The full hydraulic test to 120 psi (just over 8 bar) on the 108 mm boiler has been paused at 78 psi (just over 5 bar).

water gauges must remain parallel to one another so that no undue pressure is applied to the tube glass on assembly.

TESTING

For hydraulic tests, the builder must have a set of suitable blanking plugs to screw into all but one of the threaded bushes for the various boiler gauges and valves. These provide satisfactory pressure-tight integrity of the boiler shell. Either turn a set from hexagonal brass rod or purchase them ready made. The plugs should be fitted with a copper washer, where necessary some PTFE tape, and tightened to ensure that they do not leak. This is done after a satisfactory visual inspection of the boiler. It can then safely be subject to a hydraulic shell test. The applied pressure is twice working pressure for the initial hydraulic shell test and one-and-a-half times working pressure for all repeat tests. The pressure is applied gradually and increased in steps of not more than 10% once it exceeds the working pressure. The test pressure must hold for as long as necessary to allow thorough examination of the whole boiler for signs of distortion, damage or leakage and evidence of joint failure. The boiler test will last at least ten minutes at full test pressure. Any modifications or repairs, which might affect the structural integrity of the boiler, will necessitate repeating this test at twice working pressure.

Builders must indelibly mark their boiler with their chosen unique identification number in a suitable place that is readily visible on the installed boiler. It is easy to stamp the owner's marking on the firebox or fix a small brass plate to it. This number must never be altered. The form and position of the marking must not damage or compromise the boiler structure. All certification will

Photo 3. This boiler plate shows the name, the test and working pressure as well as the date.

Photo 4. A boiler identification plate with the date of initial testing.

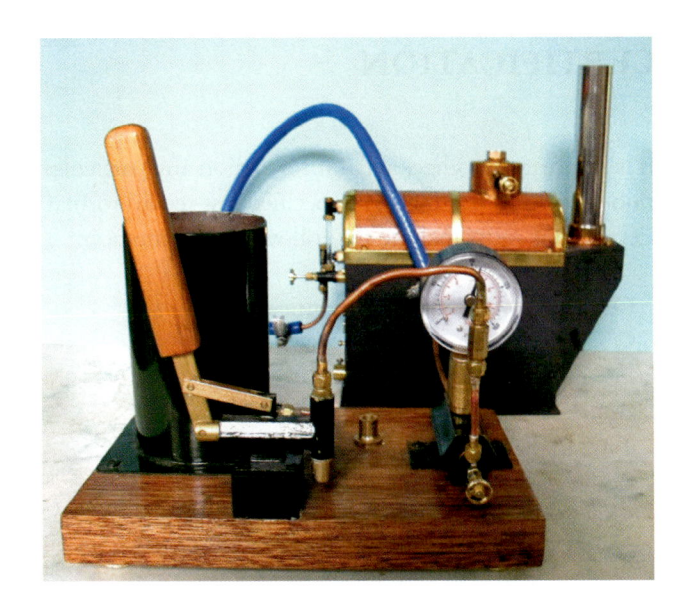

Photo 5. Hydraulic test on 3" horizontal boiler at 90 psi (6 bar) without safety valve and pressure gauge.

Photo 6. A home-made safety-valve adjusting tool.

use this number. Before allocating a permanent number, builders should check whether their club has a preferred boiler-numbering method.

After adding the cladding, burner and fittings, except the safety valve, the inspector will undertake a further hydraulic test at one-and-a-half times working pressure to prove the structural integrity of the interface and the boiler fittings. This includes the pressure gauge. If the gauge does not cover the full range required by the test, disconnect it and fit a blank. Ensure that the siphon is not blocked by applying low hydraulic pressure to see that water is ejected from the siphon before blanking the joint. This is followed by a steam test before the boiler can be operated.

Every four years a further hydraulic test is repeated at one-and-a-half times working pressure. Again the boiler is tested with its fittings, excluding the safety valve.

HYDRAULIC TEST PROCEDURE

The process is carried out using a test gauge which has, within the previous two years, been checked and calibrated to an acceptable standard. Any errors identified on the calibration record will be taken into account when subsequently using the gauge for test or calibration.

The boiler pressure gauge is checked against the test gauge. If not already marked, the boiler's pressure gauge will be compared with the test gauge and marked with the working pressure of the boiler as a red indelible line on the dial of the gauge or an immoveable point on the bezel if the dial is inaccessible. Pressure gauges for small models with a link and lever mechanism are only accurate to ±10% full range output. Any gauge which cannot be red lined within these limits must be replaced.

It is recommended that a stop valve is positioned between the test pump and the boiler under test so that the pump can be isolated from the boiler and test gauge. In situations where a large-capacity test pump is used on a small boiler it is suggested that a safety relief valve is fitted immediately after the pump, set to a value just above the required test pressure. This is to prevent any possibility of damage to the boiler under test due to inadvertent over pressurisation.

The test should be carried out in quiet environment so that the failure of any internal component, such as a stay, may be heard. The test is carried out in a place where no significant change in the boiler temperature occurs during the test. Any test out-of-doors should be carried out in a shaded location away from direct sunlight. The boiler is fully filled with water as near as possible to the ambient air temperature but between 7°C and 21°C. It is vented to exclude any air pockets. The test must be carried out away from people not directly involved with the test. There must be no hammer testing or shock loading while the boiler is under pressure.

Any loss of pressure is fully investigated. Slight loss from blanking plugs and fittings may be allowed. The boiler fittings should be checked for integrity, thread quality and dezincification to eliminate any risk of subsequent detachment. Pressure loss which cannot be accounted for, or which is at an unacceptable level, means the boiler has failed the test. A boiler which shows signs of any form of failure must be repaired and then subject to an appropriate repeat hydraulic test with a pass or fail certificate being issued.

STEAM TEST

Immediately after the completed boiler and fitting have passed the hydraulic test at one-and-a-half times working pressure, the inspector will carry out the steam test. Fill the boiler with distilled water, preferably also de-ionised

Set the safety valve to open at or below the working pressure of the boiler. Photo 6 shows a home-made

46 BOILER TESTING

Photo 7. Adjusting the safety valve on a 108 mm boiler.

safety-valve adjusting tool. It is bent from a length of 18 gauge (1.2 mm) piano wire glued into a wooden handle.

The boiler is steamed at the maximum firing rate of the ceramic burner or gas-torch together with its natural gas supply. The test continues for sufficient time to satisfy the inspector that stable conditions have finally been attained.

Then the operation of the safety valve is checked to ensure that it functions at the working pressure of the boiler and that the pressure does not rise by more than 10% of the working pressure during safety-valve operation. If it fails to open at the correct pressure, it must be re-adjusted. If it fails the test it must be replaced. A steam test is required annually.

Photo 8. The 3" horizontal-boiler safety valve blowing at 45 psi (3.1 bar).

CERTIFICATION

It is important to check what information any particular club requires and if there is a specified test-record format. Certificates must include the following information:

Organisation issuing the certificate.
Owner's name.
Location of test.
Boiler number.
Type of boiler.
Boiler volume in litres.
Boiler material.
Construction date.
Examination and hydraulic-test date.
Examination and steam-test date.
Examination result.
Certificate expiry date.
Working pressure.
Test pressure applied.
Parts not examined.
Any repairs needed and timescale for completion.
Confirmation of safety valve operation.
Date of report.
Name and signature of inspector and any witness.

In addition, some or all of the following data may be included:

Fuel type.
Pressure-gauge range.
Safety-valve set point in bars.
Bar/litre size.
Date of initial hydraulic and steam tests.
Pressure gauge reading.
Safety valve lifts at bar or psi.
General condition of boiler.
Re-tests with dates.

Membership of a well-established model engineering club, affiliated to one of the major national regulating bodies, will provide the benefit of access to experienced boiler inspectors. They will be able to offer guidance during construction, testing and record keeping.

BOILER WATER

Boilers should use distilled water when steaming to avoid scale building up and reducing efficiency. Chapter 8, Page 106 gives more information about suitable types of water. Despite every effort to minimise deposits of scale

Photo 9. A 2" (51 mm) test gauge that reads up to 11 bar (160 psi). It is fitted with a ¼" ME adaptor.

inside the boiler, there will inevitable be some build up over time. To establish the degree of scaling, remove two fittings and pass small flexible inspection torch, such as a Bend-A-Light or Sealey flexible LED inspection torch through the safety-valve hole threaded $5/16$" ME. Then put your eye to the second fitting and look for any build up of white scale. This is readily removed with a commercial de-scaling fluid (available from DIY stores for cleaning the inside of kettles and irons). Follow the instructions on the bottle but first remove all the fittings and install blanking plugs, leaving the one for the safety valve open. Put a small amount of a de-scaling solution into a three-quarters full boiler and heat to boiling. Leave it to stand for twenty-four hours, then fully drain the boiler and rinse out well with clean water.

MAINTENANCE

Each time the boiler is steamed check:
- The safety valve operates at the correct pressure.
- For leaks or weeps from fittings, bushes and pipes.
- The water-gauge ways are clear by blowing down the glass. Confirm the water quickly returns to its right level.
- The correct operation of any feed pump that maintains or replenishes the water level in the boiler.
- The regulator/steam valve operation is smooth and can be completely closed.

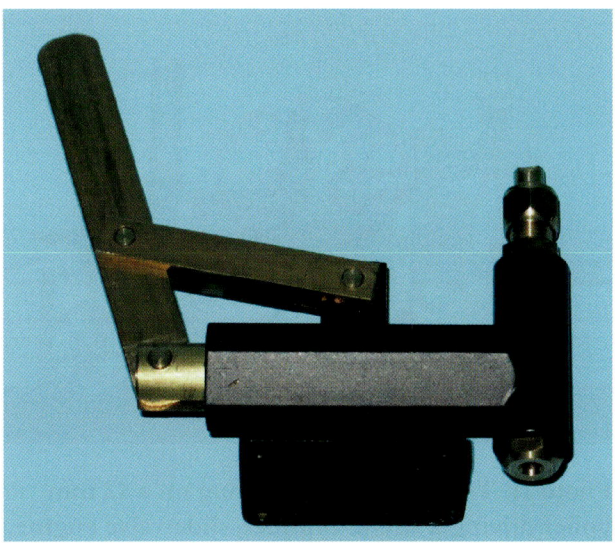

Photo 10. A commercial $3/8$" (9.5 mm) boiler-feed pump will pressurise a boiler for hydraulic test.

To ensure safe and reliable boiler operation, its general condition needs to be visually inspected on an annual basis and a steam test completed. Remove any scale that may have accumulated inside. Then fill with water, light the burner and confirm to the inspector that the safety valve opens at the red-line pressure. If it does not, re-adjust it. Ensure the pressure does not rise more than 10% above the red-line pressure with the burner at maximum heat output. Do not forget to update the boiler test record.

Every four years the boiler will require a further hydraulic test. This is done at one-and-a-half times the maximum boiler-operating pressure. At the same time, check that the pressure-gauge siphon is not blocked by applying a minimum hydraulic pressure to see that water comes out of it before refitting the gauge, if it has a sufficient range for the test, or fitting a blanking plug.

Copper boilers should be laid up dry to minimise the possibility of dezincification of any brass fittings. If it is possible the boiler will experience low temperatures, disconnect the pressure gauge and empty the siphon tube of water to prevent it freezing in the tube.

BOILERS THAT WILL NOT BE STEAMED IN PUBLIC

Some builders will only wish to steam their boilers in their own workshops. If these boilers are below the 3 bar/litre limit, this is acceptable. Nevertheless, some simple tests should be carried out by boiler builders. No boiler testing should be carried out with the small pressure gauge that will be fitted to the boiler. An accurate gauge of at least 2" (51 mm) diameter must be used.

48 BOILER TESTING

Photo 11. The safety valve blowing on a 42 mm boiler driving a single-cylinder, slide-valve engine.

HYDRAULIC TESTING

The aim of hydraulic testing is to prove the integrity of the boiler at twice the proposed working pressure. Testing should involve two model engineers, the builder and a friend, who should try to ensure that the builder has not made any un-noticed mistakes. The initial hydraulic test of the boiler must take place before installing any cladding or fittings.

First carefully check the boiler to ensure that it has been made of the copper of the correct thickness and that all the integral bushes and domes are made of bronze and not brass. Also, all the joints should be checked to ensure that they are satisfactory and that the silver solder has penetrated into them.

Screw blanking plugs into all but one of the threaded bushes used for the various boiler fitting. Fit the plugs with a copper washer before tightening to ensure no leaks. Mount a 2" (51 mm) pressure gauge with a range up to 160 psi (11 bar) into the last threaded bushes, with an adaptor from ¼" BSP to ¼" ME. Connect a water tank and boiler feed pump via an isolating valve to the clack-valve input to the boiler.

Remove the largest plug on top of the boiler and fill with clean water, letting any air escape until as little as possible still remains. Then apply a few strokes with the pump until water starts to run out of the top, isolate the pump and fit the final blanking plug. Now, try and work in a quiet environment so that the failure of any internal component, such as a stay, is audible. Slowly pump the boiler up to its working pressure. This only takes a few strokes of the pump. Pause, close the isolating valve and check for any leaks. Then in steps of 10%, gradually increase the pressure to twice working pressure. The boiler must be capable of holding that pressure steady without any leaks or distortion for ten minutes.

The initial hydraulic test must be at twice working pressure. Further tests are needed every four years, but at only one-and-a-half times the operating pressure.

STEAM TESTING

No testing is complete without the boiler being steamed. Thus, after successful hydraulic testing, remove the blanking plugs and finally clad the boiler with wooden planking, or any other cladding to suit its use. Also paint the fire box and smokebox as necessary. Do this before fitting the various valves and gauges but not the safety valve. Copper washers of the appropriate thickness will allow fittings like the water gauge to be correctly orientated and also provide a steam- and water-tight seal, possibly helped by PTFE tape or Heldite. At this stage carry out a further hydraulic test at one-and-a-half times working pressure. This will check the fittings do not leak. If the test pressure will exceed the maximum pressure-gauge reading, remove it and blank off the bush after applying minimum pressure to the siphon to check it is not blocked.

For the steam test, ideally, connect the boiler to the engine it is to power via a displacement lubricator. Fit the pressure gauge and safety valve. Fill the boiler with clean distilled water, leaving an air space at the top of about 10% of the total volume. Light the burner and after a few minutes, the pressure on the gauge will start to rise. Check that there are no leaks around the various fitting. If there are, turn off the burner, let the boiler cool down, and then tighten the offending fitting before resuming the steam test. As the boiler reaches its designed operating pressure, it is essential that the safety valve opens. If it does not, it must be adjusted until it releases at the correct pressure. The pressure must not rise by more than 10% with the burner at maximum output and with the steam valve to the engine closed.

Finally, open the steam valve to the engine and, after clearing the cylinders of any condensed water and warming the engine, run it and adjust the gas flow to the burner to maintain pressure in the boiler.

Carry out a steam test at yearly intervals. Inspect the boiler and associated pipe work to ensure that all is in good order. Check the boiler safety valve to ensure correct operation at the specified pressure on the gauge.

Any testing should be carried out in accordance with *The Examination & Testing of Miniature Steam Boilers (2012)*, issued by The British Model Engineering Liaison Group and updated from time to time. However, model-engineering-society inspectors will definitely not issue boiler test certificates for boilers which they have not tested. Furthermore, certificates cannot be issued retrospectively.

4: FITTINGS FOR THE BOILER

Some model engineers may think about making a few of their boiler fittings, such as safety and steam valves. This is a time-consuming process that requires detailed plans and the ability to work to close tolerances so that the assembly is able to safely withstand steam pressure.

All the various valves and gauges can be purchased as ready-to-fit items. This approach has been chosen for all the boilers in this book and no designs are provided for home-made fittings.

In the UK, boiler fittings are only supplied with imperial thread sizes, almost invariably Model Engineer (ME) threads. Metrication, it seems, has yet to touch this area of manufacture.

THREADED BUSHES

The many valves and other connections to a boiler need suitably sized threaded bushes to be silver soldered into the boiler during its construction. These items must be made of bronze and are easy to turn to the appropriate dimensions to suit the thread of the fitting. They are also relatively inexpensive to buy. Useful sizes for all of the various fittings needed on small boilers are $3/16$" x 40 tpi, $1/4$" x 40 tpi and occasionally $5/16$" x 32 tpi. All employ ME threads.

BLANKING PLUGS

For boiler testing, the majority of bushes must be blanked off, including the one for the safety valve. This task requires making or purchasing a small number of brass or bronze blanking plugs, of the appropriate thread. During testing, these plugs will be fitted with a copper washer and screwed in place to seal the boiler.

SCREW-IN FITTINGS

SAFETY VALVES

Fitting a safety valve to any steam boiler is absolutely essential. It is the safety link so that steam can blow off if the boiler reaches its maximum working pressure and either steam is not being drawn off or the burner is providing too much heat. A sufficient size is essential to avoid boiler pressure ever rising by more than 10% of the working pressure during safety-valve operation.

Safety valves come in various shapes and sizes. The safety valves shown in Photo 2 rely on a stainless-steel

Photo 1. Top, a selection of blanking plugs from $3/16$" to $5/16$" ME. Below, home-made threaded bronze bushes, one $3/16$" ME, the rest $1/4$" ME.

Photo 2. Left a tall safety valve, in the centre a short one, both $5/16$" x 32 tpi. On the right is a smaller $1/4$" x 40 tpi one.

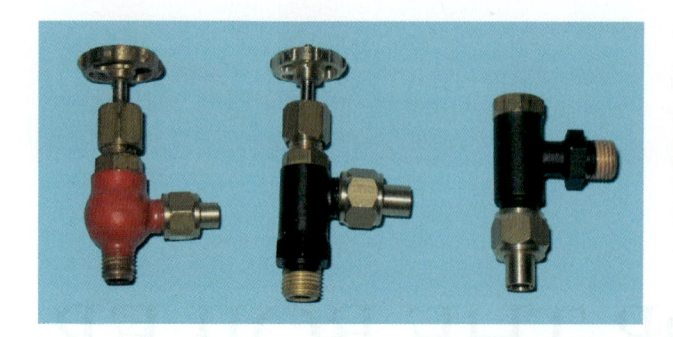

Photo 3. From left to right, a $^3/_{16}$" x 40 tpi globe valve, a ¼" x 40 tpi steam valve and a ¼" x 40 tpi clack valve.

ball that is held on its seat by a spring made of the same material. Varying the compression of the spring changes the pressure at which the safety valve blows-off. The release pressure should be set to suit the boiler and the engine it is to power. It must be adjusted to the maximum-rated working steam pressure for the boiler or below this figure.

Most safety valves used on the boilers in this book have a $^5/_{16}$" x 32 tpi ME thread. The smallest boiler has one with a ¼" x 40 tpi ME thread. Select a safety valve that exhibits minimal pressure rise with maximum flow under steam test conditions, in line with latest boiler test recommendations.

It is not easy to home-build a small safety valve. It is difficult to form a sharp seat for the valve and stop it leaking. Thus, the use of a commercial bronze safety valve from a quality supplier has much to recommend it.

BLOW-DOWN VALVES

A blow-down valve on a boiler is usually fitted as an integral part of the water gauge. It allows the boiler to be emptied of water and is also useful for clearing out any solid matter from the gauge glass. However, an

Photo 4. A 90° steam valve fitted to a radio-controlled twin-cylinder boat engine.

Photo 5. A 90° steam valve, with an attractive wooden handle, fitted to a mill engine.

independent valve may be fitted in a separate threaded bush if preferred.

CHECK OR CLACK VALVES

In order to introduce further water into a hot boiler, a one-way valve is needed. A check or clack valve is a one-way valve that serves exactly this purpose. It has a ball that is lifted off its seat by the pressure of the water being pumped in but is otherwise held on its seat by a spring or gravity and the pressure inside the boiler. It should be fitted low down in the boiler so that the cold water is rapidly heated by the burner.

STEAM VALVES

Steam valves can usefully be divided into two types. The first is the screw-down stop valve which has a circular hand wheel that is turned anti-clockwise to open the valve and screwed down clockwise to close it. One common type is the globe valve. It has a spherical body shape with its two halves separated by an internal baffle. The valve has an opening to form a seat and a movable plug can be screwed onto the seat to close the valve. The plug is connected to a stem, which is operated by screw action from the hand wheel.

The other type of valve is employed as a regulator or radio-controlled valve and turns on and off with a simple 90° movement of the valve lever. These valves may be in the form of rotary plug valves with a hole through the centre or globe valves with a very coarse thread in the stem.

Both types of valve can be purchased for straight 180° fitting or with the input at 90° to the output.

PRESSURE GAUGES

Most model-size pressure gauges use a Bourdon tube. It consists of a C-shaped tube that is sealed at one end and open to boiler pressure at the other. As the pressure increases elastic distortion of the tube causes it to

BUILDING SMALL BOILERS 51

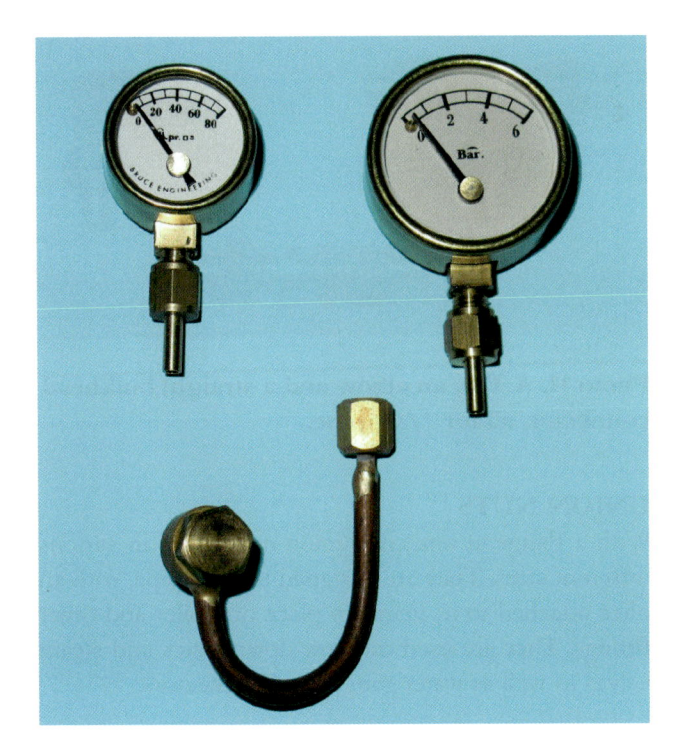

Photo 6. Left, a ¾" (19 mm) diameter gauge reading psi, right a 1" (25 mm) diameter gauge reading in bar and below a syphon.

unwind. This movement is proportional to steam pressure and is used to move the pointer.

Model pressure gauges can be bought to read in psi or in bar. The range of the gauge should extend at least 50% beyond the maximum operating pressure of the boiler. For small boilers, a ¾" (19 mm) or 1" (25 mm) gauge reading 0 - 60, 0 - 80 psi or 0 - 6 bar is suitable. The working pressure should be marked on it in red. The glass is easily removed and replaced to do this.

Siphon tube

As steam temperatures may damage the Bourdon tube in a pressure gauge, it is common practice to install the gauge at the end of a siphon tube. The siphon tube fills with water when the boiler is filled and transmits the steam pressure the gauge. Thus the Bourdon tube is isolated it from the highest steam temperatures. The siphon tube is normally U-shaped.

WATER GAUGES AND GLASSES

The level of the water in any boiler is a very important factor and the ability to monitor the level enables the user to ensure that the boiler never runs dry.

Carefully cut the glass for the water gauge to length. There are two simple ways of doing this. The first is by using a rotary abrasive cutting disc in a small hand-held electric drill. Alternatively, using a V-block to hold the tube, score around it with a triangular needle file and

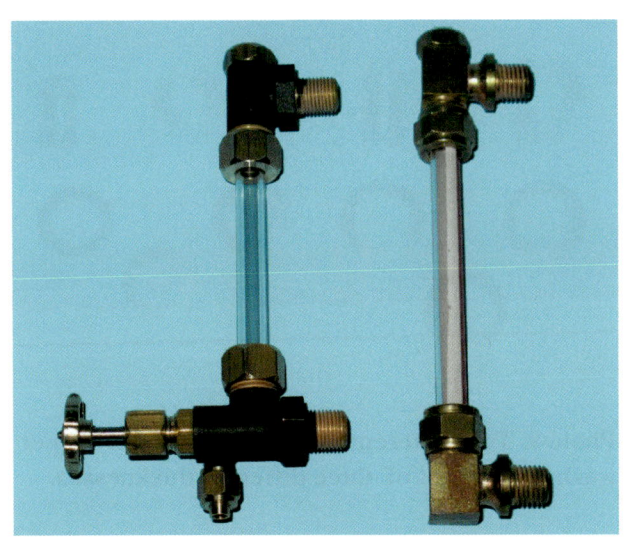

Photo 7. Two water gauges, on the left one with a blow-down valve, on the right one without.

snap off the end. Hold the cut end in a gas flame to just melt the end to a smooth finish.

The size of gauge suitable for the boilers in this book, apart from the smallest horizontal one, is ¼" x 40 with 5 mm glass, with or without a blow-down valve. The smallest boiler needs a $3/16$" x 40 one with 4 mm glass; a size not normally available with a blow-down valve.

OTHER FITTINGS

COPPER TUBE

Soft and readily bent copper pipe comes in a range of sizes, of which the most suitable for use with small boilers are $1/8$", $5/32$" and $3/16$" (3 - 5 mm) sizes. All the boilers described employ $5/32$" (4 mm) pipe to carry water to the boiler, steam from the boiler to the engine and exhaust from the engine. This is an ideal size for boilers under 3 bar/litres capacity.

Photo 8. Soft copper tube for connecting the boiler to the engine is available in many sizes.

52 FITTINGS FOR THE BOILER

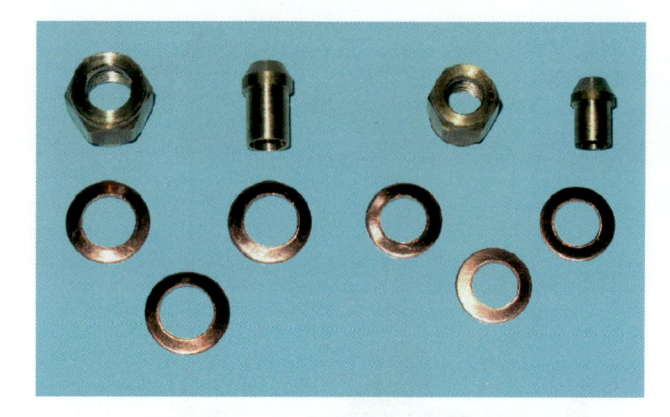

Photo 9. Two different size nuts, olives and copper washers, the last of three different thicknesses.

COPPER WASHERS
There are many different sizes and thicknesses of copper washers. They are used to seal the various fittings into the boiler bushes. ¼" washers are suitable for most fittings but ³/₁₆" are needed for the pressure gauge and ⁵/₁₆" ones for the safety valve. Additional washers of the required thickness may be needed to ensure that fittings like water gauges and clack valves are correctly orientated on the boiler.

CONNECTING PIPES
Connecting a boiler to a steam engine requires running neat copper pipework; often bent to shape. This is easily done using an external bending spring. These come in a range of sizes to suit different diameter pipes. They can be fitted over pipes to stop them kinking when they are bent by hand. Alternatively, use a pipe-bending tool.

To connect the pipe to the various fittings, the pipes must be fitted with olives with nuts; both of a size to match that of the pipe. When connecting a pipe to any union on a fitting, the nut must first be threaded on the pipe, followed by an olive. The olive is then carefully silver soldered to the pipe if a steam one. It may be soft soldered if it is only a water pipe. Chapter 2 Pages 41 and 42 shows how an olive is silver soldered to a pipe.

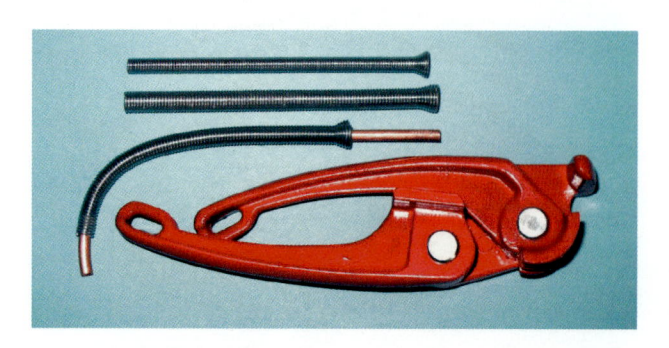

Photo 10. The right-size spring fitted over a pipe bent to shape and an alternative pipe-bending tool.

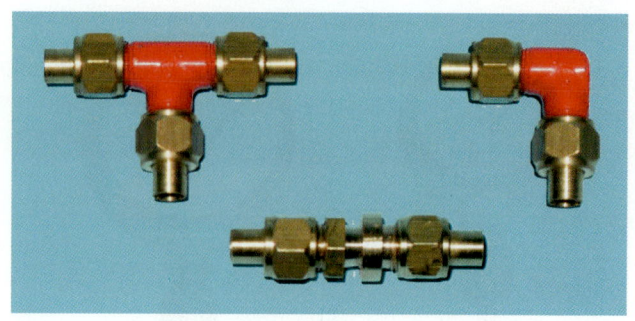

Photo 11. A Tee, an elbow and a straight bulkhead connector, all for ⁵/₃₂" pipe.

UNION NUTS
With a flange at one end, union nuts come in various different sizes. They are designed to hold pipe, with an olive attached to it, firmly in place on boiler and other fittings. They are used on blow down, clack and steam valves as well as water gauges and connectors.

STRAIGHT CONNECTORS
Sometimes the pipe has to run through a metal hole, such as the exhaust feeding into the boiler smoke box. Even the best modellers will occasionally find the length of copper pipe that is needed to run a steam or water connection is too short. A straight or bulkhead connector is the solution to these two problems.

ELBOWS
To avoid the necessity of bending copper pipe through a tight angle of 90°, an elbow of a size to match the pipe will do the same task very tidily.

TEES
It is not unusual to use a boiler to drive more items than just a steam engine. Examples include a steam whistle and a steam-powered boiler feed pump. These will require a Tee connection where the steam pipe to the engine divides to feed another component.

SEALING JOINTS

In most cases, joints can be made steam and water proof by tightening the olive, soldered on the copper pipe, into its fitting. The occasional leak can be stopped by using an appropriate tape or sealant. Fittings that screw into threaded bushes in the boiler are sealed with copper washers, sometimes also with some sealant.

PTFE TAPE
There are times when a fitting or nut has to fit a thread with a steam-tight seal. An easy way to do this is to wrap

Photo 12. A hand-operated boiler feed pump is needed for filling most boilers.

a few turns of PTFE tape or sealing cord around the thread before completing the joint. Take care as fragments of PTFE tape can block pipes and clack valves.

COMPOUNDS FOR STEAM FITTINGS

Loctite 567 Master Pipe Sealant is ideal for sealing steam fittings. It is designed to lock and seal metal tapered threads and fittings. It cures when confined in the absence of air between close-fitting metal surfaces. Loctite Loc 'n Seal 242 thread-locking and sealing compound is also fine for sealing and aligning boiler fittings. Loctite Multi-gasket 574 is suitable for most steam joints. These Loctite products all work up to 150°C. Alternatives are Heldite with a range up to 350°C, or Boss White, a versatile pipe-jointing compound widely used in the plumbing industry. It works well up to 200°C and 7 bar.

BOILER FEED PUMPS

For all but the smallest boiler, the normal method of filling them with water is to use a hand pump for the first and subsequent fills. Sometimes a mechanically driven feed pump, powered by the steam engine, is employed to keep the boiler topped up after it has initially been filled. Continuing to heat a boiler when it has run out of water will quickly destroy it. It is also hazardous both to person and to property.

The smallest boilers may also be filled by removing the safety valve from its threaded bush so water can be fed in. This is usually done with a large (50 or 100 ml) syringe with short length of silicon-rubber tube attached.

BYPASS VALVES

When using an engine-driven boiler feed pump, a bypass valve allows the rate of water transfer to be controlled. This can be fitted across the water output connection and the source of water of any engine-driven feed pump

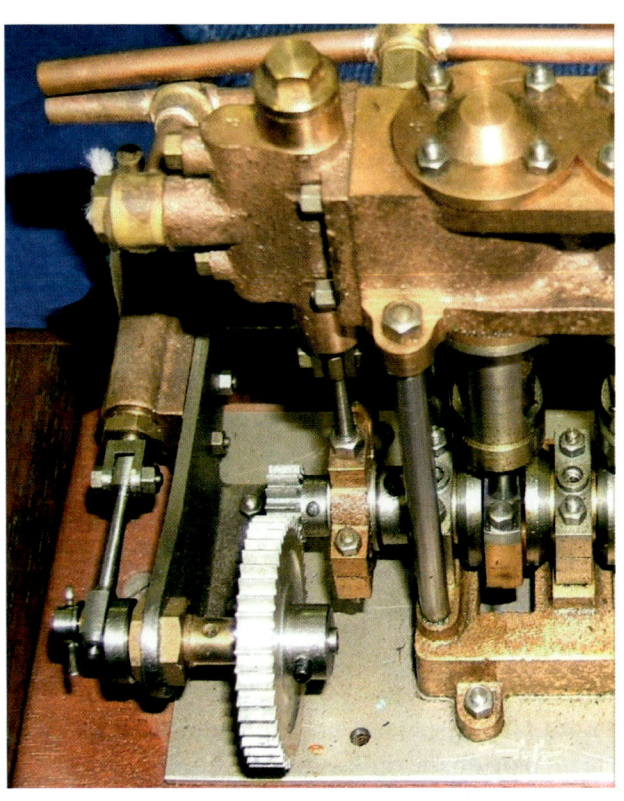

Photo 13. An engine-driven boiler feed pump that a twin-cylinder engine powers via a pair of gears.

so that, hopefully, the water level in the boiler stays fairly steady. The valve is similar to a globe valve but with a stud on the bottom so it can be fixed to the engine-mounting plate or the water tank. Some trial and error will be necessary to achieve the required valve setting.

AUTOMATIC BOILER CONTROL

In order to save steam, and thus fuel, boilers can be fitted with an automatic boiler-control system. This turns down the gas pressure to the burner when the boiler pressure rises above a pre-set figure. It then increases the gas again when the pressure falls. This is ideal in remote applications, such as radio-controlled boats, where the engine may spend periods either stopped or running at very slow speed. However, there is still a degree of uncertainty in the use of these systems, due mainly to difficulties in controlling the burner and measuring the pressure. There is more information in the next chapter.

LUBRICATORS

A modicum of oil inside the cylinder of any engine is essential to provide adequate lubrication. The obvious

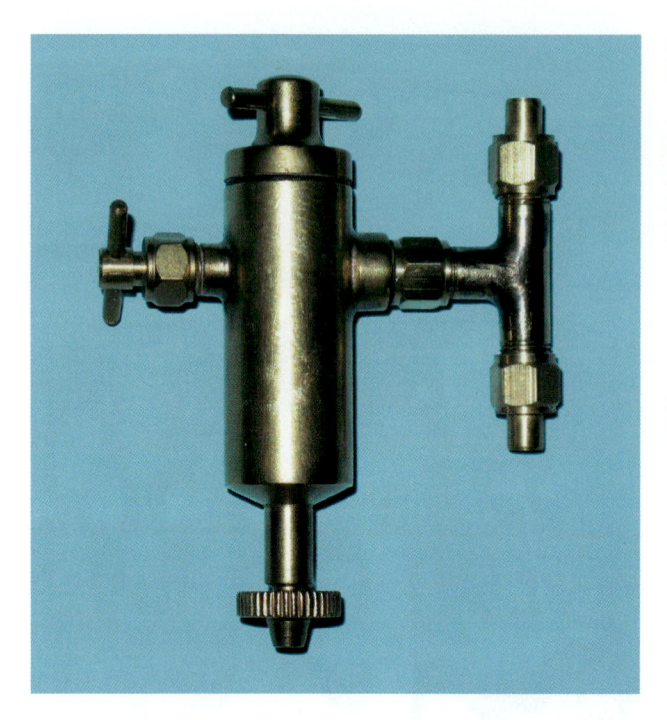

Photo 14. A displacement lubricator showing the steam pipe on the right, normally fitted horizontally, and the oil rate adjuster opposite.

way to achieve this is to mix the oil with the steam entering the cylinder. There are two well-established ways of doing this.

DISPLACEMENT LUBRICATORS
The most popular type of lubricator for the size of engines likely to be driven by the boilers in this book is the displacement lubricator. It relies on water condensing in the lubricator and, as oil floats on water, the oil is very gradually displaced into the steam flow to the cylinder. Oil is filled at the top of the lubricator and water drained from a valve at the bottom. The rate of oil release is set by the adjusting valve fitted to the side of the lubricator and by the temperature of the lubricator body.

MECHANICAL LUBRICATORS
A mechanical lubricator is only common on larger models, such as traction engines, steam lorries and locomotives. This type of lubricator employs a mechanically driven pump to force small quantities of oil into the steam flow.

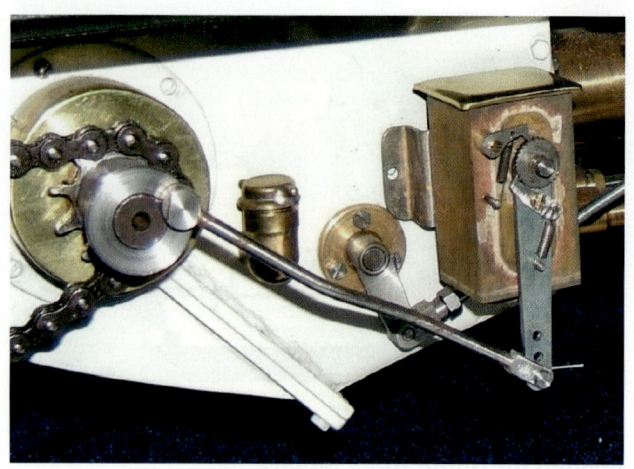

Photo 15. A mechanical lubricator fitted to an under-type steam lorry.

Whilst this is a good way of lubricating the cylinders and pistons, it is much less likely to be used with an engine powered by a small boiler.

STEAM CYLINDER OIL
To lubricate the piston, cylinder and valve gear of any engine, steam oil is placed in the lubricator connected to the engine. Steam oil is mineral based and contains oxidation inhibitors and around 5% acid-less tallow or synthetic fatty acid. For the size of engine likely to be driven by a small boiler, oil to ISO 460 is probably the right viscosity, though thinner oil may be needed for smaller engines. At the pressures the boilers are designed to run, the steam is unlikely to cause oil problems.

Steam oil enters the steam flow into the cylinders where it is atomized and emulsifies. It is carried with the steam to all the internal surfaces that the steam touches. Since these surfaces are usually slightly cooler than the steam a small amount of condensation takes place and whatever oil is emulsified within the condensate is deposited on the exposed surface.

Inevitably the steam will carry some oil through to the engine's exhaust. An oil separator, described in Chapter 8, is essential for boats as well as for some vertical boilers; those where steam is fed up the chimney. This is to avoid oil dripping down the fire tubes onto the ceramic burner and damaging it.

5: HEAT SOURCES

All the boilers described in this book are powered by liquefied petroleum gas (LPG). While it is feasible to employ coal as a fuel for heating water, it makes boiler construction significantly harder. Also, coal is really only practical for static use with small boilers as it needs an operator present to stoke the fire. Methylated spirits burners provide remarkably little heat output and, as a result, a very low rate of steam production. Coal and methylated spirit have therefore been excluded as heating sources for the boilers described in this book.

LIQUEFIED PETROLEUM GAS

Of all the different types of LPG a mixture of propane and butane, sometimes also with isobutane, is the normal fuel used for heating all the model boilers in this book, burned either in a ceramic burner or a gas torch. The gas is readily acquired in small containers from DIY, camping and caravan-equipment stores.

BASIC SAFETY NOTICE

LPG is potentially dangerous if some essential safety precautions are not observed.

There are two approaches to providing gas for a burner. Use a small disposable canister or fit a refillable gas tank and load it with gas from a disposable can.

• Connectors and their associated pipes need to be properly installed and frequently inspected.

• The gas is denser than air and will pool in any enclosed area such as a workshop, vehicle or the inside of a model. Therefore, always refill tanks in the open air.

• Always use a butane/propane mix. Once a gas tank has been filled, or if a burner fails to ignite and the gas has to be turned off, allow some time for any spilled gas to disperse before attempting to light or re-light the boiler.

• Ensure the gas valve is always shut off after use and the connection to a disposable can is removed.

BURNERS

All the vertical boilers and the horizontal water-tube one are heated by a ceramic burner. The other two horizontal boilers employ small Sievert gas torches.

Photo 1. A disposable gas canister that provides gas to a horizontal marine boiler.

Photo 2. A 2" (51 mm) diameter, 3½" (89 mm) long refillable gas tank.

56 HEAT SOURCES

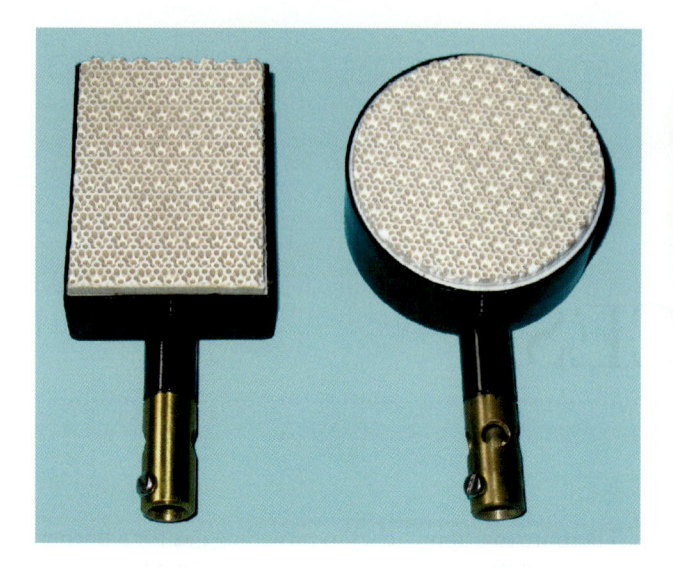

Photo 3. Left, a 2" x 2¾" ceramic burner for a 3" horizontal boiler. Right, a 2¾" circular one for larger vertical boilers.

CERAMIC BURNERS

Relative to their size small ceramic burners are an efficient method of heating the water in a boiler. Bix burners are available commercially in a range of both circular and rectangular sizes. Popular dimensions for the boilers described in this book are:

2" round burner – 2¹/₈" (54 mm) diameter.
2¾" round burner – 2⁵/₈" (67 mm) diameter.
2" x 2¾" (51 x 67 mm) burner.

Typically, all these burners are 1¹/₈" (29 mm) high.

The right size of burner for any particular boiler is important. For each of the boilers in this volume, the most appropriate size of burner is recommended.

Jets

For these ceramic burners, different size gas jet can be fitted. They screw into the jet holder with a little sealant on the thread. The holder is secured in the ceramic burner input tube by a small screw. A No 8 gas jet is recommended for the smaller round burner and the rectangular one. For the 2¾" diameter one, a No 10 or No 16 gas jet seems to be the best although a No 8, 12 or 16 is recommended by the manufacturer.

Photo 4. A gas jet and one fitted to a jet holder.

Photo 5. The initial adjustment of the jet holder in the burner.

Adjusting the burner

Before mounting a burner in a boiler, screw and seal the required size of jet into the jet holder and connect the gas to the holder. Then slide the holder into the brass mixer gas tube. Adjust the jet position in the tube to leave the air holes two-thirds closed, with the end of the burner sticking out of the brass mixer tube by about 8 mm (⁵/₁₆") and then tighten the adjusting screw. Slowly turn on the gas and light the burner. Set the gas valve to give a reasonable size of flame.

Allow the burner to warm up for half a minute. Loosen the screw and move the jet to get a stable blue flame, with small blue cones burning over the ceramic surface, and retighten the screw. This will ensure the optimum air/gas mixture. Check valve and pipe connections with soapy water to ensure there are no gas leaks.

Turn off the gas, allow the burner to cool and install it in the boiler. It is essential that plenty of fresh air can enter the firebox. All the vertical-boiler fireboxes have ample air holes around their perimeter. The 3" horizontal boiler has a large slot beneath the firebox door for air.

A yellow flame shows insufficient air. The jet holder needs moving out, but not so far as to give a blue flame moving on the burner surface because of too much air. This can result in overheating of the burner and an increase in noise.

A partially blocked jet or leaking gas around the jet threads can also cause problems and make it impossible to correctly adjust the burner.

Photo 6. The view through the air holes of a vertical boiler showing small blue cones of flame just after lighting the burner.

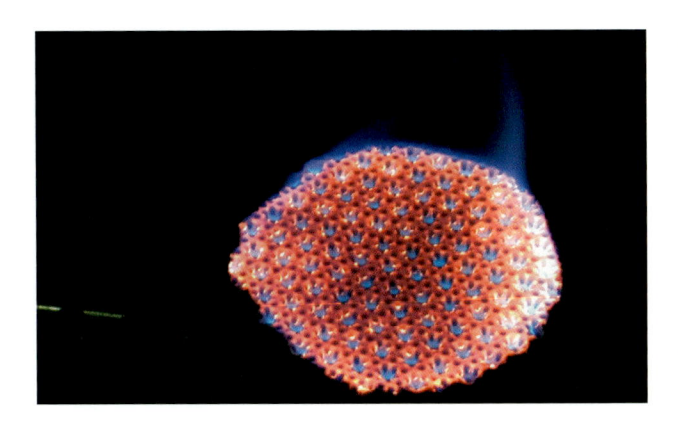

BUILDING SMALL BOILERS

Photo 7. The glowing heat from a well-adjusted ceramic burner.

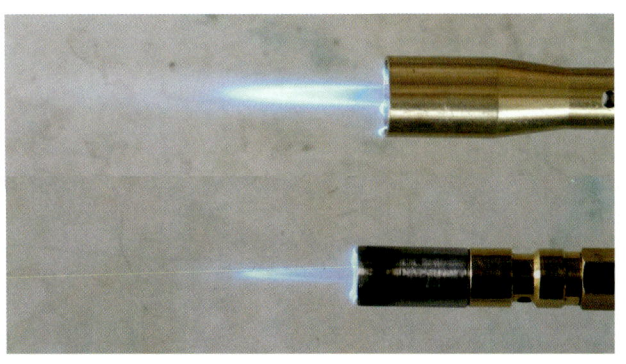

Photo 9. Top, the Sievert 8720 burner. Below the 8842 burner with its flame-end unscrewable casing shortened by 2 mm ($^5/_{64}$") to increase flame spread.

GAS TORCHES

It is not possible to fit ceramic burners in the flues of two of the horizontal boilers described in Chapter 7. The solution is to use a small gas torch. There are several on the market that can operate a horizontal boiler with a 15 mm flue. The 54 mm boiler uses the Sievert Light Line 872001 burner. It is a 12.5 mm ($^1/_2$") burner, with an external diameter of 14 mm and a claimed heat output of 0.75 kW. The 42 mm boiler is fitted with the 884204 Light Line burner, with one minor change. It is a 9 mm burner, with an external diameter of 11 mm and a claimed heat output of 0.25 kW. Both burners are shown in Photo 8.

The simple modification to the 8842 is to turn 2 mm ($^5/_{64}$") off the length at the flame end of the burner's unscrewable steel cover. This alteration broadens the flame near the burner and also slightly reduces the overall length of the flame. The adapter that is used to connect the burners to a gas supply, rather than the handle of a small gas torch, is straightforward to make. The same adapter will fit both torches. It is described on Page 59.

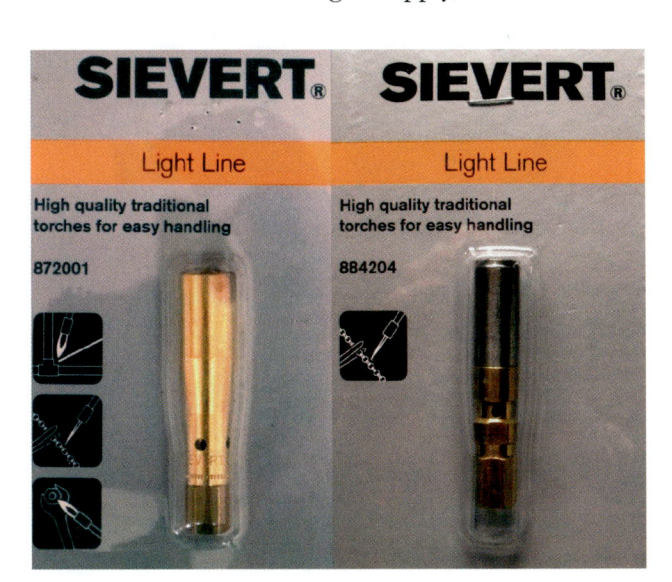

The size and type of burner, and the size of the flue have been tested for heating effectiveness and the results are described in the Appendix. Do not try the 8842 burner in the 54 mm boiler. It produces insufficient heat. However, the 8720 could be used with the 42 mm boiler to increase the rate of steam production. Both burners need good gas pressure to perform at their best.

BURNER MOUNTS

Drawing 1 shows a two-part burner mount, which may be used with the ceramic burners likely to be fitted to the boilers in this book. The layouts of the slightly different type of mounts for the two sizes of gas torch are shown on Pages 93 and 96.

For ceramic burners, the critical dimensions are the diameter of the hole and its height from the bottom of the mount. Both of these measurements need to match

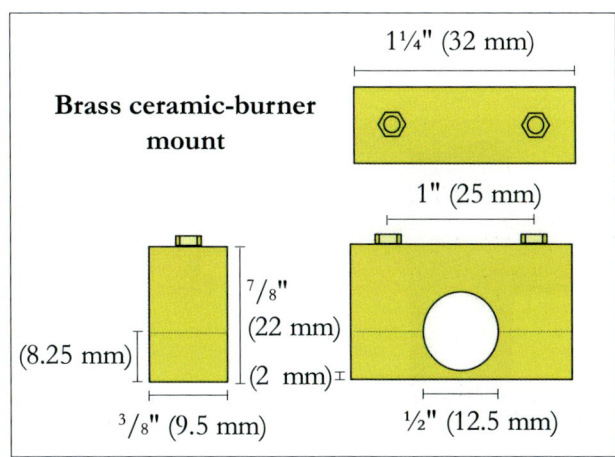

Photo 8. The Sievert 8720 and 8842 Light Line burners for heating small horizontal boilers.

Drawing 1. The mount for 2" and 2¾" diameter round and 2" x 2¾" rectangular ceramic burners.

58 HEAT SOURCES

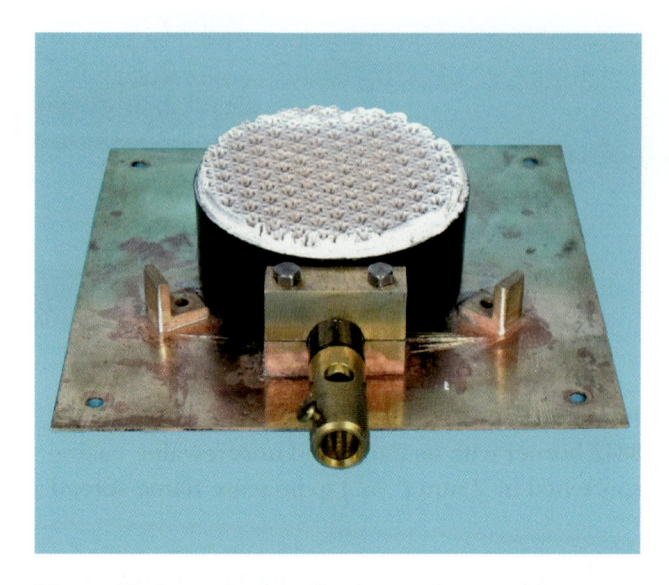

Photo 10. A vertical-boiler base plate and burner.

the dimensions of the burner. The mount is fixed to the boiler base plate. It clamps the burner firmly in place and ensures it is in the correct position. Photo 10 shows a typical example of a burner with mount attached to a base plate for a vertical fire-tube boiler.

The mount for a gas torch is cut from a strip of ¾" (19 mm) x ⅜" (9.5 mm) brass, with its length and hole position to suit the installation. It is drilled to fit the diameter of the burner, with holes in the sides tapped to take 8BA (M2) grub screws. An example is shown in Photo 11.

GAS CONTAINERS

Gas can be purchased in a variety of sizes of small, disposable self-sealing tin containers. The more compact sizes are often ideal as a direct gas source for heating a small static boiler or one fitted in a boat with sufficient space and a boiler feed pump.

Three practical sizes of gas containers are:

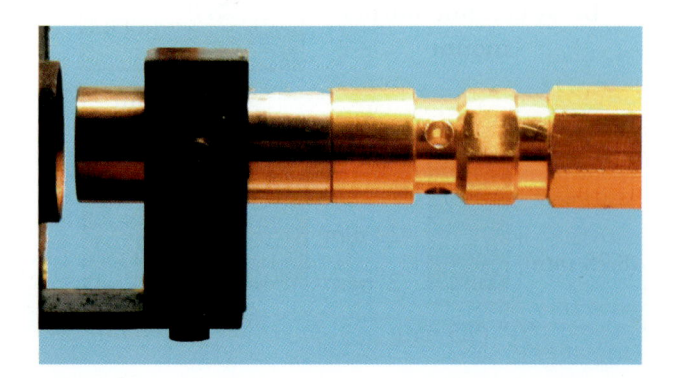

Photo 11. A mount for the Sievert 8842 burner just outside a flue. Grub screws secure the burner.

Photo 12. Two nominal 100 g and 230 g disposable containers of a propane/butane mixture.

	Diameter	Height	Weight of gas
C100	3½" (90 mm)	2¾" (70 mm)	100 g (3½ oz)
C250	4¼" (108 mm)	3¼" (83 mm)	230 g (8 oz)
C500	4¼" (108 mm)	5¼" (133 mm)	440 g (15½ oz)

Alternatively, a small commercial gas tank may be purchased and filled from a larger disposable tin. Although in principle, it is possible to build a home-made, refillable gas tank from copper tube, testing is required to a very-high pressure, which needs special

Photo 13. A small refillable gas tank, 2" (51 mm) diameter and 1¾" (44 mm) high.

BUILDING SMALL BOILERS

Photo 14. A connector to a gas valve for a throw-away canister, a connector to a gas torch and a jet holder with screw-in jet and with the jet removed.

Photo 15. A nozzle to fill refillable gas tanks. It screws onto the top of disposable gas cans.

equipment. Construction of such a tank in the home workshop is definitely not recommended.

Tanks like the one shown in Photo 13 are primarily intended for use with small marine, rail or stationary applications such as a steam crane where a large gas tank with piping would look out of place. They are made of non-sparking brass and copper that is silver soldered. The tanks are available in several sizes, designed for use with up to 60/40 butane/propane mix. They are tested to a pressure of 360 psi (25 bar) and come with a test certificate. Three different sizes are widely available from several model engineering suppliers:

- 2" (51 mm) diameter by 1¾" (44 mm) high.
- 2" (51 mm) diameter by 3½" (89 mm) long.
- 2" (51 mm) diameter by 5" (127 mm) long.

Any refillable gas tank will incorporate a fitting for a filler nozzle that is a push fit into it. This will enable gas to be transferred to it from a larger disposable gas cylinder into the gas tank. A typical example is shown in Photo 15.

PIPE WORK AND VALVES

Care is needed when connecting a gas source to a boiler burner to ensure that the joints are all gas tight. A manual gas valve that screws onto a disposable gas tank, or a similar valve fitted to a refillable gas tank, controls the amount of gas flowing. Copper pipe can be used to connect the gas to the burner and ⅛" outside diameter is the norm. One end usually terminates in a manual screw fitting that goes onto the gas valve; the other a gas jet holder. For connection to a gas torch, thread a short length of ⅜" (10 mm) brass hexagonal rod M8 x 0.75 to fit the burner. Centre drill M3 (⅛") two-thirds of the way through, then cross drill ⅛" to fit the gas pipe and silver solder the pipe in place.

A manual gas valve will only allow the heat input to be set to approximately match the expected quantity of steam required by the engine. A radio-controlled valve driven by a servo will allow rather better boiler-pressure management. There are also commercial gas regulators that adjust the gas flow, depending on the steam pressure in the boiler.

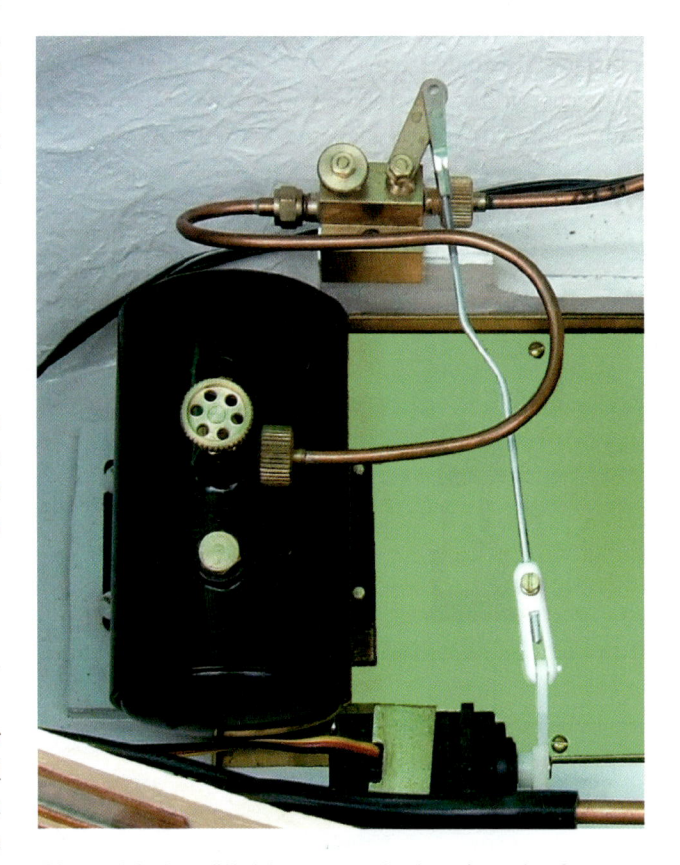

Photo 16. A refillable gas tank showing the Stuart servo-controlled gas valve feeding the burner.

60 HEAT SOURCES

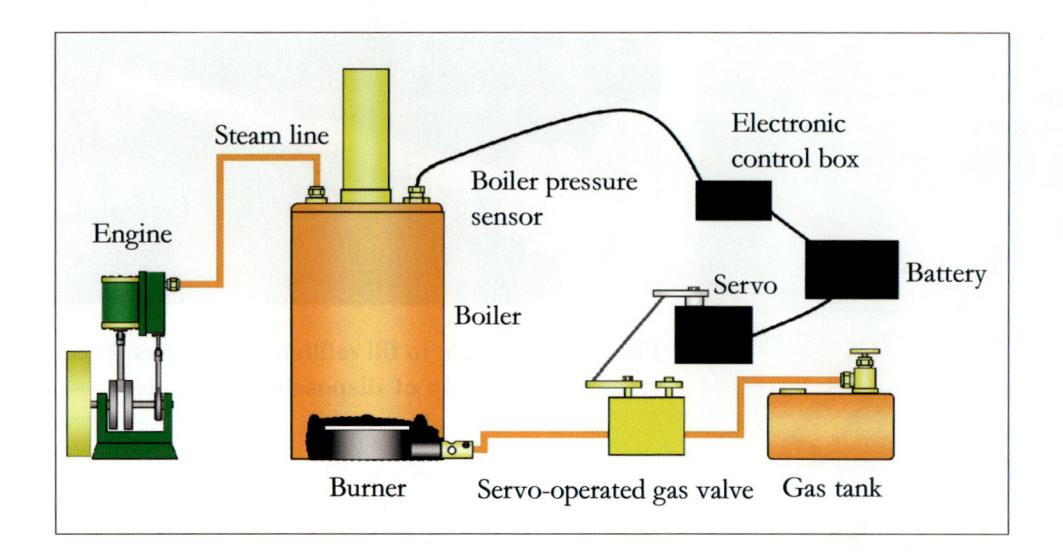

Drawing 2. The Stuart electronic gas pressure control system.

AUTOMATIC GAS VALVES

Stuart offers electronic gas valves that automatically control gas flow to the burner by monitoring boiler pressure. Once sufficient pressure is reached the gas flow is reduced to just a pilot, conserving gas and water. The system comprises an electronic control box, a pressure sensor, a servo-operated gas valve, pipe and a battery.

Forest Classics offers the Bix boiler-pressure regulator while both Hielscher in Germany and Anton in France produce similar mechanical solutions employing a flexible membrane. These regulators automatically vary the burner flame to try and maintain the selected boiler pressure. An adjustment screw sets the desired pressure. In practice, it may be tricky to ensure the burner operates satisfactorily under the changing gas settings.

IGNITERS

Although matches or a lighter can be used to ignite boiler burners, a better solution with less risk of scorched hands, is to use an igniter like the one illustrated in Photo 17. It uses lighter fuel (butane) that is readily topped up. Its gas is ignited by a piezo-electric crystal. A vertical boiler is easily lit by removing the chimney, holding the lit igniter to the chimney mount and turning on the gas. A distinctive 'pop' sound will indicate that the burner has lit. The ceramic burner in the horizontal water-tube boiler should be lit through the door at the burner end.

A gas torch should have its end just 3 mm ($1/8$") clear of the flue with the grub screws tightened. The igniter is applied to the gap as the gas is slowly turned on. A roaring sound will confirm that the burner has lit.

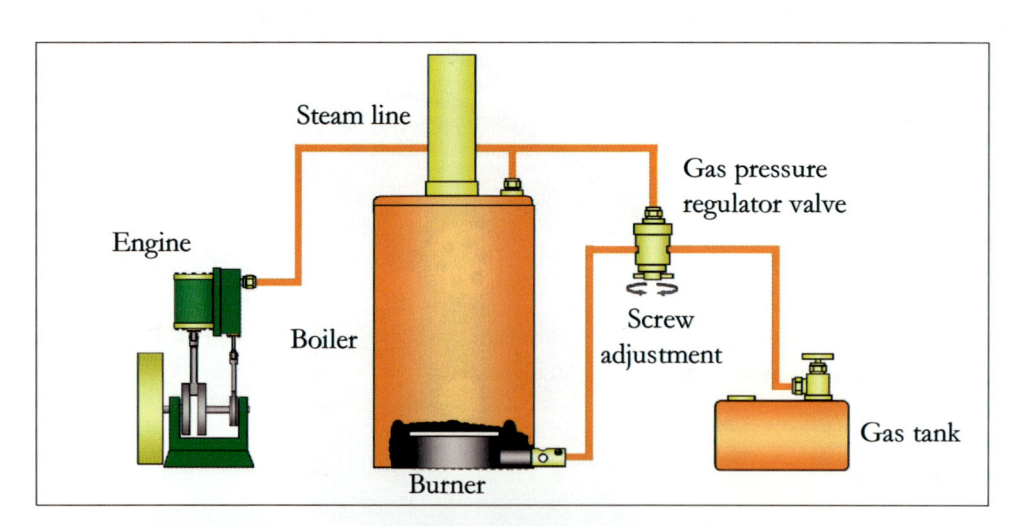

Drawing 3. A typical mechanical gas pressure control system.

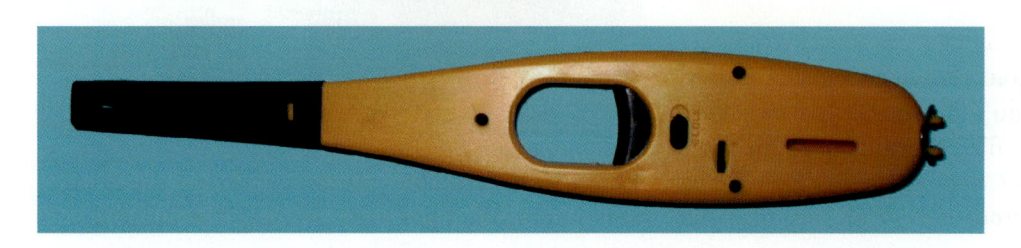

Photo 17. A handy butane-powered igniter with piezo-electric spark.

6: VERTICAL-BOILER DESIGNS

OVERVIEW

This chapter describes three relatively small but powerful vertical boilers that can readily be home-built. Chapter 2 shows how all can safely be silver soldered in a single session without any step soldering. Careful assembly is needed to ensure that all the boiler parts are securely held in place for soldering. While these boilers all fall within the 3 bar/litre limit they will still need basic independent testing if they are to be steamed publically.

These boilers use round C106 hard-drawn copper tube for their barrels. The Appendix shows that 16 gauge (1.6 mm) copper tube will meet the strength requirements. The flanged plates are also made from copper sheet. For all the three boilers described, 16 gauge copper has adequate strength.

The length of any boiler may be reduced and the position of the threaded bushes altered. Each vertical boiler needs a base plate to match its particular application. Page 76 shows various solutions. These may have to be modified to suit the intended use of the boiler.

Photo 1. Details are provided of how to build these three vertical boilers.

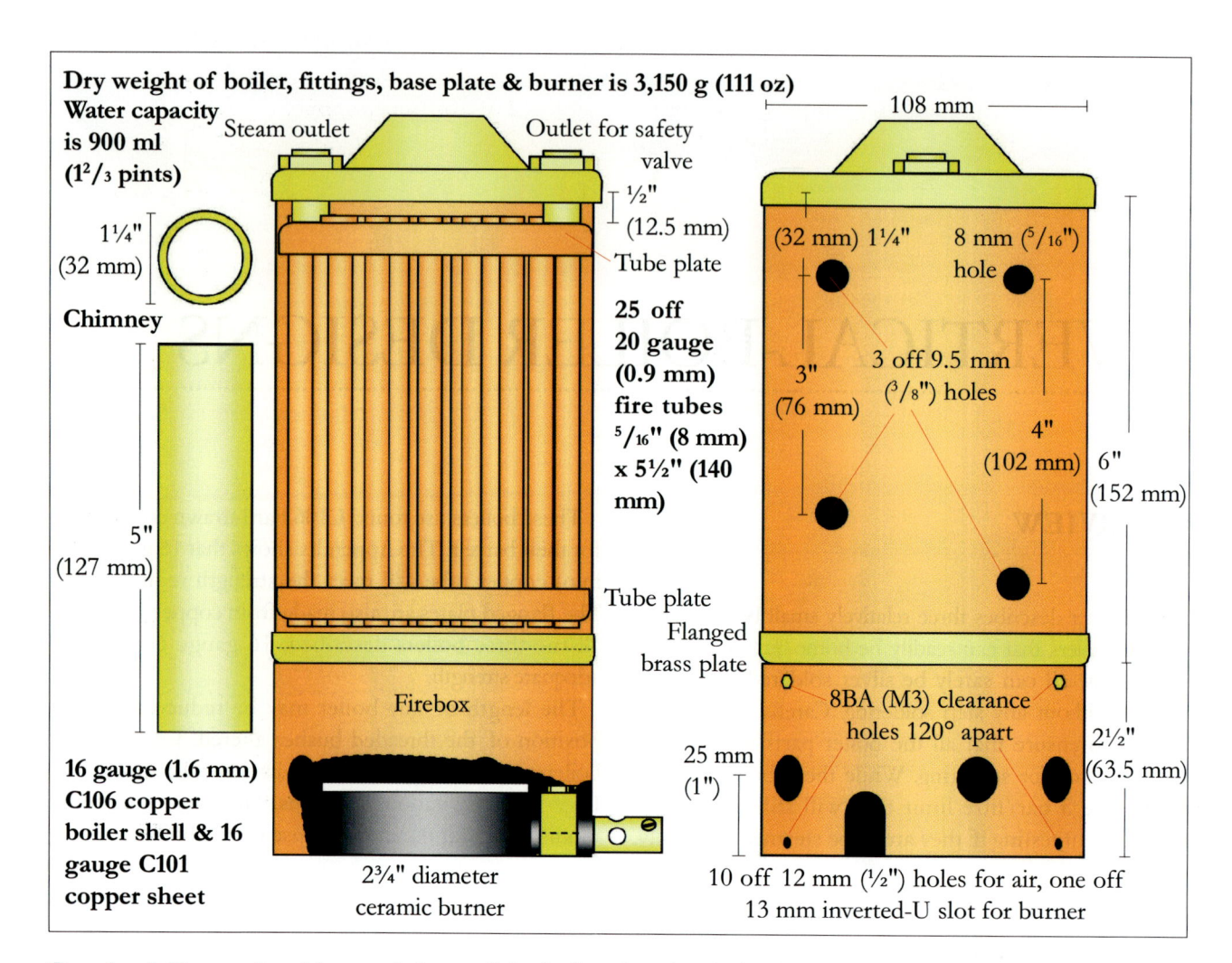

Dry weight of boiler, fittings, base plate & burner is 3,150 g (111 oz)
Water capacity is 900 ml (1²/₃ pints)

Steam outlet
Outlet for safety valve
1¼" (32 mm)
Chimney
5" (127 mm)
16 gauge (1.6 mm) C106 copper boiler shell & 16 gauge C101 copper sheet

½" (12.5 mm)
Tube plate
25 off 20 gauge (0.9 mm) fire tubes ⁵/₁₆" (8 mm) x 5½" (140 mm)
Tube plate
Flanged brass plate
Firebox
2¾" diameter ceramic burner

108 mm
(32 mm) 1¼"   8 mm (⁵/₁₆") hole
3" (76 mm)   3 off 9.5 mm (³/₈") holes
4" (102 mm)   6" (152 mm)
8BA (M3) clearance holes 120° apart
25 mm (1")   2½" (63.5 mm)
10 off 12 mm (½") holes for air, one off 13 mm inverted-U slot for burner

Drawing 1. External and internal views of the boiler showing holes for burner air and securing base plate.

108 mm (4¼") VERTICAL BOILER

This efficient boiler, originally designed to power a static steam engine, has 25 fire tubes and a separate firebox. The advantage of a separate firebox is that it allows the boiler lagging strips to butt at both ends against 1.6 mm (¹/₁₆") brass flanges. The boiler and firebox shells may also be cheaper if an off-cut can be obtained for the firebox. The fire tubes obviate the need for a flue. The boiler is 285 mm (11¼") tall including fittings, with the chimney adding a further 65 mm (2½").

Building this vertical boiler starts by a obtaining a 6" (152 mm) length of 108 mm 16 gauge copper tube for the boiler and a 2½" (63.5 mm) length of the same diameter tube for the firebox. The boiler shell has three 9.5 mm (³/₈") and one 8 mm (⁵/₁₆") diameter hole drilled in its side to fit the threaded bosses for the pressure gauge, clack valve and water gauge. The firebox has ten 12 mm (½") holes at 30° intervals drilled 25 mm (1") from the bottom and a eleventh hole drilled in the centre of the 60° gap but only 22 mm (⁷/₈") from the bottom. Open this up to 13 mm using a drill or a round file, followed by making a pair of cuts from the base to the hole with a hacksaw to form an inverted U-shape. Finally, bevel down the top of the firebox from the outside at an angle of 30° with a sanding drum in a small hand-held drill, so that it fits the curve of the flanged brass plate that attaches to it.

The smoke box and firebox tops are 5¼" (133 mm) diameter circles of 16 gauge brass sheet, annealed and flanged. Form them over a 108 mm wood block to give a ³/₈" (9.5 mm) flange. Skim the inside in the lathe to fit over the boiler shell. Mill a hole 48 mm (1⁷/₈") diameter in the smoke box cover and one in the firebox top 95 mm (3¾"). Two holes in the smoke box at 42 mm pcd are for the outlets to the steam and safety valves.

Cut out two discs of 16 gauge copper plate around 5" (125 mm) diameter for the pair of fire-tube plates. Anneal and form them over the wood block now reduced to 101.6 mm to provide a ³/₈" (9.5 mm) flange. Drill twenty-five holes ⁵/₁₆" (8 mm) and three holes ¹/₈" (3 mm) in both plates for the threaded rods. Then drill the further two holes only in the top plate for the steam

BUILDING SMALL BOILERS

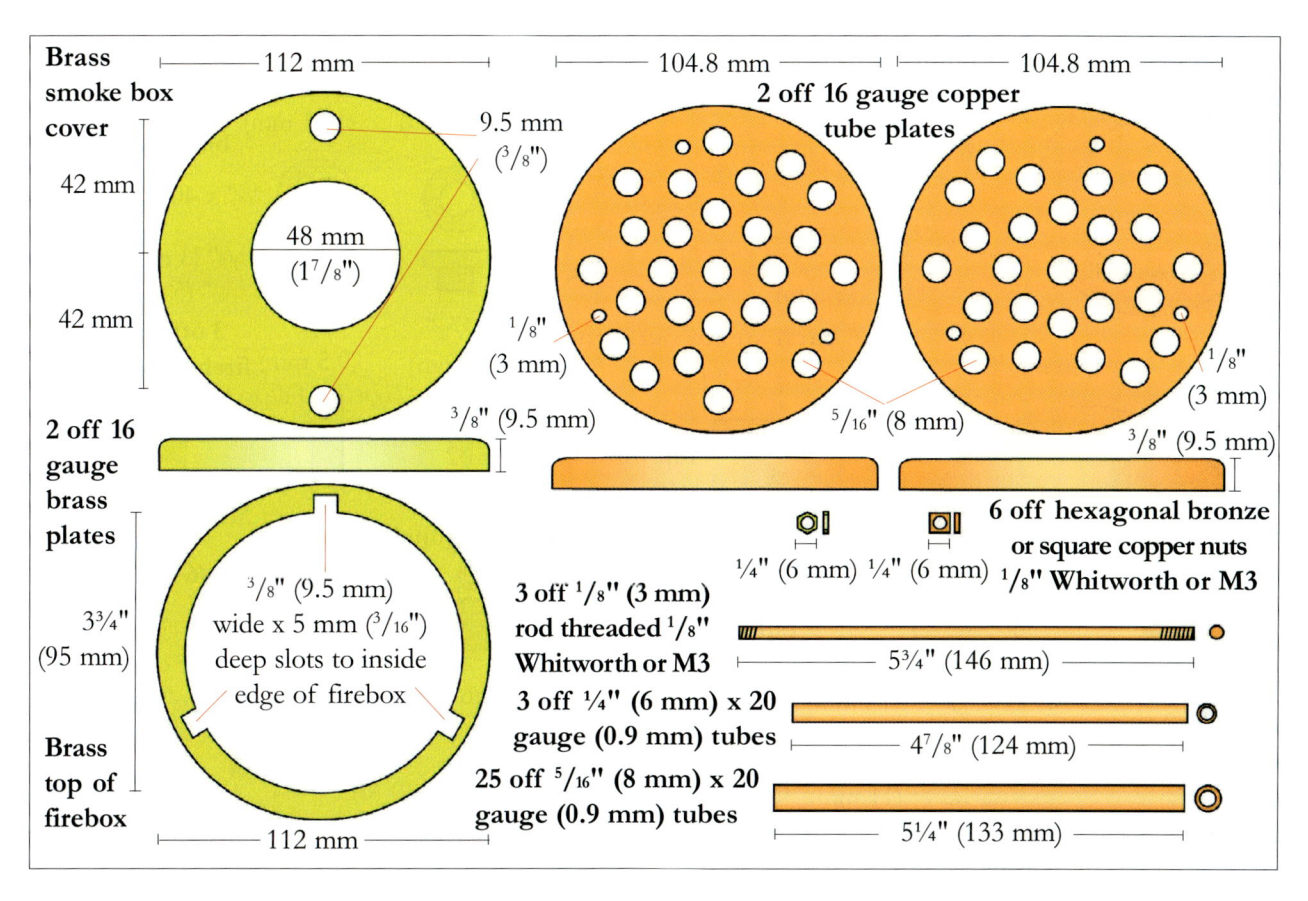

Drawing 2. Two brass and two copper plates with various other component parts of the boiler.

and safety valve fittings. Skim both of the plates in the lathe to fit in the boiler shell.

The 25 fire tubes are 5¼" (133 mm) long and are made from ⁵/₁₆" (8 mm) diameter 20 gauge (0.9 mm) copper tube. Lightly flare all the tubes at one end so that they will not pass right through the holes in the tube plates. There are also three ⅛" (3 mm) rods, threaded at each end and fitted with copper or bronze nuts. These run through small tubes that hold the tube plates in place during assembly and soldering. The rods are 5¾" (146 mm) long and are threaded BSW ⅛" x 40 (M3) for ⅜" (9.5 mm) along one end and ½" (12.5 mm) at the other. The tubes are ¼" (6 mm) diameter, 4⅞" (124 mm) long with at least ⅛" (3 mm) clearance for the copper rods. These rods and tubes do not form part of the structural strength of the boiler. Test assemble the tube plates and the spacing rods and their tubes and tighten the six nuts. Insert the assembly in the boiler shell so the plates are the right distance from the ends of the boiler shell. The flanges will slightly overlap three of the holes for threaded bushes. Mark where the flanges

Holes in boiler shell	Position from top	Angle
1 x 6 mm	9 mm	0°
1 x 9.5 mm	32 mm	140°
1 x 8 mm	32 mm	190°
1 x 9.5 mm	108 mm	140°
1 x 9.5 mm	134 mm	190°
3 x 2.85 mm	150 mm	0°, 120°, 240°
Firebox	**from bottom**	
10 x 12 mm	25 mm	At 30° intervals
1 x 13 mm	12 mm	0°

Table 1. Details of the holes to be pre-drilled in the boiler shell and firebox.

Holes	Radius	Angle
1 x 8 mm	Centre	0°
8 x 8 mm	18 mm	0°, 45°, 90°, 135°, 180°, 225°, 270°, 315°
8 x 8 mm	30 mm	19°, 71°, 113°, 157°, 199°, 252°, 295°, 339°
10 x 8 mm	42 mm	0°, 35°, 54°, 90°, 135°, 180°, 216°, 235°, 270°, 315°
3 x 3 mm	42 mm	121°, 250°, 345°

Table 2. The tube-plate-hole positions; the red ones only in the top plate. Do make a mirror pair.

64 VERTICAL-BOILER DESIGNS

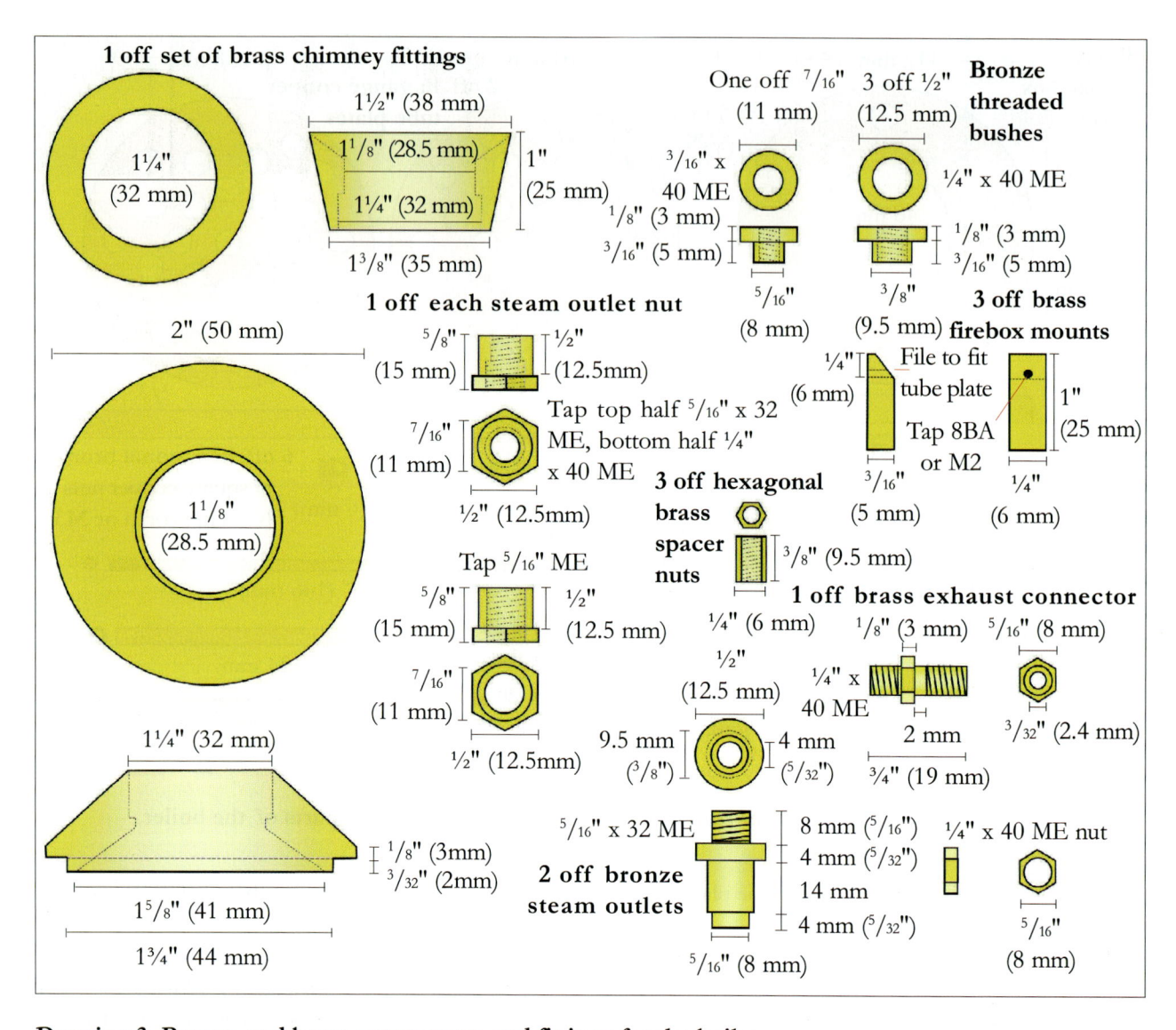

Drawing 3. Bronze and brass components and fittings for the boiler.

overlap the holes and, after disassembling the parts, file U-shaped slots in the flanges to clear the holes for the threaded bushes.

Heat for the boiler is provided by a circular 2¾" diameter ceramic gas burner, mounted on a base plate at the bottom of the firebox.

Photo 2. The set of components needed to make the 108 mm vertical boiler.

Photo 3. Top left, the four bronze bushes, top right the two bronze outputs connectors and nuts to the steam and safety valves, bottom left to right the three brass firebox connectors, their bolts and the exhaust pipe-to-pipe connector parts.

Twelve components are made from bronze or brass. The four threaded bushes must be bronze, one to fit an 8 mm ($5/16"$) hole with a $3/16"$ x 40 ME thread and three to go into 9.5 mm ($3/8"$) holes with a $1/4"$ x 40 ME thread. These bushes may be purchased or turned in a lathe and tapped. Turn the two identical steam outlets from $1/2"$ (12.5 mm) bronze rod 30 mm long, with the top end threaded $5/16"$ x 32 ME and the bottom end turned down to $5/16"$ (8 mm), with a hole $5/32"$ (4 mm) through the centre. Turn the two brass steam outlets nuts and tap one $5/16"$ x 32 right through and the other $5/16"$ x 32 one end and $1/4"$ x 40 at the other.

The exhaust connection into the smoke box is a homemade $5/32"$ pipe-to-pipe bulkhead connector but with the length on one side increased from 5 mm to 9 mm to accommodate a second $1/4"$ ME nut to hold it to the boiler shell. The three firebox connectors are lengths of $3/16"$ x $1/4"$ (5 x 6 mm) brass strip with one end filed at an angle to fit tightly to the tube plate.

The chimney is a 5" (127 mm) length of $1\frac{1}{4}"$ (32 mm) brass tube. Turn the boss on top of the smoke box cover that houses the chimney from a piece of 2" (50 mm) round brass. Also turn the flared chimney top from a piece $1\frac{1}{2}"$ (38 mm) x 1" (25 mm). The top may also be formed from a short length of copper tube. Silver solder the boss to the smoke box cover and the top to the chimney.

The firebox is the first component to be assembled and this requires a jig comprising three lengths of 25 mm (1") angle iron approximately 220 mm ($8^2/3"$) long, each with a 12 mm ($1/2"$) wide slot milled in it, 150 mm ($5^7/8"$) from one end to accommodate the firebox cover. Temporarily fit the brass cover firmly in place on the boiler shell having first cleaned the outer edge with wire wool. Then place the firebox on top of the brass ring with the three jig bars held in place with three 120 - 140 mm ($4\frac{3}{4}"$ - $5\frac{1}{2}"$) jubilee clips. Place the whole assembly

Photo 4. The firebox jig is made from three lengths of angle iron.

upright on a flat surface and carefully tap down the firebox to ensure it fits well on the brass disk. Run some Tippex or Snopake typewriter correcting fluid around

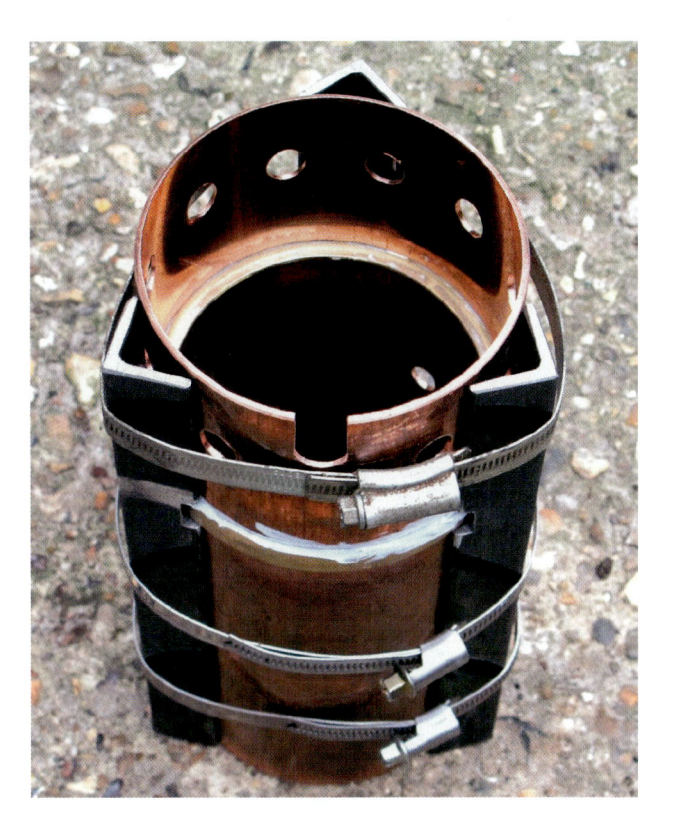

Photo 5. The firebox held in place on the boiler by the firebox jig and three jubilee clips.

66 VERTICAL-BOILER DESIGNS

Photo 6. The firebox, with the brass ring soldered in place, and drilled with 11 air holes and the inverted-U slot for the burner connection.

the outside of the brass to stop silver solder flowing onto it. If any fluid has seeped inside the firebox, remove it with a scriber. Then coat the interior brass to copper interface with flux, heat the outside of firebox and brass ring in a hearth with a gas torch and apply silver solder around the joint. After cooling, remove the jig and boiler shell, taking care as the copper is very

Photo 7. The firetube and plate assembly ready for insertion in the inverted boiler shell.

Photo 8. The bare boiler after silver soldering and cleaning.

soft; the heat has just annealed it. The firebox is now complete but must be thoroughly cleaned by soaking in pickle, then washed in clean cold water and dried.

To prepare the boiler for silver soldering, clean the shell and tube plates by soaking in pickle and then rinse in clean water. Use steel wool for further polishing of these items as well as cleaning the other parts. First assemble the two tube plates with the three rods in their tubes and tighten up the six nuts so the structure is rigid with the bottom tube plate on top. It is essential to have the tube plates correctly orientated relative to each other. Then insert the tubes through the bottom plate, the unflared ends first. Start with the centre tube and work outwards to make it easier to locate the other end of the fire-tubes in their correct holes. The assembly will then look like Photo 7 and it is essential that the tubes extend 3 mm ($1/8$") below the lower plate.

Carefully test fit the whole assembly in the inverted boiler shell, remembering to keep the fire tubes vertical at all time. Accurately position the assembly so the semi-circular slots in the flanges align with the holes in the boiler shell. Once satisfied all fits nicely, remove the entire tube assembly, remove all the tubes and mix up some flux. Apply the flux to all the parts, which are to be soldered, before re-assembling them and fitting them back in the boiler shell. Paint rings of flux where the tube-plate flanges fit. More flux may need to be added around the perimeter of the tube plates after assembly.

BUILDING SMALL BOILERS 67

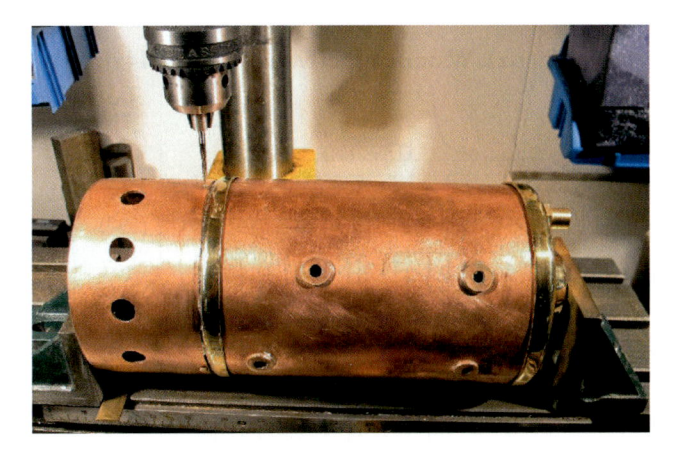

Photo 9. The setup for drilling and tapping the holes for bolting the boiler to the firebox.

Hold the threaded bushes in place by twisted galvanised wire or home-made jubilee clips. Then bolt the three brass strips, with flux behind them, to the bottom of the boiler shell, making sure that they stick up vertically. Adjust the spacer nuts to ensure that the top tube plate is exactly ½" (12.5 mm) from the end of the shell.

Stand the inverted boiler vertically in the hearth and heat up until applied silver solder melts. Run the solder thoroughly around the outside of the tube plate, around each fire tube and the three nuts on the ends of the copper rods, as well as around the two threaded bushes at that end of the boiler. Remove the heat and without delay carefully turn the boiler over using tongs. Ttake off the three spacer nuts, place the two fluxed steam outlet in their holes and repeat the exercise at the top end.

When cool, carefully examine every joint to ensure complete penetration and adhesion of the silver solder. Cut off any excess length of the three copper rods at each end of the boiler, pickle it and rinse it in cold water. Finish cleaning it with wire wool ready for inspection and hydraulic testing.

After a satisfactory test, fit the firebox to the bottom of the boiler shell. First file off the heads of the bolts that held the three brass mounting strips on the bottom of the boiler. Also file three ¼" (6 mm) slots inside the brass firebox ring so the ³⁄₁₆" x ¼" (5 x 6 mm) mounting strips, can pass through. Mark the position of the centre of these brass blocks on the outside of the firebox and fit onto the boiler shell. Drill three holes 1.8 mm and tap 8BA (or 1.65 mm and M2) so the firebox is firmly held in place with three brass bolts.

Photo 9 shows the set up for drilling, using three angle plates, one at each end and one 'hidden' behind the boiler shell. A strip of brass below the bottom of the firebox keeps it level. Push the boiler by hand against the rear angle plate while drilling. Then remove the firebox and polish the brass outside. To fit the firebox

Photo 10. Two completed boiler, each with its burner and different base plate.

permanently to the boiler, apply ceramic heat-resistant sealant/glue to the inside of the brass ring to prevent heat leaking out and discolouring the wooden lagging. Then re-attach the firebox and bolt it securely in place.

The boiler is ready to be lagged with wooden strips, fixed in place with superglue. Sand them to provide a smooth finish, give three coats of clear varnish and then fit three brass boiler bands. Make the base plate to suit the particular installation required (see Page 76). Fit a 2¾" diameter round ceramic burner and bolt in place. The firebox needs a couple of coats of heat-resisting black paint. Also apply this to the base plate. To fit the base plate, drill and tap three 6BA or M3 holes through the firebox 6 mm from the bottom and 120° apart. Do attach a plate to the firebox with details of the boiler, or use letter and number punches to impress the details into it. After a successful second hydraulic test at 72 psi (5 bar), the boiler is finally ready for its initial steam test. This process has already been described in Chapter 3. It can then be attached to an engine ready for use.

68 VERTICAL-BOILER DESIGNS

Dry weight of boiler, fittings, baseplate & burner is 2,800 g (99 oz). Water capacity is 810 ml (1.44 pints)

Steam outlet · Outlet for safety valve

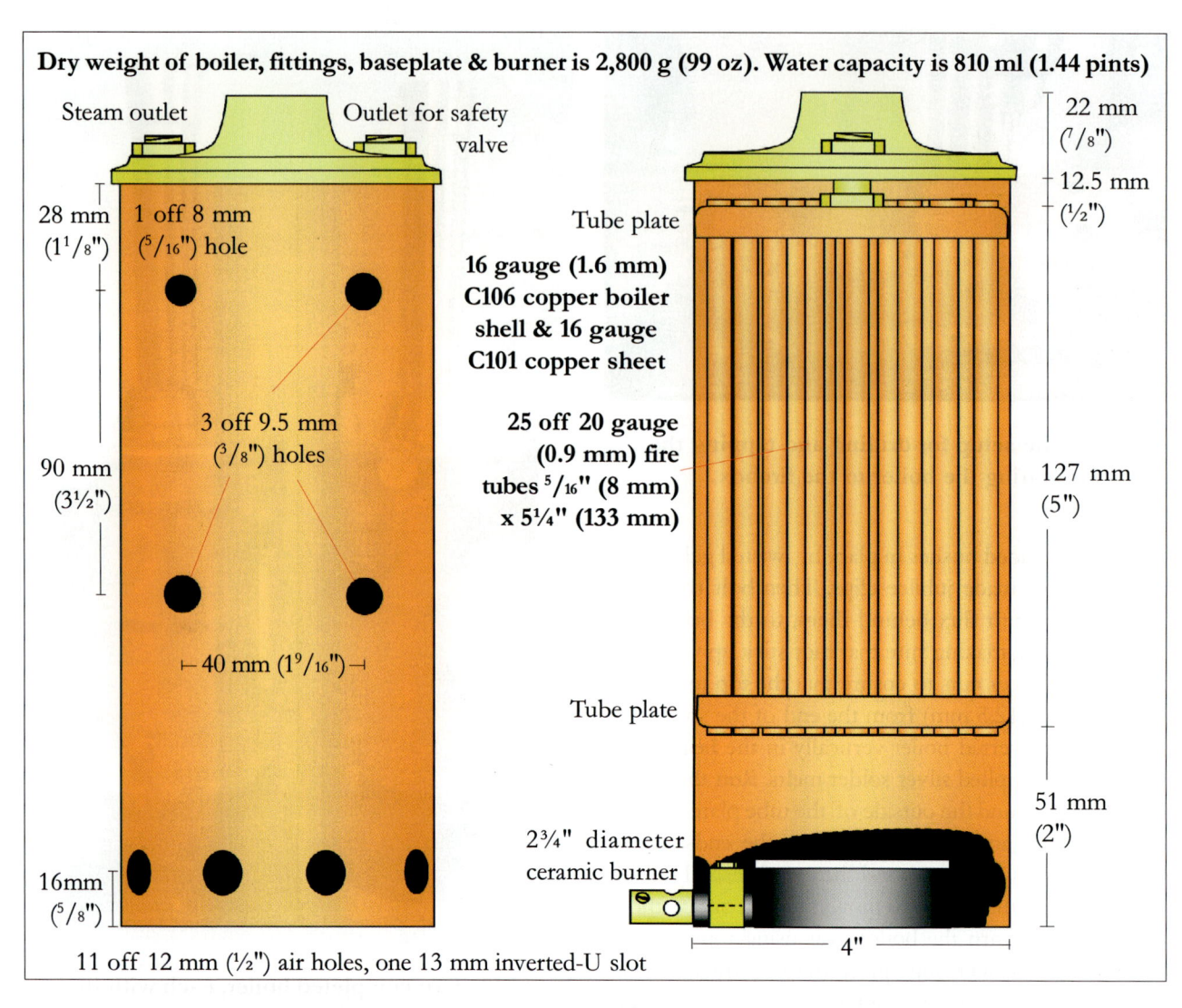

28 mm (1 1/8")
1 off 8 mm (5/16") hole
90 mm (3 1/2")
3 off 9.5 mm (3/8") holes
40 mm (1 9/16")
16 mm (5/8")
11 off 12 mm (1/2") air holes, one 13 mm inverted-U slot

Tube plate
16 gauge (1.6 mm) C106 copper boiler shell & 16 gauge C101 copper sheet
25 off 20 gauge (0.9 mm) fire tubes 5/16" (8 mm) x 5 1/4" (133 mm)
Tube plate
2 3/4" diameter ceramic burner

22 mm (7/8")
12.5 mm (1/2")
127 mm (5")
51 mm (2")
4"

Drawing 4. The 4" boiler shell, smoke-box cover, tube plates, fire tubes and burner.

Photo 11. The various component parts that make up the 4" boiler pressure vessel.

4" (102 mm) VERTICAL BOILER

This slightly narrower vertical boiler is ideal for marine use. Unlike the previous boiler, its firebox is part of the boiler shell. It is 10 1/4" (260 mm) tall with fittings plus a further 1 3/8" (35 mm) for the chimney. It uses a 7 1/2" (190 mm) length of 4" (102 mm) diameter 16 gauge copper tube; the bottom 2" (51 mm) forms the firebox. It was inspired by and is a much simplified version of Stan Bray's similar size boiler that was coal fired with a water-cooled firebox.

It is fitted with 25 fire tubes 5 1/4" (133 mm) long, made from 5/16" (8 mm) diameter 20 gauge (0.9 mm) copper tube. The top of the smoke box can be made in two ways. Turn a casting, available from GLR Kennions, to shape in a lathe or make a flanged brass smoke-box cover in the same way as that for the 108 mm boiler described on Page 62. A 2 3/4" circular ceramic burner fits in the firebox and is held in place by a split mount attached to a base plate.

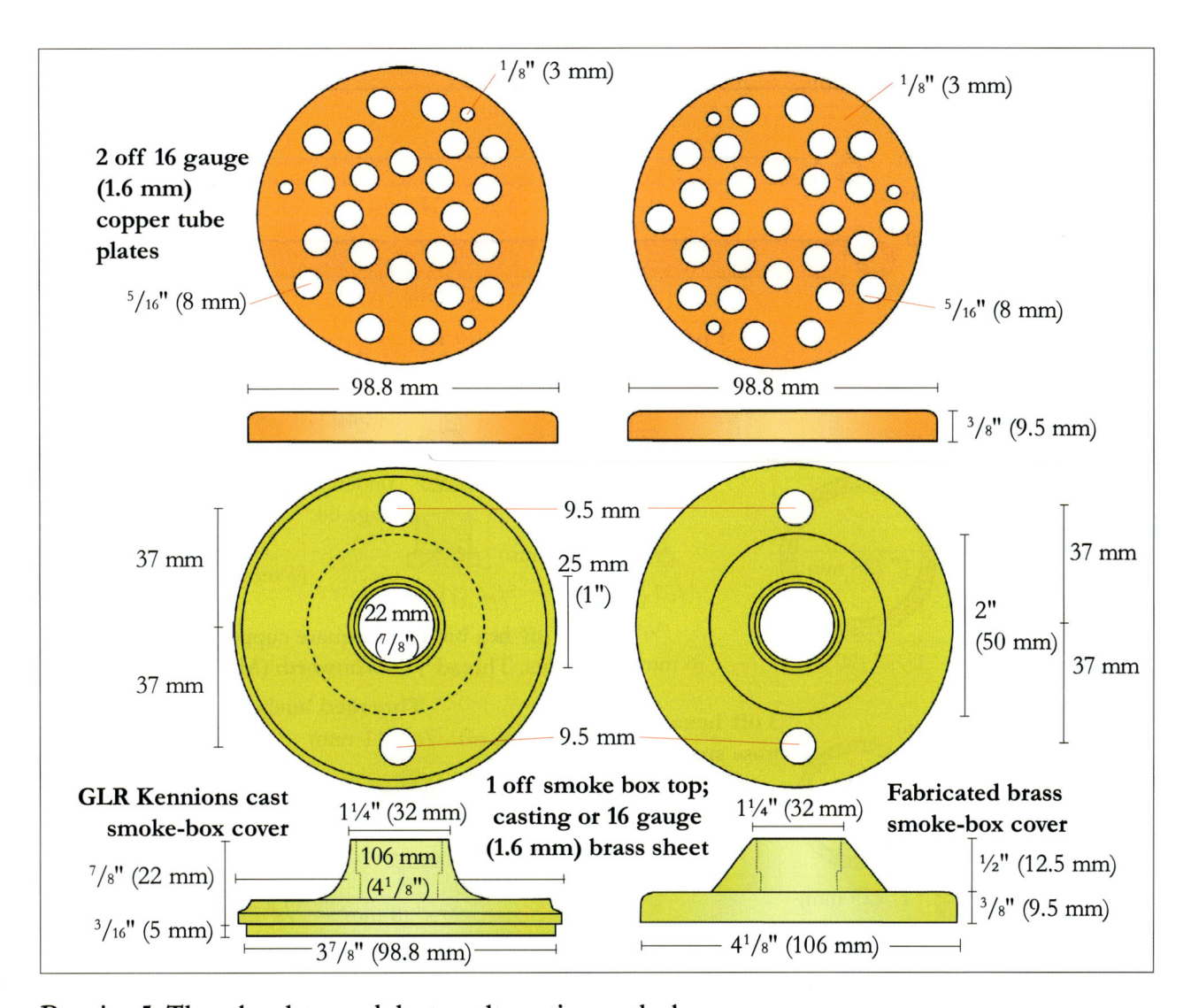

Drawing 5. The tube plates and the two alternative smoke box covers.

Carefully drill four holes in the squared-off boiler tube for the two gauges and clack valve; also eleven holes to ventilate the burner and a twelfth one filed to form an inverted-U for the burner. Form a mirror pair of flanged plates from 16 gauge copper discs 4¾" (120 mm) diameter over a 3¾" (95.6 mm) diameter wooden block. Drill both of the plates with twenty-five holes ⁵/₁₆" (8 mm), then two further holes of the same size for the steam outlet and safety valve. Both plates have three ¹/₈" (3 mm) holes for the spacer-tube rods. In the lathe, skim the pair of plates to fit inside the boiler shell.

Cut the twenty-five fire tubes to 5¼" (133 mm) length and then slightly splay out one end of each one, checking that the flared end will not pass through the holes in the flanged plates. Cut the three smaller spacer tubes and rods to length, thread the rods for ³/₈" (9.5 mm) along one end and ½" (12.5 mm) at the other and make copper or bronze nuts to fit. Carry out a test assembly of the flanged plates. Insert it in the boiler shell in the correct position and mark where the flanges need small semi-circular sections removed to clear the threaded bushes. Remove this small amount of amount of copper from the flanges with a round file.

There are several conventional machining jobs. The easiest are the two connecting units, their nuts and the four threaded bushes. The smoke-box cover is a relatively

Holes	Radius	Angle
1 x 8 mm	Centre	0°
8 x 8 mm	18 mm	0°, 45°, 90°, 135°, 180°, 225°, 270°, 315°
8 x 8 mm	29 mm	19°, 57°, 123°, 161°, 199°, 237°, 303°, 341°
10 x 8 mm	37 mm	0°, 38°, 76°, 104°, 142°, 180°, 218°, 256°, 284°, 322°
3 x 3 mm	37 mm	10°, 102°, 237°

Table 3. The location of the tube-plate holes; the red ones only in the top plate. Make a mirror pair.

70 VERTICAL-BOILER DESIGNS

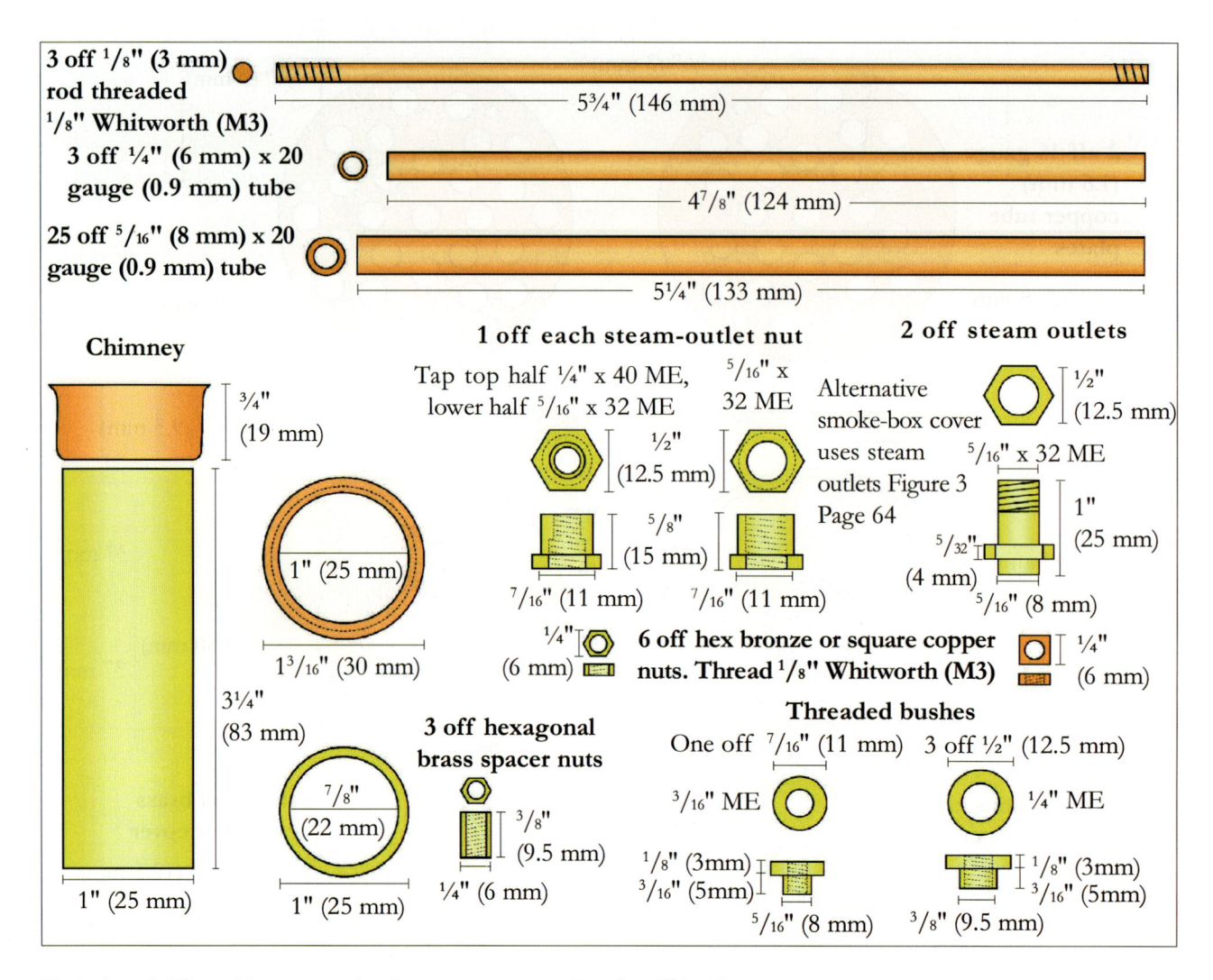

Drawing 6. The chimney and other components for the 4" boiler

straightforward task. The casting needs a profiling tool to obtain a smooth curve on its top surface. Bore the hole for the funnel and drill holes and mill flat spots for the connecting units to the safety valve and steam output. The casting is held in place by tightening the nuts on the two connecting units soldered to the top tube plate.

Mount the alternative flanged brass smoke box lid on the outside jaws of a 3-jaw chuck and turn the edges; then face the top. Also turn a chimney mount and silver solder it in place prior to polishing the complete unit.

The chimney can be either thin-walled copper or brass tube, embellished with a flared top. The chimney shown is brass tube with a piece of central-heating pipe flared in to fit the top of the tube.

To prepare the boiler for soldering, clean the various component parts first in a pickle, then rinse in cold water. Clean smaller items with wire wool. Assemble the tube plates, their spacer tubes and rods, with the bottom plate on top. Tighten the nuts until the assembly is firm and then insert the fire tubes from the firebox end. During assembly, coat the areas to be joined with flux before placing the plates with tubes in the boiler shell. The firebox end of the boiler will be silver soldered first. Adjust the brass spacer nuts to ensure the top tube plate is ½" (12.5mm) from the top of the boiler shell. At this stage do not fit the steam-outlet connectors. Insert the four threaded bushes, flux the joints and hold in place with twisted wire. Place the whole boiler assembly in the hearth, firebox up, and solder the bottom tube plate, fire tubes, threaded rods and nuts in place; also the bottom two threaded bushes. Without delay, use tongs to carefully turn the boiler over, remove the brass spacer nuts and insert the two well-fluxed steam connectors. Silver solder the top end of the boiler, including the two top threaded bushes. Pickle the boiler, wash in clean cold water ready for hydraulic testing. This was done to 120 psi (8.3 bar).

Then lag the boiler and attach the smoke box cover, the various fittings and a base plate (described on Page 76). The boiler can now have its second hydraulic test at 80 psi (5.5 bar). Check the burner operates correctly and fit it to the base plate. The boiler is finally ready for its first steam test and connection to an engine.

BUILDING SMALL BOILERS 71

Photo 12. The tube plate and fire tube assembly ready to fit in the boiler tube.

Photo 13. The soldered-up boiler before cleaning.

Photo 14. The inside of the firebox immediately after silver soldering and before cleaning.

Photo 15. The completed boiler with mahogany planking and boiler fittings.

72 VERTICAL-BOILER DESIGNS

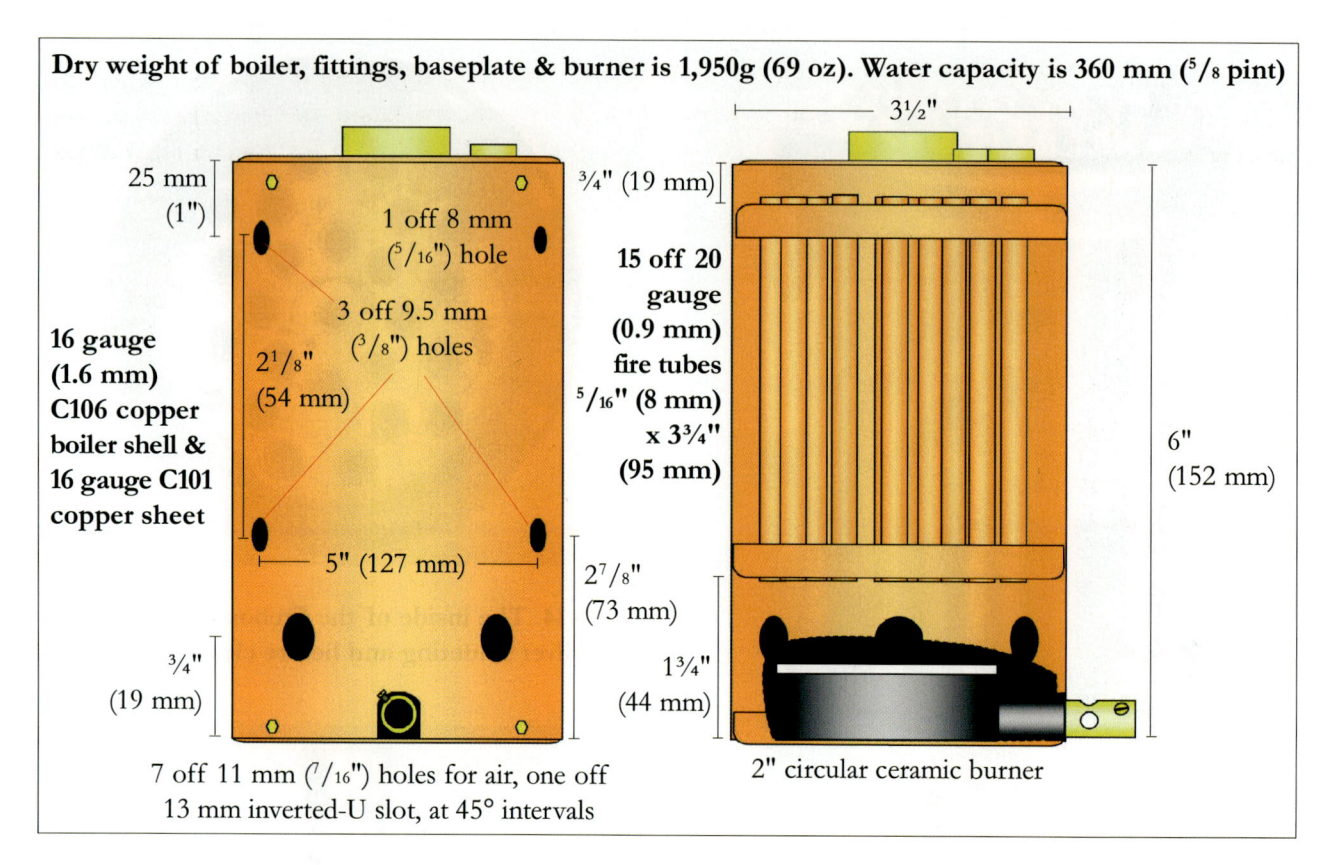

Dry weight of boiler, fittings, baseplate & burner is 1,950g (69 oz). Water capacity is 360 mm (⁵/₈ pint)

- 25 mm (1")
- 16 gauge (1.6 mm) C106 copper boiler shell & 16 gauge C101 copper sheet
- 1 off 8 mm (⁵/₁₆") hole
- 3 off 9.5 mm (³/₈") holes
- 2¹/₈" (54 mm)
- 5" (127 mm)
- ³/₄" (19 mm)
- 7 off 11 mm (⁷/₁₆") holes for air, one off 13 mm inverted-U slot, at 45° intervals
- ³/₄" (19 mm)
- 15 off 20 gauge (0.9 mm) fire tubes ⁵/₁₆" (8 mm) x 3³/₄" (95 mm)
- 2⁷/₈" (73 mm)
- 1³/₄" (44 mm)
- 3½"
- 6" (152 mm)
- 2" circular ceramic burner

Drawing 7. External and internal views of the 3½" vertical boiler.

3½" (89 mm) VERTICAL BOILER

This smallest vertical boiler is only 7" (180 mm) tall excluding the chimney. It is gas heated and was installated in a miniature steam lorry to replace the vertical water-tube version, which never produced enough steam. As a result, it has an off-centre chimney with the steam outlet and safety valve on the same side of the smoke box. The pressure and water gauges are on opposite sides of the boiler. There are fifteen fire tubes and the boiler is ideal for smaller models or where space is limited.

The boiler shell plus firebox is a 6" (152 mm) length of copper tube drilled with holes for threaded bushes; three 9.5 mm (³/₈") and one 8 mm (⁵/₁₆"). The firebox has seven 11 mm (⁷/₁₆") air holes and one 13 mm opened up to an inverted U-shaped slot for the burner connection. The tube plates, the smoke-box cover and the base plate are copper. Make these parts from 16 gauge copper discs 4¹/₈" (105 mm) in diameter, flanged over a wooden form 82.5 mm (3¼") in diameter. Drill fifteen holes ⁵/₁₆" (8 mm) in both plates as mirror images, then two more in the top plate for the steam outlets. Both plates have three small spacer-rod holes. In the lathe, skim both flanges to fit the boiler shell. Then bore the hole for the chimney.

The fire tubes are ⁵/₁₆" (8 mm) diameter 20 gauge (0.9 mm) copper tube and are 3³/₄" (95 mm) long.

Slightly widen one end so that they will not pass right through the holes in the tube plates. There are also three ¹/₈" (3 mm) rods, 4¼" (108 mm) long, threaded ¹/₈" Whitworth (M3) for ¼" (6 mm) at one end, ½" (13 mm) at the other and fitted with copper or bronze nuts. ½" (13 mm) long brass hexagonal nuts screw onto the longer threaded ends of the copper rods to ensure the top tube plate is exactly ¾" (19 mm) from the top of the boiler shell. These rods run through ¼" (6 mm) x 3³/₈" (86 mm) tubes that hold the tube plates in place when soldering the boiler. Assemble the flanged plates with the spacer tubes, insert them in the boiler shell in the correct orientation and mark the flanges where they need small semi-circular sections removed to clear the threaded bushes. A round file will remove these small segments.

Holes	Radius	Angle
1 x 8 mm	Centre	0°
6 x 8 mm	18 mm	0°, 60°, 120°, 180° 240°, 300°
10 x 8 mm	34 mm	15°, 55°, 95° 140°, 175°, 210°, 255°, 290°, 317°, 345°
3 x 3 mm	37 mm	35°, 115°, 235°

Table 4. The holes to be drilled in the mirror pair of tube plates, those in red only in the top plate.

BUILDING SMALL BOILERS 73

1 off 20 gauge (1.6 mm) copper base plate, smoke-box cover and pair of tube plates.

³⁄₈" (9.5 mm)
85.8 mm
85.8 mm

1¼" (32 mm)
⁷⁄₈" 22 mm
10 mm
½" (13 mm)   25 mm (1")

⁵⁄₁₆" (8 mm)
¹⁄₈" (3 mm)
¹⁄₈" (3 mm)
⁸⁄₁₆" (8 mm)

3 off ¹⁄₈" (3 mm) rods threaded ¹⁄₈" Whitworth (M3)

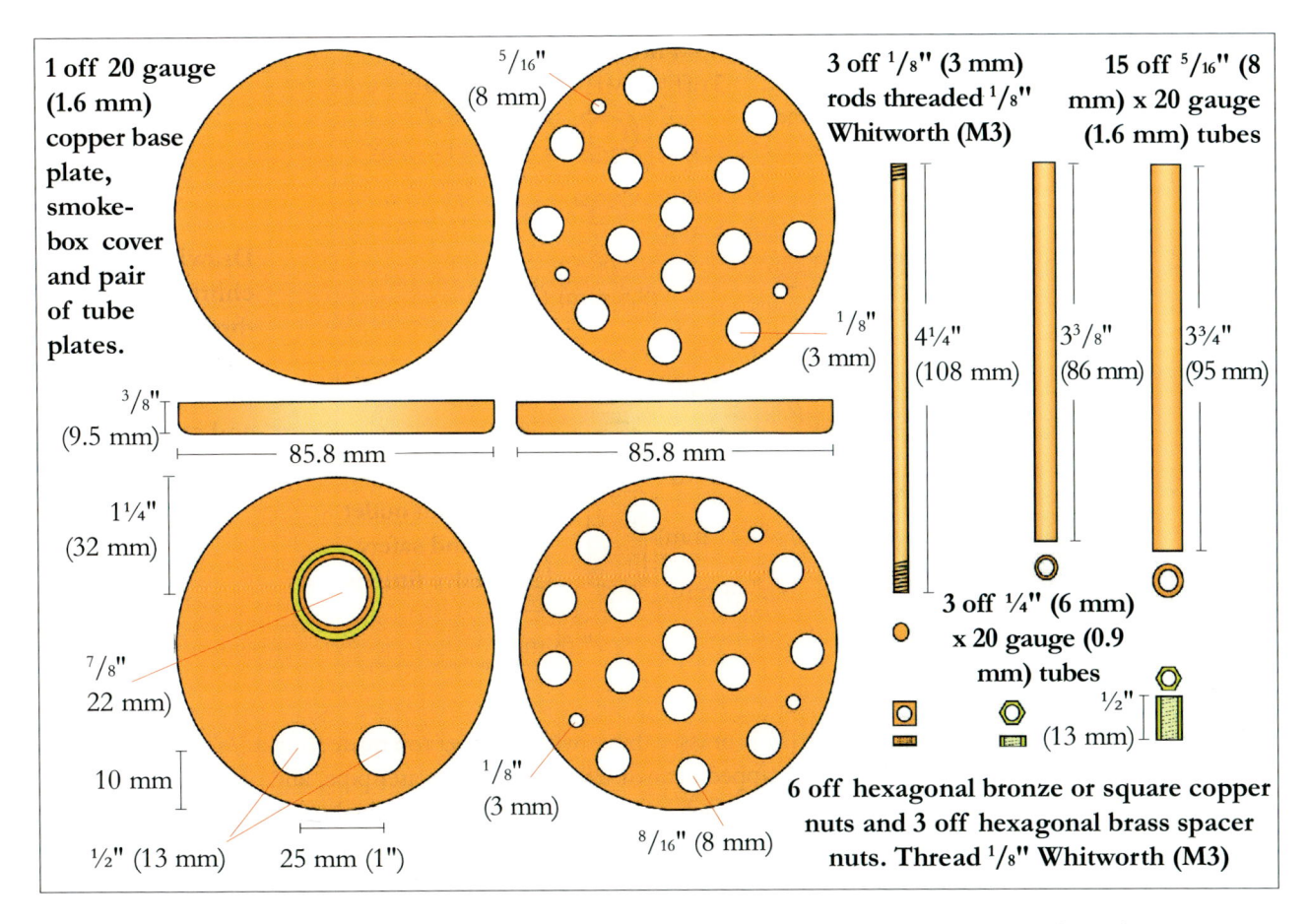

4¼" (108 mm)

15 off ⁵⁄₁₆" (8 mm) x 20 gauge (1.6 mm) tubes

3³⁄₈" (86 mm)   3¾" (95 mm)

3 off ¼" (6 mm) x 20 gauge (0.9 mm) tubes

½" (13 mm)

6 off hexagonal bronze or square copper nuts and 3 off hexagonal brass spacer nuts. Thread ¹⁄₈" Whitworth (M3)

Drawing 8. The tube plates, smoke-box cover, base plate, fire tubes, spacer tubes, rods and nuts.

The smoke-box cover has three holes. The one for the chimney is located 1¼" (32 mm) from the edge, is bored ⁷⁄₈" (22 mm) diameter, with a ring of brass silver soldered to it that holds the brass chimney. Opposite the chimney are two ½" (13 mm) holes through which the bronze fittings for the safety valve and steam outlet protrude.

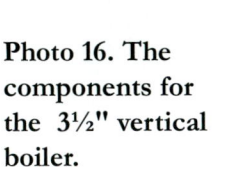

Photo 16. The components for the 3½" vertical boiler.

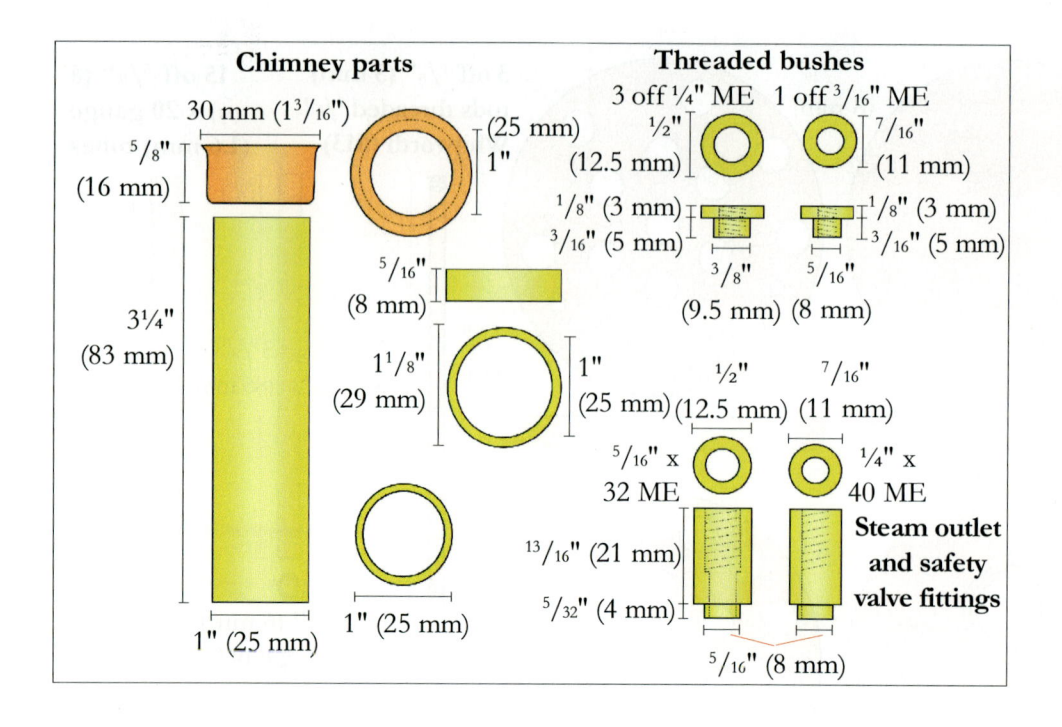

74 VERTICAL-BOILER DESIGNS

Drawing 9. The chimney parts, threaded bushes, and fittings for the safety valve and steam outlet.

This cover is held in place with three 6BA (M3) brass bolts. These fit into threaded holes drilled and tapped in the plate flanges and boiler shell $1/8$" (3 mm) from each end. A 2" circular ceramic burner fits in the firebox. The baseplate (see Drawing 11 on Page 77) has strips of brass, silver soldered to the baseplate, drilled and tapped 6BA (M3) fix it to the boiler. A clamp holds the burner.

The chimney is a $3¼$" (83 mm) length of 1" (25 mm) thin-walled copper or brass tube. The chimney shown is brass with a copper top made from a $5/8$" (16 mm) length of 28 mm copper water pipe, annealed and then flared out at the top and in at the bottom.

Before silver soldering the boiler, soak the body and pair of tube plates in pickle, wash in cold water and dry. Further cleaning of all items is readily undertaken with steel wool. The two tube plates are assembled, with the bottom tube plate on top and correctly orientated relative to each other, with the three rods in their spacer tubes and the six nuts tightened. This will give a rigid structure. Fit the unflared ends of the tubes through the bottom plate. Start at the centre and work outwards to ease locating the bottoms of the tubes in their correct holes. The complete assembly is shown in Photo 17.

Photo 17. The flanged tube plates and fire tubes assembly ready for inserting into the boiler shell.

Photo 18. The boiler firebox before pickling.

BUILDING SMALL BOILERS 75

Photo 19. The flanged copper smoke-box cover with chimney and brass mounting ring.

Test fit the assembly in the inverted boiler shell, always keeping the fire tubes vertical. If all fits nicely, remove the entire assembly and take out the tubes. Mix up some flux and apply it to all parts to be soldered before re-assembling them. More flux may be needed around the perimeter of the tube plates. Twisted wire holds the threaded bushes in place. Screw the long brass bolts onto the copper rods in the smoke box and adjust until the

Photo 21. The completed boiler with wooden lagging, ceramic burner and boiler fittings.

tube plate is ¾" (19 mm) from end of the boiler shell. Stand the boiler vertically, still up-side-down, in the hearth and heat it until the flux liquefies and the silver solder melts. Run the solder around the outside of the tube plate, each fire tube, threaded rod and nut, as well as around the bottom pair of threaded bushes. Using tongs, quickly but carefully turn the hot boiler the right way up. Flux and insert the two bronze steam-outlets, and repeat the same soldering tasks for the top-half parts.

Allow the boiler to cool and carefully check all the joints to see that the silver solder has flowed into them. Pickle the boiler and rinse in cold water so that it is clean. Once pressure tested at 120 psi (8.3 bar), it is time to bolt the smoke-box cover in position. Install the wooden planks, boiler bands and the various fittings ready for a second hydraulic test at 90 psi (6.2 bar). Finally attach the burner to the base, check the flame and bolt the base plate to the boiler ready for its first steam test.

Photo 20. The silver-soldered boiler with plugs in the threaded bushes after hydraulic testing.

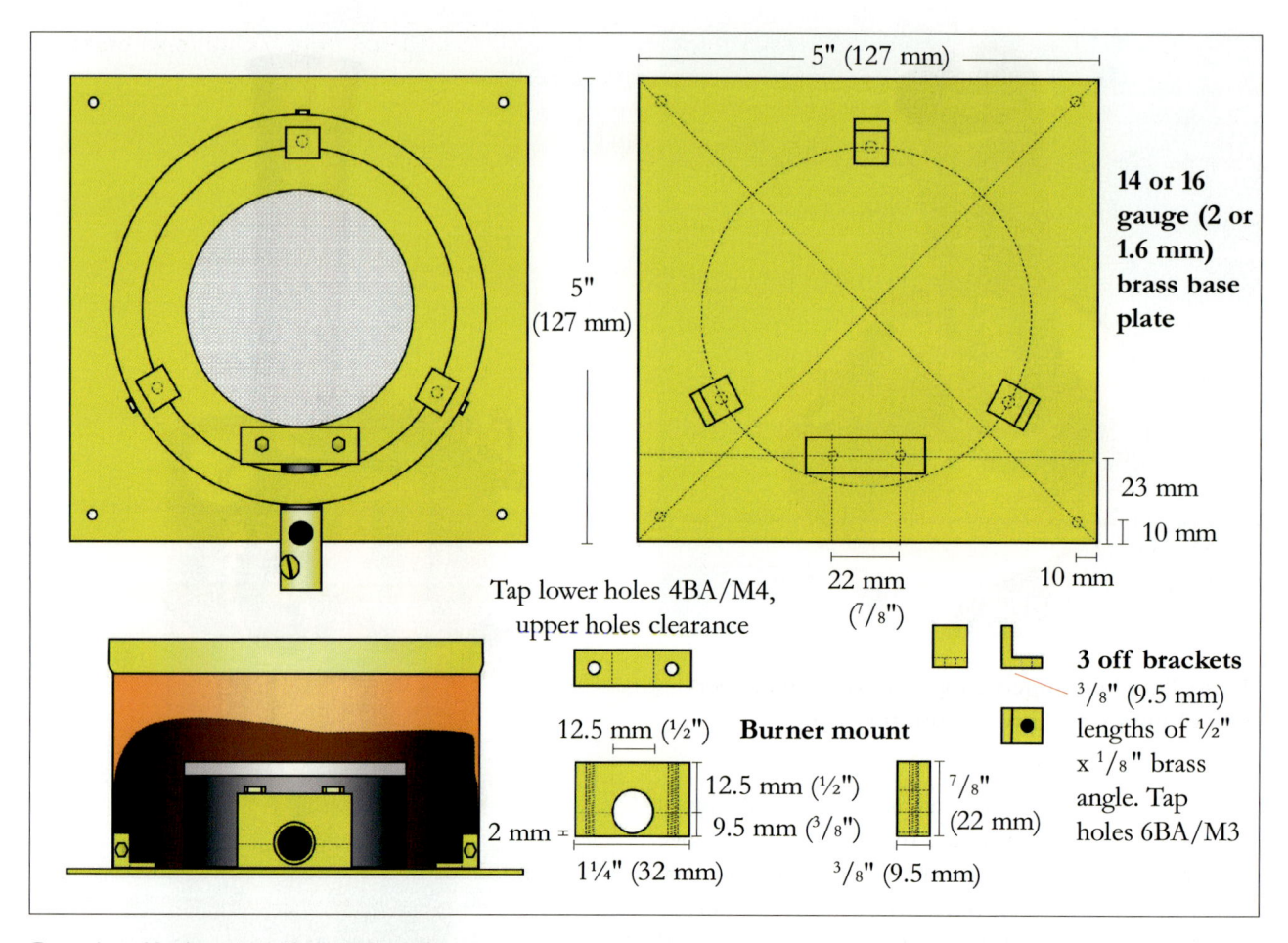

Drawing 10. A square base plate, burner mount and brackets for the 108 mm and the 4" vertical boilers.

OPTIONAL BASE PLATES

Fixing a vertical boiler down, whether it drives a static engine or is located in a moving vehicle or boat, usually requires a baseplate. While these are often customised to a particular requirement, this section includes four solutions which may be altered to meet individual needs.

The optional base plate for the 108 mm and the 4" boilers consists of a 5" (127 mm) square of 1.6 or 2 mm (16 or 14 gauge) thick brass sheet with seven 6BA (M3) and two 4BA (M4) clearance holes drilled in it. For the 108 mm boiler, three holes are at 43.5 mm pcd and for the 4" one at 40.5 mm pcd so that miniature angle brackets can be held in place with small bolts. The burner-mount holes should be 23 mm from the edge in both cases. Drawing 10 shows the layout and the various brass parts.

There are several alternative solutions for permanently attaching the parts. The first involves silver soldering, either with a hand-held torch or with a small burner on a larger torch to heat the whole base plate evenly. Try to

Photo 22. A baseplate with fittings assembled ready for soldering.

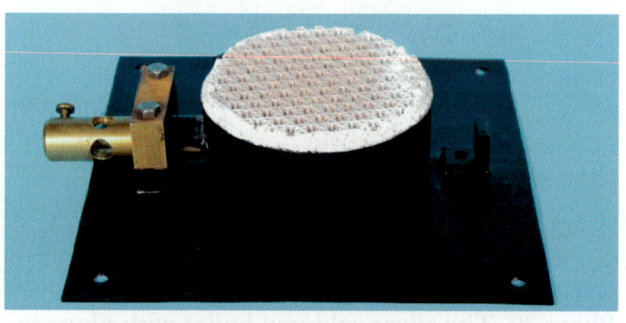

Photo 23. A finished base plate and burner clamp.

BUILDING SMALL BOILERS 77

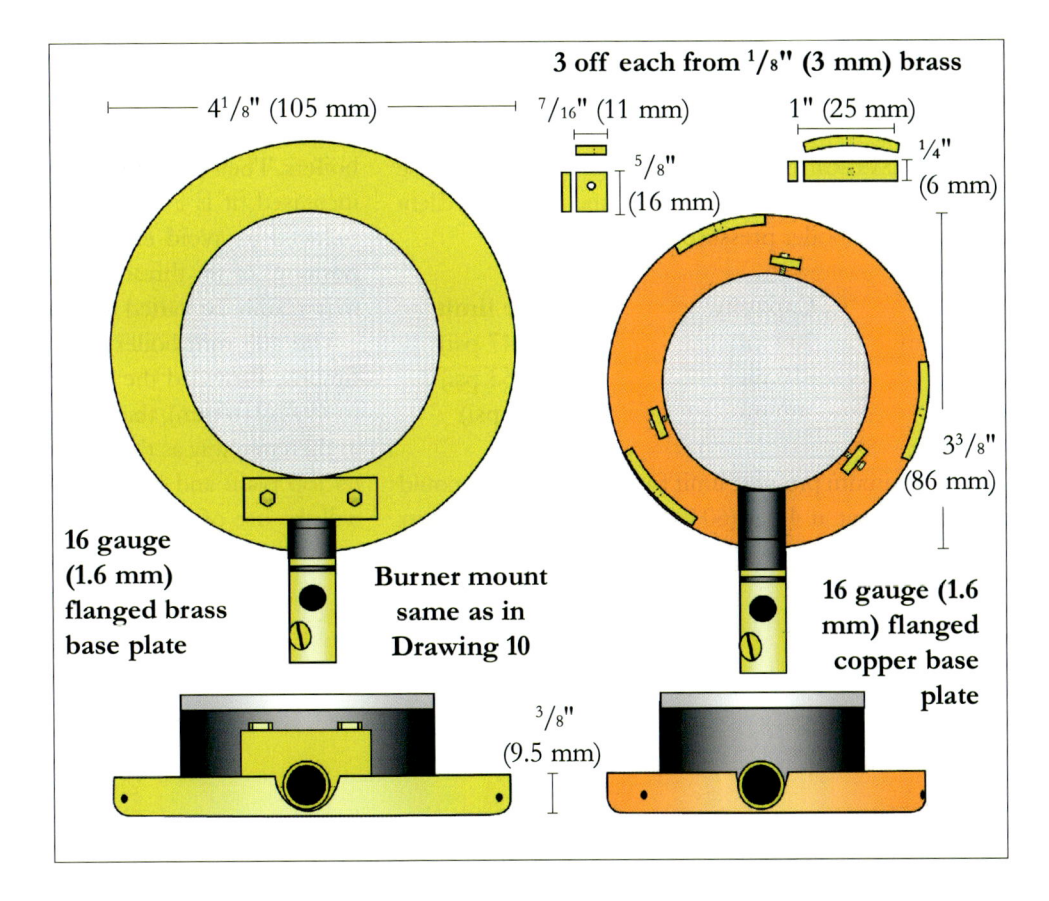

Drawing 11. Two round base plates with burner mounts for a 108 mm vertical boiler, left, and a 3½" vertical one, right.

3 off each from ⅛" (3 mm) brass

4⅛" (105 mm)   7/16" (11 mm)   1" (25 mm)

⅝" (16 mm)   ¼" (6 mm)

16 gauge (1.6 mm) flanged brass base plate

Burner mount same as in Drawing 10

3⅜" (86 mm)

16 gauge (1.6 mm) flanged copper base plate

⅜" (9.5 mm)

avoid distorting the base plate; the hand-held approach is more inclined to do so so due to uneven heating. In either case, if the base plate is screwed to a scrap of plywood, the distortion will be reduced even though the wood may catch fire!

Bolt the three brackets to the base and use studs with nuts on the bottom to hold the burner clamp in place. Silver solder the four components in place. Remove the bolts holding the brackets and burner clamp. Any bolt that cannot be removed can be filed flat on the underside of the base, while the nuts on the burner clamp can be removed and the stub of the studs filed down. Clean the base in pickle. Judicious use of a hide-faced hammer and flat hard jaws in a vice will quickly flatten any distortion in the plate. Another solution is just to use bolts to hold the parts in place with the heads countersunk into a base of 2 mm brass.

The hole in the burner clamp to fit the burner input pipe needs to match the diameter of the pipe on the actual burner being used. This will normally be ½" (12.5 mm) and located with its centre ⅜" (9.5 mm) above the base plate.

Once the base plate is complete, round off corners of the brackets to clear the boiler shell. Following a trial fit, mark the base plate with the centre of each of the three brackets so that their position is visible with the shell in position. Mark the three hole positions to be drilled in the boiler firebox, 5/16" (8 mm) up from the base plate and drill tapping holes through. Thread to suit 6BA or M3 bolts.

One alternative to a square base plate is a circular one that is flanged to fit inside the firebox. This is better when installing a boiler in a steam lorry. It will require three short lengths of ⅛" (3 mm) brass strip tapped 6BA or M3 as well as three 1" x ¼" (25 x 6 mm) lengths of ⅛" (3 mm) brass strip bent to match the curve of the flange These are all silver soldered in position on the base plate. The burner is held in place by three 6BA (M3) bolts screwed into the burner-mounting plates and gently adjusted to grip the burner casing. Drill and tap three holes 6BA or M3, spaced at 120° around the perimeter, and ⅛" (6 mm) up from the bottom of the firebox to hold the base plate in place.

Photo 24. A well-used circular base plate and burner from a 3½" vertical boiler.

CONCLUSIONS

The three vertical boilers described in this chapter use very similar construction techniques and all are excellent steamers. The boiler pressure limits are:

Boiler	Capacity	Pressure limit
108 mm	900 ml	3.3 bar (47 psi)
4"	810 ml	3.7 bar (53 psi)
3½"	360 ml	4 bar (60 psi)

The maximum pressure limit for all these boilers could in theory be set at 4 bar (60 psi); half the hydraulic test pressure of 8 bar (120 psi). In practice it must be set at the lower pressure defined by the water capacity.

Readers may, within limits, modify the designs of the boilers. Their height may be increased or reduced but if increased, it is essential that the operating pressure is reduced to avoid exceeding the 3 bar/litre limit. The positions of the threaded bushes and the chimney mounts may readily be varied to suit the planned installation.

The 108 mm boiler does not have to use a separate firebox. Provided the boiler shell is increased in length to 8½" (216 mm), the boiler can be built as a single unit in the same way as the 4" boiler. In this case, the firebox, its top plate and the mounts will not be required, nor will the use of a ceramic filler be needed.

7: HORIZONTAL-BOILER DESIGNS

OVERVIEW

This chapter describes three small horizontal boilers that are suitable for home-building. They are a 3" (76 mm) horizontal water-tube boiler, together with 54 mm ($2^1/_8$") and 42 mm ($1^2/_3$") single-flue boilers. The water-tube boiler is heated by a ceramic burner while the other two boilers employ gas torches and internal flues.

Like the vertical boilers, Chapter 2 demonstrates how all three horizontal boilers can safely be silver soldered in a single session without any step soldering. Careful assembly is needed to ensure that all the parts of the boiler are securely held in place in the hearth before starting soldering. Every one of these boilers falls within the 3 bar/litre limit but they still need some relatively straight-forward independent testing. Chapter 3 gives full details of how hydraulic and steam testing is carried out.

All three boilers have relatively low profiles. The largest can be fitted to a variety of steam-powered boats. All three are well suited to powering a static steam engine. The two smallest boilers may also readily be configured and fitted to suitably sized designs of Gauge 1 and 16 mm narrow-gauge locomotives.

Photo 1. Three rather different horizontal boilers; two for static or locomotive use.

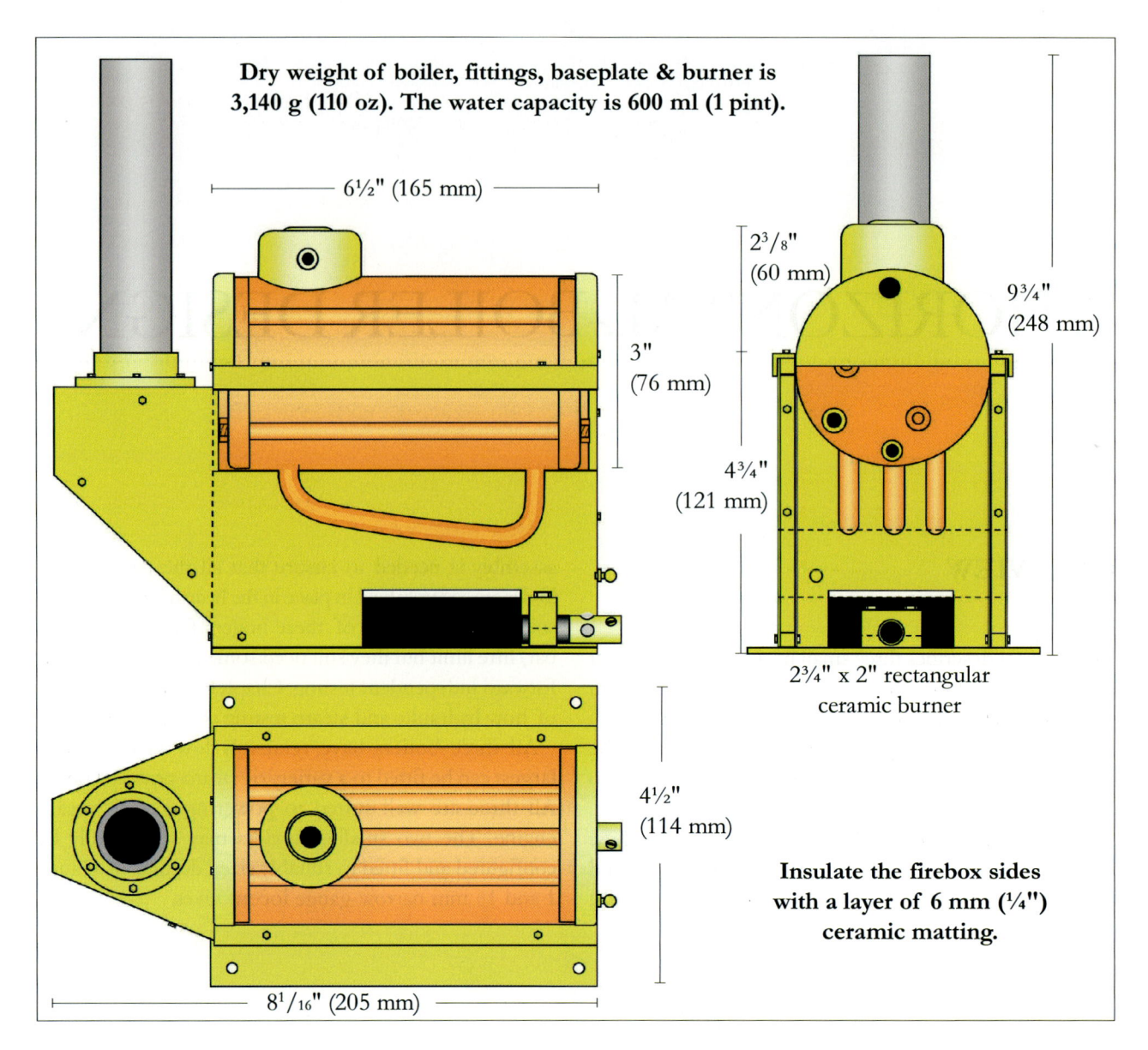

Dry weight of boiler, fittings, baseplate & burner is 3,140 g (110 oz). The water capacity is 600 ml (1 pint).

6½" (165 mm)

3" (76 mm)

2³⁄₈" (60 mm)

9¾" (248 mm)

4¾" (121 mm)

2¾" x 2" rectangular ceramic burner

4½" (114 mm)

Insulate the firebox sides with a layer of 6 mm (¼") ceramic matting.

8¹⁄₁₆" (205 mm)

Drawing 1. Three views of the boiler showing the internal stays, the water tubes and ceramic burner.

3" (76 mm) HORIZONTAL BOILER

This horizontal boiler is designed for marine or static use and employs three water tubes beneath the boiler shell, giving a water capacity of 600 ml (1 pint). The maximum working pressure for this boiler is 4 bar (60 psi). The pressure vessel sits in a brass casing. It is heated by a rectangular ceramic heater. While it is rather less efficient than the vertical fire-tube boilers described in Chapter 6, it benefits from having a lower centre of gravity. Its height is 6⁷⁄₈" (175 mm) to the top of the steam dome. It is well suited to being used in model boats.

The boiler uses a 152 mm (6") length of copper tube with flanged end caps supported by three ³⁄₁₆" (5 mm) bronze longitudinal stays. It has three 8 mm (⁵⁄₁₆") copper water tubes, underneath the boiler but just above the burner, to increase the rate of steam production. On the top is a bronze steam dome that connects to the safety valve, pressure gauge and steam outlet valve. Two bronze threaded bushes on one of the end plates allow a water gauge to be fitted while a third is provided for a clack valve. The firebox is made from a sandwich of 6 mm (¼") ceramic matting between two layers of folded brass sheet, which are bolted together. The ceramic mat is easily cut to size and helps to insulate the heat in the firebox. A door gives access to the burner for lighting. The other end of the firebox terminates in a stainless-steel chimney.

The water tubes beneath the boiler shell are formed from three 9" (230 mm) long lengths of 8 mm (⁵⁄₁₆") copper tube. Chapter 1, Pages 22 - 24 gave details of how to bend them to shape. Three identical water tubes are required with the centres of their open ends 4" (102 mm) apart. The ends of the tubes can then be cut

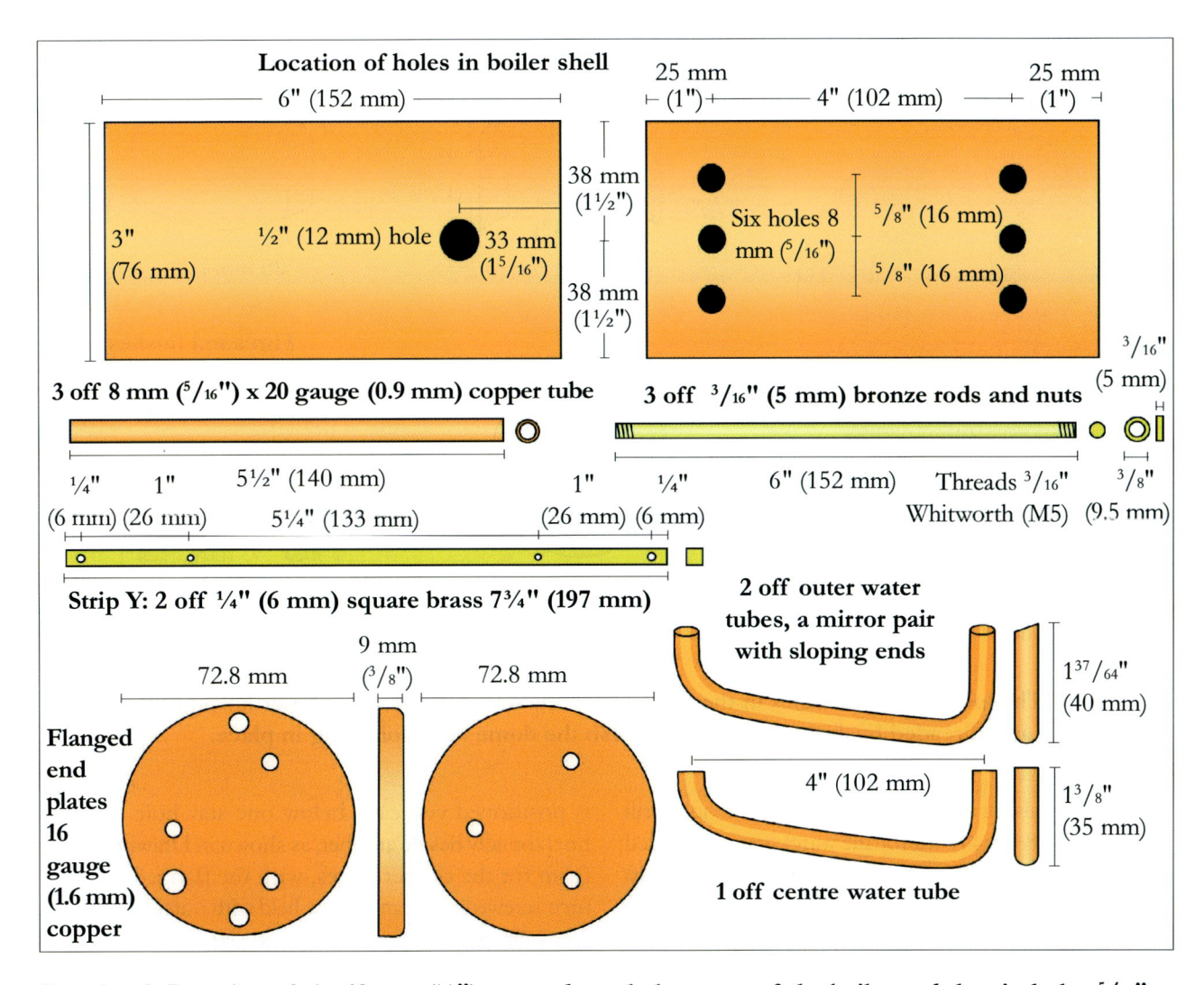

Drawing 2. Location of the 12 mm (½") steam dome hole on top of the boiler and the six holes ⁵/₁₆" (8 mm) for the three water tubes in the 3" horizontal boiler. Also shown are the boiler end plates, water tubes, stays, spacer tubes and brass strips along the sides of the boiler.

to length, noting that the outer tubes have longer ends than the centre one. Cut the ends of the centre tube square and both ends of the outer pair at an angle of about 30° to provide a mirror pair.

The boiler has seven holes drilled/milled in the shell. The pairs of holes for each tube are exactly 4" (102 mm) between centres. The holes for the centre tube are located on the centre line of the boiler shell while the outer two tubes have an 8 mm (⁵/₁₆") gap between them and the centre tube. This is shown in Drawing 2. The 12 mm (½") hole on the top of the boiler is for the steam dome.

A 7¾" (197 mm) length of ¼" (6 mm) square brass is fixed to each side of the boiler, with its upper surface at the boiler centre height, to support it on its firebox. Two steel jigging pieces hold them in place for silver soldering. Later cut them to the same length as the boiler shell.

The half of the boiler above the firebox has a brass cover at each end, formed from a disc of 16 gauge brass 4" (100 mm) in diameter. It is annealed and flanged over a 76.2 mm (3") wooden form. The disc is then held in a lathe chuck using internal jaws and the top and the flanges trimmed to give a smooth finish all over. Mark the disc centre line and then saw it exactly in half. Some slight trimming of the height of each half may be required to give a snug fit when installed. Drill a 10 mm hole centrally in one of the flanged discs to clear the top water-gauge fitting.

To make the boiler end plates, turn the wooden form down to 69.6 mm diameter and over it flange two 16 gauge (1.6 mm) copper discs, 4" (100 mm) in diameter. Then in turn mount each flanged disc, with the wooden form inside, on a rotary table. Hold the disc and its form firmly in place with a steel strip over the top, which has a pair of holes drilled at 3½" (89 mm) between centres (see photo 25 on Page 20). A laser centre/edge finder mounted in the chuck is a useful aid in ensuring that the disc is correctly centred. Then move the milling table 18.3 mm (²³/₃₂") and drill three ³/₁₆" (5 mm) holes

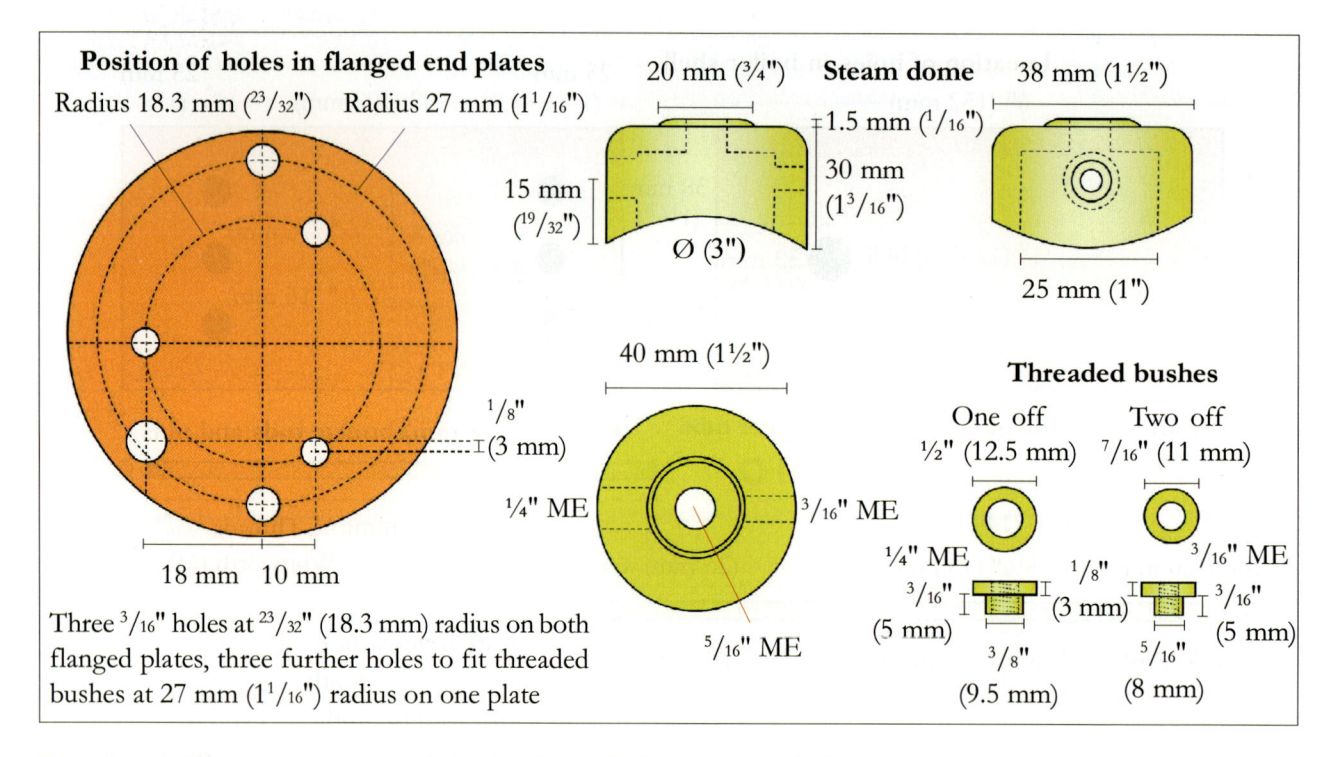

82 HORIZONTAL-BOILER DESIGNS

Position of holes in flanged end plates
Radius 18.3 mm (²³/₃₂")   Radius 27 mm (1¹/₁₆")

Steam dome — 20 mm (¾"), 1.5 mm (¹/₁₆"), 15 mm (¹⁹/₃₂"), 30 mm (1³/₁₆"), Ø (3"), 38 mm (1½"), 25 mm (1")

40 mm (1½"), 1/8" (3 mm), ¼" ME, ³/₁₆" ME, 5/16" ME

Threaded bushes
One off ½" (12.5 mm), Two off ⁷/₁₆" (11 mm)
¼" ME, ³/₁₆" ME, ³/₁₆" (5 mm), 1/8" (3 mm), ³/₁₆" (5 mm), 3/8" (9.5 mm), 5/16" (8 mm)

18 mm   10 mm

Three ³/₁₆" holes at ²³/₃₂" (18.3 mm) radius on both flanged plates, three further holes to fit threaded bushes at 27 mm (1¹/₁₆") radius on one plate

Drawing 3. The location of the holes in the end plates; one only has the three inner holes. Make the steam dome and threaded bushes from bronze. Polish the dome after soldering in place.

at 120° intervals for the stays. On one end plate only, drill the two ⁵/₁₆" (8 mm) holes for the water gauge threaded bushes 54 mm (2⅛") apart on a centre line parallel to one pair of stay holes. Drill one further 9.5 mm (³/₁₆") hole for the threaded bush for the clack valve. This one is positioned vertically below one stay hole and it is horizontally beside another, as shown in Drawing 3. The form for the copper plates, with the flanged plates in turn screwed to it, can then be held with outside jaws of a 3-jaw chuck to trim the flanges to size.

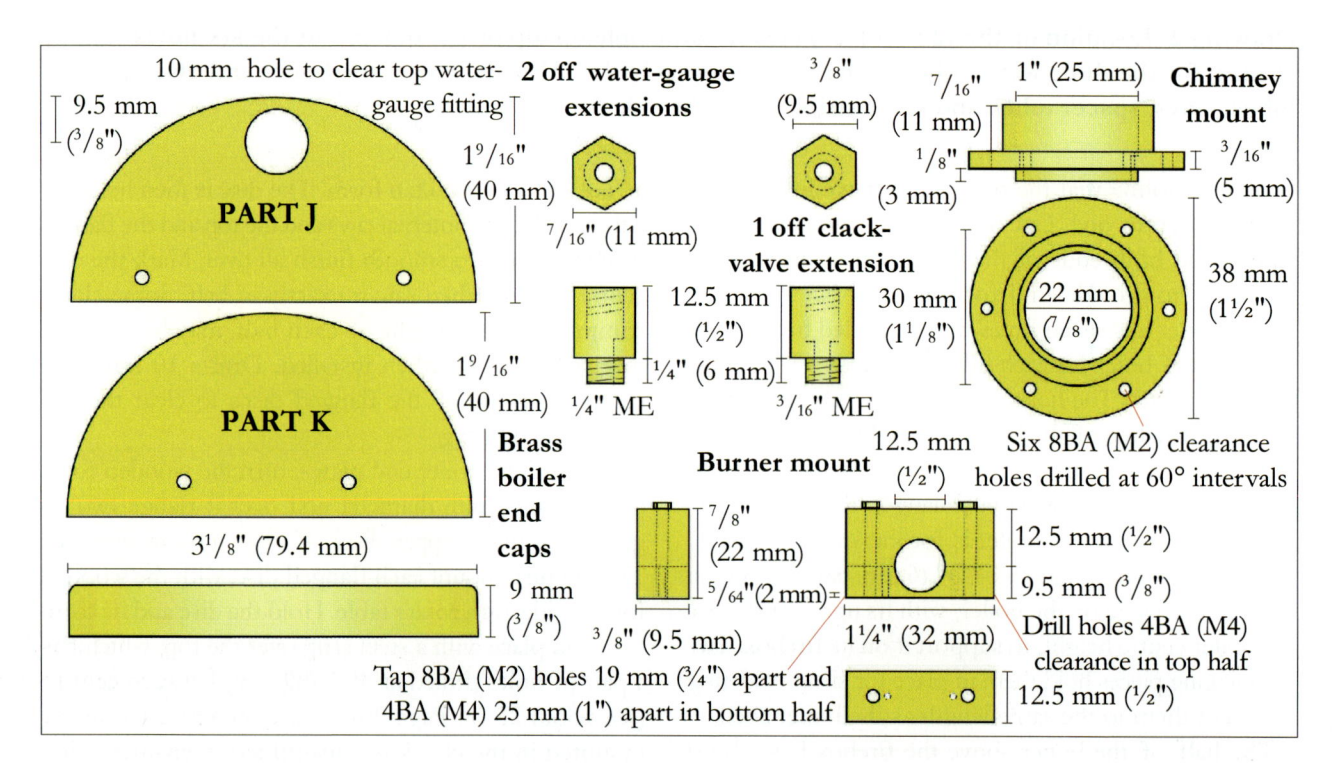

PART J — 9.5 mm (³/₈"), 10 mm hole to clear top water-gauge fitting, 1⁹/₁₆" (40 mm)

2 off water-gauge extensions — ⁷/₁₆" (11 mm), ¼" ME

1 off clack-valve extension — 12.5 mm (½"), ¼" (6 mm), 30 mm (1⅛"), ³/₁₆" ME

Chimney mount — 3/8" (9.5 mm), ⁷/₁₆" (11 mm), 1" (25 mm), 1/8" (3 mm), ³/₁₆" (5 mm), 22 mm (⁷/₈"), 38 mm (1½")

PART K — 1⁹/₁₆" (40 mm), 3⅛" (79.4 mm)

Brass boiler end caps — 9 mm (³/₈")

Burner mount — ⁷/₈" (22 mm), ⁵/₆₄" (2 mm), 3/8" (9.5 mm), 12.5 mm (½"), 1¼" (32 mm), 12.5 mm (½"), 9.5 mm (³/₈"), 12.5 mm (½")

Tap 8BA (M2) holes 19 mm (¾") apart and 4BA (M4) 25 mm (1") apart in bottom half

Six 8BA (M2) clearance holes drilled at 60° intervals

Drill holes 4BA (M4) clearance in top half

Drawing 4. The brass boiler end caps, threaded extensions, chimney and burner mounts. The end caps and chimney should be polished. Hole locations in Parts J and K must match those in Parts G & F.

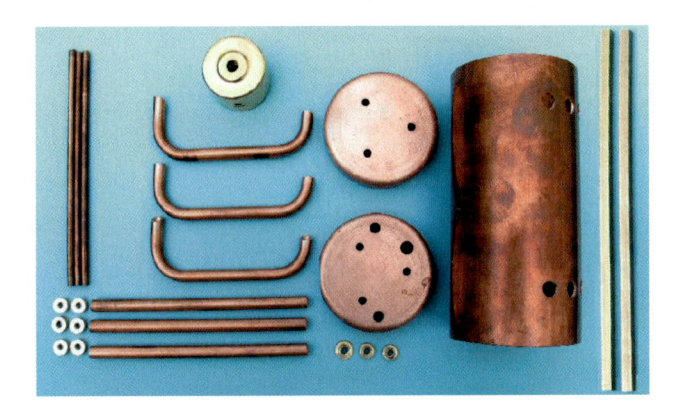

Photo 2. The set of parts for the 3" horizontal boiler pressure vessel.

Photo 4. The setup for milling one side of the brass angle Strip Z.

The steam dome is turned, drilled and tapped from 40 mm (1½") diameter round bronze bar. The chimney mount is a short ¾" (19 mm) length of 1½" (40 mm) round bronze or brass bar. Bore it ⁷/₈" (22 mm) and then enlarge one end to 1" (25 mm) for a depth of ⁷/₁₆" (11 mm) to fit the chimney. This is illustrated in Drawing 4.

Cut the three 6" (152 mm) lengths of ³/₁₆" phosphor bronze rod for the stays and thread ³/₁₆" (5 mm) for a distance of ¼" (6 mm) from each end of the rod. The three spacer tubes are 5½" (140 mm) long and have an external diameter of ⁵/₁₆" (8 mm) to give clearance for the stays inside.

Cut eleven different brass strips:
Strip U: 1 off ⅜" (9.5 mm) x ¼" (6 mm) x 3½" (89 mm)
Strip V: 2 off ¼" (6 mm) square x 5¹³/₁₆" (148 mm)
Strip W: 2 off ¼" (6 mm) x ⅜ (9.5 mm) x 4¼" (108 mm)
Strip X: 2 off ¼" (6 mm) square x 4" (102 mm)
Strip Y: 2 off ¼" (6 mm) square x 7¾" (197 mm)
Strip Z: 2 off ⅜" (9.5 mm) x ¹/₁₆" (1.5 mm) thick angle x 6³/₁₆" (157 mm)

Grip each pair of Strips Y and Z together in a machine vice with a scrap piece of 1 mm brass sheet between the strips. Mill 0.5 mm (0.02") off one side of Strip Z so that the angle will securely hold the firebox sides.

Clamp Strips Y and Z together with equal amounts of Strip Y protruding each end. Drill 8BA or M2 tapping-size holes 1¼" (32 mm) from each end of Strip Y. Tap the holes in Strips Y and open those in Strips Z to clearance size. Then drill a further 2 holes 6BA (M3) clearance ¼" (6 mm) from the end of each Strip Y to hold the strips in place during silver soldering.

Make two 4" (102 mm) long steel spacers ½" (12.5 mm) x ¼" (6 mm) to hold Strips Y in exactly the correct orientation against the boiler shell. These jigging strips are bolted to each end of Strips Y with 6BA (M3) steel bolts so the brass strips are the right distance apart; precisely 3" and with the same amount sticking out each end beyond the boiler shell.

Soldering up the boiler requires several other jigging parts to hold everything in place. The two flanged end plates are held in position by the three longitudinal stays with spacer tubes slipped over them. The stay rods are threaded ³/₁₆" Whitworth (M5) and the plates are secured with round nuts. They may be visible and will look better than hexagonal ones. They only need to be finger tight.

The water tubes sit on a Scanalex former with a pair of water-tube offcuts to hold them in place. These parts

Photo 3. Other firebox parts include the front and rear hemispherical end plates, the chimney mount and the three extension pieces for the water gauge and clack valve.

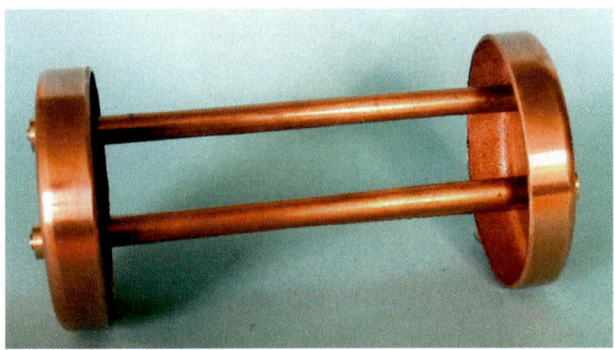

Photo 5. The stays and spacer tubes fitted to the end plates, bolting them together.

84 HORIZONTAL-BOILER DESIGNS

Photo 6. The boiler is jigged by two steel strips, two offcuts of water tube and a Scanalex former.

are shown in Photo 6. The two Strips Y, the steam dome, the water tubes and their jigging parts are held in place with twisted 1 mm (20 gauge) wire.

To silver solder the boiler, place it vertically in the hearth, supported on blocks either side of Strips Y. First deal with one end plate, its threaded bushes, stays, boiler-support strips and the three water-tube joints at that end. Then turn the boiler over and solder the other end plate, stays, boiler-support strips and water-tube joints in place. Finally turn the boiler to a horizontal position to solder the steam dome. When cool, carefully inspect all the joints and then remove the wire clips and jigging pieces. Rinse in hot water to remove any remaining flux, place in pickle to clean the boiler and rinse again with clean water. Cut the ends of the ¼" (6 mm) square Strips Y back to the length of the boiler shell. Now the boiler is ready for independent inspection and its first hydraulic test.

FIREBOX PARTS

Eleven pieces of the firebox casing are cut from 20 gauge (1.6 mm) brass sheet using a bandsaw, nibbler or hacksaw. The twelfth, the Base, is cut from 14 gauge (2 mm) brass.

Photo 8. The soldered and cleaned boiler with the steam dome and Strips Y cut to length.

The dimensions, shown in Drawing 5, do include bend allowances. The parts comprise the left and right outer walls (Parts B), which have 30° bends part way along their length, and the left and right inner walls (Parts A). The firebox door is top-hinged to Part G with small doll's-house brass butt hinges. Its knob is a brass stud from a radio-control ball-joint link or made from wood. Parts E and C cover the top and bottom chimney end of the firebox. The top one has a 1" (25 mm) hole cut in it, over which the chimney mount is bolted. Also bolted to it is Part F, bent to 90° and with one edge filed to clear the chimney mount. The hemispherical flanged-brass disc, Part K, attaches to it. Fold the ³/₈" (9.5 mm) tabs on Parts E and the side ones on Part C to 90°. Bend the front and rear tabs of Part C and sides of Part D only 60°. Once bent, the tabs will be about ¼" (6 mm) wide and should be held securely in place and drilled to clear 8BA (M2) bolts. The Warco vice brake shown in

Drawing 7. The water tubes held in place for silver soldering with a block of Skamolex.

Photo 9. The set of parts for the firebox and smoke box of the 3" horizontal boiler.

BUILDING SMALL BOILERS 85

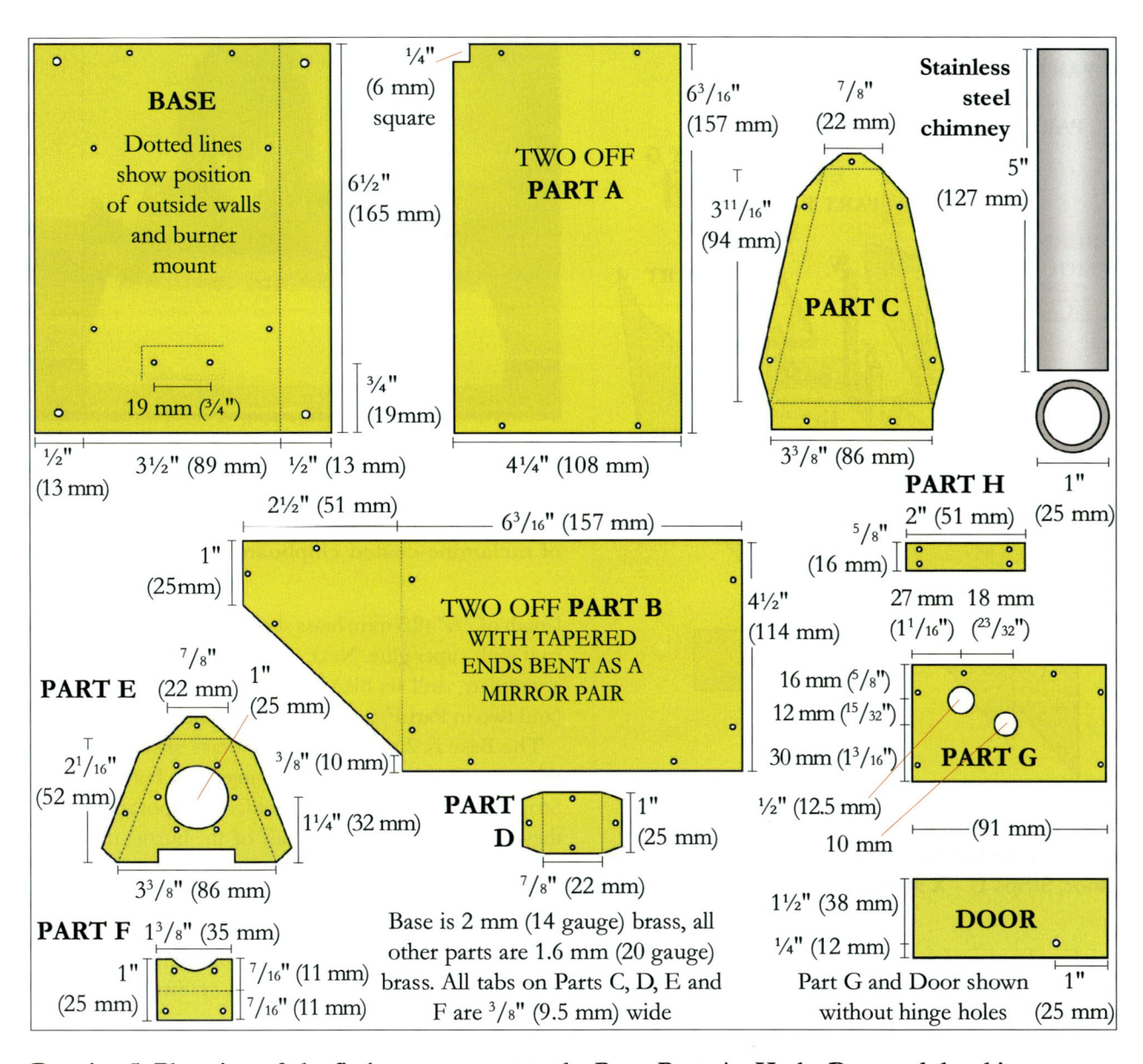

Drawing 5. Plan view of the firebox components; the Base, Parts A - H, the Door and the chimney.

Photo 10 is a relatively inexpensive way of folding the parts. Otherwise a mini bending brake will do the job.

After Part E has been folded, cut a piece of scrap wood to fit inside it. Mount it on a drilling or milling

Photo 10. Bending the third tab on Part E of the firebox using the Warco vice brake.

Photo 11. The set up for making the chimney opening in Part E with a hole saw.

86 HORIZONTAL-BOILER DESIGNS

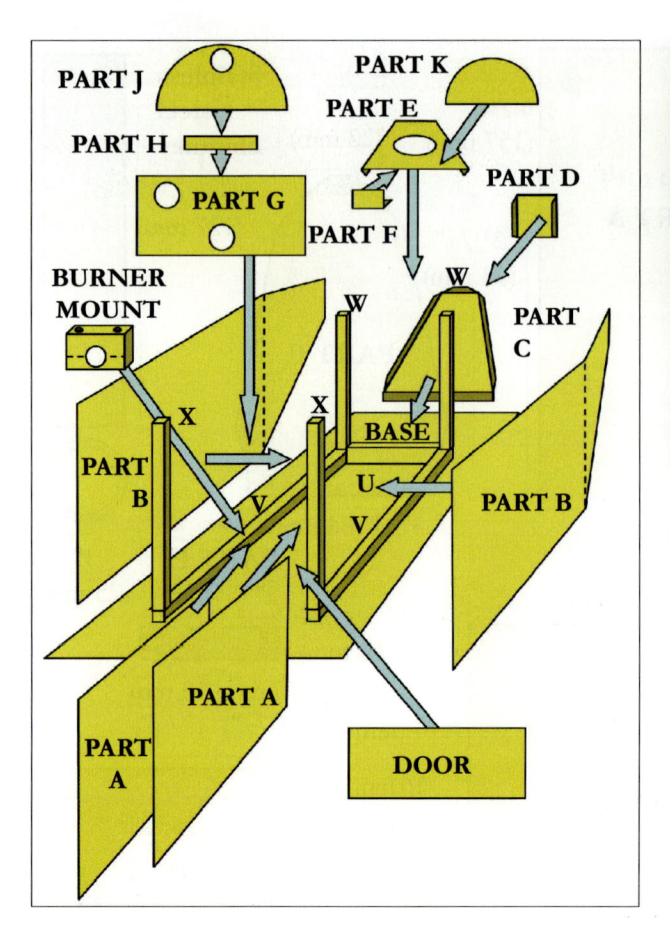

Drawing 6. An exploded view of the firebox showing the location of Parts A - K, the Base, the Door, Strips U - X and the burner mount.

Photo 12. Drilling the Base and Strips V, both of which are located with superglue; the strip being drilled is clamped, with the baseplate, on a piece of melamine-coated chipboard.

machine by clamping it to the table. Using a 1" (25 mm) hole saw drill the hole for the chimney mount. Part F, a length of ³/₈" (9.5 mm) brass sheet, bent to 90°, is attached to it with super glue. Next, using the chimney mount as a template, drill six 8BA (M2) clearance holes in Part E (and two in Part F) so the mount can be bolted to them.

The Base is 2 mm (14 gauge) brass sheet; the extra thickness allowing the use of countersunk bolts to attach Strips U, V and the burner holder. Temporarily fasten these strips and the bottom half of the burner mount to the Base with just two or three blobs of gel superglue. Place the whole lot on a short length of chipboard or MDF on the milling table, clamp each part in place, then drill and tap 8BA or (M2) holes on the centre-line of the strip 50 mm (2") in from each end of Strips V, 15 mm

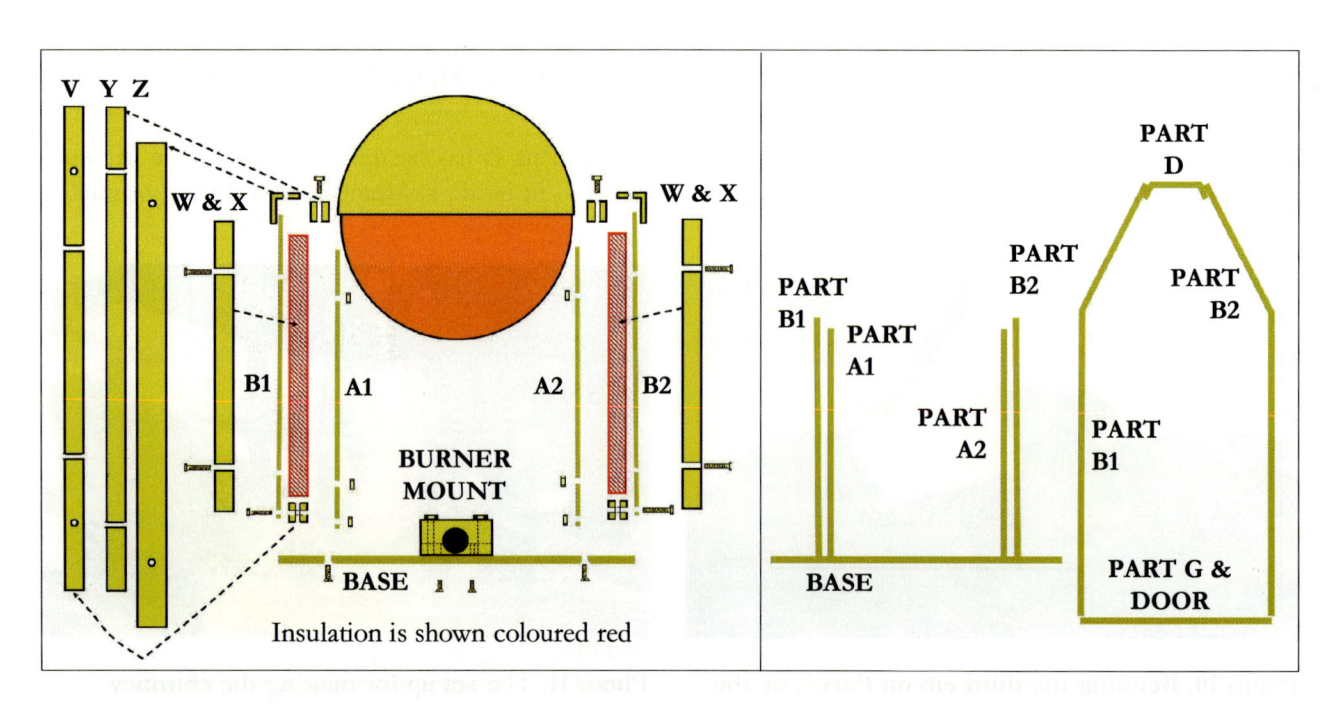

Drawing 7. An exploded view of the basic parts that make up the firebox and how they are folded.

BUILDING SMALL BOILERS

Photo 13. Drilling and tapping Parts A, B and Strips V. The assembly is clamped to the milling table and Parts A and B secured with a pair of clamps. The side of the Base fits in a table slot.

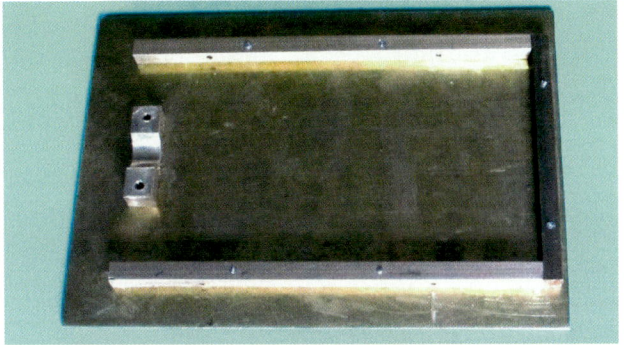

Photo 15. The Base with Strips U, V and the bottom half of the burner mount.

(½") in from each end of Strip U and 19 mm (¾") apart on the burner mount. The strips are then removed from the Base with a little heat. The holes in the Base are opened to 8BA (M2) clearance and countersunk. The setup is shown in Photo 12. Exactly the same process is used to attach the burner to the Base. It is positioned centrally ¾" (19 mm) from the door.

A similar procedure is followed with Parts A, B and Strips V and W with further 8BA (M2) clearance holes drilled. These are on the centre-line of the strips; the vertical ones 1" (25 mm) and the bottom ones 1½" (38 mm) from each end. Parts A needs their top edges chamfered with a file to an angle of about 60° to fit against the boiler shell.

Clamp Part C in place with the firebox assembly stood with its funnel end on top in order to drill and tap two 8BA or M2 holes through it into Strip U, and open to clearance in Part C, enabling the bottom of Part C to be bolted in place. Using clamps, hand drill two pairs of 8BA or M2 clearance holes in Parts B and C and bolt Part C in place. Clamp Part D in position, hand drill the same size holes and bolt in place, followed by Part E. This is shown in Photo 14. Hemispherical Part K bolts to Part F. Drill a 10 mm hole in hemispherical Part J to clear the top end of the water gauge fitting and bolt to Part G using Part H.

Superglue Part G to Strips X, drill and tap 8BA (M2) ½" (12 mm) from each end and then open up the holes in Part G to clearance size. The Door is top hinged to Part G using small dolls' house hinges and appropriately sized nuts and bolts. A hole is also needed for a small knob to open the door.

ASSEMBLING THE FIREBOX

Once all the holes in the various parts have been drilled to size and tapped as required, the parts can be disassembled and any burrs removed before assembly

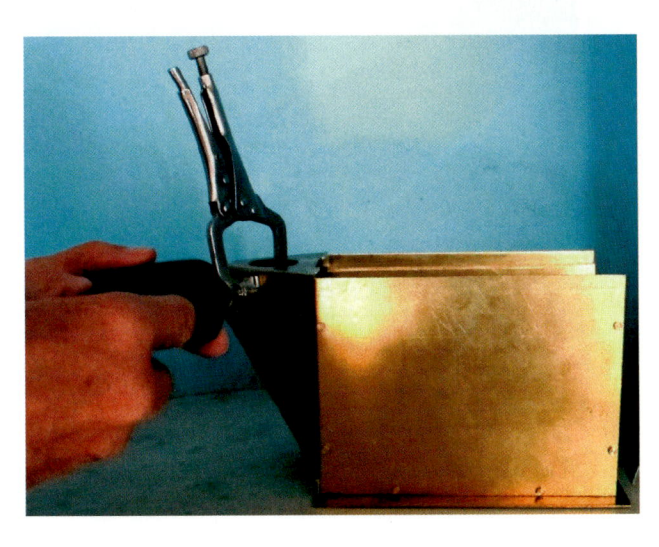

Photo 14. Part E clamped in place while a hand-held electric drill is used to make the fixing holes.

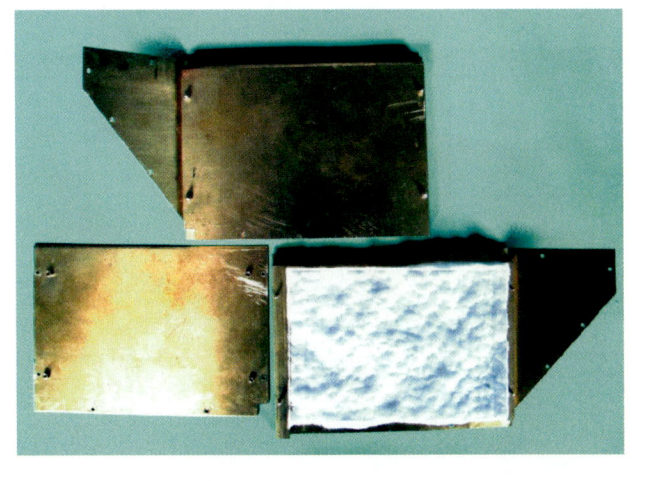

Photo 16. One pair of sides, Parts A and B assembled, the other pair ready for assembly with the ceramic insulation cut to size.

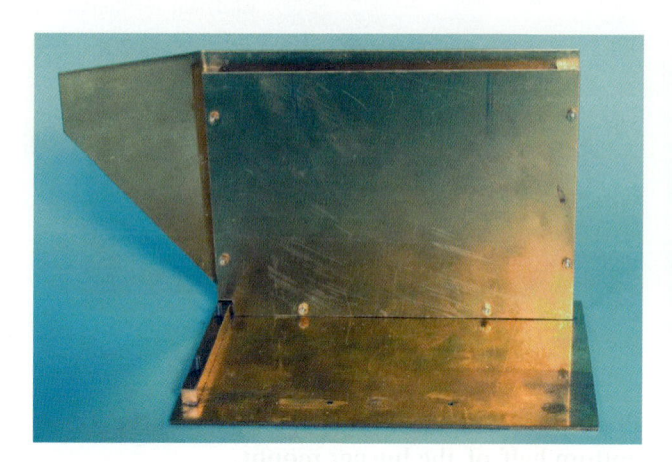

Photo 17. Parts A and B bolted to the Base.

of the combined firebox and smoke box commences. Start with the Base and bolt Strips U, V and the burner mount to it. Next, with scissors, cut two pieces of 6 mm (¼") ceramic boiler insulation 5½" x 4" (140 x 102 mm). Pass four bolts though Part B and strips W and X, then fit the piece of insulation between the strips, flush with the top of Part B and with 6 mm (¼") space at the bottom for Strip V. Then fix Part A in place with nuts on the bolts. Bolt the assemblies of both pairs of Parts A and B, Strips W and X to Strips V already on the Base.

Bolt Part C to Strip U and then to both Parts B. Next attach Part D in place. Bolt the door hinges to Part G and the Door with 12BA (M1) nuts and bolts after drilling locating holes in them. At this point, the assembly needs preparation for painting by first sand blasting all the exterior surfaces (see Photo 68 on Page 32). Temporarily bolt Parts E, G and the door in place for this and mask the top to stop sand affecting the insulation.

Remove these parts once sand blasting is complete. Bolt the chimney mount to both Parts E and F, bolt the hemispherical flanged brass disc K to Part F and bolt

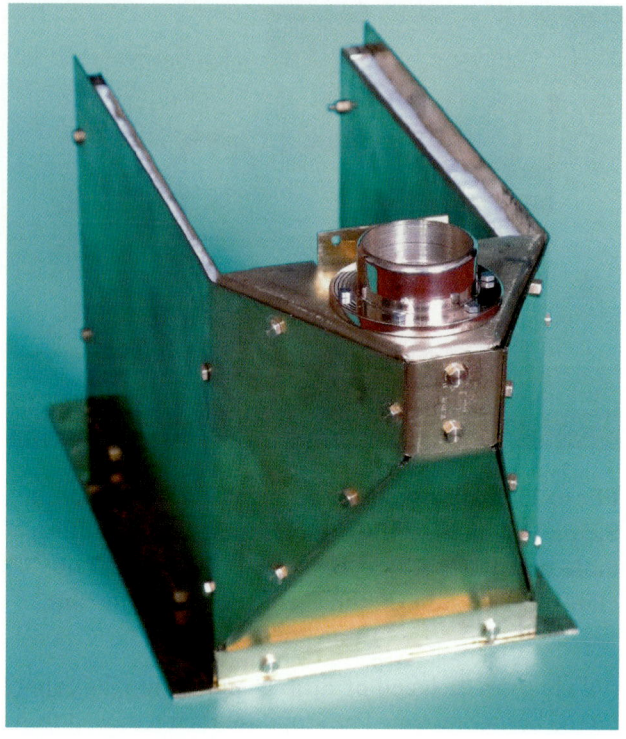

Photo 19. The sides, Parts A and B, the ceramic insulation and Part C, D, E and F bolted in place.

these parts to Parts B and D; a somewhat fiddly process. Once these are bolted firmly in place, any air leaks at the chimney end of the firebox should be filled with ceramic glue/filler. Then, slide the hydraulically tested copper boiler in place and bolt down the brass angle Strips Z.

Bolt the other hemispherical flanged brass disc, Part J to Part G via Part H. Finally, bolt in place Part G with

Photo 18. Both sides with the insulation in position and Part C bolted in place.

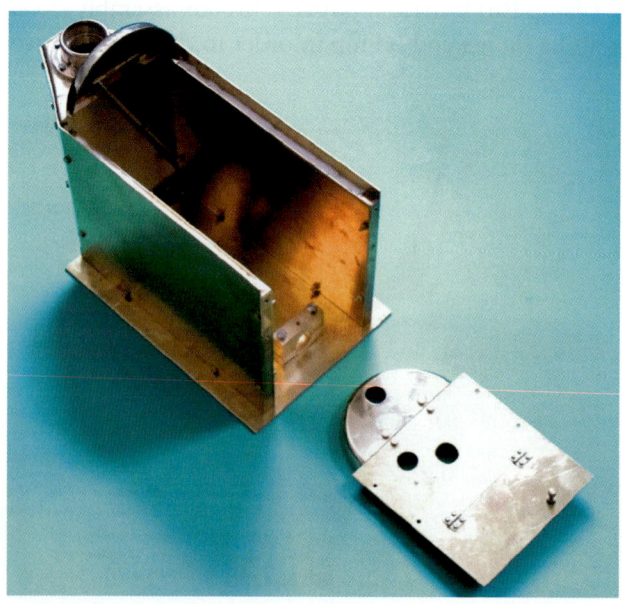

Photo 20. Complete firebox with Part G, H, J and the Door ready to hold the boiler is in position.

Photo 21. The finished boiler showing stainless steel chimney fitted in its brass mount and the planked top half of the boiler shell.

the Door and its hemispherical brass strip attached to it. The boiler is now held securely on its firebox.

Paint the outside of the firebox with several coats of heat-resisting black paint, apart from the boiler shell, the hemispherical brass discs, the brass angle strips that hold the boiler in place and the chimney mount. These parts should all be polished before they are fitted. The process of sand blasting and painting is described in Chapter 1 on pages 31 and 32.

Wooden planking is cut to length and sanded to fit around the steam dome. It is super glued to cover the top half of the boiler shell and, after sanding and several coats of varnish, fitted with a central brass boiler band, with its ends bent at right angles. The ends are clamped to Strips Z and then holes drilled and tapped 8BA (M2). The holes in the band themselves must be opened to clearance size so that it can be bolted in place.

This particular firebox configuration requires the three extension pieces, two for the water gauge and one for the clack valve. Made from hexagonal brass, screw them in place with copper washers at each end. Then fit and tighten the water gauge and clack valve. Attach the pressure gauge, steam and safety valves to the steam dome and install the burner in its mount.

The boiler is finally ready for its second hydraulic test at 90 psi (6.2 bar). If this is successful, it can be followed by a steam test. Only then can it be connected to a suitable engine.

90 HORIZONTAL-BOILER DESIGNS

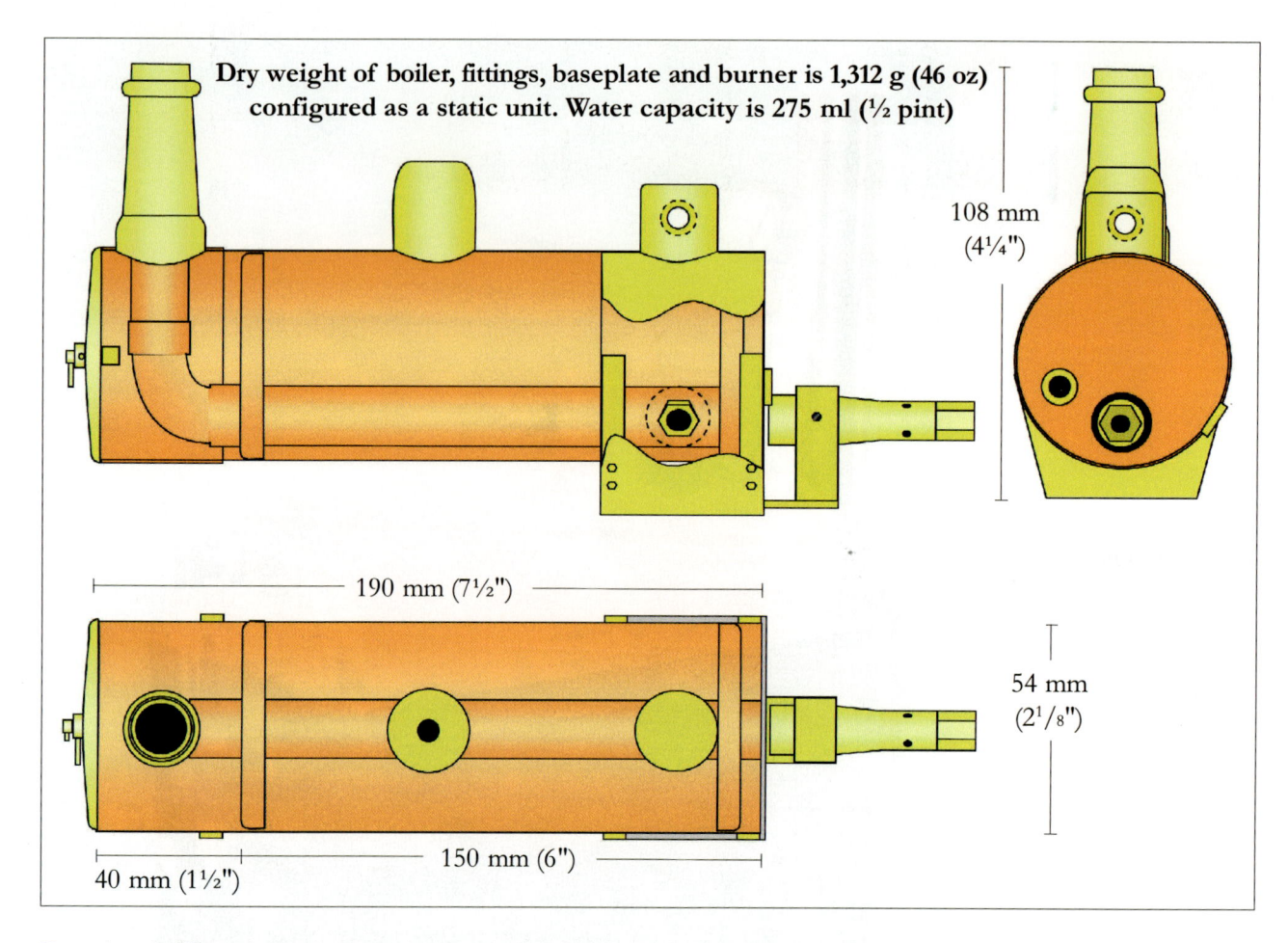

Drawing 8. Three views of the basic 54 mm boiler, showing the flue running along its length.

Dry weight of boiler, fittings, baseplate and burner is 1,312 g (46 oz) configured as a static unit. Water capacity is 275 ml (½ pint)

108 mm (4¼")
190 mm (7½")
54 mm (2⅛")
150 mm (6")
40 mm (1½")

54 mm (2⅛") HORIZONTAL BOILER

This small horizontal boiler may well prove attractive to smaller-gauge locomotive builders. It would also be ideal as a static boiler driving a small twin-cylinder engine. It is built around a 190 mm (7½") length of 54 mm diameter 18 gauge (1.2 mm) copper tube with a flue made from 15 mm diameter 20 gauge (0.7 mm) copper pipe; both widely used for plumbing (EN 1057 type X). Four or five holes are needed in the boiler barrel; one for the chimney, two for the safety valve and the steam domes, one at the burner end of the boiler for the water gauge and one for the front mount of the static boiler.

Two flanged plates are required so turn a suitable wooden form from a piece of hardwood to 48.4 mm (1²⁹⁄₃₂") diameter. Make the flanged copper end plates from 76 mm (3") discs of 16 gauge (1.6 mm) copper sheet. Turn them to diameter, held on the form in the lathe by pressure from a length of wood around 25 mm (1") diameter pushed by a rotating centre. Check that the boiler barrel will just slide over them.

The flanged end plates need a 15 mm hole to fit the flue tube. Each end plate is in turn fitted to the wooden form and the assembly clamped to a milling table. Then carefully mill or drill the 15 mm hole with its outer edge 5 mm (³⁄₁₆") from the outer edge of the flange. This is described in detail in Chapter 1, Page 20. Also drill a ³⁄₈" (9.5 mm) hole in one plate for a threaded bush.

Form the smoke box door from a 60 mm (2½") disc of 16 gauge annealed brass, pressed to shape in a form tool. Sizes of the form-tool parts are given in Drawing 2 on

Photo 22. The copper and bronze parts of the boiler that will be soldered together.

BUILDING SMALL BOILERS 91

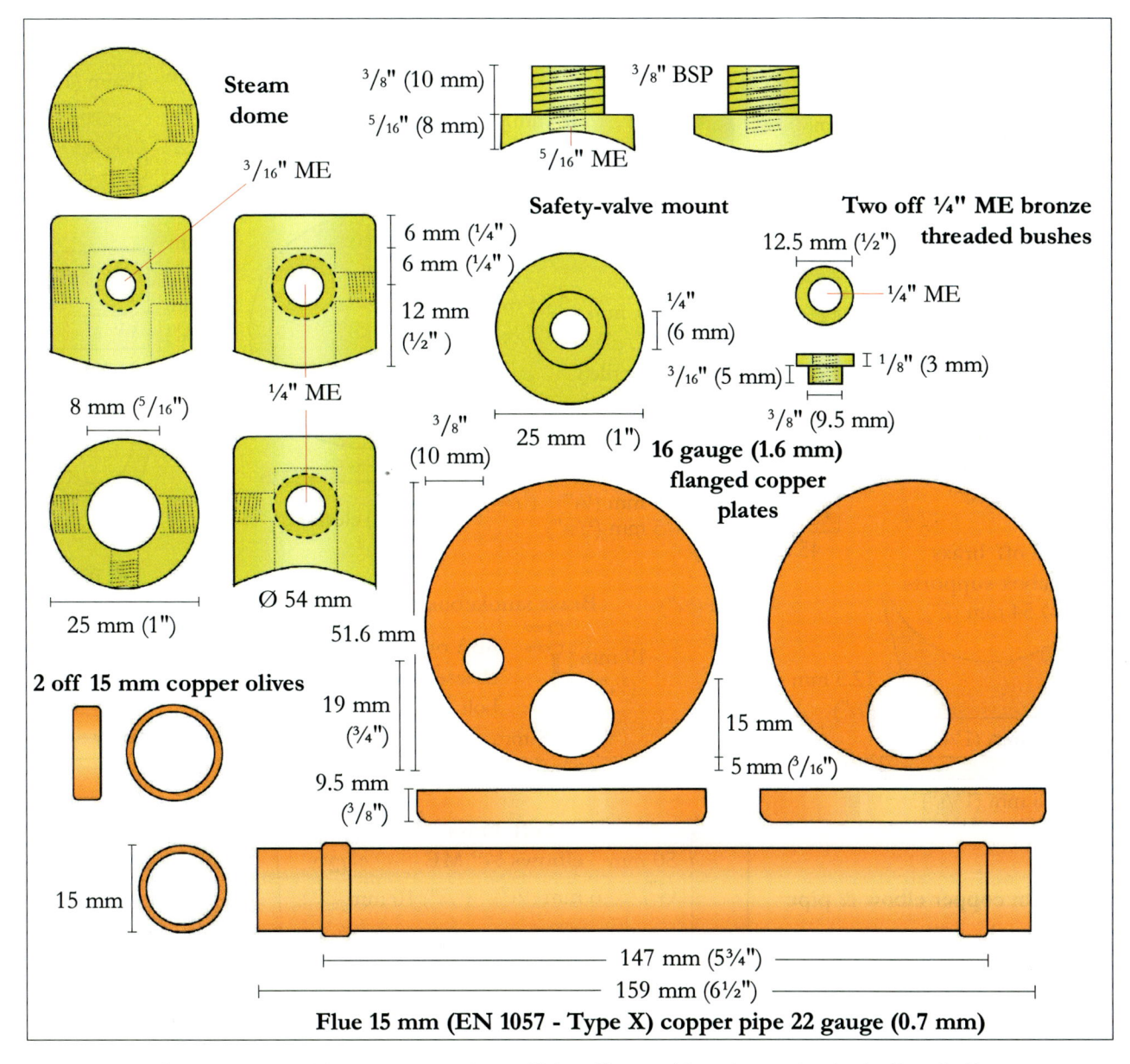

Drawing 9. The copper and bronze parts that will be silver soldered to or in the boiler shell.

Page 28. Recess the wooden form to fit the door and centre drill 2.3 mm ($^3/_{32}$"). Hold it in the lathe on the form with a bolt and pressure from a rotating centre via the same length of wood. Trim to 56.4 mm ($2^7/_{32}$") diameter.

The flue is a length of 15 mm copper pipe with a copper olive fitted at each end to space the end plates. Chapter 1, Page 21 shows how this is done.

Heating is provided by a Sievert 8720 Light Line burner. Make a fitting, described in Chapter 5, Page 59, to connect it to a gas pipe. The burner is held in a mount that can be customised to the boiler application.

The boiler has two bronze domes. One, made in two halves that screw together, houses the safety valve and is mounted half way along the top of the boiler. The other dome and a threaded bush are at the burner end. This steam dome feeds the pressure gauge, the top of the

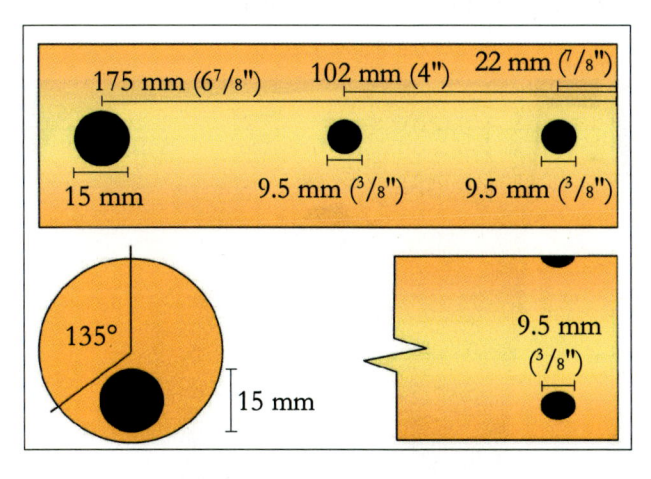

Drawing 10. Hole positions and the sizes in the boiler shell. The static one has a 6BA/M3 clearance hole under the centre of the chimney hole.

92 HORIZONTAL-BOILER DESIGNS

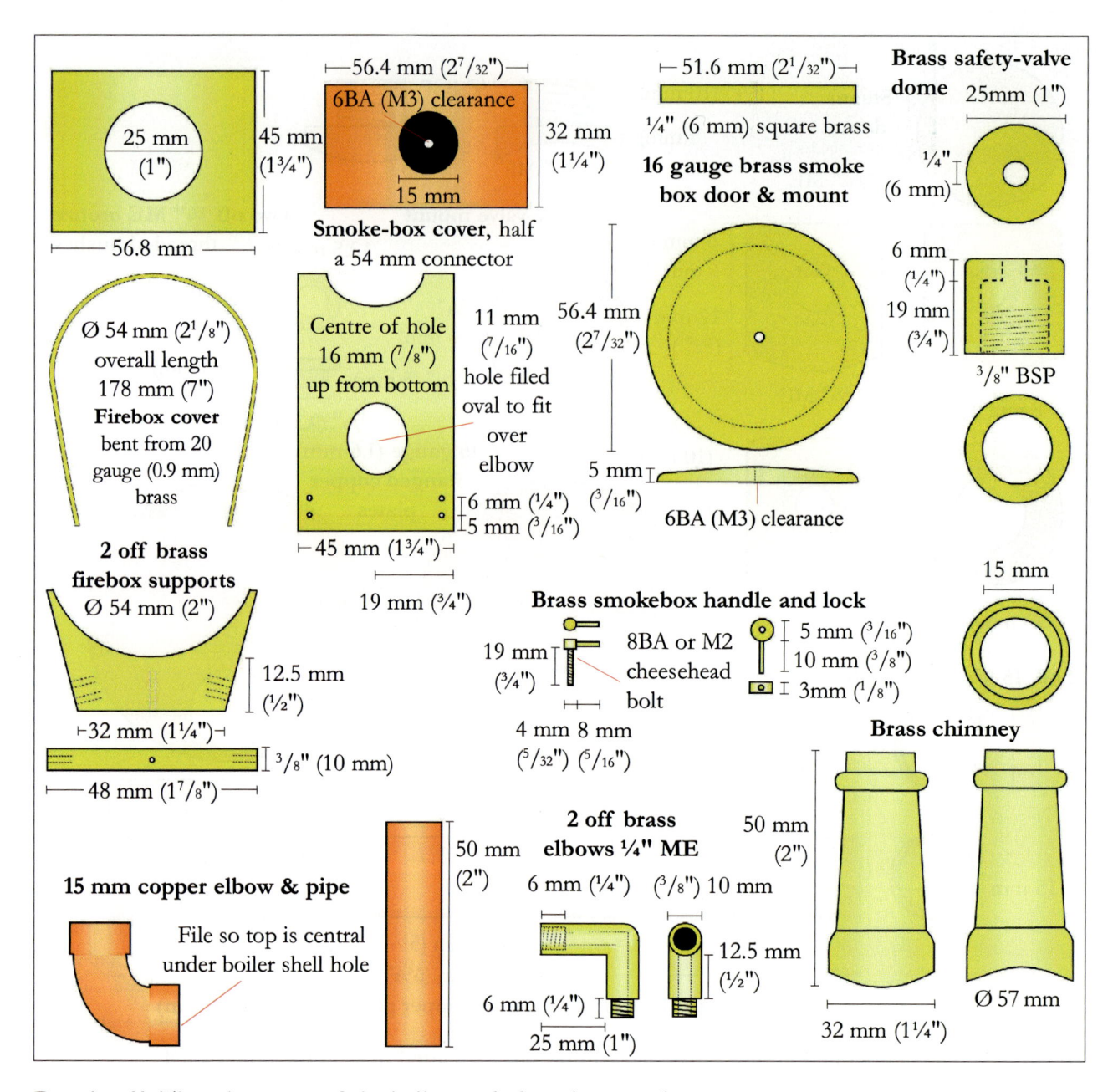

Drawing 11. The other parts of the boiler made from brass and copper.

Photo 23. The boiler ready for soldering. Rings of silver solder have been placed on the upper plate.

Photo 24. The boiler after soldering and pickling.

BUILDING SMALL BOILERS 93

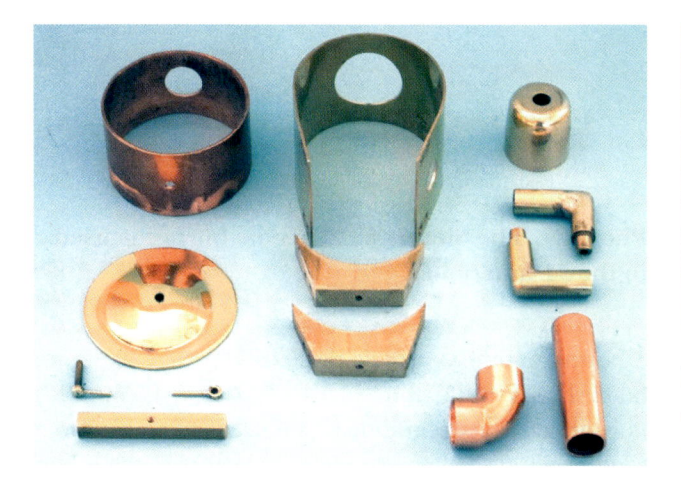

Photo 25. The parts added to the boiler after it has been silver soldered and pressure tested.

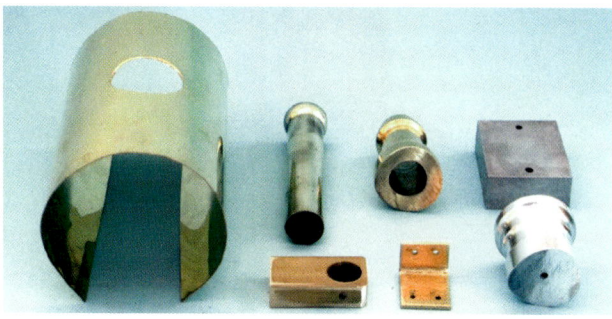

Photo 26. The optional boiler cladding, choice of chimneys, burner mount and supports for the static version of the boiler.

water gauge and the steam outlet. The threaded bush, near to the bottom of the boiler shell, is for connection to the bottom of the water gauge via an elbow. The clack valve is connected to a threaded bush in the plate at the burner end of the boiler.

Prepare the boiler for silver soldering by carefully cleaning all these components. Then apply flux to each component as they are assembled in place. It is important to secure these parts in position with wire. A piece of metal rod, 25 mm (1") diameter and 40 mm (1½") long ensures the end plate at the smoke-box end is correctly located. The boiler is placed vertically in the hearth, burner-end upwards, resting on the metal rod and ensuring that the rod is well clear of the flue. Silver solder the endplate, threaded bush and flue at that end, the steam dome, threaded bush on the side and the central safety-valve dome. Quickly turn the hot boiler over, stand it on the burner end and silver solder the second end plate and flue. Once all the parts have been soldered, the boiler is cleaned, first in hot water, then in pickle and finally rinsed in cold water, ready for independent pressure testing to 120 psi (8.3 bar).

Following a successful test, fit the various smoke-box components. Cut a 54 mm copper connector in half lengthways and slide it over the boiler shell. Drill a 15 mm hole through the two layers, 15 mm (⁵/₈") from one end, and a 6BA (M3) clearance hole directly below on the other side to attach the boiler to its mount. A plain 15 mm copper elbow has its flue end filed so its upper end lines

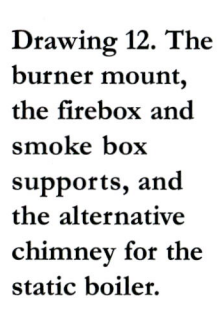

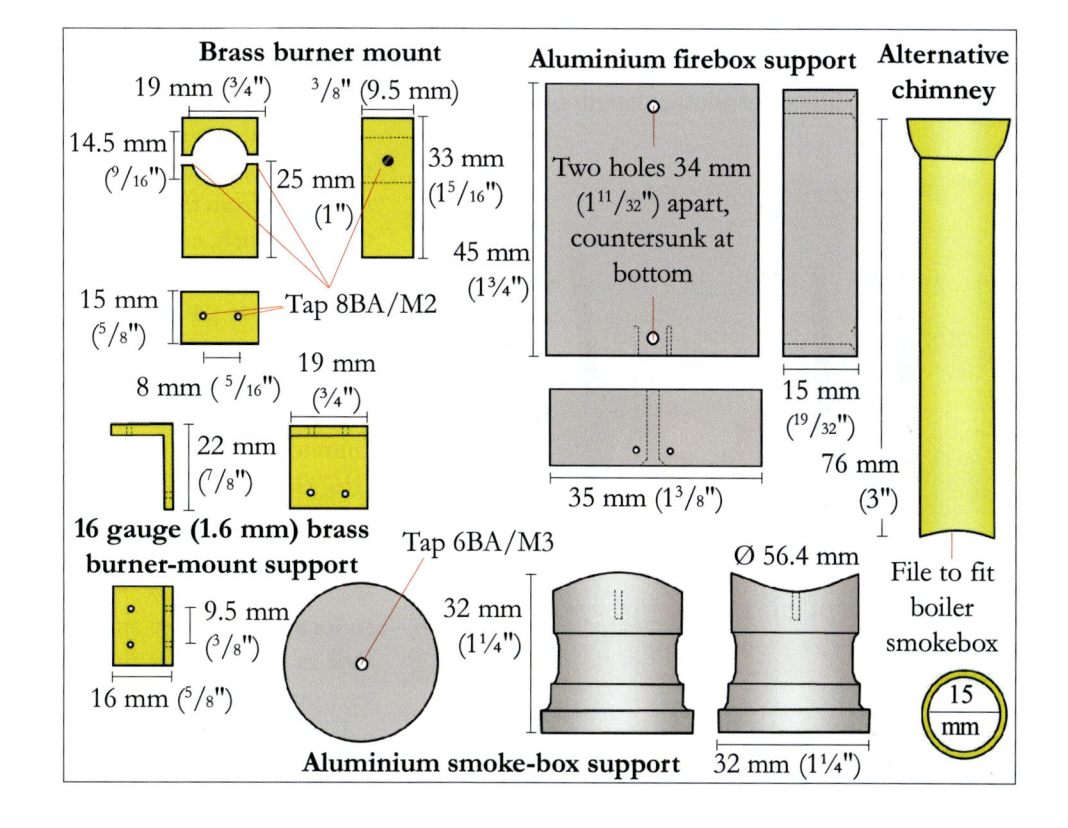

Drawing 12. The burner mount, the firebox and smoke box supports, and the alternative chimney for the static boiler.

Photo 27. The smokebox parts glued in place.

Photo 29. The Sievert 8720 needle burner is used in the 54 mm boiler.

up with the hole in the top of the boiler. The elbow, and the vertical length of copper tube fitted to it, project 12.5 mm (1") above the smoke box cover. Attach them using ceramic adhesive/filler. The chimney is a tight fit over the copper tube It is filed at the bottom to fit the smoke-box curve and glued in place.

The brass smoke-box door attaches to a strip of ¼" (6 mm) square brass strip with its ends chamfered to fit the curvature of the boiler shell. Centre drill and tap it 8BA or M2. The door is held in place by a handle made from a suitably sized slotted cheese-head screw with a short length of 1.5 mm (¹⁄₁₆") brass wire silver soldered in the slot. The handle is locked in position by a short length of 5 mm (³⁄₁₆") brass rod drilled and tapped to fit and then cross drilled for another length of brass wire.

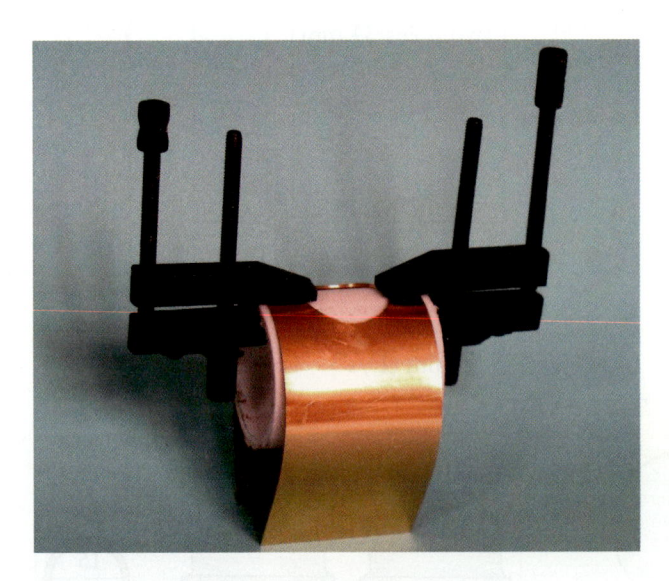

Photo 28. Bending the firebox around a short length of 42 mm plastic waste pipe.

Form the firebox from a piece of 20 gauge (0.9 mm) brass sheet 178 x 45 mm (7" x 1¾"). It has a 25 mm (1") hole drilled in its centre that then needs to be filed to a slightly elliptical shape so that it will fit over the steam dome. To bend the sheet to shape, clamp it to the top of the smoke-box end of the boiler and gently start to bend it around the curve of the boiler. Remove it and repeat the exercise over a 42 mm form. This can be a short length of plastic waste-pipe tube or copper tube with the sheet held with tool-maker's clamps, as shown in Photo 28. With care a perfect fit can be achieved.

Exactly the same technique is used to drill the hole in the centre of the boiler cladding and to form it to fit around the boiler when used in a locomotive.

The two ³⁄₈" (10 mm) brass firebox supports for the boiler are fly cut to fit around its curve. Cut the sides to an angle and finished by milling to shape and height. Drill holes in the brass firebox cover for attaching it to the brass ends by pairs of 8BA or M2 bolts on each side. In addition, drill a ⁷⁄₁₆" (11 mm) hole for an elbow to screw into the threaded brass bush on the side of the boiler. This hole needs to have some metal filed away top and bottom to accommodate the angle of the fitting relative to the side of the firebox.

The safety valve fits inside the centre dome with the top of the dome screwed on. The clack valve mounts on the end plate. The water gauge runs down one side of the boiler from the side of the steam dome to the lower threaded bush, each via an elbow. The steam valve is on the other side of this dome; in the middle is the syphon and pressure gauge.

Boiler installation

If the boiler is fitted to a steam locomotive, turn its chimney to shape from a 50 mm (2") length of 30 mm (1¼") brass rod with a hemispherical section fly cut to fit the smoke box. It must have a 15 mm hole in its centre to fit over the 15 mm copper tube projecting up from the smoke box. A customised saddle is required to locate the boiler smoke box between the frames as well as a mount for the burner. Details will inevitably vary depending on the layout of the chosen locomotive.

For a static engine, the support under the smoke box can be turned to an elegant shape from a short length of

Photo 30. The boiler fitted to a 2-2-2 twin-cylinder locomotive.

1½" (40 mm) round rod, which is fly cut to fit the smokebox cover. In addition, a short length of 45 x 35 mm (1¾" x 1⅜") rectangular metal fits under the firebox, held in place by a pair of countersunk 6BA or M3 bolts. However, the lower steam elbow must be fitted before this part is bolted in place. The burner mount also bolts onto this block. The chimney is a length of ⅝" (15.9 mm) diameter thin-wall brass tube with a 15 mm internal diameter, splayed out at the top. This is done by annealing the brass and then hammering a suitable round steel object into one end of the tube. A large ball bearing or the ball of a ball-pein hammer is ideal for this purpose. In both cases, the smoke box is painted with two coats of black, heat-resistant paint while the rest of the boiler can either be planked with strips of wood, clad with brass over a thin layer of insulation and painted, or the copper can just be painted with a heat-resisting paint.

The burner, illustrated in Photo 29, is held in a ¾" (19 mm) x ⅜" (9.5 mm) brass burner mount. It has a 14.5 mm (⁹⁄₁₆") hole and grub screws hold the burner so there is a 3 mm (⅛") gap between it and the flue. The mount bolts to the firebox base via a small brass bracket. At last it is time for the second independent hydraulic and steam tests.

The locomotive boiler, however, will have to wait until the appropriate stage in construction is reached before the boiler is submitted for these two tests to be completed

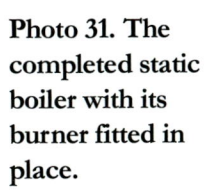

Photo 31. The completed static boiler with its burner fitted in place.

Dry weight of boiler, fittings and burner mount is 955 g (34 oz) configured as a portable unit. Water capacity is 130 ml (¼ pint)

100 mm (3¹⁵/₁₆")

42 mm (1²/₃")

122 mm (4¹³/₁₆")

30 mm (1³/₁₆")

Burner mount

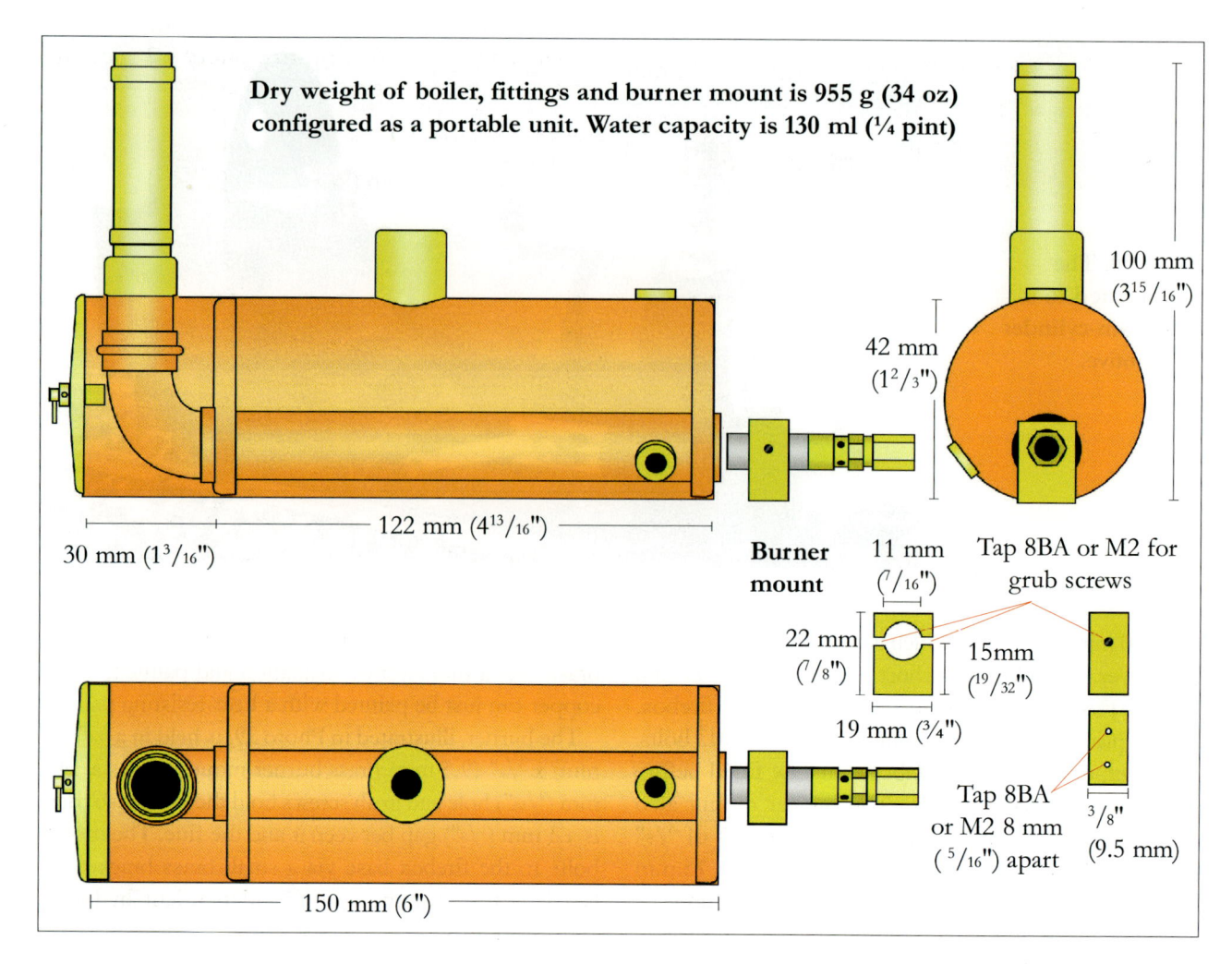

11 mm (⁷/₁₆")

Tap 8BA or M2 for grub screws

22 mm (⁷/₈")

15mm (¹⁹/₃₂")

19 mm (³/₄")

Tap 8BA or M2 8 mm (⁵/₁₆") apart

³/₈" (9.5 mm)

150 mm (6")

Drawing 13. Three views of the boiler pressure vessel showing the flue, end plates, burner and its mount.

42 mm (1²/₃") HORIZONTAL BOILER

The smallest boiler described can be fitted in 32 mm narrow-gauge live-steam locomotives. It can also be configured as a portable or static boiler. It is relatively easy to build and is very similar in construction to the 54 mm (2") boiler. It is made from two lengths of copper tube. The outer shell and flue are respectively lengths of 42 mm diameter 18 gauge (1.2 mm) and 15 mm 22 gauge (0.7 mm) EN 1057 type X copper plumbing tube.

The first task is to make a wooden form 36.4 mm diameter. Then make the flanged copper end plates from 60 mm (2³/₈") discs of 16 gauge (1.6 mm) copper sheet. Once formed turn them to diameter, held in place on the form in the lathe by pressure from a rotating centre via a short length of round wood. Keep checking until the boiler barrel will just slide over each end plate as the right diameter is reached.

Having formed the flanged end plates, it is time to cut a 15 mm hole to fit the flue tube, exactly 5 mm (³/₁₆") along a radius from the edge of the flange. Photo 26 on Page 20 shows how to clamp the assembly to a milling table. Lock the table and gently cut the hole with a 15 mm drill or slot mill. Remove the first flanged plate, clamp the second plate and again cut a hole in it 5 mm (³/₁₆") from the edge.

Photo 32. The boiler pressure-vessel parts; the drilled boiler shell and, from left to right, the flue, the two threaded bushes, the steam dome, the chimney and the two end plates.

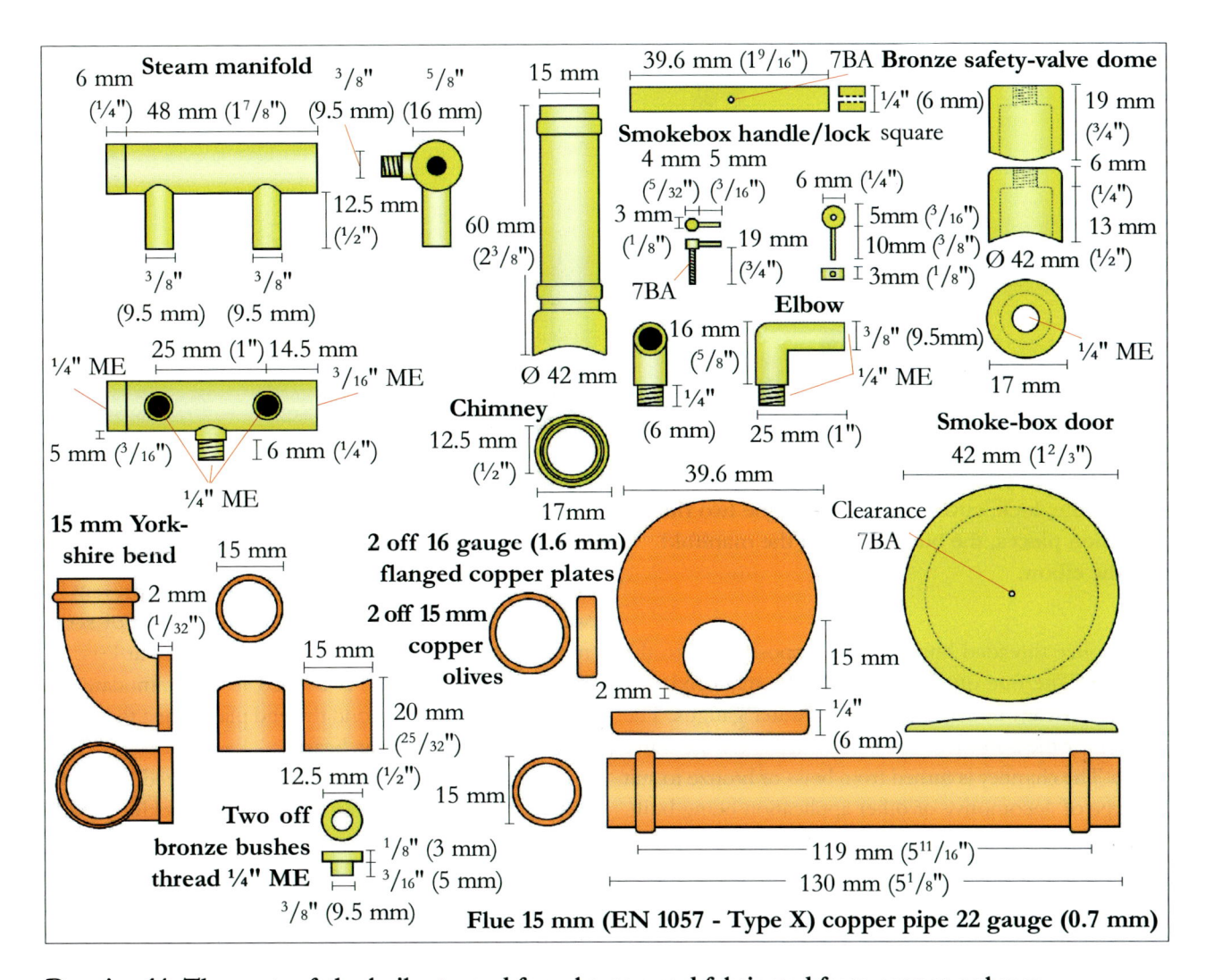

Drawing 14. The parts of the boiler turned from bronze and fabricated from copper or brass.

The flue is a length of 15 mm water pipe. It has a copper olive fitted at each end to space the flanged end plates in their correct positions. Their outside edges are exactly 119 mm (5$^{11}/_{16}$") apart. Locate the first olive in place with a straight 15 mm plumbing compression fitting to squeeze it in place. To fit the second olive, first partly saw through the compression joint so it can easily be sawn right through and removed once the second olive is securely in place. How to do this is illustrated in Chapter 1 on Page 21.

Once this task is complete, make the brass smoke-box cover for the boiler. Cut out a disc of 16 gauge (1.6 mm) brass just under 50 mm (2") diameter. A simple steel forming tool is shown in Photo 54 and Drawing 2 on Page 28. Anneal the brass plate, fit it in the female form and place the male part inside the form. Compress the two parts of the form in a vice to shape the curved smoke box door with a line around it. Drill a 2.5 mm (0.1") hole in the centre and recess the wooden form to fit the door. Then bolt the brass disk to the form and placed it in the lathe. With a length of round wood pressed against the disc with a rotating centre, turn to the exact diameter of the boiler tube. This provides a convincing front of a locomotive smoke box.

The boiler has a bronze steam dome for the safety valve mounted half way along the top of the boiler and

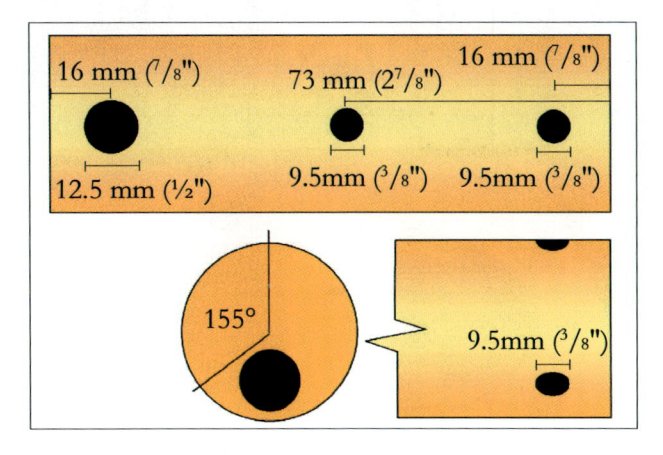

Drawing 15. The location and the sizes of the holes in the boiler shell.

Photo 33. The other parts of the boiler; the smoke-box handle, lock, cover and brass bar, the two flue extension pieces, the burner holder, the manifold and the elbow.

Photo 35. The boiler after silver soldering and pickling. It is like this for its first hydraulic test.

two bronze threaded bushes at the opposite end to the chimney. The one on the top is for the manifold that feeds the steam outlet, pressure and water gauges. The other, near the bottom of the boiler shell is for the water gauge. The chimney is turned from brass or bronze to suit the type of locomotive or other application being built.

Carefully wire the components in place after fluxing, ready for silver soldering. The design of chimney shown, in particular, needs extra support at its top to prevent its weight tilting it downwards. In addition, a piece of scrap metal at least 3 mm ($1/8$") thick, with a hole at least 16 mm ($5/8$") in diameter, is needed to accommodate the flue that sticks out beyond the end plate when the boiler is stood vertically in the hearth.

Once all the parts have been silver soldered, clean the boiler, first in hot water and then in pickle. Finally rinse it well in cold water, ready for its first pressure test up to 120 psi (8.3 bar).

The manifold is a length of ½" (12.5 mm) round bronze bar 48 mm ($1^7/8$") long. Drill a 10 mm hole almost its whole length and then a 4 mm hole from the other end that is threaded $3/16$" ME. Also drill three ¼" (6 mm) holes into the manifold, two 1" (25 mm) apart, the third half way between, offset 90°. Open up to $3/8$" (9.5 mm) to a depth of 3 mm ($1/8$"). Then silver solder a further 6 mm (¼") length of ½" (12.5 mm) round bronze bar, pre-drilled and threaded ¼" ME, to the open end. At the same time, silver solder in place two lengths of $3/8$" (9.5 mm) round bronze that have been pre-drilled and tapped ¼" ME and one with a ¼" ME male thread.

The water gauge runs down one side of the boiler with the pressure gauge and its syphon beside it, while the steam and clack valves are on the other side. The bottom fitting for the water gauge is an elbow with the shorter arm threaded male and the longer one female; both ¼" ME.

Cut a short length of ¼" (6 mm) square brass bar, with its ends chamfered, to fit across the centre of the smoke box. Drill and tap the centre of the bar 7BA (M2.5) to hold the smoke-box cover in place. Make a handle from a 7BA (M2.5) slotted cheese-head screw with 1.5 mm ($1/16$") brass wire silver soldered in the slot. The handle lock is 5 mm ($3/16$") brass rod. Drill and tap it to fit the handle, cross drill it and silver solder in a short length of

Photo 34. The funnel, safety-valve dome and bushes held in place with soft 1 mm galvanised wire.

BUILDING SMALL BOILERS 99

Photo 36. The finished boiler ready to be clad and fitted in a locomotive chassis.

brass wire. A 15 mm Yorkshire elbow has one end cut so there is only 2 mm showing beyond the solder band. The fitting is then heated to remove all the soft solder. A short length of 15 mm pipe has one end filed to a curve so, with the pipe in the elbow, both fit in the smoke box connecting the flue to the funnel. Then fix them in place with high-temperature ceramic filler glue. At the same time, with the smoke-box cover attached, the square brass rod is glued in place and the whole assembly left vertically, smoke box upwards for the adhesive to dry. Then the smoke box cover is unscrewed and further filler added between the ¼" square rod and the 90° bend. The smoke box is painted with black heat-resisting paint.

Boiler heat is provided by a modified Sievert 8842 torch connected to a gas pipe. The modification is described in Chapter 5 Page 57. The rectangular mount is ¾" x ³/₈" (19 x 9.5 mm) brass with a 10.5 mm hole drilled to fit the burner and 8BA (M2) grub screws to hold it.

Clad the rest of the boiler with strips of wood, followed by several coats of varnish for protection. For a locomotive, the cladding can be wooden planks with brass boiler bands or thin brass sheet curved over a layer of insulation.

Photo 37. A Sievert 8842 needle burner is used to heat the 42 mm boiler.

Boiler installation

The way the boiler is finished will depend on its how it is to be used. Will it be fitted to a locomotive or will it be employed to power a static engine? Examples are shown of the boiler fitted in a typical 32 mm narrow-gauge locomotive and in a portable configuration.

For a narrow-gauge locomotive to run on 32 mm rails, the clad boiler, complete with gauges and valves, is ready to be mounted on the frames. Cradles located on the frames should have a curve fly cut in them to suit the diameter of the clad boiler. In the example illustrated in

Photo 38. The pressure and water gauges, the steam and clack valves.

Photo 39. No 9, a freelance home-built 32 mm narrow-gauge locomotive with a 42 mm boiler.

Photo 38, the diameter is 46 mm (1$^{13}/_{16}$"). The burner mount is bolted in position on the footplate, located so that the burner is central in the flue and just 3 mm ($^1/_8$") clear of the flue. With connections made to the cylinders of the engine, the clack valve and the burner, the boiler is ready for its second hydraulic and steam tests.

For a relatively stationary installation Photo 41 shows a portable configuration. Form the two boiler mounts from a single 5" (125 mm) length of 2" x $^3/_8$" (50 x 10 mm) brass strip. Fly cut each end to give a hemispherical cut out 22.5 mm ($^7/_8$") radius to exactly fit the planked boiler shell. Cut the strip in half to form two matching mounts. The sides also have indentations side fly cut in them, 25 mm (1") from the top and with a radius of 25 mm (1"). The upper sides have ¼" slots milled to allow the boiler banding to be inset. The front mount has the area below the curved cut outs removed and the centre bottom drilled and tapped 6BA (M3). The mounts are held apart by a $^5/_{16}$" (8 mm) brass rod. The front axle is a length of ¼" (6 mm) square brass which is centre drilled 6BA or M3 clearance, with each end drilled 8BA or M2 for the axles. The rear mount has holes drilled $^1/_8$" (3 mm) up from the bottom and tapped 8BA (M2). The axles are 8BA or M2 bolts with short lengths of brass tube slipped over to fit the Lego wagon wheels shown in Photos 40 and 41. The front ones are 28 mm diameter and the rear ones 34 mm. They are fitted on the axles, followed by an 8BA or M2 'lock' nut to hold each bolt to the chassis. It is probably easiest to bolt the parts of the frame together, apart from the wheels and front axle, prior to painting. Etch prime and then give two coats of enamel paint followed by two of varnish to protect the paint.

The boiler is held to the frame by the boiler bands which are attached to the mounts by 8BA or M2 bolts. Shape the band to fit around the boiler, attach the band with the first bolt and then smooth it down firmly so the second hole can be marked on the band. Drill the clearance hole and re-attach the band, again using fingers to line up the second hole.

Fit the brass burner mount to a short length of ¾" (20 mm) wide 16 gauge (1.6 mm) brass which has a 90° bend. This attaches to the chassis with two 8BA bolts. Two coats of heat-resistant paint on the smoke box, boiler burner end and mount finish the boiler. It is finally time for the second hydraulic test to be done at 90 psi (6 bar) followed by a steam test and connection to an engine.

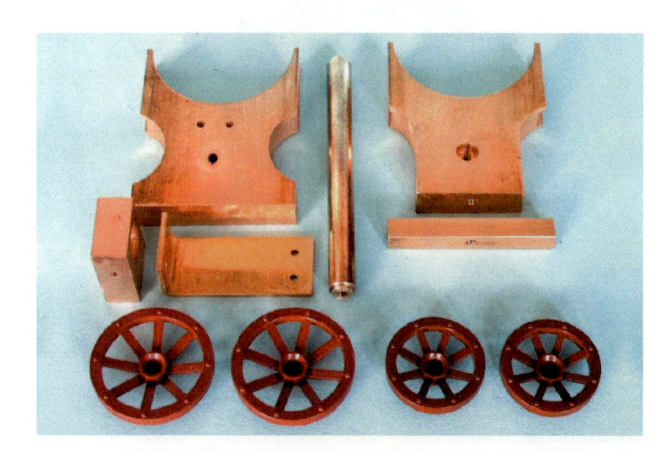

Photo 40. The additional parts for the portable boiler configuration, including the Lego wagon wheels.

BUILDING SMALL BOILERS 101

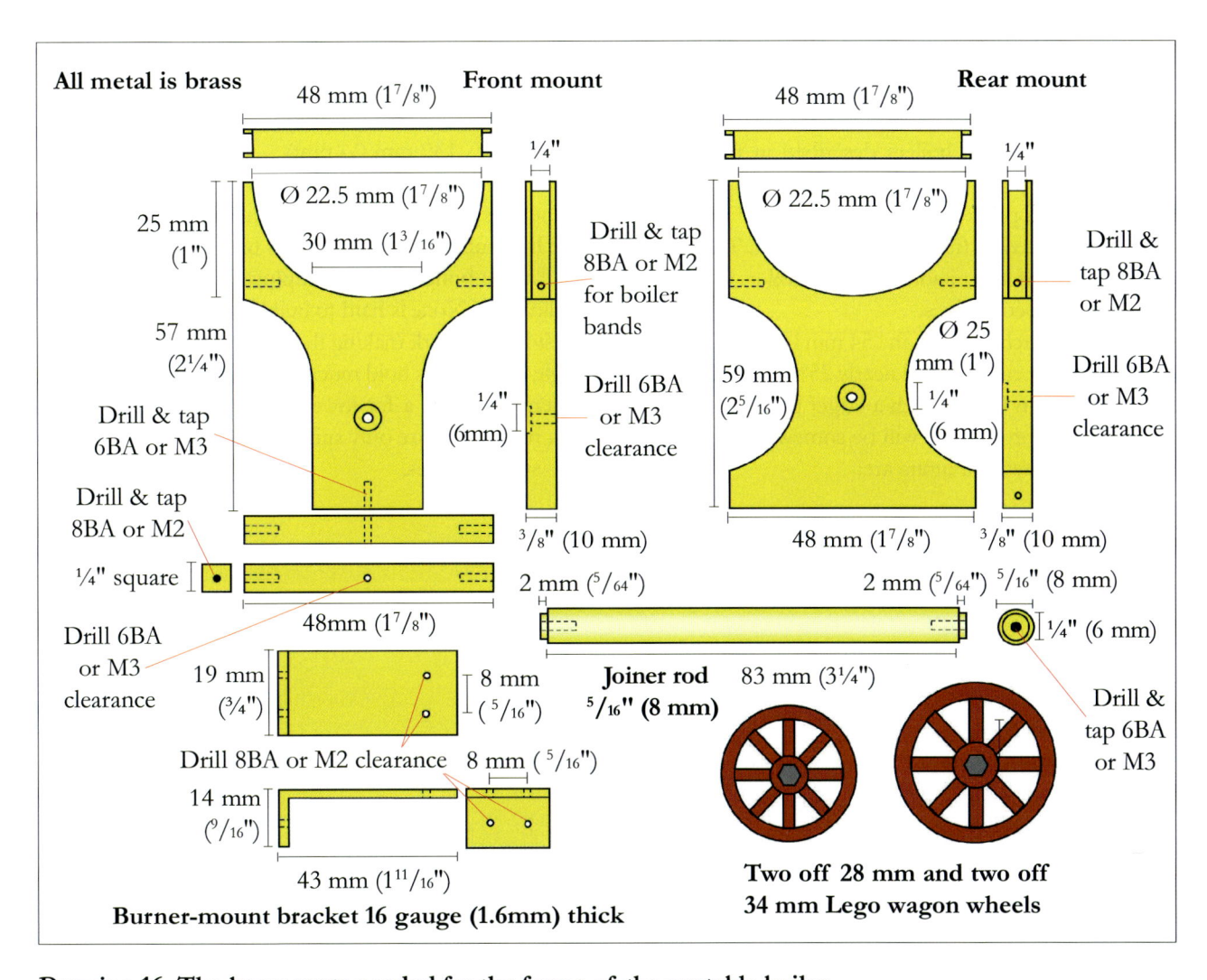

Drawing 16. The brass parts needed for the frame of the portable boiler.

Photo 41. The completed boiler configured as a portable unit.

CONCLUSIONS

The three horizontal boilers described in this chapter have quite low profiles and are relatively squat. All three can drive appropriately sized static engines. The largest one is well suited to fitting in a steam boat. The 54 mm and 42 mm ones are suitable for use as boilers for smaller-gauge steam locomotives.

Using gas-torch burners, the 54 mm boiler has roughly twice the water capacity and nearly 25% greater flue area than the 42 mm boiler. With a larger burner as well, its rate of steam production will be somewhat higher.

The boiler pressure limits are:

Boiler	Capacity	Pressure limit
3"	600 mm (1 pint)	4 bar (60 psi)
54 mm	275 mm (½ pint)	4 bar (60 psi)
42 mm	130 mm (¼ pint)	4 bar (60 psi)

The pressure limit is set for all these boilers at half the first hydraulic-test pressure of 8 bar (120 psi).

All three boilers can be employed in static or mobile applications. None is hard to build but the largest involves considerable work making the fire/smoke box. The two single-flue boilers hold much less water than all the other boilers and have a far lower rate of steam-generation. As a result, they are only suitable for providing power to very small engines.

8: OPERATING BOILERS

Once the boiler has been successfully tested, it is time to prepare for putting it into service driving a model steam engine. This will usually involve some sort of mounting as well as connecting pipe-work from the boiler to the engine via a lubricator, and to ancillaries such as a boiler feed pump or whistle. Pipe-work may also be needed via an oil separator and back to the boiler chimney.

The key issue, however, is whether the boiler is a good match for the engine it is to drive. This will depend on the steaming rate of the boiler and the steam consumption of the engine. The boiler capability depends on the area of water in contact with copper being heated and the effective heat output of the burner.

For a vertical boiler, the effective heating area is the area of the bottom tube plate plus the area of the vertical fire tubes exposed to water in the boiler. A figure for the latter can be taken as around half their total length. The actual figure depends on the amount of water remaining in the boiler.

For the horizontal water-tube boiler it can be taken as the surface area of the water tubes plus one third of the surface area of the boiler shell. For the horizontal single-flue boilers with just an internal flue, it can be taken as two-thirds of the flue area. The figures for all the boilers are detailed in the Appendix.

INSTALLING THE BOILER

If the boiler is driving a static engine, a good solution is to make a flat metal base for the boiler and mount both the engine and the boiler on a suitably sized hardwood stand. This may be varnished or covered with tiles. What is normally important is that the hardwood is protected from the heat of the burner; less of a problem with a single-flue boiler.

For a boiler that will be fitted in a mobile application such as a boat, lorry or locomotive, a simple customised method of installation will need to be devised. For a boat, firmly attach the boiler base plate to the lowest deck. For a lorry boiler with a round base-plate in the bottom of the firebox, bolt it to the chassis. In the case of a locomotive, mount it on top or between the frames.

CONNECTING TO AN ENGINE

Copper pipework is employed to connect the engine to the boiler. The connection runs from the steam valve at the top of the boiler to the input joint of the engine it is driving. Connections to all the boilers in this book are made with $5/32"$ copper pipe. However, $1/8"$ copper tubing could be fitted to the smallest two boilers providing the fittings match this size of pipe.

Regardless of the engine being powered, the steam from the boiler will need to pass through a lubricator that feeds oil into the valve gear and cylinders. With the

Photo 1. A 3½" fire-tube boiler mounted between the frames of a steam lorry.

104 OPERATING BOILERS

Photo 2. A displacement lubricator fitted to a Stuart D10 engine.

Photo 3. The set of parts for an oil separator.

sizes of boilers in this book, a displacement lubricator is normally the best solution. There will also be pipe work from the engine exhaust to the boiler chimney or to an exhaust pipe, normally via an oil separator.

LUBRICATION

While not strictly a part of any boiler, two types of oil will be required for the engine parts and its lubricator. The first type of oil is a normal machine oil, such as 3-in-1, that is applied to the various bearings and visible moving parts. The second type is steam oil.

The steam output to the engine should be routed via a displacement or mechanical lubricator. This will minimise wear between the piston or piston ring and the cylinder bore as well as any valves. The lubricator requires steam oil of relatively high viscosity (ISO 460). This type of oil has additives so that it forms an emulsion with water to spread the lubricant in the cylinders and valves. Several model engineering suppliers include it in their catalogues.

OIL SEPARATORS

Particularly for boilers installed in model boats, a means of separating the steam oil from the exhaust steam is essential. It is often a legal requirement for operating on the many ponds, lakes and other waterways in the UK to avoid polluting them.

Making a small oil separator is simple once the methods used for constructing a boiler have been mastered. It is not a pressure vessel but its construction is very similar to a small boiler. Carefully follow the instructions given in Chapter 2 when silver soldering it.

It works by taking the engine exhaust and spraying it, in a circular pattern, around the walls of the separator. The oil drops will come out of suspension and fall to the bottom of the separator, with some steam condensing to water. The exhaust steam will exit from the top of the separator. At the end of each run, the condensed

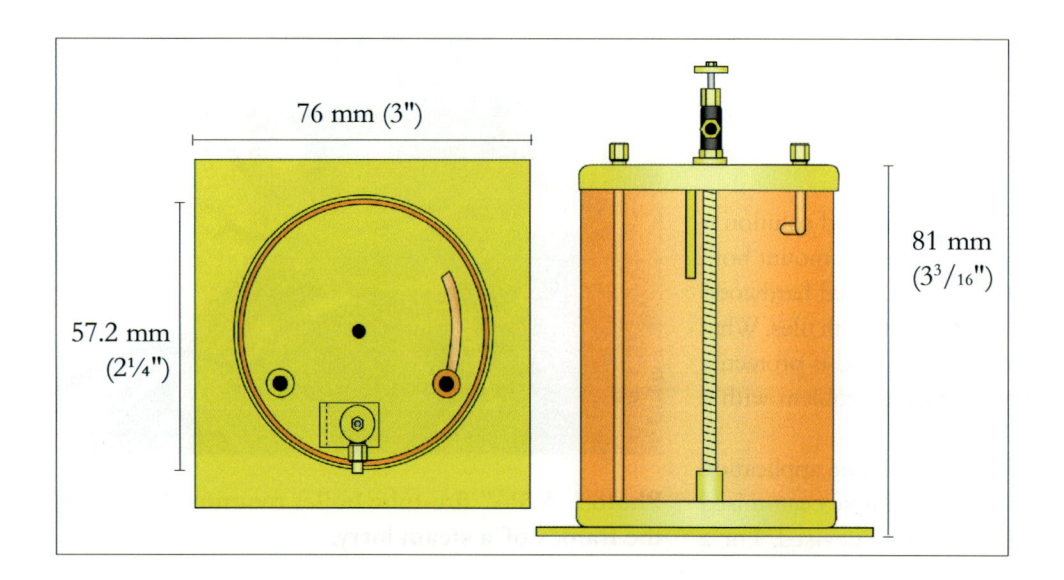

Drawing 1. The internal layout of an oil separator made from a 3" (76 mm) length of 54 mm copper tube.

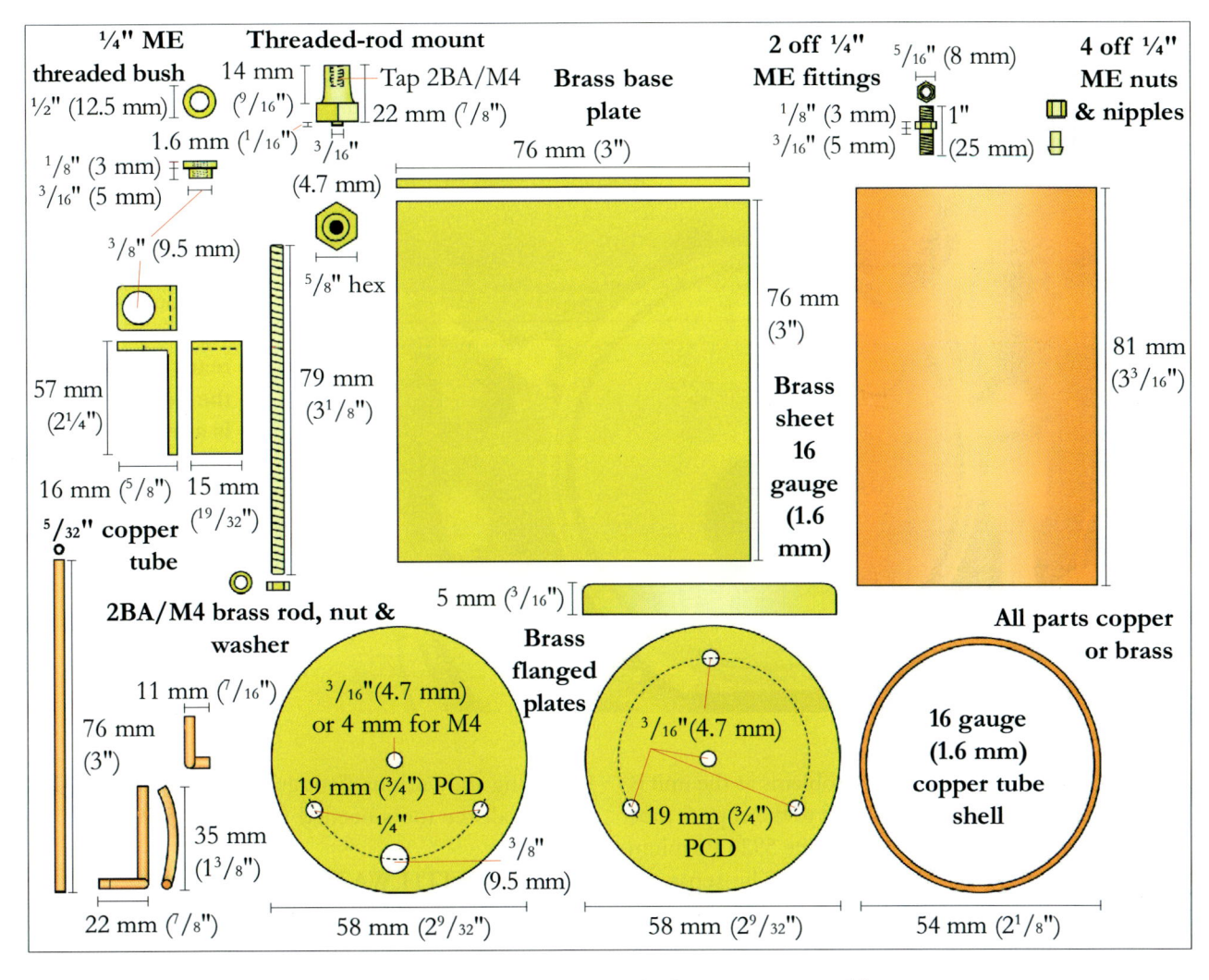

Drawing 2. The separate parts of an oil separator, made from copper and brass.

oil/water mixture should be emptied. In use, this is done by closing the steam outlet valve, removing the bung from a rubber pipe connected to the emptying output and feeding it into a suitable container. Open the steam to the engine for a few seconds until the water/oil mixture stops coming out.

It is easy to make a separator from a short length of copper tube. The top and bottom of the unit are flanged brass plates; held in place with a bolt. Permanently silver solder a flat brass plate to the bottom flanged plate. There are three connectors on the top; one for the exhaust from the engine, one for the cleaned steam output via a valve and one for emptying the unit. There is also a baffle between the steam input and exhaust.

The example described uses a 75 mm (3") length of 54 mm copper tube but both the diameter and the

Photo 4. The sub-assemblies of an oil separator.

Photo 5. A pair of completed oil separators.

Photo 6. A 3½" fire-tube boiler in a steam lorry with the roof and chimney removed ready for lighting the boiler. There is a manually operated boiler-feed pump at the top of the picture.

height can be varied without any problems as the unit is not stressed. The end caps are sealed to the copper tube with silicon gasket sealant, such as Loctite 5920 Premium Silicone Copper Gasket Maker/Sealant. The separator may be lagged with hardwood strips glued in place.

STEAMING THE BOILER

At last the boiler is installed. It is ready to be steamed and connected to the engine it will power. It is a good idea to have a check-list of all the essential items; water, gas, igniter and a range of spanners for tightening and loosening the various fittings and connections. Also include all the tools needed for the engine.

FILLING WITH WATER

Do not just fill a boiler with tap water. Most districts have some degree of hardness in the water that will quickly scale up the inside of the boiler and ruin its performance. Undoubtedly, it is best to use distilled water, readily bought on the internet in 5 litre (1 gallon) or larger plastic containers. Alternatives to consider are well-filtered rain water, de-ionised water, which is available from DIY and car-accessory stores, or softened tap water. They are all reputed to be less than ideal for use in copper

Photo 7. A launch fitted with a 3½" fire-tube boiler heated by a ceramic burner fed from a throw-away gas canister. It powers a Puffin twin-cylinder, double-acting engine with a bore and stroke of $^7/_{16}$" (11 mm) and an engine-driven boiler-feed pump.

Photo 8. The gauge glass shows the boiler is around half-full of water.

boilers but individual experiences show conflicting results. The user should assess the varied information available and then choose which water to use.

Whichever is selected, always try and stick with the same type of water when filling up the boiler.

Photo 10. A small 16 mm narrow gauge 0-2-0 locomotive, fitted with a 42 mm boiler that powers two small oscillating cylinders.

While the smallest two horizontal boilers may be filled with a large syringe, the use of a boiler feed pump, connected to a clack valve, will allow all the boilers to be filled by a hand pump. The steam output valve must be closed while the boiler is being filled to avoid also filling the engine's cylinders with water.

Check the level on the water gauge, and if a bubble occurs in the gauge, tilt the boiler to remove the bubble and then continue filling. The filled water level should be about 10 - 15 mm (½") below the top tube plate for vertical boilers and a similar distance below the top of the boiler shell for the 3" horizontal boiler.

For the smallest two single-flue boilers the figure should be about 6 mm (¼"). Some boilers, once they are steaming, will have their water topped up by an engine-driven feed pump.

Photo 9. The bubble in the gauge glass must be removed to get an accurate reading.

Photo 11. A free-lance 2-2-2 locomotive design fitted with a 54 mm boiler and driving two double-acting cylinders.

108 OPERATING BOILERS

Photo 12. A well-set-up ceramic burner.

FILLING WITH GAS
If a disposable gas canister is used, simply connect it to the fitting with the gas valve closed. If the gas tank is a refillable one, press the filler nozzle of a full or part-used canister into the tank-filling valve and gas will flow until the tank is full. Almost inevitably, some gas will leak out and be lost from the nozzle/valve interface, so wait for a few minutes for it to disperse.

Note that a refilled gas tank will be very cold and may well have frosty condensation on its exterior. For this reason, it is desirable to fit the tank in a place where it can get some warmth but at the same time is well isolated from the boiler burner.

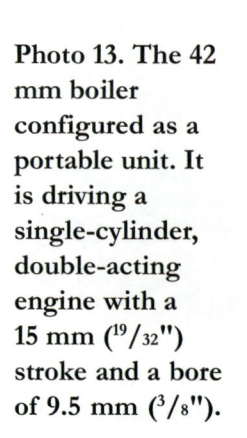

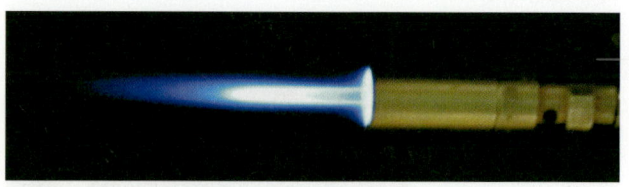

Photo 14. The right flame from a gas torch.

SETTING UP THE BURNER
Before putting a ceramic burner in the boiler, place it on a flat surface and fit the recommended jet in its holder, sealing the joint. Insert the nozzle into the mixer gas tube. Slide the jet holder in the mixer gas tube to leave the air holes two-thirds closed. About 8 mm ($^5/_{16}$") of the jet holder should be sticking out of the mixer tube. Loosely tighten the securing screw. Connect the gas to the burner gas pipe, turn it on and light the burner. Test all the pipe joints and unions in the gas line between gas supply and the burner. This is easily done using a soapy water solution applied with a small paint brush and checking there are no bubbles with the gas flowing.

With the burner lit, move the jet holder until there is a stable blue flame and secure the jet holder in the mixer gas tube. This gives the optimum air/gas mixture. A yellow flame shows insufficient air, while a blue one moving on the surface of the burner, indicates too much air. There are full details in Chapter 5. Turn off the gas, allow the burner to cool and install it in the boiler.

For boilers heated with a gas torch, no setting up is necessary except to fit the torch so that its burner end is 3 mm ($^1/_8$") outside the end of the flue.

LIGHTING THE BURNER
Care is needed lighting a gas burner. For a vertical boiler, remove the chimney, turn on the gas and place a lit igniter in the chimney hole. A popping sound confirms that the gas has lit. For the horizontal water-tube boiler, open the firebox door and light the burner. If the gas

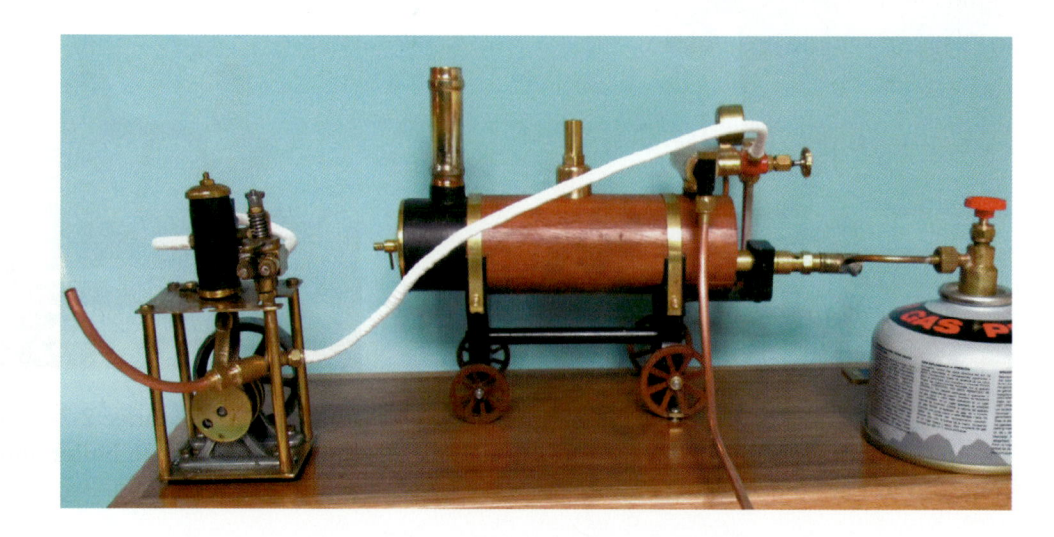

Photo 13. The 42 mm boiler configured as a portable unit. It is driving a single-cylinder, double-acting engine with a 15 mm ($^{19}/_{32}$") stroke and a bore of 9.5 mm ($^3/_8$").

Photo 15. A 3½" fire-tube boiler in a steam lorry. The red glow from the circular 2" ceramic burner is visible through the chimney. The engine is a oscillating twin-cylinder, double-acting engine with a bore and stroke of $^7/_{16}$" (11 mm).

Photo 17. The 54 mm boiler powering a small double-acting mill engine with a ½" (12.5 mm) bore and ¾" (19 mm) stroke.

does not ignite quickly, turn it off. Wait a few minutes for any gas accumulation in the firebox to disperse before trying again. It is important that the burner operates correctly. The white element of a ceramic burner should glow red.

For a torch, slowly turn on the gas and light with a flame in the gap between flue and torch. If necessary loosen the grub screws to slightly withdraw the burner for lighting. Then move it back to give a 3 mm ($^1/_8$") gap. Retighten the screws. Look for a strong blue flame with a pale centre.

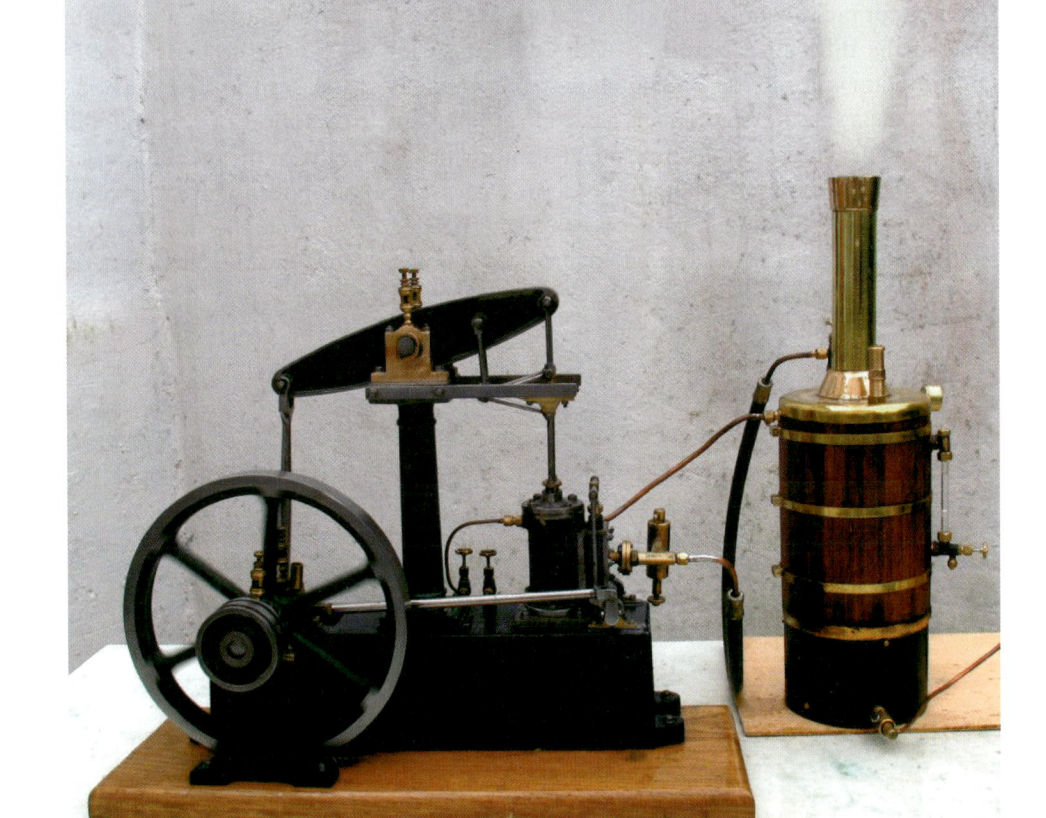

Photo 16. The 108 mm boiler driving a Stuart beam engine that has a bore of 1" (25 mm) and a stroke of 2" (50 mm).

RAISING STEAM

It will take quite some time before the pressure on the gauge starts to rise; the time depending mainly on the water capacity and heating efficiency. It will then increase fairly quickly until full operating pressure is reached and the safety valve starts to lift. Open the steam valve and start to open any manually or radio-controlled regulator. Then gently turn over the engine by hand if it is cold. Beware of hydraulic locking with water in the cold cylinder. Open any drain valves if fitted. Once steam is entering the engine, it will quickly warm up, the drain valves can be closed and the engine will run. Assuming the boiler is well matched to the engine, pressure should be maintained in the boiler.

MAINTAINING PRESSURE

It is essential at all times to keep an eye on the boiler water level as serious damage can occur if a boiler is run dry. A boiler is both a steam generator and a steam reservoir. A nearly full boiler will have little space to store steam so that initially pressure may fall rapidly once the regulator is opened. This highlights the importance of not over-filling a boiler. It also emphasises the need to match the boiler and engine combination. Some advice on the size of engine that the boilers in this book can power is given in the Appendix on Page 118.

It is important to set the gas flow to match the rate at which the engine is consuming steam. This is readily done manually in static installations but more care is required for radio-controlled models, particularly boats. One of the difficulties here is that the rate of steam consumption will vary depending on how the engine is driven and its speed. An automatic gas-control valve can be fitted, which senses boiler pressure and automatically adjusts the gas flow to maintain the desired pressure. Regardless, any boat should have less gas than is needed to empty the boiler of water. An engine-driven boiler feed pump should be fitted to draw water from an auxiliary tank and keep up the water level in the boiler.

FINISHED WITH ENGINES

Once the steaming session is over, use steam pressure to empty the oil separator ready for future use. The

Photo 18. The 3" horizontal boiler driving a Stuart S50 mill engine with a $^5/_8$" (16 mm) bore and 1¼" (32 mm) stroke.

steam and gas valves should be closed, the boiler allowed to cool and then emptied of water, ready for the next steaming session. Do not leave a boiler part-filled with water for any length of time.

If a disposable gas canister is fitted, this should also be disconnected and safely stored. Take care with the disposal of empty canisters. A refillable tank needs its gas valve securely closed.

After the first year of operation, check the general condition of the boiler and the opening of the safety valve at the correct pressure. Remove any scale by filling the boiler with water and a small amount of a de-scaling solution, then boiling it. Leave the contents in the boiler for a whole day before draining and rinsing it out with clean water.

The boiler will need to be inspected and a steam test carried out once a year. Do not forget to update the boiler record. Every four years it is important to carry out a hydraulic test at a pressure that is 50% higher than the maximum boiler-operating pressure.

… BUILDING SMALL BOILERS

APPENDIX

INTRODUCTION

An HSE (Health and Safety Executive) information sheet (Entertainment sheet No 12) is aimed at model engineers operating miniature railways, miniature traction engines or miniature road vehicles as a hobby activity, either under the patronage of a club, a society or as individuals. It is relevant to small boilers where the activity takes place in a public place, when the Health and Safety at Work etc Act 1974 (HSW Act) applies. Providing the testing and regular maintenance described in Chapter 3 are followed there should be no problems.

Individual insurance is highly recommended to cover any boiler. A suitable policy will include third-party damage caused by boilers that do not exceed the 3 bar-litre limit and also gas tanks with a capacity of not more than 250 ml. Walter Midgley is a leading provider of insurance of this type and exhibits at many model engineering shows.

The following section provides the safety calculations used for the boiler designs in this book. It reasonably assumes that any model engineer building one of these boilers will carefully follow the requirements for good silver-soldered joints and boiler testing.

The figures quoted by KN Harris in *Model Boilers & Boilermaking*, Martin Evans in *Model Locomotive and Marine Boilers*, Tubal Cain in *The Model Engineer's Handbook* and Basil Markham in *Model Engineer Vol 159 No 3813*, the last for tube collapse pressure, have been a basis for all the calculations. Where either just imperial or just metric units simplify calculations, these units are used and the 'other' equivalents not quoted.

SAFETY CALCULATIONS

All the boilers described in Chapters 6 and 7 have had their strength calculated for safe operation at the designed steam pressure, set by the safety valve. They have also all been hydraulically tested to 120 psi (8.3 bar). A safety factor of 8 has been included in the calculations, a figure widely applied to model boilers.

The first consideration is the ultimate tensile strength (UTS) of the materials being used. The UTS of copper is 25,000 psi, that of silver-soldered joints in copper can be taken as $0.8 \times 25,000$ psi = 20,000 psi. The UTS of phosphor bronze, used for stays in the 3" horizontal boiler is 38,000 psi.

BOILER SHELL

Consider first the copper tube that forms the boiler shell. Its required thickness comes from the following formula:

Plate thickness in inches =
$$\frac{\text{outside diameter} \times \text{safety factor} \times \text{working pressure}}{2 \times \text{UTS of metal (copper)} \times \text{temperature allowance}}$$

Filling the formula in with actual figure for the six different tube diameters, with a temperature allowance of 0.8 (recommended for copper boilers working between 60 and 100 psi), the figures come out as follows:

108 mm vertical boiler
$$\frac{4\tfrac{1}{4} \times 8 \times 60}{2 \times 25,000 \times 0.8} = 0.051"\ \text{Thinner than 17 gauge}$$

4" vertical boiler
$$\frac{4 \times 8 \times 60}{2 \times 25,000 \times 0.8} = 0.048"\ \text{Exactly 18 gauge}$$

3½" vertical boiler
$$\frac{3\tfrac{1}{2} \times 8 \times 60}{2 \times 25,000 \times 0.8} = 0.042"\ \text{Thinner than 18 gauge}$$

3" horizontal boiler
$$\frac{3 \times 8 \times 60}{2 \times 25,000 \times 0.8} = 0.036"\ \text{Exactly 20 gauge}$$

As 16 gauge copper tube is widely available, it is the ideal solution for these four boilers. For the smallest two boilers:

54 mm horizontal boiler

$$\frac{2.125 \times 8 \times 50}{2 \times 25{,}000 \times 0.8} = 0.021"\text{ Just thinner than 24 gauge}$$

42 mm horizontal boiler

$$\frac{1.65 \times 8 \times 50}{2 \times 25{,}000 \times 0.8} = 0.02"\text{ Exactly 25 gauge}$$

Half hard EN 1057 type X (previously BS 2871 Table X) tubes with a 54 mm or 42 mm outside diameter have a wall thickness of 1.2 mm (18 gauge) and are cleared to a maximum working pressure of 27 bar (368 psi) and 35 bar (515 psi) respectively.

5/16" (8 mm) water tubes

$$\frac{0.313 \times 8 \times 60}{2 \times 25{,}000 \times 0.8} = 0.0037"\text{ Just thicker than 43 gauge}$$

For standardisation with the fire tubes, the water tubes on the 3" horizontal boiler are 20 gauge (0.914 mm).

SWG (Standard wire gauge) is still widely employed in the UK for sheet metal gauges. The sizes and metric equivalents are given in Table 1.

FIRE TUBES AND FLUES

The next requirement is to decide the size of any fire tubes and flues. The formula just given for the tube that forms a boiler shell does not apply because a tube will collapse under a significantly lower external pressure than the same tube will burst under internal pressure. However, a collapsing tube will not cause a devastating external boiler explosion. On the other hand, there is the corrosive effect of the burner gases to consider but for gas heating, this is not a significant factor. This is equally true both for fire tubes and flues.

SWG	Imperial	Metric
14 gauge	0.080"	2.032 mm
15 gauge	0.072"	1.829 mm
16 gauge	0.064"	1.626 mm
17 gauge	0.056"	1.422 mm
18 gauge	0.048"	1.219 mm
19 gauge	0.040"	1.016 mm
20 gauge	0.036"	0.914 mm
21 gauge	0.032"	0.813 mm
22 gauge	0.028"	0.711 mm
23 gauge	0.024"	0.609 mm
24 gauge	0.020"	0.508 mm

Table 1. Useful SWG (Standard wire gauge) sizes.

5/16" (8 mm) fire tubes

For fire tubes working at 80 - 120 psi, the literature suggests that 5/16" x 22 gauge is considered very safe at boiler pressures of up to 60 psi. However, 5/16" (8 mm) tubes of 20 gauge (0.914 mm) are used that increase the safety factor. A more mathematical approach by Basil Markham states that stress of 3,000 psi should not be exceeded in the formula:

$$\text{Stress} = \frac{\text{test pressure} \times \text{outside diameter}}{2 \times \text{wall thickness}}$$

putting in actual figures for 5/16" (8 mm) at 120 psi:

$$\text{Stress} = \frac{120 \times 0.313}{2 \times 0.036} = 521.67 \text{ psi}$$

This shows that 5/16" x 20 gauge tubes will only be loaded to 17.5% of Markham's recommended stress.

Flues

The following figures for tubes and flues, taken from Martin Evans book and are for boilers running at 80 - 120 psi (5.5 - 8.3 bar). This gives an additional safety factor of two for the horizontal boilers with a flue tube, which are only cleared to run at a maximum of 60 psi (4 bar).

5/16"	22 gauge
1/2"	20 gauge
5/8"	20 gauge
7/8"	18 gauge

It is noteworthy that despite these recommendations, Markham quotes Evans' Stirling locomotive as using 7/8" tubes of 20 gauge! Once again, Markham's formula is applicable.

The internal flues of both the horizontal boilers are 15 mm copper tubes that run the length of the boiler, fit in the bottom section and contain the burner flame.

These flue tubes are made from standard household copper pipe to EN 1057 - Type X, which is 0.7mm (0.028") thick, approximately 22 gauge.

$$\text{Stress} = \frac{120 \times 0.591}{2 \times 0.028} = 1266.43 \text{ psi}$$

This shows that the load on the flue, which is 15 mm diameter and 0.7 mm thick, approximately 22 gauge, is only 42% of Markham's recommended stress.

END PLATES

The flanged end plates are flat and their strength needs to be treated rather differently. For a start, Martin Evans suggests they should be 25% thicker than the boiler shell.

BUILDING SMALL BOILERS 113

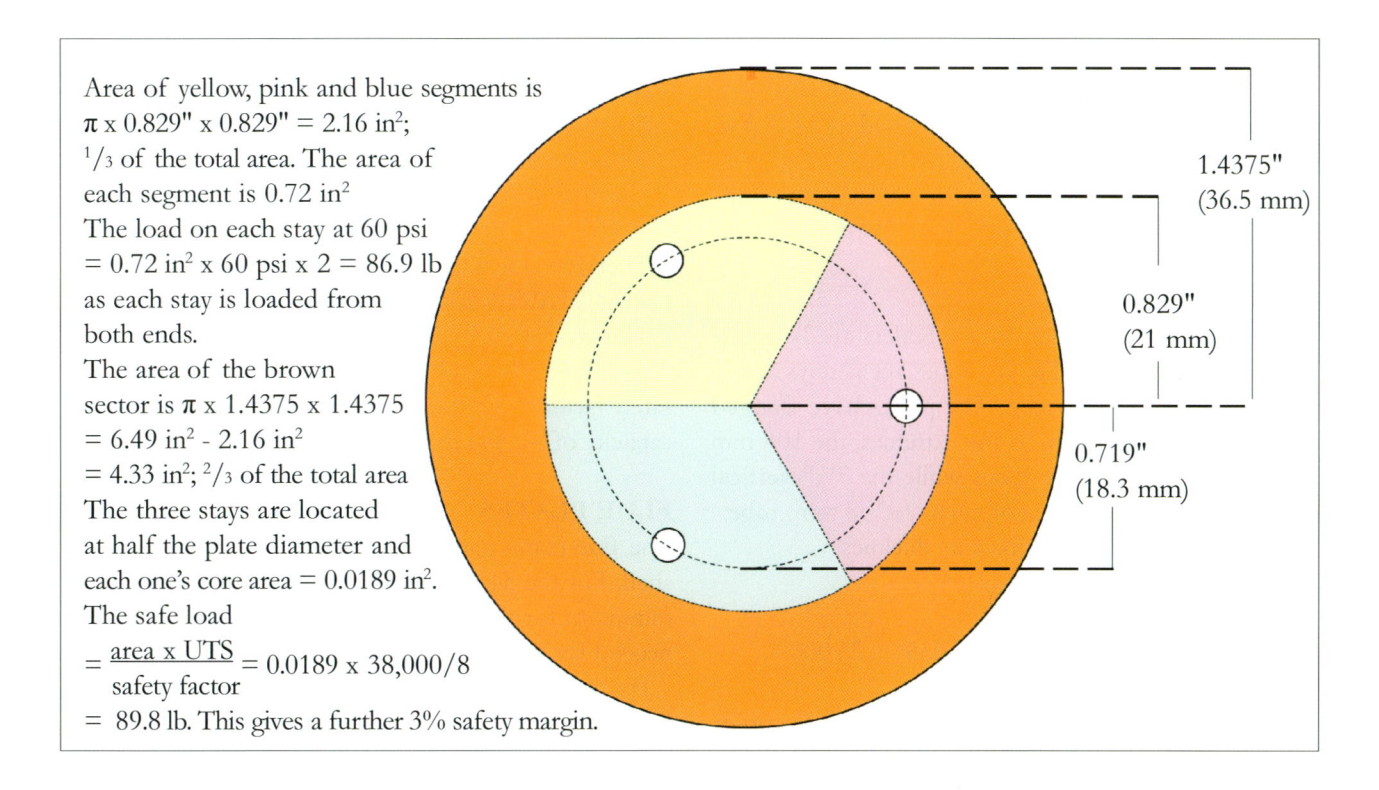

Area of yellow, pink and blue segments is
π x 0.829" x 0.829" = 2.16 in²;
1/3 of the total area. The area of
each segment is 0.72 in²
The load on each stay at 60 psi
= 0.72 in² x 60 psi x 2 = 86.9 lb
as each stay is loaded from
both ends.
The area of the brown
sector is π x 1.4375 x 1.4375
= 6.49 in² - 2.16 in²
= 4.33 in²; 2/3 of the total area
The three stays are located
at half the plate diameter and
each one's core area = 0.0189 in².
The safe load
= $\frac{\text{area x UTS}}{\text{safety factor}}$ = 0.0189 x 38,000/8
= 89.8 lb. This gives a further 3% safety margin.

1.4375" (36.5 mm)
0.829" (21 mm)
0.719" (18.3 mm)

For the 3" horizontal boiler, 20 gauge or 0.036" is the minimum requirement for the boiler shell so the end plates should be at least 0.045" thick, so 18 gauge copper plate is the minimum. Thus 16 gauge is fine and the plates have flanged ends that are 3/8" (9.5 mm) wide.

Load on 3" horizontal boiler end plates

The area of the end plate is 3" (76.2 mm) diameter less twice metal thickness (1.6 mm x 2) =
  π x 36.5 x 36.5/25.4 x 25.4 = 6.488 in²
  Total load on each end plate is 6.488 in² x 60 psi = 389 lb x 8 for safety factor = 3,114 lb
  Assuming 1/3 of the load is carried by stays and 2/3 by the rim, each rim will have to support a load of 2,076 lb.
  The depth of flange is 3/8" but only 1/4" is flat, so assuming 50% silver solder penetration = 1/8".
  Perimeter of rim = π x 2.874" = 9.03".
  Area of soldered rim = 9.03" x 0.125" = 1.129 in².
  The load carrying capacity of the silver-soldered rim = 1.129 in² x 20,000 psi = 22,580 lb against a calculated load, including safety factor of 2,076 lb.

Stays

The stays will have to carry a load of 2,076 lb (they carry one-third of the load from both end plates).
  Area of 3/16" rod after threads are cut ME 3/16" x 40) = 0.0189 in². (*Model Engineer's Handbook* page 4.5.)
  The load that each phosphor bronze rod can carry = 0.0189 in² x 38,000 psi = 718 lb.
  So 3 stays can carry 2,154 lb, against a required load including safety factor of 2,076 lb.

Stay spacing

The stay spacing used = 0.719" x 2 Cos 30° (0.866) = 1.245". The required stay spacing can be derived from the formula:

$$\text{Pitch} = \frac{\text{Diameter}^2 \text{ x UTS x 3}}{\text{Pressure x Safety factor x 4}}$$

For the 3" horizontal boiler, the stays are of 3/16" rod (0.155" diameter after threads cut). The maximum working pressure is 60 psi and the safety factor is eight. Thus

$$\text{Pitch} = \sqrt{\frac{0.155 \times 0.155 \times 38,000 \times 3}{60 \times 8 \times 4}} = 1.426"$$

Thus, with the actual spacing of 1.245" there is an additional safety factor of over 12%.

Hydraulic test of 3" horizontal boiler

Thinking about distortion under test at 120 psi, it is worth considering the actual load at twice the working pressure without a safety factor to see if the end plates will distort.
  Total load on each end plate is:
  6.488 in² x 120 psi = 778 lb.
  Assuming 1/3 of the load is carried by stays and 2/3 by the rim, the rim will carry 519 lb; the stays also 519 lb.
  Annealed copper start to yield at 10,000 psi.
  Assume silver solder starts to yield at 8,000 psi.
  Phosphor bronze starts to yield at 25,000 psi.
  The rim will start to yield at 1.129 in² x 8,000 psi = 9,032 lb versus load of 519 lb.

Each stay will start to yield at 0.0189 in² x 25,000 psi = 472.5 lb.

Three stays together will start to yield at 1417.5 lb compared with a load of 519 lb.

Thus, there should be no noticeable distortion on the boiler end plates under hydraulic test. There was none.

TUBE PLATES

All the tube plates for the vertical boilers are 16 gauge (1.6 mm copper plate). The fire tubes act as stays and in all cases are closely spaced. The plates have flanged ends ³/₈" (9.5 mm) deep. At the extremes, the 108 mm vertical boiler has 25 fire tubes while the 3½" vertical one has 15. The metal area of each ⁵/₁₆" (8 mm) tube:

= the perimeter of the tube x its thickness

$$= \frac{\pi \times 8 \times 0.914}{25.4 \times 25.4} = 0.0356 \text{ in}^2$$

Thus the support provided = 0.0356 x 25,000 = 890 lb.

25 tubes can take a total load of 890 x 25 = 22,250 lb.
15 tubes can take a total load of 890 x 15 = 13,350 lb.

The depth of flange is ³/₈" but only ¼" is flat, so assuming 50% silver solder penetration, the depth = ¹/₈".

108 mm boiler

The end-plate area (108 mm diameter less 3.2 mm)

$$= \frac{\pi \times 52.4 \times 52.4}{25.4 \times 25.4} = 13.37 \text{ in}^2$$

Less the area of each ⁵/₁₆" (8 mm) diameter fire tubes, which has a diameter of 0.313". The area of these 25 fire tubes

= π x 0.156 x 0.156 x 25 = 1.91 in².

The effective area of the bottom tube plate is:
13.37 in² - 1.91 in² = 11.46 in².
Perimeter of rim = π x 4¼" = 12.96"
Area of rim = 12.96" x 0.125" = 1.62 in².
The load carrying capacity of silver-soldered rim:
= 1.62 in² x 20,000 psi = 32,400 lb.

Therefore, the total load carrying capacity of each tube plate = 32,400 + 22,250 = 54,650 lb.

The area of each tube plate = 12.96 in².

At 60 psi, the load = 60 x 12.96 = 777.6 lb x 8 for safety factor = 6,621 lb, against a calculated load carrying capacity of 54,650 lb.

3½" boiler

The end-plate area (3½" {88.9 mm} diameter less 3.2 mm)

$$= \frac{\pi \times 42.85 \times 42.85}{25.4 \times 25.4} = 8.942 \text{ in}^2$$

Less the area of each ⁵/₁₆" (8 mm) diameter fire tubes, which has an internal diameter of 0.313". The internal area of these 15 fire tubes

= π x 0.156 x 0.156 x 15 = 1.15 in².

The effective area of the bottom tube plate is:
8.94 in² - 1.15 in² = 7.79 in².
Perimeter of rim = π x 3½" = 10.99"
Area of rim = 10.99" x 0.125" = 1.37 in².
The load carrying capacity of silver-soldered rim
= 1.37 in² x 20,000 psi = 27,493 lb.

Therefore, the total load carrying capacity of each tube plate = 27,493 + 13,350 = 40,843 lb.

The area of each tube plate = 7.79 in².

At 60 psi, the load = 60 x 7.79 = 467.4 lb x 8 for safety factor = 3,739 lb, against a calculated load carrying capacity of 40,843 lb.

FLUE PLATES

The flue plates should be 25% thicker than the boiler shell. For the 54 mm boiler, 0.024" or 23 gauge is the minimum for the boiler shell, so 0.030" or 21 gauge is needed for the end plates.

For the 42 mm boiler, 0.02" or 24 gauge is the minimum for the boiler shell, so 0.025" or just thicker than 23 gauge is the minimum for the end plates.

Thus 16 gauge copper plate is more than sufficient for both boilers. The plates have flanged ends that are ³/₈" (9.5 mm) wide.

The 15 mm flue area = π x 15 mm x 0.7 mm
= 32.99 mm² = 0.051 in². So it can carry a load along its length of 0.051 x 25,000 = 1287.4 lb.

54 mm boiler

The plate area $= \frac{\pi \times 25.4 \times 25.4}{25.4 \times 25.4} = 3.14 \text{ in}^2$

The load is 3.14 in² x 60 psi = 188 lb x 8 safety factor = 1,507 lb.
Perimeter of rim = π x 2.125" = 6.68"
Area of rim = 6.68" x 0.125" = 0.835 in² so the load carrying capacity of silver-soldered rim
= 0.835 in² x 20,000 psi = 16,692 lb.

The load carrying capacity of the flue is 1,287 lb so the total load carrying capacity of the flue plate is 1,287 + 16,692 = 17,979 lb against a load of 1,507 lb.

42 mm boiler

The plate area $= \frac{\pi \times 19.4 \times 19.4}{25.4 \times 25.4} = 1.83 \text{ in}^2$

The load is 1.83 in² x 60 psi
= 110 lb x 8 safety factor = 880 lb.
Perimeter of rim = π x 1.65" = 5.19"
Area of rim = 5.19" x 0.125" = 0.65 in² so the load carrying capacity of silver-soldered rim:
= 0.65 in² x 20,000 psi = 13,000 lb.

The load carrying capacity of the flue is 1,287 lb so the total load carrying capacity of the flue plate is 1,287 + 13,000 = 14,287 lb against a load of 880 lb.

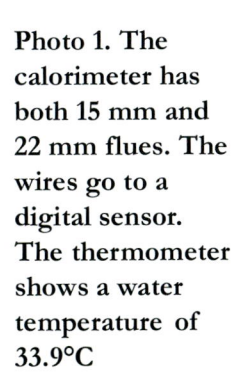

BUILDING SMALL BOILERS

Photo 1. The calorimeter has both 15 mm and 22 mm flues. The wires go to a digital sensor. The thermometer shows a water temperature of 33.9°C

BURNER HEAT OUTPUT

The boilers described in this book either use a ceramic burner or a needle-point burner to provide the heat input.

NEEDLE-POINT BURNER COMPARISON

A calorimeter was constructed from a biscuit tin, a 15 mm and a 22 mm flanged connector. Two lengths each of 15 mm and of 22 mm copper tube soft soldered together with a pair of 90° elbows provide flues and chimneys. Each flue is 190 mm (7½") long to the centre of the chimney. A hole was drilled at each end of the tin for the flange connectors and the flues were connected to them by their compression joints.

The calorimeter was filled with 1,500 ml of water for five tests run, first with a Sievert Light Line 884204 burner, followed by a Sievert Light Line 872001 burner and a Primus 8704 needle burner. Two different flue sizes were tested. The hot water was replaced by cold water at the end of each test. A digital thermometer measured the water temperature.

The heat absorbed by the water is as follows:
$Q = mc\Delta t$ where:
Q = heat gained by water in kJ (Calculated).
m = mass of water (kg).
c = specific heat of water (4.186 kJ/kg°C {or °K}).
Δt = temperature difference (°C or °K).

The rate of heat supplied by burner is:
$P = Q/t$ where:
P = heat output of burner/tube combination (kW).
Q = Heat gained by water (kJ).
t = Time in seconds.

1. **Unmodified Sievert 8842 burner in 15 mm flue:**
Start temperature: 12.0°C.
10 minute temperature: 22.1°C.
15 minute temperature: 26.9°C.

The water was heated from 12.0°C to 26.9°C in 900 seconds.
Thus $Q = 1.5$ kg $\times$ 4.186 kJ/kg°C $\times$ 14.9°C = 93.71 kJ.
Output of burner/fire tube combination:
    $P = 93.71$ kJ/900 s.
So the heat input = 0.104 kW.

2. **Modified Sievert 8842 burner in 15 mm flue:**
Start temperature: 11.5°C.
10 minute temperature: 23.6°C.
15 minute temperature: 28.6°C.

Thus $Q = 1.5$ kg $\times$ 4.186 kJ/kg°C $\times$ 17.1°C = 107.37 kJ.
Output of burner/fire tube combination:
    $P = 107.37$ kJ/900 s.
So the heat input = 0.12 kW.

Photo 2. From left to right, the nozzles of Sievert 8842 and 8720 Light Line needle burners.

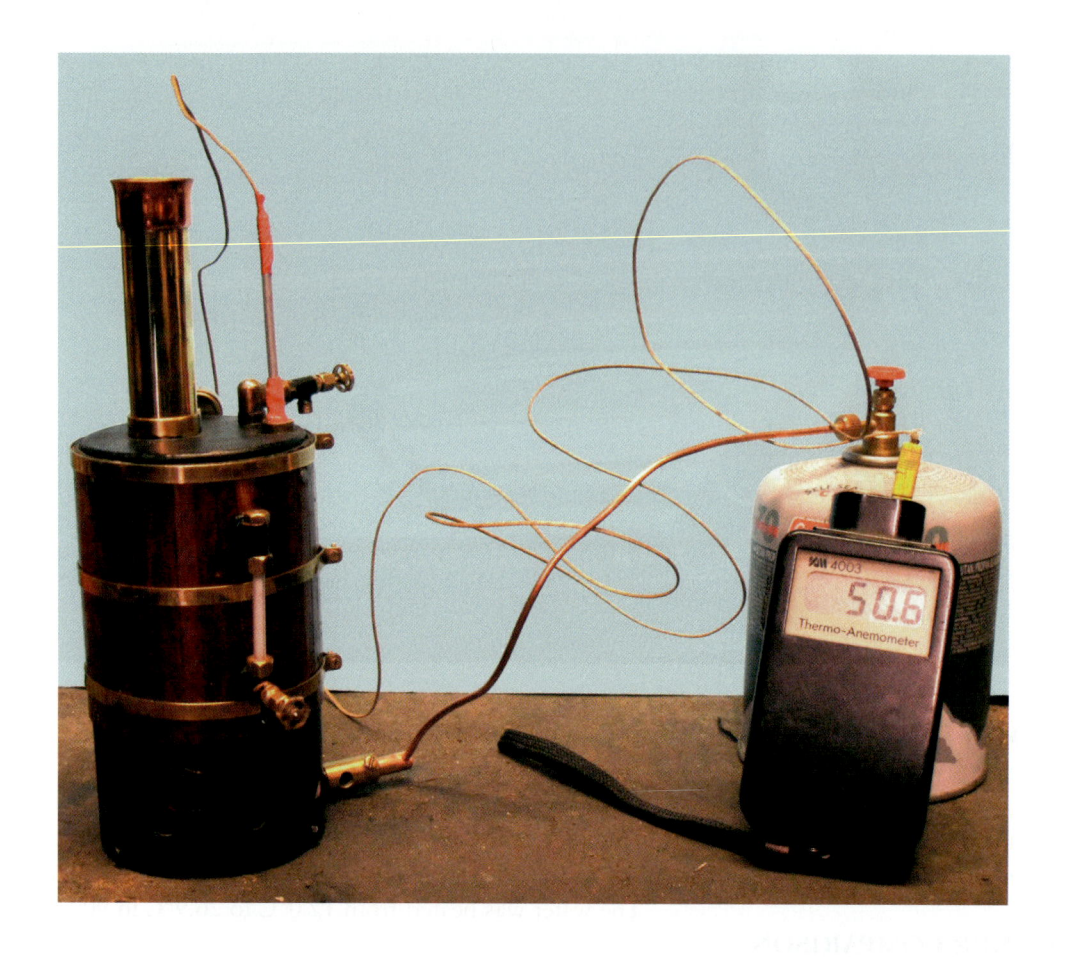

Photo 3. The set up for measuring the heat input to the 3½" boiler from its ceramic burner, with a temperature sensor connected to a digital readout.

3. **Unmodified Sievert 8720 burner in 15 mm flue:**
Start temperature: 14.0°C.
10 minute temperature: 40.0°C.
15 minute temperature 50.0°C.

Thus Q = 1.5 kg x 4.186 kJ/kg°C x 36.0°C = 226.04 kJ.
Output of burner/fire tube combination:
P = 226.04 kJ/900s.
So the heat input = 0.25 kW.

4. **Modified Sievert 8842 needle in 22 mm flue:**
Start temperature: 11.5°C.
10 minute temperature: 20.5°C.

Thus Q = 1.5 kg x 4.186 kJ/kg°C x 9.0°C = 56.51 kJ.
Output of burner/fire tube combination:
P = 56.51 kJ/600s.
So the heat input = 0.094 kW.

5. **Unmodified Primus 8704 burner in 22 mm flue:**
Start temperature: 21.3°C.
10 minute temperature: 71.5°C.

Thus Q = 1.5 kg x 4.186 kJ/kg°C x 30.3°C = 315.21 kJ.
Output of burner/fire tube combination:
P = 315.21 kJ/600s.
So the heat input = 0.53 kW.

Tests 1 gave less heat input than Test 2; both in a 15 mm flue. Test 4 in a 22 mm flue provided a much lower heat input than Test 2. Test 3 produced about twice the heat of Test 2 in the 15 mm flue. Test 5 produced flames from the end of the flue even with the gas significantly turned down.

The results led to the choice of the Sievert Light Line 8720 in a 15 mm flue for the 54 mm boiler. The modified Sievert 8842 needle burner in a 15 mm flue was chosen for the 42 mm boiler. The modification involved removing 2 mm ($^5/_{64}$") from the output end.

CERAMIC BURNER TESTING
To test the heat input to a boiler from its ceramic burner, a type K thermocouple was inserted through the safety-valve fitting. A measured amount of water was added and the time taken to raise its temperature was measured.

3½" vertical boiler
The boiler was filled with 360 ml of water and its 2" ceramic burner with a No 8 jet was lit.
Start temperature: 19.5°C.
5 minute temperature: 87.5°C.

Q = 0.36 kg x 4.186 kJ/kg°C x 68.0°C.
Q = 102.47 kJ.

Photo 4. What is the heat input to the 54 mm boiler fitted with a Sievert 8720 Light Line burner? Using a digital thermometer helps to get accurate results.

Output of burner/boiler combination
    P = 102.47 kJ/300 seconds.
So the heat input to the water = 0.34 kW.

4" vertical boiler
This boiler was filled with 550 ml of water and its 2¾" ceramic burner with a No 10 jet was lit.
    Start temperature: 19.5°C.
    4 minute temperature: 84.7°C.

Q = 0.55 kg x 4.186 kJ/kg°C x 65.2°C.
Q = 150.11 kJ.
Output of burner/boiler combination:
    P = 150.11 kJ/240 seconds.
So the heat input = 0.63 kW.

NEEDLE-POINT BURNER TESTING
To measure heat-input rate by a Sievert 8720 burner into the 54 mm boiler, the same thermocouple was inserted into the safety-valve fitting, with 250 ml water. The time was again measured for the temperature to rise a given amount.

54 mm boiler
Start temperature: 25.9°C.
5 minute temperature: 81.9°C.

Q = 0.25 kg x 4.186 kJ/kg°C x 56.0°C.

Q = 58.60 kJ.
Output of burner/boiler combination
    P = 58.60 kJ/300 seconds.
So the heat input to the water = 0.195 kW.

The calorimeter, which has no lagging that would minimise unwanted heat loss, was used to measure only the comparative performance of the burners. The actual performance of the 8720 burner in the calorimeter differed from the figure it achieved when fitted to a boiler. The latter figure is the more accurate one as it is provides a better representation of actual operating conditions.

BOILER STEAM PRODUCTION

The main variables affecting the steam output of a boiler are the surface area of water exposed to the heat, the rate of heat transfer from the burner to the water and the pressure in the boiler. All the figures below apply at a pressure of around 3 bar (44 psi).

The latent heat of evaporation of water at boiling is 2.26 kJ/g. This means that once the water is boiling:
The 2" ceramic burner with a 0.34 watts output
= 340 x 60 = 20.4 kJ/min could in theory evaporate:

$$\frac{20.4}{2.26} = 9.03 \text{ g water/min}$$

At 3 bar, 1 g of water produces 461 ml of steam.

Thus 9.03 grams of water give 4,161 ml of steam. The equivalent figures for the 2¾" burner with a 630 watts output is 7,710 ml of steam. These figures are based on the measured heat transfer to the water in the boilers.

Similar figures for the Sievert Light Line 8720 burner are the evaporation of 5.2 g of water/min. This figure is equivalent to the production of 2,387 ml of steam/min. For the 8842 burner the figure is 2 g of water/min equivalent to 922 ml of steam/min.

The warm-up time of a full boiler will be the longest. For a full vertical boiler, the rate of steam production will be highest, due to the area of water exposed to heat. This rate will reduce as the water is consumed. However, a full boiler will initially have little space to store steam and thus may have problems delivering sufficent steam to the engine.

The steam production rate will not vary as much for a horizontal boiler as the water level has less impact.

BOILER AND ENGINE SIZES

All the figures given below are theoretical. For practical purposes, when sizing an engine to a boiler, halving the suggested performance will help account for other losses. These are dominated by steam temperature and pressure changes between the boiler and cylinder.

Taking some typical engines, the double-acting Stuart Mill engine has a ⁵⁄₈" (15.88 mm) bore and a 1¼" (31.75 mm) stroke. The steam it will therefore consume can be calculated from the cylinder volume.

$$\pi \times 0.794^2 \times 3.175 \times 2 = 12.57 \text{ cc/rev}.$$

It should be possible to run it at up to 600 rpm on a 108 mm or 4" vertical boiler heated by the 2¾" ceramic burner. These boilers can provide around 7,710 ml of steam per minute. The speed would be about 300 rpm on a 3½" vertical or 3" horizontal boiler fitted with the 2" burner. These should produce some 4,161 ml of steam per minute.

The 108 mm or 4" vertical boiler should run the Stuart D10, with a ¾" (19.05 mm) bore and stroke giving a volume per rev of 21.72 cc, at around 350 rpm; the Stuart Beam engine with a 1" (25.4 mm) stroke and 2" (50.8 mm) bore and a volume per rev of 51.5 cc at up to 150 rpm.

The 3½" vertical or 3" horizontal boiler should steam a Stuart 10V or 10H of ¾" (19.05 mm) bore and stroke and a volume of 10.86 cc/rev at over 350 rpm.

The 54 mm boiler should provide around 2,386 ml of steam/minute. The PM Research double-acting mill engine has a ½" (12.5 mm) bore and ¾" (19 mm) stroke. The volume of steam needed per rev is 4.66 cc/rev. This could be run at some 500 rpm

The 42 mm boiler should provide around 922 ml of steam/minute. The modified double-acting Wilesco engine has a 15 mm (¹⁹⁄₃₂") stroke and a bore of 9.5 mm (³⁄₈"). The volume of steam needed per rev is 1.06 cc/rev so it should be possible to run it at over 800 rpm.

It is arguable that the steam is cut off early by the valve gear, reducing steam consumption. In theory, this may be true, in practice other losses exceed any cut-off savings in small model engines.

To summarize, the theoretical approximate maximum engine speed can be calculated as follows. The speed in rpm equals the boiler steam-production rate in millilitres per minute divided by the engine capacity in cubic centimetres, the number of cylinders and the number of steam inputs per revolution (for double-acting engines).

LIST OF USEFUL ADDRESSES

Anton Fabrice BRETAGNE
Mécaniques & Accessoires ANTÓN
La Jarrie
F -17380 PUY DU LAC
FRANCE
fabrice.bretagne.perso.neuf.fr

Blackgates Engineering
Unit 1 Victory Court, Flagship Square,
Shaw Cross Business Park
Dewsbury.
West Yorkshire, WF12 7TH, UK
www.blackgates.co.uk

C & W Berry Ltd
262 Golden Hill Lane
Leyland
PR25 2YH, UK
www.cwberry.com

Chronos Ltd
Unit 14, Dukeminster Estate
Church St, Dunstable
LU5 4HU, UK
www.chronos.ltd.uk

Clevedon Steam
2 The Penns
Clevedon
North Somerset, BS21 5AN, UK
www.clevedonsteam.co.uk

College Engineering Supply
2 Sandy Lane, Codsall
Wolverhampton
WV8 1EJ, UK
www.collegeengineering.co.uk

CuP Alloys
Matrix Business Centre
Novel Way, Dinnington
South Yorks, S25 3QB, UK
www.cupalloys.co.uk

Distilled Water Supplies
Unit 1, Airfield Road Trading Estate,
Airfield Road, Podington
Northamptonshire
NN29 7XA, UK
www.buydistilledwater.co.uk

Forest Classics
Unit 11D, Main Offices
New Dunn Works
Sling
Coleford
Gloucestershire, GL16 8JD, UK
www.forest-classics.co.uk

GLR Kennions Limited
Estate Office, Hobbs Cross Business Centre
Epping
Essex, CM16 7NY, UK
www.modelmakingsupplies.co.uk

Hamilton Gas Products
2 Balloo Place
Balloo Industrial Estate
Bangor
Northern Ireland, BT19 7BP, UK
www.gasproducts.co.uk

Johnson Matthey Plc
5th Floor
25 Farringdon Street
London, EC4A 4AB, UK
www.matthey.com/about/preciousmetals.htm

Lutz Hielscher Technische Spielwaren
Schmiedestraße 52
D-42279 Wuppertal
GERMANY
www.hielscher-dampfmodelle.de/cms/index.php

Maccsteam Ltd
79 Victoria Road
Macclesfield
Cheshire, SK10 3JA, UK
www.maccsteam.com

MainSteam Models
58, Oxford Road
Dewsbury
West Yorkshire, WF13 4EH, UK
www.mainsteam.co.uk

Noggin End Metals
83 Peascroft Road
Norton
Stoke on Trent, ST6 8HG, UK
www.nogginend.com

Northern Association of Model Engineers
www.normodeng.org.uk

APPENDIX

Polly Model Engineering Limited
Atlas Mills
Birchwood Avenue
Long Eaton
Nottingham
NG10 3ND, UK
www.pollymodelengineering.co.uk

RDG Tools Ltd
Grosvenor House
Caldene Business Park
Burnley Rd
Mytholmroyd
West Yorkshire, HX7 5QJ UK.
www.rdgtools.co.uk

Reeves 2000
Appleby Hill
Austrey
Warks, CV9 3ER, UK.
www.ajreeves.com

Shesto Ltd
Unit 2, Sapcote Trading Centre
374 High Road
Willesden
London
NW10 2DH, UK.
www.shesto.co.uk

Silverline Tools Ltd
Boundary Way, Lufton Trading Estate
Yeovil
Somerset, BA22 8HZ, UK.
www.silverlinetools.com

Southern Federation of Model Engineering Societies
www.sfmes.co.uk/public

Stuart Models
Grove Works
West Road
Bridport
Dorset, DT6 5JT, UK
www.stuartmodels.com

The Distilled Water Company
Unit C, 2 Endeavour Way
Durnsford Road Industrial Estate
Wimbledon
London, SW19 8UH, UK
www.thedistilledwatercompany

Toolbank
Long Reach, Galleon Boulevard
Crossways Business Park
Dartford,
Kent, DA2 6QE, UK
www.toolbank.com

Tracy Tools Ltd
Unit 1, Parkfield Industrial Estate
Barton Hill Way
Torquay, TQ2 8JG, UK.
www.tracytools.com

Walker Midgley Insurance Brokers Ltd
Yorkshire Bank Chambers
Fargate
Sheffield, S1 2HD, UK.
www.walkermidgley.co.uk

INDEX

16 mm, 9, 74, 79, 81, 98
32 mm, 3, 4, 6, 34, 35, 63, 65, 73, 83, 96, 99
3 bar/litres, 8, 43, 44, 47, 51, 61, 78, 79

A
Automatic boiler control, 13, 53

B
Bend-A-Light, 47
Bix, 56, 60
Blanking plug, 38, 44, 46 - 49
Blow-down valve, 31, 50, 51
Boiler barrel, 11, 13, 90, 96
    Feed pump, 8, 11, 43, 47, 48, 52, 53, 58, 103, 107, 110
    Single flue, 2, 3, 5, 11, 13, 79, 103
    Water, 46
Boss White, 53
BS 2871, 13, 112
BSP, 43
Butane, 8, 30, 33, 34, 42, 55, 59, 60
Bypass, 8, 53
Bypass valve, 53

C
C101, 13, 72
C106, 13, 61
Ceramix, 32
Certificate, 43, 46
Certification, 46
Check or clack valve, 50
Cladding, 11, 13, 25, 26, 43, 45, 48, 94, 99
Clarke, 10, 34
Cleaning, 11, 15, 24, 25, 32, 40, 47, 66, 67, 74
Coal, 1, 8, 55, 65
Combustion chamber, 6, 7
Connecting to an engine, 103
Connector, 8, 11, 52, 55, 65, 70, 72, 93, 105, 116
Copper washer, 8, 31, 44, 48, 49, 52, 53, 89
CuP Alloys, 33, 119
CZ108, 13

D
Displacement, 11, 37, 48, 53, 54, 104
Displacement lubricator, 48, 53, 54, 104
Drilling, 2, 9, 13, 19, 20, 24, 67, 85, 88
DZR, 3

E
Easy-flo flux, 36, 40
EN 1057, 13, 21, 90, 96, 112
Evans, 2, 111, 112

F
Farmer, 2
Feed pump, 8, 11, 42, 43, 47, 48, 52, 53, 58, 103, 107, 110
Filling, 11, 13, 53, 106 - 108, 110, 111
    with gas, 107
    with water, 11, 13, 46, 106
Fire brick, 10, 35
Flanging, 14 - 16
Flue, 7, 23
Flux, 36

G
Galloway tube, 3
Gas torch, 10, 11, 33, 57
Gauge 1, 3, 4, 6, 13, 79, 90
Glue, 67, 87, 93

H
Handle, 19, 28, 33, 40, 47, 57, 94
Health and Safety, 111
Heldite, 31, 48, 53
High temperature, 2, 10, 26, 32, 33
Horizontal boiler, 6, 79, 80, 90, 96
HSE, 111
Hydraulic test, 43 - 48, 113

I
Insulation, 10, 29, 88, 95, 99
ISO 460, 54, 104

J
Jets, 56

L
Laser, 19, 20, 81
Lego, 100
Lock, 19, 96, 98
Locomotive, 2 - 4, 6, 26, 79, 90, 94 - 96, 98, 99, 102, 103
Loctite, 53, 106
Lubrication, 58, 104
Lubricators, 53, 54

M
Machine Mart, 10, 34
Maintaining pressure, 110
Maintenance, 47
Markham, 111, 112
Matting, 26, 80
MDF, 14, 86
Mechanical lubricator, 11, 54, 104
Mercaptan, 33
Metcote, 32
Methylated spirit, 8, 55
Metrication, 12, 49

O
Oil separator, 104
    Steam, 11, 54, 104

P
Paint, 26, 31, 32, 37, 67, 95, 100
Pickle, 11, 24
Pipe work, 11, 43, 48, 59, 104
PM Research, 119
Pressure gauge, 51
    limit, 101
Propane, 8, 10, 15, 30, 34, 42, 55, 59
PTFE, 8, 26, 31, 44, 48, 53

R
Rectifying leaks, 39
Reeves, 33, 120

S
Safety, 42
    calculations, 111
    precautions, 10
    valve, 49
Sealant, 21, 32, 53, 56, 67, 106
Sealey torch, 47
Sealing, 8, 53, 58
SEM, 32
Shesto, 33, 120
Sievert, 10, 30, 33, 55, 57, 91, 117, 118
Silver soldering, 10, 33, 37
Silver-flo, 10, 36
Single-flue boiler, 2, 3, 5, 11, 13, 79, 103
Siphon, 45, 47, 48, 51
Skamolex, 10, 39, 41
Snopake, 38, 65
Stays, 20, 113
Steam oil, 11, 54, 104
    test, 43 - 48
    valve, 11, 31, 47 - 49, 50, 52, 94, 103, 109
Straight connector, 52
Stuart, 3, 10, 59, 119
Superglue, 26, 67, 86, 87

T
Tees, 8, 52
Testing, 9, 11, 43 - 48, 116, 118
Thermalite, 10, 35, 39
Threaded bush, 49
Tipp-ex, 65
Tools, 9, 14, 25, 106

U
Union nut, 52
UTS, 111, 113

V
V-block, 14
Vermiculite, 10, 35, 41

W
Water, 11, 13, 46, 106
    gauge, 51
    tube, 22
Working pressure, 8

Y
Yarrow, 2, 3